Canadian Writers and Their Works

CANADIAN WRITERS

AND THEIR WORKS

POETRY   SERIES   •   VOLUME   TEN

 EDITED   BY

ROBERT   LECKER,   JACK   DAVID,   ELLEN   QUIGLEY

INTRODUCED   BY   GEORGE   WOODCOCK

ECW PRESS, 1992

CANADIAN CATALOGUING IN PUBLICATION DATA

Main entry under title:

Canadian writers and their works: essays on form,
context, and development : poetry

Includes bibliographies and indexes.
ISBN 0-920802-43-5 (set). — ISBN 0-55022-069-1 (v. 10)

1. Canadian poetry (English) — History and criticism.*
2. Poets, Canadian (English) — Biography.* I. Lecker,
Robert, 1951– . II. David, Jack, 1946– .
III. Quigley, Ellen, 1955– .

PS8141.C37 1992   C811'.09   C89-005234-4
PR9190.2.C37. 1992

The publication of this series has been assisted by grants from the Ontario Arts
Council and The Canada Council.

This volume was typeset in Sabon by ECW Type & Art, Oakville, Ontario. Printed
and bound by Imprimerie Gagné Ltée, Louiseville, Quebec.

Published by ECW PRESS, 1980 Queen Street East, Toronto, Ontario M4L 1J2.

The illustrations are by Isaac Bickerstaff.

CONTENTS

Introduction *George Woodcock* 5

Leonard Cohen *Linda Hutcheon* 21

Robert Kroetsch *Ann Munton* 69

Eli Mandel *Dennis Cooley* 189

John Newlove *Douglas Barbour* 281

Joe Rosenblatt *Ed Jewinski* 339

Index 397

PREFACE

Canadian Writers and Their Works (CWTW) is a unique, twenty-volume collection of critical essays covering the development of Canadian fiction and poetry over the past two centuries. Ten volumes are devoted to fiction, and ten to poetry. Each volume contains a unifying Introduction by George Woodcock and four or five discrete critical essays on specific writers. Moreover, each critical essay includes a brief biography of the author, a discussion of the tradition and milieu influencing his/her work, a critical overview section which reviews published criticism on the author, a long section analyzing the author's works, and a selected bibliography listing primary and secondary material. The essays in each volume are arranged alphabetically according to last names of the writers under study.

The editors wish to acknowledge the contributions of many people who have played an important part in creating this series. First, we wish to thank the critics who prepared the essays for this volume: Douglas Barbour, Dennis Cooley, Linda Hutcheon, Ed Jewinski, Ann Munton, and George Woodcock. We are also indebted to the production and design teams at both The Porcupine's Quill and ECW Type & Art, and to Hilda Keskin, Wiesia Kolasinska and Stephanie Termeer, who keyboarded the manuscript in its initial typesetting phase.

RL / JD / EQ

Introduction

GEORGE WOODCOCK

IT IS NOT ACCIDENTAL that three out of the five poets represented in this volume should be from the prairies and, in the long wanderings poets take nowadays, should have retained that orientation. As one of them, Eli Mandel, has put it: "My image for the prairie writer . . . is not necessarily the one who is in the west, or who stays here, but the one who returns, who moves, who points in this direction." Our very sense of the prairie in fact encourages this feeling of movement within vast but contained environment, a concept materialized as endless land and towering skies; we remember the everlasting movement of the great herds of bison and the Indians and wolves who followed them, and the very fluidity of a rural immigrant society that in less than a century emerged, flourished, and declined.

In literary terms what is striking is the way in which this change in human life on the prairie has been accompanied by a change in its writers and writing that strikingly parallels it. For decades we thought of the prairie as *par excellence* a land of fiction, the home of the Canadian realist novel, realism extending on one side into the European-derived naturalism of Frederick Philip Grove and on the other into the popular romanticism of Martha Ostenso. In this fiction the whole history of prairie rural society was re-enacted, from the harshness and loneliness of pioneer living, represented in their different ways by Grove and Ostenso and Robert J.C. Stead, through the cramped and despairing communities of duststorm depression projected by Sinclair Ross (with a touch of comic relief from W.O. Mitchell) to the almost elegiac celebration, so much of it through memory, of a vanishing way of life contained in the great Manawaka cycle of Margaret Laurence's novels.

Prairie society has indeed gone in the way the novelists perceived. The quarter-section farms, with their red barns so visible across the snow and their windbreaks around the houses, have given way to the great spreads — thousands of acres in a single holding, of agribusiness, which has ruined the prairie economy and its soil by its obstinate adherence to single cropping. The great highways that leap across the land have diminished the little elevator communities that were dotted at intervals along the railways as they have drawn farmers and shoppers and business people to the few larger centres. The deep sense of mutual concern and the practice of mutual aid that veterans of the Depression in the prairies still remember so vividly have almost vanished.

People really began to become aware of these changes in the 1960s, as I did because at that time I was travelling often by road across Canada, and each time, as the roads improved, I noticed a corresponding shrinkage of small places like the Horizon of *As for Me and My House*. Population was drying out of these small places to the cities and even out of the region, and one was no longer aware of the vital community life recorded in so many of the prairie novels and in memoirs of pre-World War II prairie life like those of Nellie McClung and Mary Hiemstra. It was undoubtedly this draining away from the present that took the vitality out of prairie novels and led to their tending towards reminiscence and nostalgia, largely recording a way of life that exists no longer.

It was as these trends became evident from the early 1960s that the naissance of poetry in the prairies began, and in place of the jejune, derivative verse that had once been written there, a strange flowering began to emerge from the roots of what seemed like a dying society. Surprising at first sight, the development seemed less so on reflection, when one caught the large cargo of elegy and melancholy that these new poets were carrying, and realized how well it tuned with the changing spirit of prairie communities as the settlers' sense of challenge moved over to a kind of despairing acceptance of the recurring inevitabilities of drought and debt, loneliness and a one-crop economy. While novels are appropriate to societies with the sense of a shared future — as the prairies were even in the Depression when one shared what one had as well as one's misfortunes and frail hopes, poetry tends to flourish where people feel isolated, where the community loses its vitality and its solidarity. The Romantic period was also the time of the industrial revolution, that great breeder of alienation. The legions of American poetry, led by Whitman, broke forth after the Civil War, and the first real poetic movement in Canada was almost coterminous with the Northwest Rebellion and

6

the early clashes it created between Quebec and the rest of Canada. And in the 1960s a sense of unease and isolation, though a different kind from what the pioneers had experienced, was reappearing on the prairies; the social community was beginning to lose its vitality and solidarity as the economic basis for living became yearly — even monthly — more precarious.

But isolation and alienation — paradoxically — create their own community, that of the people who recognize their condition, and in this case accept the prairie for what it still is. A place of space and distance, a place of time and of pasts hidden deeply before record, whose intimations elude the historian; perhaps only the poet can uncover them. This is what John Newlove did in his poem, "Prairie," an early model in this genre, in which he is talking of the intangibility of history and even of geography in that landscape made for wanderers and as mirage-ridden as a desert, which men have vainly tried to lock into geometrical patterns resembling those of cities. He sees the past as

> men roaming
> as beasts seen through dips
> in history, fostered by legend,
> invented remembrance. Scenes shake,
> the words do not suffice . . .

And he sees himself as prairie man in a strangely illusive world:

> never
> to be at ease, but always migrating
> from city to city
> seeking some almost seen
> god or food or earth or word.[1]

John Newlove was the first of these prairie poets to achieve a degree of acceptance through poems that gained him a reputation for dark pessimism and for a kind of tenderness that always seemed to verge on cruelty. In some ways, in their ease of phrasing, in their felicitous colloquialism, in their easily running rhythms, in their philosophizing pretensions, Newlove's poems resemble those of Al Purdy without being strictly derivative. And if there is any writer whom one can regard as the real precursor of the prairie movement in verse,

7

it is surely Purdy, that inveterate wanderer, who wrote of another rural society — that of southern Ontario — which proceeded within a century from success to decay. There was really nothing in the prairie past before the 1960s of a poetic tradition — oral or written — that might offer an inspiration to new writers: nothing, for instance, like the outport tradition of songs in Newfoundland. And that is why one senses the presence of Purdy, perhaps as an example rather than as a model, behind so many of these poets.

Apart from the western poets discussed in this volume — Mandel and Kroetsch as well as Newlove — a whole school of prairie poets has appeared; immediately names like those of Lorna Crozier, Ken Mitchell, Glen Sorestad, Andy Suknaski, come to mind. They run their own prairie magazines, their own little presses, their own conferences, and have created, in the past twenty years or so, a literary milieu of their own in which all the classic prairie virtues of mutual aid and mutual regard can re-emerge and flourish.

In this volume, as in others of *Canadian Writers and Their Works* relating to recent Canadian poetry, one encounters the division between poets who have emerged through the academy and have to cast off a burden of scholarship before their real poetic quality stands out, and those who have been unencumbered by such beginnings. Both John Newlove and Joe Rosenblatt belong to the strong Canadian tradition of the autodidactic, non-academic poet, which includes such powerful names as Al Purdy and Milton Acorn and Alden Nowlan, as P.K. Page and Gwendolyn MacEwen, while Leonard Cohen was never greatly influenced by his university training and slid out from under the academic shadow via decadence into pop art.

But Eli Mandel, for example, was so closely involved in the academic-poetic milieu of the 1950s, that in the beginning, as happened to James Reaney and Jay Macpherson, he was treated as member of a kind of mythopoeic school influenced by Northrop Frye. In the mind of what teacher-critic this strange notion arose I have no idea, but it became almost a cliché in literary magazines for a while. I criticized it strongly when I wrote the chapter on "Poetry" in the 1976 edition of the *Literary History of Canada*. Northrop Frye in his "Conclusion" to that edition took up my remark, one of the rare occasions on which we agreed in public:

. . . among the many things I am grateful for and deeply appreciate, one is the fact that the phrase 'the Frye school of

8

mythopoeic poetry' is so briefly dismissed by Mr. Woodcock. There is no Frye school of mythopoeic poetry; criticism and poetry cannot possibly be related in that way.[2]

Dennis Cooley, I note with relief, remarks that the "identification of Mandel as some acolyte of a Frygian school of writing" is "common but somewhat misleading." As Frank Davey has pointed out, Eli Mandel was profoundly affected by the "Second World War, and the horrors of the Jewish concentration camps," and his work remains "characterized by macabre images of suffering and destruction, and by a pervasive pessimism."[3] But such elements, while they lend themselves to mythopoeic treatment, do not emerge from critical trends or literary fashion; they proceed in Mandel's case from experience, deeply felt even if vicariously undergone.

What is perhaps most interesting in Mandel is the prosodic shift that took place in mid-career. Cooley traces this to the influence of Warren Tallman, whom Mandel encountered during the 1960s. Tallman, who finds mention in other volumes of this series, was an interesting semi-shaman figure, neither poet nor critic, but influential as a kind of missionary who arrived to teach at the University of British Columbia in 1956, already well acquainted personally and through their work with the poets of the Beat era in San Francisco, such as Kenneth Rexroth, Robert Duncan, and Allen Ginsberg. Tallman allied himself with the young poets who were editing Tish (George Bowering, Frank Davey, Fred Wah, and others) and encouraged them in following that perennially revived urge among poets to simplify and get back to the spoken tongue. In one amazing week, deeply influential in the development of western Canadian poetry, Tallman brought a group of his Americans — Ginsberg and Duncan, Levertov and Olson, to Vancouver for talk and reading sessions with Canadian writers. (Rexroth, with whom Tallman had now fallen out, was not invited.)

When Mandel came a little later to Vancouver, he fell under the spell of Tallman's considerable charisma and his passionate argument. Then, as Cooley remarks, "the gates were opened to a drastic shift in his writing. For the first decade he had enlisted in an aesthetic of overriding structures, heavy symbolic import, and grand rhetoric. Mandel now moved into more modest measures in which the poet or his surrogate no longer acted as supreme makers, apart from and superior to their society."

What indeed we see in Mandel's evolution is the shift from the grandiose bard of his early imagination, distancing himself into mythical structures from which he can address the world in anger, to the poet sensitive to his world and considering it meditatively, yet never surrendering his sense of the creating power of the imagination, for, as Cooley also justly remarks, Mandel displays in everything he has written "a profound sense that literature invents life and invests it with pattern and meaning."

It is this Mandel, moving away from the hyperbolic to the minimal, who turned back to the prairies and particularly the area of past Jewish settlement in Saskatchewan, as the source of his vision. One finds the search for the elemental in both life and language projected in such a splendid minimal poem as "Estevan, 1934," often anthologized but still worth quoting as a benchmark in Mandel's development.

> remembering the family we
> called breeds   the Roques
> their house smelling of urine
> my mother's prayers before
> the dried fish she cursed
> them for their dirtiness their
> women I remember too
>   how
> seldom they spoke and
> they touched one another
>
> even when the sun killed
> cattle and rabbis
>   even
> in poisoned slow air
> like hunters
>   like lizards
> they touched   stone
> they touched
>   earth[4]

John Newlove evaded being trapped early by the academy, though later like most of us he became intermittently involved. His first small book, *Grave Sirs*, was published when he was twenty-four by a couple of friendly Vancouver hand printers. With her usual felicity of phrase, Margaret Atwood has aptly summed up one aspect of Newlove's writing. "He is a loser and his proper study is loss." But Newlove is no ordinary loser; after all, he has been relatively successful and much respected in later years as a poet. As the poetry editor for McClelland and Stewart he was for a while a power in the literary world, and his life has not been without joys. Yet he writes with a consistent pessimism that seems almost constitutional, for even the gentlest of his lyric poems, the tenderest of his statements of love, is darkened with regret, with the sense of failing. One sees him as a kind of Schopenhauer in verse; for all one knows he may even have an ancient faithful dog to share his gloom.

I have always, in fact, suspected a touch of deliberation in Newlove's pessimism. It is in fact the same problem as that of Schopenhauer. How can one continue to live and to work so productively if the world is so irremediably wretched? But Newlove does continue, and a pose, as Wilde argued in various ways, can be the essence of a poem. The "man of sorrows, and acquainted with grief," may be the persona through whom Newlove can speak with effect, as he almost always does. The necessary effect of the stance on his way of writing is austerity projected into prosody. For, like other pessimists — Swift, Orwell, Samuel Butler, and among poets Rochester especially — Newlove sets out to be a plain speaker. He aims at the colloquial. He avoids as far as possible the simile and the metaphor because they lie by evasion and delay the true recording of perceptions. Yet he reminds one of the recurring importance of imagism in twentieth-century English and, since late Duncan Campbell Scott and W.W.E. Ross, Canadian poetry, for his images are necessary ones, and clear and strong.

Gary Geddes has remarked that "Newlove is Canada's most gifted and meticulous prosodist,"[5] Frank Davey has said that he has "developed one of the most direct and visually precise styles in twentieth-century poetry,"[6] and Douglas Barbour, elsewhere than in his essay in the present volume, has said that "even in the rendering of the worst aspects of the human condition, the integrity and energy of the poetry affirm life, humanity, the love the artist bears the world."[7]

Underlying these remarks is always an implication that so good a poet has not received the kind of recognition that his skills and his powers deserve. And perhaps all one can answer to that complaint is that the most perceptive Canadian critics do recognize his quality (though his behaviour has sometimes made praise difficult), that critical-historical surveys like *Canadian Writers and Their Works* take him very seriously, and that he is quite copiously included in the best anthologies. Unlike Leonard Cohen, Newlove has not sought ways to broaden and popularize his appeal, and given his evident inclinations towards reclusiveness, perhaps he may be content to gain a melancholy satisfaction from the Stendhalian privilege of being appreciated by the Happy Few for whom poetry concentrates the world's reality.

Certainly to such readers the great variety of the poetry he has achieved within his elegiac spectrum is extraordinary. As Geddes also said: "One moment he is the delicate lyricist, improving on the themes of love, beauty, and loss, moving to ever-finer discriminations of thought and feeling; the next he is the stand-up comic, employing self-deflation, hyperbole, fantasy, and — especially in the treatment of domestic or mundane subjects — a deliberate rhetorical excess and archaic diction."[8]

Talk of archaic diction reminds one how far Newlove is — if not a historical poet — at least a poet highly conscious of the past, so largely unrecorded, that plays its dominant part in one's image of the prairies. Some of his most impressive poems are long meditations like "The Pride," in which the native peoples whom white culture so long neglected come back to inhabit and shape our minds.

> Not this handful
> of fragments, as the indians
> are not composed of
> the romantic stories
> about them, or of the stories
> they tell only, but
> still ride the soil
> in us, dry bones apart
> of the dust in our eyes,
> needed and troubling
> in the glare, in
> our breath, in our
> ears, in our mouths,
> in our bodies entire, in our minds, until
> at last
> we become them[9]

The same feeling of the past of the plains and of our ancestral links with them is evident in the poetry of Robert Kroetsch. Kroetsch is of course a writer of many parts, and had made a name through his fantastic novels of the West and the North, with their larger-and-stranger-than-life heroes, even before he took seriously to poetry. He is also deeply interested in European-based deconstructionist criticism, and Ann Munton, who writes on him, seems to be a fellow believer and enlarges greatly on this aspect of his writing and thinking — so greatly that I need hardly say more, particularly since I feel that critical *theory* can bear only obliquely on the work of literature.

Critical practice is another matter, a matter less of the analysis and taxonomy towards which past academic critics like Frye and the (once) New Critics have been inclined rather than of mediation, of finding the language through which the reader can best understand the work. Of course there is a great deal of mediation in deconstructionist practice and criticism for the mysterious relation between reader (that "Dear Reader" of Victorian man of letters strangely transmogrified) lies at the heart of the process, though the destructionist in the end demands a complicity that destroys the creative role and renders literature or any other art by definition almost inconclusive.

Having said as much I prefer to talk of Kroetsch directly rather than through the glass of stance within which he has tried to encapsulate himself as a poet. Munton notes that Kroetsch entered slowly, even cautiously, into poetry, so that it is only recently his importance as a poet has been recognized, yet now, like Margaret Atwood and very few other Canadian writers, he is seen as just as important a poet as he was a novelist.

Even the titles of Kroetsch's volumes of verse show the extent to which his work is related to the concrete reality of prairie existence, observed and remembered: *The Stone Hammer Poems*, *The Ledger*, *Seed Catalogue*, *Field Notes*. Some of these are long poems, others are collections of related short poems, but Kroetsch avoids narrative on a major scale, and like many contemporary poets prefers the open-ended form that narrative, with its terminal urge, tends to negate. "System and grid" of all kinds he avoids; he seeks contradiction; he uses disjunctive association as freely as any surrealist. He is freely anecdotal, but also metaphorical, and his anecdotes often end as splendid metaphors. And in all this, whether or not he pursues or is being pursued by any of the theories that he chooses to cultivate, one senses that in his choice of the unsystematic and the open, in his predilection for unanticipated association and juxtaposition, he is more concerned than anything else to shape a kind of poetry appropriate to the prairie and to his formative experiences of it.

Frye was right when he suggested that what we must seek in considering a poem is not the critical doctrine that the poet may hold or be influenced by. We must consider it mainly or merely as poetry and decide whether the poet has succeeded in his chosen aim, which in Kroetsch's case is evidently to make a poetry appropriate to the experience of the prairie, to the sense of "space all over the place," as he has put it, to the dissolving into each other of pasts that are outside history. It is the offering of states of mind in appropriate and moving words that is the poet's task, not the exemplification of any literary theory, however congenial or striking or eccentric.

And judged in this way, Kroetsch has produced some extraordinary poems centring on personal obsessions, family history, possessions to which the hands of men had imparted poetic significance, and in this way he had developed autobiographical poetry in very original ways. *Seed Catalogue* commemorates his childhood passion for gardening and extends it into general gardener's lore; *The Ledger* takes an old family farm ledger and extracts from it the essence of a homesteader's life and his relation to the land. And there is the fine "Stone Hammer Poem," about an ancient Indian stone implement the plough threw up on his grandfather's farm.

4.
The stone maul
was found.
In the field
my grandfather
thought
was his

my father
thought was his

5.
It is a stone
old as the last
Ice Age, the

retreating ice,
the retreating
buffalo, the
retreating Indians

(the saskatoons bloom
white (infrequently
the chokecherries the
highbrush cranberries the
pincherries bloom
white along the barbed
wire fence (the
pemmican   winter[10]

It is a two-steps-forward-one-step-backward kind of poetry, of
spurts and retreats, of irrational repetitions, of catching breath, and
hesitation. It tells without narration, and though it is rich in images
— often a kind of *millefiori* of them — it is short on metaphors, yet
the whole poem and its ancient stone are transformed into a single
giant metaphor. It is alive with fresh perception united in a great
intelligent rumination as if the poet were somehow in tune with the
soul of the prairie, and it is this tuning in that makes the poems both
satisfying and original — not any critical theories the poet or others
may advance in his justification.

Joe Rosenblatt stands aside from the other poets I am here discussing, and — so far as I know — from other contemporary Canadian
poets by being a fine bestiarist. He is also in his own way a western
if not a prairie poet, for like one of his own mythical bees he has
buzzed all the way from a working class background to a rural setting
in British Columbia, whose lush and still largely unspoilt environment accords with his strongly projected sense of man's mutual
relations with the natural world and its fecund energies. But man,
compared with the animals, is the dumb loser in the great fabulist
panorama that his poems offer, far less interesting than the marvellous bee, far less aware even than the rodents, as a typical poem like
"Groundhogs & Appearances" suggests.

Oh, we're blank.
Groundhogs fade into the roots of our eyes.
Once we could light fires with hallucinations

but now we just breathe lightly
& count our memories. Have we missed an important
sensation?

Concrete images? Rabbit food?
Dare we lie down and sleep?
We're almost invisible.

Billions of rodent souls!
They've turned the System into a garbage dump,
but we're still buried alive in our bodies.
We'll close our eyes,
imagine the asterisks out in a private space.
Our images are double-parked out there.[11]

Dostoevsky used to say of nineteenth-century Russian writers that "we all came out of Gogol's *Overcoat*," and there are whole schools of Canadian poets of whom it might be said that they came out of W.C. Williams' "Red Wheelbarrow." Rosenblatt is one of them, and also one of these at least marginally affected by the voice-and-sound practices of the Black Mountaineers. Yet there has been a baroque extravagance of language and imagery to Rosenblatt's mature verse and an onomatopoeic fancifulness to his animal poems that makes him stand out very individually as a true eccentric. There is no other Canadian poet so visionary of the unity of the natural world as Rosenblatt in his fables; perhaps we need no more than one original of his kind.

Leonard Cohen as a writer has prodigally run through two reputations. His major novel, *Beautiful Losers*, was an extraordinary modern manifesto of Black Decadence, and his poetry, with its alternation of sardonic commentary on the world and a bittersweet romantic eroticism, won him a high repute among the coming poets of the 1960s. At the same time, by the late 1960s he achieved because of his songs and performances a considerable position in the world, outside poetry, of pop music. The highly ornamented and also highly formalist verse of early books like *Let Us Compare Mythologies* and *The Spice Box of Earth* also put Cohen apart from the majority of his contemporaries. He was bold in his themes, in his defiance of conventional morality, but extraordinarily conventional in the way he expressed its rebellion. The comparison with the decadents of the nineties was obvious, for his poems were often strikingly similar to those of — say — Ernest Dowson and the early Wilde, in their textural richness and their clinging nostalgia, but also in their calculated waywardness, in their cultivation of the amoral, the macabre, the cruel, not for its own sake, but for the sense of Satanic romanticism it projected. *Beautiful Losers* became as much a manifesto of decadence as Huysmans' *À rébours* had been in the late nineteenth century.

But while the perversity of content may seem to establish the experimental and radical credentials of decadent literature, in form the decadence has always tended to the conservative, the ultimate corruption into perversity of the conventional, as Beardsley's drawings and the poems of Lionel Johnson so often mocked yet revived the Augustan mode.

Cohen, it is true, at times tore away from his task of what Frank Davey has called "escaping from life by transmuting its slippery actualities into the reliable simplicities of myth and art"[12] and wrote the self-deprecating, cynical, and deliberately anti-conventional anti-poems of *The Energy of Slaves*. Yet even the poems denouncing the Holocaust and other horrors of Nazism, in *Flowers of Hitler* and elsewhere, took on largely the formalist qualities of laments and ritual denunciations.

Cohen's involvement in song writing and singing did not make his work any less conventional; on the contrary, it led him to the realm of trite emotions and facilely romantic images of nostalgia and loss and false loss that has always been the substance of popular lyrics. But whether in song or in poetry, there is always a cloying concern with the hypnotic powers of oral sound, and while the images that Cohen evokes have often — especially in *Beautiful Losers* — the naughty nastiness of an Aubrey Beardsley or the weak *carpe diem* of an Arthur Symons, in the end the poet of whom he reminds one most is that sound-drunk chanter and tamed outcast, the pussy of Putney, Algernon Charles Swinburne, with Baudelaire as the distant and ever-fascinating ancestor.

Canada has had few international poets, but perhaps Cohen in his way has been one of them with his claims to membership of that durable fraternity of the Decadence, where poetry always hovers on the verge of the poetic, art on the verge of the artful. If skill without true innovation, the gesture without the substance of rebellion, are one's criteria, then Leonard Cohen belongs. But because his immediately apprehensible excellences are so great and his ultimate impact is so slight, his achievement is likely to be the ultimate and self-created exile of the true decadent.

NOTES

[1] John Newlove, "The Prairie," *Canadian Poetry*, vol. 2, ed. Jack David and Robert Lecker (Toronto: General and ECW, 1982), p. 169.

[2] Northrop Frye, "Conclusion," *Literary History of Canada*, 2nd ed., vol. 3, ed. Carl F. Klinck (Toronto: Univ. of Toronto Press, 1976), 319.

[3] Frank Davey, "Eli Mandel," *Oxford Companion to Canadian Literature*, ed. William Toye (Toronto: Oxford Univ. Press, 1983), p. 504.

[4] Eli Mandel, "estevan, 1934:," *Canadian Poetry*, pp. 65–66.

[5] Gary Geddes, "John Newlove," *Oxford Companion*, p. 558.

[6] Frank Davey, *From There to Here: A Guide to English Canadian Literature Since 1960* (Erin, Ont.: Press Porcépic, 1974), p. 205.

[7] Douglas Barbour, "John Newlove," *Canadian Poetry*, p. 305.

[8] Geddes, p. 558.

[9] John Newlove, "The Pride," *New Oxford Book of Canadian Verse in English*, ed. Margaret Atwood (Toronto: Oxford Univ. Press, 1982), p. 343.

[10] Robert Kroetsch, "Stone Hammer Poem," *Canadian Poetry*, pp. 100–01.

[11] Joe Rosenblatt, "Groundhogs and Appearances," *Canadian Poetry*, p. 142.

[12] Frank Davey, "Leonard Cohen," *Oxford Companion*, p. 134.

Leonard Cohen
and His Works

Leonard Cohen (1934–   )

LINDA HUTCHEON

Biography

IN 1967 George Bowering wrote that "Leonard Cohen could become the Jewish Kahlil Gibran."[1] And, certainly, with McClelland and Stewart printing or reprinting a half-dozen of his books in the mid-1960s, Cohen's popular success as a poet of the times seemed assured. His early background was probably appropriate, though perhaps less exotic than these somewhat dubious accolades might have suggested. Born into a comfortable Jewish family, Cohen attended McGill University and later, briefly, Columbia University. His interest and skill in poetry writing were manifest early: McGill awarded him the McNaughton Prize in creative writing, and Louis Dudek published *Let Us Compare Mythologies* as the first book of his McGill Poetry Series in 1956. After graduation from McGill, Cohen edited a New York literary magazine called *The Phoenix*, where, in 1957, many of the poems later published in *The Spice-Box of Earth* (1961) appeared. In his early years, Cohen frequently published individual poems in literary journals — *CIV/n* (1953–54), *Forge* [McGill Univ.] (1954–56), *Prism* [Sir George Williams College] (1958), *The Tamarack Review* (1958), and *Queen's Quarterly* (1959).

Freed by a small inheritance, Cohen left North America for the Greek island of Hydra in the late 1950s. Here he lived with a Norwegian woman named Marianne and her son, and here he wrote the poems of *Flowers for Hitler* (1964) and *Parasites of Heaven* (1966). He also tried his hand at two novels: *The Favourite Game* (1963) and *Beautiful Losers* (1966). The *succès de scandale* of the latter coincided with the beginning of Cohen's career as a popular singer and songwriter. At one point, a *Melody Maker* poll listed Cohen as second only to Bob Dylan in popularity. With the help of Judy Collins and brief appearances at concerts (Newport Folk Festival and Central Park, New York) and on television (CBS's

Camera Three), Cohen soon became the darling of the pop music promoters. The publication of his *Selected Poems 1956–1968* (1968) coincided with the release of his first album, *Songs of Leonard Cohen* (1968), followed shortly by *Songs from a Room* (1969).

Leaving a quiet life in Hydra with Marianne, Cohen began both a new career and life-style — as a concert performer — and a new relationship. His new companion, Suzanne Elrod, was to be the mother of his two children (Adam Nathan and Lorca Sarah) and the "Lady" celebrated, lost, mourned, and scorned in his later *Death of a Lady's Man* (1978). With Cohen's public career came the press cult of the Cohen personality and the spate of articles on, and interviews of, the various newsworthy personae of the lonely rebel drop-out artist; the ironic, sardonic poet-lover; the vegetarian, mystic seer. As a poet, too, Cohen was at the height of his success in the late 1960s, winning the Quebec Award (1964) and the Governor General's Award (1968), which he refused with predictable irony, claiming that, while much in him strove for the honour, the poems themselves forbade it absolutely. In 1962 Cohen had announced that he would seek his audience in *Esquire* and *Playboy* — which *people* read — rather than literary magazines that only *poets* read. Nevertheless the poetic and academic establishment did not turn its back on its rebel son. In 1971 Dalhousie University awarded him an honourary Litt. D., and the next year the University of Toronto purchased his papers.

Cohen's energy in these years, however, was primarily devoted to his singing and songwriting. In 1971 Columbia Records released *Songs of Love and Hate*, and Robert Altman used Cohen's music as the score for his film *McCabe and Mrs. Miller*. In 1972 Cohen published his first new book of poems in six years — *The Energy of Slaves* — and perhaps it was the generally unfavourable reviews that confirmed Cohen in his choice of a stage career. In Europe in particular, his concerts were major cultural events, and as a result, his poems were translated into French, German, Spanish, Danish, Swedish, and Dutch. The Royal Winnipeg Ballet took *The Shining People of Leonard Cohen* on its European tour. In the next few years Cohen released three more albums: *Live Songs* (1973), *New Skin for the Old Ceremony* (1974), and *The Best of Leonard Cohen* (1975). The show *Sisters of Mercy* was a hit at the 1973 Shaw Festival in Niagara-on-the-Lake, Ontario.

The later 1970s saw a change in Cohen's life and work. After spending some time at a Zen centre in California, Cohen, now separated from Suzanne Elrod, began to write and record the album *Death of a Ladies' Man* (1977) with the help of Phil Spector (note the plural "Ladies' "; the book title is in the singular). The new sound that was born of this odd professional collaboration was greeted with mixed reactions, as was his publication of the book *Death of a Lady's Man* (1978).

When not on the road or recording in Nashville or New York for his albums *Recent Songs* (1979), *Various Positions* (1984), and *I'm Your Man* (1988), Cohen seems to have spent much of his time either in a Saint Dominique Street flat in Montreal's immigrant district or at his upper duplex near Los Angeles. The publication of *Book of Mercy* (1984), a book of "contemporary psalms," consolidated a renewal of Cohen's interest in devotional traditions dating from his earliest verse and clear in the recent songs, presented here in a prose (and quasi-narrative) form. As both Don Owen, in his NFB film *Ladies and Gentlemen . . . Mr. Leonard Cohen* (1965), and later Harry Rasky, in his CBC film *The Song of Leonard Cohen* (1980), learned, Cohen's power as a performer and personality is strong and easily (and entertainingly) documentable. The *enfant terrible* of Canadian poetry may no longer be an *enfant*, but the old desire to shock, to play, to "con," is still strong and appealing as his first video, *I Am a Hotel* (1984), suggested. His European following seems to have remained faithful, as the figures of his sales attest: as early as 1978, his book sales were already estimated at two million and his records at ten million — not bad for a former member of the Buckskin Boys who began playing the guitar to impress the girls at summer camp.

Tradition and Milieu

Critics and literary historians seem in agreement that Cohen's poetry grew out of the social and cultural milieu of Montreal in the 1950s. While taking classes with F.R. Scott and Louis Dudek at McGill, Cohen came under the influence of two of the main poetic currents of the time. Scott and the others who constituted the so-called McGill Movement in the 1930s had rejected the overblown and outdated romanticism of earlier Canadian verse and turned to the modernists for inspiration.[2] Cohen's early work shows the strong influence of

23

Eliot, Yeats, and the Metaphysical poets as well. Through Dudek, and later through Irving Layton, Cohen came into contact with the more urban and social orientation of the poets centred first on *First Statement* and later *Contact*. Desmond Pacey saw in Cohen's work their interest in expressing provocative ideas rather than developing sophisticated techniques.[3]

For Cohen, the older poet and friend Layton was also linked to another, earlier, and equally influential Montreal poet, A.M. Klein. The Jewish heritage of all three men played important, if different, roles in their work. Cohen has some of Klein's ambivalence towards his religion and race and certainly shares his feelings about the Holocaust: *Flowers for Hitler* is Cohen's version of Klein's *The Hitleriad*. But the differences are as strong as the similarities, and Cohen's obsession with the cult of the self and his erotic interest in the poet as lover grew more out of the Beat generation or the subsequent cultist, radicalized, hippy 1960s. There is certainly something of the spirit of Allen Ginsberg and Jack Kerouac in the early poetry and fiction: *Let Us Compare Mythologies* was published the same year as *Howl*.

Sandra Djwa and later Stephen Scobie have argued at length that Cohen's work should be seen in the tradition of the "Black Romantics."[4] For Djwa this means that Cohen's limitations are those of his late-Romantic decadent aesthetic: experience is narrowed and subjugated to art. *Flowers for Hitler* (given its titular echo of, and thematic link to, *Les Fleurs du mal*) was singled out for its immersion in destruction that was derivative of Baudelaire, Jean Genêt, William Burroughs, and so on.[5] While certainly the novel *Beautiful Losers* derives much from this predominantly novelistic modern tradition, there would seem to be a more complex mix in Cohen's poetry that is sidestepped by these critics in their undervaluing of Cohen's own ironic, self-conscious awareness of his decadent posing, of his "con." Scobie sees in Cohen's exulting in the darker aspects of the non-rational self in the face of what some see as the "saner" values of society, an extreme of the Romantic stress on the natural and the irrational. But surely Margaret Atwood's *The Journals of Susanna Moodie* and Michael Ondaatje's *The Collected Works of Billy the Kid* would therefore be equally "Black Romantic," yet their roots appear to be less in Genêt in particular than in the general radical ideology of the 1960s.

Cohen's aesthetic may be based in late-Romantic decadence, but it is also firmly part of contemporary pop culture. *Beautiful Losers* reveals most clearly his debt to the arts of the masses, and his own singing career testifies to his degree of involvement in that arena. Such a participation in the culture of the moment is not an implied avowal of antiliterary or antihumanistic feelings, but rather more an attempt to break down the Arnoldian class-inspired cultural hierarchies of the last century.[6] In this, Cohen partakes of a recent move in contemporary culture that has come to be called, perhaps rather misleadingly, "postmodernism."

Although Cohen was immediately recognized as one of the most promising poets of his generation, his later work, especially *The Energy of Slaves, Death of a Lady's Man,* and *Book of Mercy,* with the thematic stress on the difficulties and failures of both aesthetic expression and human emotion, puts Cohen into a rather different literary category. Eli Mandel has perhaps expressed this new position best: "Far more uncompromising than Lee or Atwood or Bowering or Ondaatje, and more scrupulous, Cohen is equally more compromised than all of them because closer to each of us, that is, to the duplicity of consciousness and history." Mandel goes on to argue for Cohen a central place in modern literature because of the tension in his work between art as a transforming, perfecting power and history as a nightmare of imperfection: "His development as a writer illustrates, as it creates, one of the main lines of development in Canadian writing, the gradual realization that art has the capacity to contain its own contradiction."[7] Cohen himself, however, see his latest work, *Book of Mercy,* as being "offensive" to those who have "too deep an investment in modernism," and aimed instead at a more common reader.[8]

In his attempt to expand both the audience and the scope of poetry, Cohen has certainly been more daring and has risked more than most of his generation. If, after the appearance of *Book of Mercy* in 1984, he may seem to many to have failed, it may be because, as Michael Ondaatje claimed in 1970, "Cohen, not his poems, has become the end product of his art. . . ."[9] First as a lyric poet, and then as a singer, Cohen has had to tread a fine line between confession and poetry, between popular personality and artistic persona. Perhaps his public has been as much to blame as his own impulses for the emphasis on the public performer turned psalmist. After all, Cohen had already published four well-received books of poetry when *Macleans* pronounced in August of 1968 that "Cohen's international reputation

LEONARD COHEN

as a troubadour now deserves to be matched by his stature as a poet."¹⁰

Critical Overview and Context

The poems that Cohen wrote as a teenager and published as *Let Us Compare Mythologies* in 1956 established his reputation as a promising, even brilliant, new voice in Canadian letters.¹¹ Allan Donaldson, Milton Wilson, and later Desmond Pacey perceived the comparison of various mythologies — Jewish, Christian, Hellenic, and so on — as the major thematic unifying force of the collection and as a much needed Canadian touch of exoticism, though it was clear that it was Cohen's Jewish background that was central to his vision.¹² The response to Cohen's particular mixture of violence and lyricism, which characterizes all of his later work as well, was not at all a positive one, though Northrop Frye appreciated Cohen's gift for the macabre ballad (Frye, p. 309). It was only in later critical overviews of Cohen's work that the style of these poems was evaluated as "vivid, exotic, and above all confident" (Scobie, p. 24) and was appreciated for its "gothic use of juxtaposition" (Ondaatje, p. 10), and its mixture of the serious and the witty, the tragic and the humorous. Of course, it was only later as well that the thematic centrality of this volume in Cohen's oeuvre could be perceived. For Ondaatje, writing in 1970, Cohen "seldom strayed too far from the ideas he blueprinted in his early work" (p.6). Certainly the main thematic constant was to prove to be the poet's self, the "I" of lyric verse in general and of the Beat style in particular. In this volume the poet is presented as having the power of myth-maker as well as comparison-maker. As in his later work, the poet as perceiver and as lover predominates, and the mind of the artist, as Ondaatje noted, is seen as more dramatic than the world outside it (Ondaatje, p. 8). Critics were able to see already in *Let Us Compare Mythologies* the same personal engagement with the reader that would later become familiar in Cohen's intimate appeal as a stage performer.¹³

Although this first book was published in 1956, its distribution was not wide until McClelland and Stewart reprinted it in 1966, after the publication of three other volumes of poetry. In 1961 they had published *The Spice-Box of Earth*, complete with drawings by Frank Newfeld. This was the first volume of Cohen's poetry to be published in the United States (by Viking in 1965) and, in fact, has proved to be his most popular single volume. With its appearance, Cohen was more widely reviewed. In the popular press, Robert Weaver and Dolores Bedingfield raved about the sensuous love poems,[14] and Arnold Edinborough, in two separate reviews, proclaimed that Cohen had now replaced Layton as Canada's major poet.[15] Others, however, such as Rosemary Eakins and Michael Hornyansky, complained of a certain lack of both clarity and coherence in the work.[16] The thematic continuities with the first volume were duly noted, especially the importance of the Jewish tradition[17] and the renewed self-consciousness of the role of the poet, with a new emphasis on the poet as lover. The mixing of the sacred and the profane, not to say obscene, was at first derided as, in Dudek's words, a combination of "sacred-oil and sewage-water"[18] but later came to be seen, by Pacey and Scobie in particular, as a paradox central to Cohen's imagination.[19] As he moved away from the biblical rhetoric of *Let Us Compare Mythologies*, Cohen was seen to be experimenting with ornate concreteness of diction, on the one hand, and a terse, spare abstraction, on the other. The latter was generally admired, while the former was attacked for its artificiality, for the subsequently overwrought and unfocused character of its imagery,[20] or most succinctly, for its "high ferment," in Milton Wilson's memorable phrase.[21] Later critics have not, by and large, disagreed with this evaluation of Cohen's formal achievement. Although Mandel admired the wit and playfulness of the verses from the start,[22] Al Purdy only liked their "casual offhand prosody."[23]

On the back cover of Cohen's next volume, *Flowers for Hitler* (1964), came the following statement:

> This book moves me from the world of the golden-boy poet into the dung pile of the front-line writer. I didn't plan it this way. I loved the tender notices *Spice Box* got but they embarrassed me a little. *Hitler* won't get the same hospitality from the papers. My sounds are too new, therefore people will say: this is derivative, this is slight, his power has failed. Well, I say that there has never been a book like this, prose or poetry, written in Canada. All I ask is that you put it into the hands of my generation and it will be recognized.

Though Ondaatje later found the dark underside of *The Spice-Box of Earth* "far nastier and far more frightening" than this new collection (Ondaatje, p. 21), the third volume did indeed change Cohen's image and his prediction of its reception was an accurate one. Dudek attacked his earlier protégé for his displaying of his "neurotic affiliations";[24] others found and continue to find the cynicism, the antipoetic unsubtlety, the artificially contrived horrors, and the "vacant posturing" to be signs of Cohen's failing powers.[25] Certainly the first reviews agreed with the poet's own claim to change in both tone and material; it was only later that critics could see that these changes were perhaps not as deep or as significant as Cohen would have liked to believe.[26]

Milton Wilson was one of the few reviewers who sought to go beyond evaluation to an understanding of the attempted change, perceiving Cohen's histrionics as important to his ironic and consciously undercut search for spiritual identity through role-playing and through an exploration of the poetic process itself.[27] Most other critics and reviewers focused on the thematic cohesion that this volume possesses through its negative vision of guilt, disgust, and anarchistic revulsion against the cruelty, greed, and hypocrisy of the twentieth century.[28] From this perspective, *Flowers for Hitler* seemed an attempt by the poet to free himself from self-absorption, to turn his attention outward and to add a public dimension to his private rhetoric. Certainly many of these poems, with their surrealistic imagery and provoking tone, were hits in the 1964 public readings Cohen gave when on tour with Irving Layton, Earle Birney, and Phyllis Gotlieb.

For all its superficial similarity to *Flowers for Hitler*, *Parasites of Heaven* (1966), Cohen's next collection, was not well received. It was generally felt to be more of the same, but with less cohesion and less of an emotional focus.[29] Later critics agreed, finding it an uneven book, one which was, in fact, parasitical on the success of *Beautiful Losers* and Cohen's concerts (Scobie, p. 63; Ondaatje, p. 57). In short, it was an attempt to cash in on his popularity. Although Ondaatje argued that the main interest of the volume was in Cohen's fascinating struggle with his material, even he felt the poems could not survive without a strong interest in Cohen as a personality, for much of the work moved back into the private world of the poet's mind. As George Bowering wrote: "He is the ultimate lyric man. That means that he shows any range of his discoveries, mundane to metaphysical, always through his consciousness of singular self."[30] The resulting move towards a private, hermetic imagery and what

Bowering saw as a mock-profundity of tone made *Parasites of Heaven* of minimal formal interest except as derivative or parasitic of his songs (the ballads, in particular) and of *Beautiful Losers* (the prose poems). Other possible reasons for Cohen's hermeticism in this volume will be discussed in the "Works" section below.

In 1968 Cohen published his *Selected Poems 1956–1968*. The very mixed reception was a direct result, I think, of his popular singing career. Fans were delighted and many European translations of the volume quickly followed its Canadian and American publication. Predictably, *Time* monitored the success of the book in these terms,[31] and equally predictably, the reviewer for the *Times Literary Supplement* found the poems juvenile and trendy: ". . . the same sort of thing has already been done better."[32] The obsessive Cohen themes were duly noted by the reviewers: "love, violence, martyrdom, sex, art, their intertwining in time with guilt, and the continuing search for an ecstatic nirvana by any or all of these means."[33] Critics were divided on other matters, however. Cohen's ironic posturing was seen either as empty or as a consistent strength;[34] his use of language was viewed either as excessive rhetoric or as "facility of style."[35] When reviewers looked for influences, they no longer nodded to Layton and Klein, though; they looked outside Canada now to Swinburne or Theodore Roethke.[36]

Later critics were able to see that the "New Poems" of the volume pointed ahead to *The Energy of Slaves* (1972) in their focus on the poet's role in relation to Cohen as private lover and Cohen as public entertainer (Scobie, p. 71). After four years' silence (a silence filled with many songs, however), the new collection was not particularly well received. And one possible reason is an amusing example of the "intentional fallacy" at work: statements about the poet's failing powers *within the poems* were taken at face value, and the Coleridgean paradox of the poems' own poetic power was ignored. The popular press was merely disappointed that Cohen's powers had failed and looked to his narcissism and rhetoric for proof — as if either were new to his work.[37] The same response came from both Britain and the United States, where Cohen's public persona still overshadowed his poetic work.[38] The songs, in fact, were often blamed for the poems' deficiencies.[39] The themes of the collection were generally seen to derive from *Beautiful Losers* and the other earlier works,[40] though the even more sexist view of women drew new attacks and new defences.[41] Other critics more acutely perceived that maybe Cohen was just pretending to sabotage his own work, perhaps in order to create yet another new image of himself, this time as antipoet.[42] Still others saw the book as part of a wider, "postmodern" trend in contemporary literature, especially in its self-consciousness about the artist's relationship to his medium and to his role.[43]

Six years later, *Death of a Lady's Man* reinforced this interpretation, and the reactions to the autoreferentiality of that work were divided. For many, the parallel poem/commentary structure and Cohen's even more intense focus on his love life and how it related to what he called his "life in art" were only self-indulgence; for others, *Death of a Lady's Man* was a major formal breakthrough in Cohen's work, the discovery of a form to mix perfectly the lyrical and the satiric.[44] One could argue that Cohen's fiction had already done the same and, in fact, that this book is the natural, if less interesting, next step after *Beautiful Losers*. Cohen himself saw the book less as a unified collection of poems than as a reference book to consult and as a documentation of a certain kind of sensibility. This oddly structured volume in many ways owes more to the prose than to the poetry of the past. And the songs are perhaps least important as formal and thematic background.

The critics' response to the "contemporary psalms" of *Book of Mercy* (1984) was as varied as could possibly be imagined. Rowland Smith saw them as combining Cohen's "well-established role as a worldly-wise sinner who has experienced all with the new role of would-be penitent."[45] He found these "catchy prayers" to be often "indulgent rather than anguished" (p. 155) but praised the "vintage Cohen" rhythms and resonances. In the end, he felt the book lacked "the control [and] the passion associated with great religious poetry of doubt" (p. 156). Joseph Kertes disagreed, comparing Cohen's renunciation of the secular life for the religious to that of T.S. Eliot, John Donne, and George Herbert and concluding that *Book of Mercy* is "one of the most honest and courageous attempts in Canadian writing to grapple with ultimate truth."[46] One man's "courageous attempt," however, is another man's "pious beseeching . . . neither living prayer nor interesting verse."[47] In this evaluation, Ron Graham sees the book as marking the failure of Cohen's literary talent, a view somewhat supported by Cohen's own statement that "recognitions of your own limitations are not without despair."[48] Many in this camp blame the perceived decline in talent on Cohen's singing career.

A brief account of the reception of Cohen's records would perhaps cast some light upon the context of Cohen's work and the critical reaction to it. In the late 1960s and early 1970s, Cohen was hailed as a rock poet comparable to Bob Dylan and John Lennon. The general response to his first two albums, *Songs of Leonard Cohen* (1968) and *Songs from a Room* (1969), was favourable, but the lyrics were praised over the guitar technique, which was felt to be rudimentary and functional. Cohen's odd voice was found to be a fairly good vehicle for the intimacy of the lyrics.[49] *Rolling Stone* panned *Songs of Love and Hate* (1971), however, for its lack of style: all Cohen did was put poems to music.[50] For some reviewers, though, this was what made Cohen special: Dylan was a songwriter first and a poet second, but Cohen was a poet first and foremost.[51] The range of opinion about the relation of the lyrics to the music in Cohen's work is vast, stretching from the belief that Cohen revised too little and that, frankly, the poems needed more revision to become good songs,[52] to the idea that the songs were more than poems put to music, that the lyrics and the music grew together to create a powerful personal utterance (Scobie, p. 127).

As Cohen began to tour, the reception of his records changed, for it was clear that he was much better live than in a studio.[53] The versions of earlier pieces that appear on *Live Songs* (1973) reveal the changes that performance brought to Cohen's songs. The themes of all of these songs tied in closely with the early poetry; many of the poems, in fact, became songs, or vice versa. Similarly, the songs of *New Skin for the Old Ceremony* (1974) picked up themes and ironic gestures of self-deprecation from the later poems and the fiction both. Reception to this (and to *The Best of Leonard Cohen*, released the next year) was cool,[54] partly perhaps because the tide of Cohen's performing success in North America was ebbing, though he continued to have a vast following in Europe. However, the reviewers were right in pointing to a certain monotony in Cohen's work, and it might well have been this awareness that lured Cohen into collaboration with Phil Spector in *Death of a Ladies' Man* (1977). The new sound was not particularly appreciated by Cohen's fans,[55] and he himself agreed in part.[56] Despite its rendering of several earlier poems into less ironic and complex pop tunes, this album is perhaps as far away as possible from the earlier poems-set-to-music in form and tone. Later albums would return somewhat to that earlier mode: *Recent Songs* (1979), *Various Positions* (1984), and *I'm Your Man* (1988).

Cohen's career as a pop singer has usually been blamed for the decline in the quantity and quality of his literary output.[57] Two book-length studies in English of Cohen's work, however, have placed the songs where they belong, firmly within the thematic continuity of Cohen's oeuvre: both Ondaatje and Scobie have provided fine thematic analyses that leave little more to be said. Scobie also offers the only extended and provocative analysis of the songs' lyrics. What has perhaps generally not been given enough attention is how Cohen is a product of a broader literary trend: the increased formal and thematic self-reflexivity of poetry today. Not since the Renaissance, perhaps, have we witnessed such a marked and *internalized* concern for the craft of poetry and its relation to the art of living. And, of course, Cohen would not stand alone in his desire to investigate the writing and the reading of literature. As *Death of a Lady's Man* tells us: "The modern reader will be provided a framework of defeat through which he may view without intimidation a triumph of blazing genius."[58]

Cohen's Works

According to Stephen Scobie, Cohen's central vision

> begins in a broken world, the world of the death-camps and the slaves, and, finding no solutions in the social and political vacuum of the fifties, it proceeds to the broken self, which it celebrates with a kind of fierce and inhuman joy. This vision provides a symbolic language which creates a hermetically sealed world, a closed-system view of reality. (p. 13)

Reading Cohen's poetry, however, I am struck less by a closed world than by one which, despite its self-referentiality, points outward to the world at large and to the reader in particular. At times, though, there is indeed a certain hermeticism in Cohen's imagery, a certain private quality to his symbolism. It is, of course, also true that this coexists with what can only be called banality, or more kindly, lyric simplicity, in both form and content. On both counts, George Woodcock sees Cohen as fundamentally conservative and conventional, not to say traditional and derivative.[59] Cohen's attraction to pop culture is therefore seen as natural because pop art is by definition conventional. While this is true, the significance of Cohen's conventionality is greater than such a dismissal allows, for the poet himself is more than aware — and within the poems themselves — of the potential for banality; in fact, he exploits it.

What Ondaatje calls Cohen's "gothic use of juxtaposition" (p. 10) is central to the poet's ironic and paradoxical vision in which everything both is and is not what it appears to be. Clichés are both trivial commonplaces *and* complex generators of poems. Pop culture is both trite and to be despised, *but* it is also all we have today. The Holocaust is both the greatest historical cruelty of our century *and* the emblem of the banality of evil, as documented by Hannah Arendt. Often this same ironic polarization or *coincidentia oppositorum* operates within a single word. The ubiquitous scar imagery, for example, of both *The Favourite Game* and the early poems contains two opposing but significant semantic units (or semes): the scar results from a healed wound and points to the past pain that was necessary to create it. It is also in itself a marking, an engraving. So, the poet must love, then leave his lover, in order to write of love and thereby leave his mark.

In his study *Semiotics of Poetry*, Michael Riffaterre has argued that every poem is formed as a transformation of a repressed semantic nucleus or matrix which produces or generates displacements throughout the text.[60] This matrix need not be actually present in the text but, like a repressed symptom (according to Freud), it will pop up in other guises. It is, however, always verbal and can be either derived from the poem itself or from a literary or linguistic convention. The particular importance of clichés — literary or verbal — is then clear, for they already exist actualized as fixed forms in the readers' minds, as part of their literary or linguistic competences. Riffaterre has argued too that these clichés are really tropes in the sense of being preserved stylistic devices. But, since the valorizing of individuality and originality in the Romantic period, we have come to regard such conventions and clichés in a pejorative light, though few would deny that they are still operative in poetry today. The central paradox of Cohen's irony is his use of deliberately un-Romantic techniques to express what are actually, as we shall see, very Romantic concepts of the role of the poet and of poetry. Similarly, inverting this procedure, he also uses deliberate romanticized clichés and tones of love to express very unromantic sentiments: "As the mist leaves no scar / On the dark green hill, / So my body leaves no scar / On you, nor ever will."[61]

According to Riffaterre, then, poems are produced by conversions and expansions of a semantic kernel, and so, to perceive the unity of difficult, seemingly chaotic poems, we must seek the matrix from which the poem derives. Many of Cohen's hermetic texts have been dismissed as simply bad poems. Scobie, for instance, claims that "The Glass Dog"[62] is just a list of incongruous details (p. 46), but in so claiming, he has perhaps fallen into the trap set by Cohen's self-conscious epigraph to the poem: *"Let me renew myself / in the midst of all the things of the world / which cannot be connected"* (*FH*, p. 70). The first part of the poem is concerned with the emptying of symbolic (human) meaning from natural objects (sky, stars, flowers), as the poet acknowledges and rejects his anthropomorphic imperialism: "I have no laws to bind / their hunger to my own" (*FH*, p. 70). Instead, the second section provides a vision of nature as that which is truly alive and therefore threatening to man. This new vision is activated by a visual pun as the *wind* becomes a *winding sheet* for humanity: "A white jewelled / wind in the shape of an immense spool of gauze / swaddled every moving limb" (*FH*, p. 71). The shroud of the dead is implied in the swaddling clothes of the helpless newborn human. In the third section, our exploitation of nature for food in order to live is both proclaimed and damned as a betrayal (Cohen was a vegetarian for a while), and the final (and only prose poem) section opens with "Creature! Come! One more chance" (*FH*, p. 72), as if God were willing to let humanity start again, amid the detritus of our betrayal of the natural. The poem ends with "Band Bang bells Bang in iron simple blue" (*FH*, p. 72). The "bells" and "vespers" of the previous section are recalled in their attempt to redeem our betrayal, but the "iron simple blue" suggests both "The Sea of Tin Cans" and also "Our Lady of the Miraculous Tin Ikon" of this same section (*FH*, p. 72). The "glass dog," like the "Tin Ikon," is humanity's creation; it is a more sinister variant of our anthropomorphizing imperialism, of our need to see the non-human — natural and divine both — as controlled, as part of our dead, "man-made" world, as the cliché has it.

Riffaterre points out that often it is not a pun (operating on two semantic levels as above) but a quoted text that will activate the reader's search for and discovery of a unifying semantic matrix. In "Congratulations," Cohen writes: "Hey Marco Polo / and you

Arthur Rimbaud / friends of the sailing craft / examine our time's adventure / the jewelled house of Dachau / Belsen's drunken fraternity" (*FH*, p. 15). That this poem occurs in *Flowers for Hitler*, with its overt Baudelairean echo of *Les Fleurs du mal*, reinforces the direct reference to the convention of the literary universe of the Symbolist poets, to that vision of low life and drugs, but here the decadence is directly and morally linked to Dachau, Belsen, and Hitler (see "Opium and Hitler," *FH*, pp. 78–79).

This technique of reading poems through the spectacles of other poems — more as an attempt to find meaning by comparing structure and function than as a search for the poet's own sources — has in recent criticism come to be called "intertextuality."[63] The intertexts of a work, then, are those other texts which can legitimately be connected to the poem being read, that is, by similarity of structure and function. The intertext, therefore, provides what Riffaterre calls the literary identity base of a text. Cohen's particular twist in most of his work, however, is to force the reader to invert, to ironize, the intertexts. *Beautiful Losers* can be read, for instance, as a parody or as an ironic inversion of the Bible, both in its overall structure and in its functional images.[64] Many of Cohen's songs are obvious ironic parodies of pop musical conventions as well.[65]

This intertextuality is a formal constant that all of Cohen's work demands of the reader, from the earliest poems to the novels and songs. The early "Ballad" in *Let Us Compare Mythologies* is almost a paradigm of both the intertextual mechanism itself and its range of reference. The poem begins on a deliberately very unballadlike note, already an ironic inversion of the conventional norm: "My lady was found mutilated / in a Mountain Street boarding house."[66] The next lines refer the reader to a more specific variant of this inverted ballad cliché: "My lady was a tall slender love, / like one of Tennyson's girls," but here she is really naked and slashed, "Dead two days" (*LUCM*, p. 46). The repetition of "My lady" suggests "Our Lady," the mother of the Redeemer, but here it is the lady herself who dies. Here the disciples are replaced by detectives, the scriptures by the tabloids. "My lady" is really "my old lady," the lover in popular parlance. Her beauty is known by all — known because of its cultural intertexts: "Body from Goldwyn. Botticelli had drawn her long limbs. / Rossetti the full mouth. / Ingres had coloured her skin" (*LUCM*, p. 47). The mixture of pop and "serious" cultural contexts here is typically Cohenesque, a deliberate democratization, a breaking of the barriers between low and high art forms. The more traditionally balladlike final stanzas begin with an echo of James Frazer (via T.S. Eliot, as we shall see) as the dead beloved is buried in "Spring-time" and all dance upon her grave (*LUCM*, p. 47).

The epigraph to Cohen's first collection signalled his awareness of and interest in the mechanism of intertextuality. It is from William Faulkner's *The Bear* and contains within itself an ironic citation of and commentary upon Keats's "Ode on a Grecian Urn":

> "All right," he said. "Listen," and read again, but only one stanza this time and closed the book and laid it on the table. "She cannot fade, though thou hast not thy bliss," McCaslin said: "Forever wilt thou love, and she be fair."
> "He's talking about a girl," he said.
> "He had to talk about something," McCaslin said. (*LUCM*, p. 7)

The ironic conjunction of love and poetry, as well as the intertextual focus, make it a perfect introduction to Cohen's work in general. The title of this first book, *Let Us Compare Mythologies*, points the reader to its intertextuality. Northrop Frye noted that there were many images in the poems "of white-goddess and golden-bough provenance" (Frye, p. 309). Certainly there are. The volume opens with: "Do not look for him / In brittle mountain streams: / They are too cold for any god" ("Elegy," in *LUCM*, p. 13). "Hanging man" imagery recurs frequently, but Frazer's linking of spring with rebirth does not appear in Cohen: (capitalized) Spring is the time of death in "Story" (*LUCM*, p. 63) and in "Ballad" (*LUCM*, pp. 46–47). The reader is forced to invert the mythic convention.[67] This is more the world, we suddenly realize, of Eliot's *The Waste Land* and its painful spring where "April is the cruellest month." Cohen's "Rededication" is perhaps his most overtly Eliotic poem in its tone and imagery, opening with:

> A painful rededication, this Spring,
> like the building of cathedrals between wars,
> and masons at decayed walls;
> and we are almost too tired to begin again
> with miracles and leaves
> and lingering on steps in sudden sun.
>
> (*LUCM*, p. 20)

Following are images recalling Eliot's vision of London and the Thames ("like hulks of large fish rotting far upbeach" [*LUCM*, p. 20]), and the poems ends with:

> We had learned a dignity in late winter,
> from austere trees and dry brown bushes,
> but Spring disturbs us like the morning,
> and we may hope only for no October.
>
> (*LUCM*, p. 20)

Since Eliot was an important poet for Cohen's Montreal predecessors — Smith and Scott — it is perhaps not surprising that the reader should read Cohen through Eliot. But I think Cohen himself was directly attracted to Eliot's own ironic reversal of literary conventions. Scobie points out that the title of one of the poems in *Flowers for Hitler*, "The Music Crept by Us" (p. 113), is from *The Tempest* (Scobie, p. 47). It is, but more significantly, I think, it is Shakespeare via Eliot's citation of him in *The Waste Land* in the context of the "Unreal" and infernal city and its river sweating oil and tar in "The Fire Sermon." Cohen's poem, after all, is about a world where ". . . the hat-check girl / has syphilis / and the band is composed / of former ss monsters" (*FH*, p. 113). Similarly, Cohen's "Fragment of Baroque" (*LUCM*, p. 52) recalls the focus and tone of Eliot's "A Game of Chess." Like Eliot's world, Cohen's is one of sterility, and the reader must read ironic versions of the ancient fertility myths through his poems.

Among the "mythologies" compared in Cohen's first collection are the Greek, Jewish, and Christian ones. Circe ("Song," p. 40) and Icarus ("Letter," pp. 36–37; "These Heroics," p. 28) meet the Golem ("Pagans," pp. 38–39) and the nuns of "Saint Catherine Street" (pp. 44–45).[68] As a reply to all, perhaps, the poem "To I.P.L." is generated by the never directly mentioned Nietzschean matrix, "God is dead": "No answers in your delightful / zarathustrian tales" (p. 54). The Bible, particularly the Old Testament, provides the major intertext for many of the poems, such as "Prayer for Messiah" (p. 18), "Prayer for Sunset" (p. 41), and "Exodus" (pp. 66–68). This is even more true of *The Spice-Box of Earth*, where over a dozen poems directly point the reader to biblical personages or images. But the ironic inversion of the intertext that the reader learned in the treatment of myths has now begun to operate on the most sacred of texts: Cohen's words challenge the Word. In "To a Teacher" (*SBE*, p. 21), there is a questioning of the value of sacrifice, of victimization in the name of what in *Beautiful Losers* comes to be seen as a "system": "A scheme is not a vision," Cohen warns in the song "Story of Isaac."[69] Perhaps because his name means "priest,"[70] Cohen likens the poet to the prophet, the outcast seer, the lone voice crying in the wilderness. Poetry replaces faith, and art, like ritual prayer, "makes speech a ceremony" ("Lines from My Grandfather's Journal," in *SBE*, p. 94).

Cohen may invert the religious tradition out of a need to resist it, but the reader perceives that the structures of that subverted faith and of others form the skeletal frame of his work. "I disdain God's suffering," he writes in "Absurd Prayer," because "men command sufficient pain" (*SBE*, p. 73), and Cohen chronicles that pain in *Flowers for Hitler*. Several contradictory poems from *Parasites of Heaven* make Cohen's position *vis à vis* his background somewhat more complicated, however. One of the prose poems begins: "In the Bible generations pass in a paragraph, a betrayal is disposed of in a phrase, the creation of the world consumes a page." Then he adds: "I could never pick the important dynasty out of a multitude. . . ." This is because he is not the man with "forehead shining" who wrote so succinctly of such significant specifics. Instead of being able to describe in his poetry the one olive tree "the story will need to shade its lovers," he claims instead: "For my part I describe the whole orchard."[71] In another poem, though, the poet sees himself as "John the Baptist . . . longing to be Him" and peddling "versions of Word" (*PH*, p. 47). In yet another, he claims: "When I hear you sing / Solomon / animal throat, eyes beaming / sex and wisdom / My hands ache from" (*PH*, p. 41). From what? Violence? Writing? Likely the latter for he feels companionship and solace with Solomon beside him, also ". . . aiming songs / at God . . ." (*PH*, p. 41).

Given Cohen's Jewish heritage, the use and even the inversion of biblical intertexts are perhaps not surprising. But the Bible is not by any means the only major source of intertextual reference for the reader of Cohen's work. All of the literary and linguistic clichés of romantic love, for instance, are also self-consciously and ironically utilized: "Gold, ivory, flesh, love, God, blood, moon — / I have become the expert of the catalogue" ("The Flowers That I Left in the Ground," in *SBE*, p. 4). The poem from which these self-conscious lines come is in fact a good example of Cohen's ability to force the reader to perceive that he is inverting a clichéd norm. It begins with an ironic reversal of both the cliché of flowers sent to lovers and also the literary (Ronsard, Spenser, Herrick, et al.) *carpe diem* / flower-picking seduction motif: "The flowers that I left in the ground, / that I did not gather for you" (p. 4). The poet also rejects the conventionalized love lyric's immortality claim (see, for example, Shakespeare's Sonnet 55), for he leaves the flowers to grow in the ground ". . . forever, / not in poems or marble" (p. 4). Like so many of Cohen's poems, however, this denial cannot mask the fact that it is in *this* poem that the flowers and the love live on. And, of course, the poet is always aware of this power: it is *he* who *lets* the flowers grow, the ships sail, "forever." The reason for his inversion of the love conventions lies in the poem: "Who owns anything he has not made? / With your beauty I am as uninvolved / as with horses' manes and waterfalls" (p. 5). As Breavman felt when confronted by Shell's natural beauty in *The Favourite Game*, the poet feels powerless to possess the naturally beautiful: he has to create in order to control. Therefore: "I breathe the breathless / I love you, I love you — / and let you move forever" (*SBE*, p. 5). The lover's controlling "let" is the revealing verb, once again.

A similar concept of art is presented in "When I Uncovered Your Body" where a contrast is set up between the woman's "single challenge of personal beauty" and the poet's ability to understand it only through the conventions of art, through "memories of perfect rhyme" or through seeing it as if it had been painted or "carved in stone." The poet had thought that *he* could ". . . bestow beauty / like a benediction . . ." but has to face the fact that ". . . the real and violent proportions of your body / made obsolete old treaties of excellence, / measures and poems" (*SBE*, p. 31). The love poem clichés are inverted by Cohen because the reality of love here demands it. New images are needed — often themselves inversions: in "Celebration," fellatio is presented as an ancient rite, ending with the poet toppling "with a groan, like those gods on the roof / that Samson pulled down" (*SBE*, p. 55).

Cohen also plays with more specific lyric conventions, and here the reader discovers that the intertextual references are more precise. The closing lines of Dylan Thomas' "Fern Hill" echo in "Prayer for Messiah" ("O sing from your chains where you're chained in a cave" [*LUCM*, p. 18]) and in "Portrait of the City Hall" ("Listen, says the mayor, listen to the woodland birds, / They are singing like men in chains" [*FH*, p. 15]). Yeats is perhaps an even clearer intertextual reference for most readers or critics,[72] especially in "The Girl Toy" with its recalling of "Sailing to Byzantium"'s image of the artist as the timeless golden bird that keeps the "drowsy Emperor" awake. Cohen literalizes Yeats's image: the girl is a golden "toy more precious than his famous golden birds" and it is her mechanical but potent sexuality that keeps the emperor awake. Here, however, the focus is on time and on the painful contrast that Yeats sought to escape: "he obese and old, / she lovely as a pendulum." He weeps and spits blood, cutting "his aging lips on a jewelled eye," and she hums and sings him "a ballad of their wedding feast" (*SBE*, p. 48). This is more than just an allusion to Yeats; it is an inversion that is a reply to his desire for art and the artist to be free of "those dying generations." In "Montreal 1964,"Cohen again recalls this context but on a different note: *"Canada is a dying animal / I will not be fastened to a dying animal"* (*FH*, p. 35; Cohen's italics). But he is so fastened, as, of course, was Yeats. Other echoes of Yeats also have to be inverted by the reader: the "Leda and the Swan" imagery of "depraved swans" and "celestial assault" occurs in a poem called "The Boy's Beauty." Here the woman's quivering thighs and "legendary flanks" are part of the communal sexual fantasies of a "thousand clumsy poets" (*SBE*, p. 47).

The intertextual references to John Donne's verse, on the other hand, are references the reader learns *not* to invert. In Donne, as in Eliot, Cohen seems to have found a poet of polarities, of ironic reversals of convention. (Eliot's championing of the Metaphysical poets for their complexity is likely relevant here.) Scobie (p. 24) points to Donne's technique of startling opening lines as used in Cohen's early verse: "How you murdered your family / means nothing to me / as your mouth moves across my body" ("Letter," in *LUCM*, p. 36). "The Fly" (*LUCM*, p. 60) is obviously a modern and simplified variant of Donne's "The Flea," and in "The Flowers That I Left in the Ground," Cohen writes, "I go for weariness of thee" (*SBE*, p. 4), inverting, for once, the opening lines of Donne's "Song": "Sweetest love, I do not go, / For weariness of thee." The inversion is necessary for Cohen here, because only when the poet has left the lover can poetry begin — for him, at least. When Cohen writes, in "I Long to Hold Some Lady," that "There is no flesh so perfect / As on my lady's bone" (*SBE*, p. 59), the odd word "bone" acts as a signal to the reader of the Donne intertext of "The Relique" ("A bracelet of bright haire about the bone"), which in turn determines the otherwise unmotivated final image of the poem: "Cold skeletons go marching / Each night beside my feet" (*SBE*, p. 59). The poem's imagery of worshipping priests and pilgrims also recalls the secular love/divine love play in poems such as "The Canonization" and "The Funerall," as well, of course, as the Song of Solomon. Such polarities are part of Cohen's vision, and I think he sensed in the work of Donne, like that of Eliot, a kinship with the structures of his own creative mind and its ironic paradoxes.

Cohen's imagination, however, is definitely a contemporary one, like his reader's. It is an imagination formed not only of this serious or "highbrow" poetry but also of more low-art modes. The imaginative power of popular art forms like movies is manifest in poems such as "You Are the Model" (*PH*, p. 58) and, even more overtly, in "Order" (*FH*, p. 86). The heroes of comic books are, in "A Migrating Dialogue," as fascist and sadistic as Hitler: "Captain Marvel signed the whip contract. / Joe Palooka manufactured whips. / Li'l Abner packed the whips in cases. / The Katzenjammer Kids thought up experiments" (*FH*, p. 72). Cohen also plays with the cliché as a form of *popular* verbal speech. "The Failure of a Secular Life" inverts the banality of the social and verbal clichés of the breadwinner coming home from a hard day's work: "The pain-monger came home / from a hard day's torture." When his wife "hit him with an open nerve / and a cry the trade never heard," the man who brings home the bacon quits his job — "A man's got to be able / to bring his wife something" (*FH*, p. 53).

The complexity of Cohen's manipulation of pre-established verbal commonplaces can be seen in "A Kite Is a Victim," the first poem of *The Spice-Box of Earth*. Scobie has seen the kite symbol here as a kite, a poem, a lover, and, following Ondaatje, the ego and all that is free in us (Scobie, p. 27; see Ondaatje, p. 16). Finally, the kite represents the "other." While all of this is true, there is something else operating on a purely formal level in the poem. The basic semantic units or semes are dual and paradoxical as always: they are semes of attachment and independence. These semes are first activated in what is known in semiotic terms as a kite "code," but there is then a transfer to other codes — that of a fish, a poem, and finally, with a variation, a moon code. The text itself is a rhetorical *amplificatio* or a Riffaterrian expansion of a series of clichés organized by those two semantic matrices. The early part of the poem is structured by the unspoken but implied expressions "high as a kite" and "free as a bird." But kites are, significantly, attached by strings, and so another set of clichés becomes operative: "tied down," "to string along," but also "no strings attached." These again recall the dual matrix of attachment and independence but as transcoded to a love relationship where the soaring soul of the lover traditionally transcends the earth. In an artistic code, poetic "flights of fancy" leave the poet "flying high" but he must "come down to earth" ("A kite is the last poem you've written"). But the "travelling cordless moon" escapes the poet's control and as such can indeed have the power to make him "worthy and lyric and pure" (*SBE*, p. 1).

The paradoxical dualities or polarities of control and freedom that structure this poem are paradigmatic not only in the sense that they recur in all Cohen's work in the master/slave thematic but also in the sense that they recall the structure of the inversion technique that Cohen's irony puts into operation on almost all formal levels of the text. We can see it again in the opening of the short poem "Folk" in *Flowers for Hitler*: "flowers for hitler the summer yawned / flowers all over my new grass" (p. 81). That the flowers are for "hitler" (in lower case to suggest his banal normality in a world of cruelty) negativizes an otherwise conventionally positive image. The "summer yawned" out of boredom, perhaps, or out of a culpable acceptance of trivialized evil. But the verb "yawned" also suggests, in poetic convention, the chasm or abyss that has infernal connotations (especially when reinforced here by "hitler") and also contains a suggestion of some mystery that the mind cannot fathom. This negativizing of images continues in the next line where the implied cliché is of something being spilled "all over my new dress," only here it is flowers growing "all over my new grass."

A technique related to this one is Cohen's use of puns which, as we have seen, allow him to operate in two codes simultaneously. Like Donne, he plays on the verb "to die" in both a sexual and a mortal way. He also puns on "to lie" in the sense of a sexual lying with someone and the inevitable telling of lies that accompanies that act. In the song "Leaving Greensleeves" on the album *New Skin for the Old Ceremony*, Cohen admits: "I sang my songs, I told my lies, to lie between your matchless thighs."[73] Similarly, the version of "Bird on the Wire" on the *Live Songs* album, which differs from that on *Songs from a Room*, offers this variation: "If I, if I have been untrue, it was just that I thought a lover had to be some kind of liar too."[74]

This same punning occurs in the title of *Death of a Lady's Man*. While "death" retains its intended Metaphysical ambiguity, a "Lady's Man" is either a philanderer, a man who controls women, or a man who belongs to, and is ruled by, a lady. Like the image of the kite, that of the lady's man contains within it a dual semantic determination. This reinforcement, followed by ironic inversion of conventional norms, is again typical of Cohen's imagination that can contain such polarities as the traditional religion of the spirit *and* that parody of it, the religion of the flesh, beauty *and* violence, evil *and* banality, egotism *and* self-disgust.

In *Death of a Lady's Man*, Cohen claims that the book grew out of two other manuscripts: "My Life in Art" and "The Woman Being Born." These two titles could well act as succinct summaries of the dual stances of Romantic or postmodernist self-awareness in Cohen's oeuvre: the poet as public artist figure and the poet as private lover. Cohen is both Romantic and postmodernist in his obsession with the poet's powers and in his focus on the process of creation. Ondaatje wrote that in *Let Us Compare Mythologies*, "Cohen's mythmaking process is . . . presented naked and blatant to the reader" (p. 12) as he writes of the "power of translating raw beauty into metaphors" (p. 21). While this is true, there has been an increased complexity in his poetry's modes of self-reflexiveness from the blatant early version in "These Heroics," where the poet's main identity is that of the failed flyer, the lover: "if I could ruin my feathers / in flight before the sun; / do you think that I would remain in this room, / reciting poems to you, / and making outrageous dreams / with the smallest movements of your mouth?" (*LUCM*, p. 28).

Many of Cohen's subsequent self-conscious poems present the poet posing. And the pose involves the Romantic paradox typified best perhaps by Coleridge's "Dejection: An Ode": the lament about the poet's failing powers, his inability to write poetry, resounds through the lines of a poem whose very existence undercuts the self-deprecation. Similarly, the dissolution of self in Cohen's poetry is always expressed by a voice that suggests a potent sense of self. Note the postponing future tense of his renunciation in "Style": "I will forget my style / I will have no style" (*FH*, p. 27). The poet wants to look to his work as a way of stopping time, wanting to believe the poetic convention that art fixes and eternalizes, but there is a note of panic and desperation — "Poems! break out!" — as he realizes

43

art's limitations: "Can't I live in poems? // Hurry up! poems! lies! / Damn your weak music! / You've let arthritis in! / You're no poem / you're a visa" ("On the Sickness of My Love," in *FH*, p. 51).

Like his *Künstlerroman The Favourite Game*, many of Cohen's poems actually narrate the creative process itself. *Parasites of Heaven* contains many such poems. In "Clean as the Grass," the poet comes ". . . to this page // . . . documenting the love of one / who gathered my first songs" (*PH*, p. 26). In "I wonder if my brother will ever read this," we are told that "heroes and near-heroes . . . disdain to implore the horizontal world with words and organizing metaphors" but that the poet lacks such heroic "balance" and must instead "blunder among [his] tetherings" (*PH*, p. 29). Language and its structures are both the free-flying kite and the string that binds the poet's expression: "These notebooks, these notebooks! / Poetry is no substitute for survival. / In the books beside my bed / I used up my will like an alphabet" ("These notebooks, these notebooks!" in *PH*, p. 61). Recalling "The Cuckold's Song" in *The Spice-Box of Earth* ("I repeat: the important thing was to cuckold Leonard Cohen. / I like that line because it's got my name in it" [p. 42]), "He was beautiful when he sat alone" asserts: "It is not a question mark, it is not an exclamation point, it is a full stop by the man who wrote Parasites of Heaven" (*PH*, p. 67).

This self-reflexiveness reaches a peak in *The Energy of Slaves*. The volume opens with an address to the reader: "Welcome to these lines."[75] The second and third poems are variants on each other, as the "light fell on this poem" and on the name of a tortured man who is first avenged and then forgotten ("I threw open the shutters," pp. 10, 11). In the next poem we are first told that "This is the only poem / I can read / I am the only one / can write it," and finally that "I learned to write / what might be read / on nights like this / by one like me" ("This is the only poem," p. 12). Because of this introversion, it is not likely that we will fail to heed the next poem's request: "If you ever read this / think of the man writing it" ("All men delight you," p. 13). We could continue in this vein, for almost every poem contains some reference to the life-giving processes of writing or reading the poem itself:

> I dress in black
> I have green eyes
>   in certain light

If others try to write this
death to them
death to anyone
if he or she unseal this poem
in which I dress in black

and bless your eyes
who hurry from this page
Put a green-eyed man
out of his misery and rage.

("I dress in black," p. 70)

The complexity of the reader/writer relationship here is also found in other poems that sing skilfully of the poet's lost skill: "I am no longer at my best practising / the craft of verse" ("I am no longer at my best practising," p. 24). Why continue? "I have no talent left," he writes, "I can't write a poem anymore / You can call me Len or Lennie now / like you always wanted / I guess I should pack it up / but habits persist / and women keep driving me back into it" ("I have no talent left," p. 112). While the last statement points to the centrality of the lover in the poet's identity, it is also true that for Cohen, as for his fictional hero Breavman in *The Favourite Game*, poetry grows out of past, lost love, out of "emotion recollected in tranquillity." The irony of the identity of the poet as lover lies in this: "With Annie gone, / Whose eyes to compare / With the morning sun? // Not that I did compare, / But I do compare / Now that she's gone" ("For Anne," in *SBE*, p. 64). The poet needs his lover for inspiration ("Because you are close" ["Owning Everything," in *SBE*, p. 34]), but that familiar paradox of independence and attachment reasserts itself and forces the poet to flee, for he has been robbed by love's proximity of his necessary aesthetic distance, his "strangerhood." This is the irony of love for Cohen in "The Stranger Song" and "Winter Lady"[76] (the songs from *McCabe and Mrs. Miller*) and also in many of the poems of *Parasites of Heaven*: "May I survey the emptiness / that serves as field for the complete embrace?" ("The stars turn their noble stories," in *PH*, p. 40). Among the "New Poems" in the *Selected Poems 1956–1968* are many that point both back and ahead. "The reason I write / is to make something / as beautiful as you are"[77] recalls *The Favourite Game* but anticipates as well *Death of a Lady's Man*. Reminiscent of *Beautiful Losers*, these poems address the beloved: "you know I am a god / who needs to use your body / who needs to use your body / to sing about beauty / in a way no one / has ever sung before" ("I Met You," in *SP*, p. 227).

For Cohen the poet is *not* like ordinary men. Scobie misses the self-conscious irony when he misinterprets "I Wonder How Many People in This City" (*SBE*, p. 11) as a testament that the poet is like all the others, a lonely loser (Scobie, p. 29).[80] Rather, although they too look out the window, *only he*, the poet, goes back to his desk and "write[s] this down." This is both the irony and the affirmation of the poet's identity. Only the poet can transform loneliness and even pain into art. He may, indeed, even will pain by deliberate separation from his beloved, as in "Owning Everything" (*SBE*, p. 34) and "Travel" (*SBE*, p 52). The poet is, after all, the naming Adam and in some ways every woman's first man: "You live like a god / somewhere behind the names / I have for you" ("You Live Like a God," in *SP*, p. 229). He creates, through naming, eternal monuments: "I name this mountain after him" ("There Are Some Men," in *SBE*, p. 8).

The poet, in Cohen's case, is the named as well as the namer. As mentioned earlier, his own surname means "priest," and this is a name he shares with the other males of his family, all of them (except the poet?) condemned to dissatisfaction: "Must we find all work prosaic / because our grandfather built an early synagogue?" ("Priests 1957," in *SBE*, p. 70). "Lines from My Grandfather's Journal," which ends *The Spice-Box of Earth*, presents this family figure as poet, as confessing journal writer, and as creator of a dictionary — a role which drove him "back to Genesis. Doubting where every word began" (p. 84).

This personal artist figure joins the ranks of favourite painters (Van Gogh, Chagall) and Canadian poets (Klein, Layton) whom Cohen addresses in his poems. As part of this community, the poet-priest must act too as the conscience of society. Despite the seemingly private focus of Cohen's lyrics, there is a consistent argument for a certain public responsibility that receives its fullest expression in *Flowers for Hitler*. The epigraph to the volume is from Primo Levi: "If from the inside of the Lager, a message could have seeped out to free men, it would have been this: Take care not to suffer in your own homes what is inflicted on us here" (p. 11). The first poem, "What I'm Doing Here," is both a personal confession ("I refuse the universal alibi") and a direct address to the reader: "I wait / for each one of you to confess" (p. 13).

In many of the poems that follow, Cohen neutralizes and compli-
cates the simple, clichéd, negative connotations of Naziism by
making the Nazis like us and making us more like the monsters of
history than we care to be: "All There Is to Know about Adolf
Eichmann" (*FH*, p. 66) asserts Eichmann's frightening normality,
and "A Migrating Dialogue" ends with:

Braun, Raubal and him
[Hitler and his ladies][79]
(I have some experience in these matters),
these three humans,
I can't get their nude and loving bodies out of my mind.

(*FH*, p. 74)

One of the techniques of reader involvement used by Cohen in many
of these poems is the direct address, suggesting a desire for moral
collusion between poet and reader. In "The Genius" (*SBF*, pp.
78–79) the poet claims that "For you / I will be . . ." a series of
historical clichés: the ghetto jew, the apostate jew, the banker jew,
the Broadway jew, the doctor jew, and finally the Dachau jew. By
The Energy of Slaves ("Welcome to these lines" [p. 9]) and *Beautiful
Losers* ("Welcome to you who read me today"),[80] the poet's role
goes beyond that of a moral conscience and becomes, in a sense, the
paradoxically controlled controller — the creator: "This is the poem
we have been waiting for / n'est-ce pas / . . . / You are a detail in it"
("This is the poem we have been waiting for," in *ES*, p. 114). In
Death of a Lady's Man there is a subtle play between the attacking
first-person plural voice of the commentaries and the attacked
first-person singular of the poems. Readers, as controlled controllers
themselves, are self-consciously a motivating factor in the book, as
the poet acknowledges: "I'm ashamed to be in the rays of your
reading eyes" (p. 87). We are shown original drafts, revisions, and
even comments upon both, but we are also given orders: *"go back
and read THE DOVE"* (p. 118).

Death of a Lady's Man has been considered in the treatment of
Cohen's fiction (in this same series)[81] because in many of its themes
and structures it is the logical culmination of the particular formal
self-reflexiveness of *The Favourite Game* and *Beautiful Losers*. The
same argument, however, could be made for any of Cohen's books
of poetry, regardless of their date of publication — with the exception

of *Book of Mercy*, as we shall see. While this is one way of saying that there has been a creative continuity to Cohen's imagination, it is also to say that the poetry is in some significant way only a handmaiden to the prose. While Cohen's reputation as a novelist was slow in establishing itself, today it is the two novels (but in particular *Beautiful Losers*) that stand as his most important contributions. In that second novel, Cohen found the form that finally allowed him to integrate all of his concerns. More significantly for this study, though, *Beautiful Losers* provides the single most relevant intertext for all of Cohen's poetry. It is a key to much of the seeming hermeticism mentioned at the start.

All of the major themes of *Beautiful Losers* appear in Cohen's early books of verse and in his early songs: the teacher and the disciple, the religion of the spirit and that of the flesh ("Abelard proved how bright could be / the bed between the hermitage and nunnery" ["The Priest Says Goodbye,"in *SBE*, p. 37]), the new sainthood ("Alexander Trocchi, Public Junkie, Priez Pour Nous," in *FH*, pp. 45–47), the tyrannies of history (of time and of naming), the systems we construct and their victims. Bizarre plot and character details are even prefigured, and *Beautiful Losers*' predilection for radio, comic books, and the movies is also present (in *Flowers for Hitler* alone, see: "Style" [pp. 27–28], "A Migrating Dialogue" [pp. 72–74], "Order" [p. 86], "One of the Nights I Didn't Kill Myself" [p. 120]). The nameless narrator's awareness of his bodily functions ("The food that will not obey" ["The True Desire," in *FH*, p. 61]), his profession and his yearnings ("I have been reading too much history / and writing too many history books / Magic moves from hand to hand . . ." ["Independence," in *FH*, p. 84]), and his sense of being a beautiful loser ("If I must lose, let me lose like thee!" ["The Commentary," in *FH*, p. 90]) are all in the poems written before the novel, as are F.'s teachings ("I am the flesh teacher" ["To the Indian Pilgrims," in *FH*, p. 112]) and Catherine's uncle's cure ("I embrace the changeless" ["Disguises," in *FH*, p. 118]). However, not until *Beautiful Losers* was Cohen able to pull all of these themes together and do so with that rather astonishingly original voice.[82]

Parasites of Heaven, published the same year as *Beautiful Losers*, can be seen as a companion to the novel in theme, style, and form. Certainly many of the prose poems could almost fit in the novel; in fact some of them read as if they might, at some point, actually have been part of it. The volume itself opens with a very telling short poem:

So you're the kind of vegetarian
that only eats roses
Is that what you mean
with your Beautiful Losers.
        ("So you're the kind of vegetarian," in *PH*, p. 11)

Even without the capitalization, the reader is not likely to miss the
connection. The ending of the novel also acts as an important gloss
that helps us make sense of Cohen's obsession in *Parasites of Heaven*
with images of the sky and of stars ("One night I burned the house
I loved" [p. 18], "Terribly awake I wait" [p. 28], "I wonder if my
brother will ever read this" [p. 29]). In "Somewhere in my trophy
room," the "impossible trophy" is "the bright, great sky, where no
men lived" (p. 49), and in "Here was the Harbour, crowded with
white ships," we learn that the sky "demands stories; of men the sky
demands all manner of stories, entertainments, embroideries, just as
it does of its stars . . ." (p. 45). The specific and oddly worded
expression "black star" of an earlier poem ("Desperate sexual
admirals," in *PH*, p. 32) makes this last image a little clearer in that
it punningly points to the apocalyptic Ray Charles movie in the sky
that ends *Beautiful Losers*. "Here was the Harbour . . ." continues:
"The sky does not care for this trait or that affliction, it wants the
whole man lost in his story, abandoned in the mechanics of action
. . ." (p. 45). Whether lost "in his story" or in history, the poet's
relation to the blank sky is like that of the novel's black star.
    The hermetic (bad?) poems of *Parasites of Heaven*, in fact, often
do not even make very much sense without the novel as a meaning-
generating intertext for the reader. *The Energy of Slaves*, because of
its acute self-consciousness, stands more on its own but shares, once
again, the themes and also the tone of much of *Beautiful Losers*:

I wore of medal of the Virgin
round my throat
I was always a slave
Play with me forever
    Mistress of the World
Keep me hard
Keep me in the kitchen
Keep me out of politics.
        ("I wore a medal of the Virgin," in *ES*, p. 36)

49

Furthermore, much of the muddle (or complexity) of *Death of a Lady's Man*'s form and content is dissolved when the volume is viewed as a continuation of the structural and thematic self-reflexiveness of the novel. That Cohen himself was aware of this close relationship may be inferred from a remark in one of the later sections of *Death of a Lady's Man* regarding the inherently narrative quality of this seemingly fragmented work: "The transmission is weakest in those passages where the reader is swept along in the story and the insights and the flow of events" (p. 184). In this book, in fact, the very form is in some way the major theme, and the reader is its self-conscious and intended actualizer.

With *Book of Mercy* (1984) something new appears to occur. There are still certain continuities with *Beautiful Losers* and the earlier poetry, of course. We find the same confusion of addressees and speakers, of the shifting shifters of I/you/he/we. The teacher/learner relationship with a "Friend"[83] suggests the F./narrator interaction. Certain images — the tearing of the veil (No. 3) and the "famous mechanical salvation" (No. 13) — suggest links to important motifs in the earlier novel. The general paradox of being a "beautiful loser" is echoed, as in *The Energy of Slaves*, in the constant theme of failure: "In the eyes of men he falls. . . . It is sad, they say. . . . But he falls radiantly toward the light. . ." (No. 8).

Here too we find the obsessive focus on the self,[84] from the initial opening "I" to the number of sections or psalms: fifty (the number of years of Cohen's life as he writes). The biblical syntax, diction, and imagery of the very early verse reappears here, once again in the context of creation and naming, of "searching among the words" (No. 4) — a phrase set in apposition to "begging for mercy." In this book, however, it is the specifically Jewish tradition that is invoked through references to Israel, David, Bathsheba, Abraham, Ishmael, and Moses. Cohen reinvokes the meaning of his surname (priest), but this time to emphasize the singer/psalmist: he is a David figure. The "sisters of mercy" from the early song are masculinized, within this tradition, into a male deity to whom the psalms are addressed. The female muse has only a minor presence here as the "angel of song" (No. 4).

There has clearly been a change in Cohen's perspective. Gone is the irony that marked even his most serious moments. Gone is the almost manic need to control, especially by writing. Here the stress is on being controlled — "You *let* me sing . . ." (No. 19; emphasis added)

— and on surrender to mercy — "Remove your creature's self-created world. . ." (No. 48). The ironically juggled dualities of independence and attachment that underpinned all the previous work seem to be resolved into an acceptance of attachment, even a desiring of it. F.'s "connect nothing" becomes a yearning for "absolute unity" (No. 20).

The songs written in these years do not manifest the same loss of what had become a characteristic Cohen irony. In "Tower of Song," from *I'm Your Man* (1988), the man with the less than perfect voice sings: "I was born like this, I had no choice. I was born with the gift of a golden voice."[85] In this light, it is tempting to see *Book of Mercy* as a kind of "sport" or aberration. Or perhaps it is, instead, yet another version of the *I Ching* that he claimed he wanted to write with *Death of a Lady's Man*. There is no doubt that he is still, as he once said, peddling "versions of Word" ("I am too loud when you are gone," in *PH*, p. 47), while trying to write "the fiction of [his] absence" (*DLM*, p. 210). In the previous book, he had told the reader: "All the Messiahs agree / You're not supposed to be looking for me" (*DLM*, p. 211). Yet the reader does, for the self-consciousness of Cohen's poetry is not just a textual autorepresentation: always beside this intertextual postmodernism is a very Romantic and personal self-awareness that *Book of Mercy* underlines most strongly. Like Coleridge, Cohen may feel that his "genial spirits fail" at times, but he too sings on, a pop-singer's guitar replacing the formerly requisite Aeolian harp — a "fitter instrument," perhaps, for our own particular "Mad Lutanist."

NOTES

[1] George Bowering, "Inside Leonard Cohen," rev. of *Parasites of Heaven*, *Canadian Literature*, No. 33 (Summer 1967), p. 71.

[2] See Peter Stevens, ed., *The McGill Movement*, Critical Views on Canadian Writers (Toronto: Ryerson, 1969).

[3] *Creative Writing in Canada: A Short History of English-Canadian Literature*, 2nd ed. (Toronto: Ryerson, 1961), p. 236.

[4] Sandra Djwa, "Leonard Cohen: Black Romantic," *Canadian Literature*, No. 34 (Autumn 1967), pp. 32–42; Stephen Scobie, *Leonard Cohen*, Studies in Canadian Literature, No. 12 (Vancouver: Douglas & McIntyre, 1978), esp. pp. 1–3. All further references to this work ("Scobie") appear in the text.

[5] See also George Woodcock, "The Song of the Sirens: Reflections on Leonard

Cohen," in *Odysseus Ever Returning: Essays on Canadian Writers and Writing*, New Canadian Library, No. 71 (Toronto: McClelland and Stewart, 1970), pp. 93–110.

[6] My argument here is with Eli Mandel in his "Cohen's Life as a Slave," in *Another Time*, Three Solitudes: Contemporary Literary Criticism in Canada, No. 3 (Erin, Ont.: Porcépic, 1977), p. 128. This point is more fully developed in my paper "The Carnivalesque and Contemporary Narrative: Popular Culture and the Erotic," *University of Ottawa Quarterly*, 53, No. 1 (Jan.–March 1983), 83–96.

[7] Mandel, "Cohen's Life as a Slave," p. 135.

[8] Doug Fetherling, interview with Leonard Cohen, *Books in Canada*, Aug.–Sept. 1984, p. 30.

[9] Michael Ondaatje, *Leonard Cohen*, New Canadian Library, Canadian Writers Series, No. 5 (Toronto: McClelland and Stewart, 1970), p. 60. All further references to this work ("Ondaatje") appear in the text.

[10] Rev. of *Selected Poems 1956–1968*, *Maclean's*, Aug. 1968, p. 60.

[11] Margaret Avison, "Poetry Chronicle," rev. of *Let Us Compare Mythologies*, by Leonard Cohen, and six other books, *The Tamarack Review*, No. 1 (Autumn 1956), pp. 78–85, and Desmond Pacey, "A Group of Seven," rev. of *Let Us Compare Mythologies*, by Leonard Cohen, and six other books, *Queen's Quarterly*, 63 (Autumn 1956), 438–39, found Cohen's start a brilliant one; on the more cautious side of "promising" were Northrop Frye, rev. of *Let Us Compare Mythologies*, in "Letters in Canada 1956: Poetry," *University of Toronto Quarterly*, 26 (April 1957), 308–09 (all further references to this work ["Frye"] appear in the text); Milton Wilson, "Turning New Leaves," rev. of *Let Us Compare Mythologies*, *The Canadian Forum*, March 1957, pp. 282–84; and D.G. L[ochhead], rev. of *Let Us Compare Mythologies*, by Leonard Cohen, *The Bull Calf and Other Poems*, by Irving Layton, and *Even Your Right Eye*, by Phyllis Webb, *Dalhousie Review*, 36 (Winter 1957), 425, 427.

[12] Allan Donaldson, rev. of *Let Us Compare Mythologies*, *The Fiddlehead*, No. 30 (Nov. 1956), p. 30; Wilson, "Turning New Leaves," p. 282; Desmond Pacey, "The Phenomenon of Leonard Cohen," *Canadian Literature*, No. 34 (Autumn 1967), p. 5.

[13] Michael Gnarowski, Introd., *Leonard Cohen: The Artist and His Critics*, ed. Michael Gnarowski, Critical Views on Canadian Writers (Toronto: McGraw-Hill Ryerson, 1976), pp. 4–5.

[14] Robert Weaver, "Leonard Cohen's 'Spice-Box' Presents Sombre Vision," *Toronto Daily Star*, 10 June 1961, p. 29; Dolores Bedingfield, "Montrealer's Love Songs Win Praise," rev. of *The Spice-Box of Earth*, *The Globe and Mail*, 17 June 1961, p. 9.

[15] Arnold Edinborough, rev. of *The Spice-Box of Earth*, *The Canadian Reader*, 2, No. 9 (July 1961), 5–6; "Elegant Forms," rev. of *The Spice-Box of Earth*, *Saturday Night*, 14 Oct. 1961, p. 45.

[16] Rosemary Eakins, "Cohen's Poems Show Grace and Skill," rev. of *The Spice-Box of Earth*, *Entertainment and the Arts* [*The Montreal Star*], 3 June 1961, p. 8; Michael Hornyansky, "Festive Bards," rev. of *The Spice-Box of Earth*, by Leonard Cohen, and five other books, *The Tamarack Review*, No. 21 (Autumn 1961), p. 81.

[17] Some reviewers found these Jewish poems among the best of the volume; see Hornyansky, "Festive Bards," p. 80; and Stephen Vizinczey, "Leonard Cohen," rev. of *The Spice-Box of Earth*, *Exchange*, 1, No. 1 (Nov. 1961), 71. Later critics tended to find them rather provincial in the light of his subsequent work; see, for example, Ondaatje, p. 23.

[18] "Three Major Canadian Poets — Three Major Forms of Archaism," rev. of *The Spice-Box of Earth*, by Leonard Cohen, *The Devil's Picture Book*, by Daryl Hine, and *The Swinging Flesh*, by Irving Layton, *Delta*, No. 16 (Nov. 1961), p. 25.

[19] Paccy, "The Phenomenon of Leonard Cohen"; Scobie, esp. pp. 36, 39.

[20] See David Bromige, "The Lean and the Luscious," rev. of *The Spice-Box of Earth*, *Canadian Literature*, No. 10 (Autumn 1961), p. 87; and Hornyansky, "Festive Bards," p. 80.

[21] Rev. of *The Spice-Box of Earth*, in "Letters in Canada 1961: Poetry," *University of Toronto Quarterly*, 31 (July 1962), 432.

[22] Eli Mandel, "Turning New Leaves," rev. of *The Spice Box of Earth*, by Leonard Cohen, and *The Devil's Picture Book*, by Daryl Hine, *The Canadian Forum*, Sept. 1961, p. 140.

[23] Al Purdy, "Leonard Cohen: A Personal Look," *Canadian Literature*, No. 23 (Winter 1965), p. 11.

[24] "Peripatetic Poets Show Their Wares," rev. of *Flowers for Hitler*, by Leonard Cohen, *The Laughing Rooster*, by Irving Layton, *Near False Creek Mouth*, by Earle Birney, and *Within the Zodiac*, by Phyllis Gotlieb, *Entertainments* [*The Montreal Star*], 31 Oct. 1964, p. 8.

[25] The quotation is from Brian McCarthy, "Poetry Chronicle," rev. of *Flowers for Hitler*, by Leonard Cohen, and seven other books, *The Tamarack Review*, No. 36 (Summer 1965), p. 73. See also: A.J. Arnold, "Leonard Cohen — Disturbing Contrasts," rev. of *Flowers for Hitler* and *The Spice-Box of Earth*, *Congress Bulletin* [Canadian Jewish Congress], 19, No. 1 (Jan. 1965), 3; Desmond Pacey, "Three Books of Canadian Verse," rev. of *Flowers for Hitler*, by Leonard Cohen, *Black and Secret Man*, by Eli Mandel, and *The Colour of the Times*, by Raymond Souster, *The Fiddlehead*, No. 64 (Spring 1965),

pp. 71–75; rev. of *Flowers for Hitler, Canadian Poetry*, 28, No. 2 (Feb. 1965), 38; and more recently, Ondaatje, pp. 39, 43.

[26] See, for example, Purdy, "Leonard Cohen: A Personal Look," p. 14.

[27] Milton Wilson, rev. of *Flowers for Hitler*, in "Letters in Canada 1964: Poetry," *University of Toronto Quarterly*, 34 (July 1965), 352–54.

[28] See B.W. Jones, rev. of *Flowers for Hitler*, by Leonard Cohen, and four other books, *Queen's Quarterly*, 72 (Winter 1965–66), 695–96; Pacey, "The Phenomenon of Leonard Cohen," p. 16; and Ondaatje, p. 40.

[29] See Alan Pearson, "Leonard Cohen's New Work," rev. of *Parasites of Heaven, Entertainments* [*The Montreal Star*], 10 Dec. 1966, p. 8; Robert A. Smith, rev. of *Parasites of Heaven, Quarry*, 16, No. 2 (Jan. 1967), 44; Hugh MacCallum, rev. of *Parasites of Heaven*, in "Letters in Canada 1966: Poetry," *University of Toronto Quarterly*, 36 (July 1967), 361–62; and Francis Sparshott, "Turning New Leaves (1)," rev. of *Parasites of Heaven, The Canadian Forum*, July 1967, pp. 85–86.

[30] Bowering, "Inside Leonard Cohen," p. 71.

[31] "Black Romanticism," rev. of *Selected Poems 1956–1968, Time* [Canadian ed.], 13 Sept. 1968, pp. 92, 96, 98.

[32] Rev. of *Selected Poems 1956–1968*, by Leonard Cohen, and four other books, *Times Literary Supplement*, 24 July 1969, p. 828.

[33] Douglas Barbour, "Canadian Books," rev. of *Selected Poems 1956–1968*, by Leonard Cohen, and four other books, *Dalhousie Review*, 48 (Winter 1968–69), 567.

[34] Respectively, Miriam Waddington, "A Showman in His Images' Grip," rev. of *Selected Poems 1956–1968, The Globe Magazine* [*The Globe and Mail*], 27 July 1968, p. 13; and Barbour, p. 567.

[35] Respectively, Waddington, p. 13; and Hugh MacCallum, rev. of *Selected Poems 1956–1968*, in "Letters in Canada 1968: Poetry," *University of Toronto Quarterly*, 38 (July 1969), 340.

[36] See Barry Callaghan, "Leonard Cohen: Heavy, Heavy, Heavy Hangs His Sense of Evil," rev. of *Selected Poems 1956–1968, The Telegram* [Toronto], 27 July 1968, p. 49; and Chad Walsh, "Poets, Out of Their Shells," rev. of *Selected Poems 1956–1968*, by Leonard Cohen, and six other books, *Book World* [*The Washington Post*], 28 July 1968, p. 4.

[37] See Merle Shain, "Hurry Marita. Hear the Gathering Volleys of Foreboding," rev. of *The Energy of Slaves, The Globe and Mail*, 11 Nov. 1972, p. 33; and Marni Jackson, "He's Bored, Bitter and Out of Love," rev. of *The Energy of Slaves*, by Leonard Cohen, *Incision*, by Robert Flanagan, *Selected Poems*, by Raymond Souster, and *Cannibals*, by Stanley Cooperman, *Toronto Daily Star*, 25 Nov. 1972, p. 64.

38 "Along the Fingertip Trail," rev. of *The Energy of Slaves, Times Literary Supplement*, 5 Jan. 1973, p. 10; Calvin Bedient, "A Soft Confusion, a Hard Clarity," rev. of *The Energy of Slaves*, by Leonard Cohen, and *No Jerusalem But This*, by Samuel Menashe, *The New York Times Book Review*, 18 Feb. 1973, pp. 26–27.

39 David Lehman, "Politics," rev. of *The Energy of Slaves*, by Leonard Cohen, *Monster*, by Robert Morgan, *Debridement*, by Michael S. Harper, and *Burning the Empty Nests*, by Gregory Orr, *Poetry* [Chicago], 123 (Dec. 1973), 173–78. Other negative reviews were those of Christopher Levenson, rev. of *The Energy of Slaves, Queen's Quarterly*, 80 (Autumn 1973), 469–71; and Michael Hornyansky, rev. of *The Energy of Slaves*, in "Letters in Canada 1972: Poetry," *University of Toronto Quarterly*, 42 (Summer 1973), 368.

40 Beverly Smith, "By Self Possessed," rev. of *The Energy of Slaves, Books in Canada*, Nov.–Dec. 1972, pp. 52–53; Patricia Morley, "Solitary Adventure, or Shared Pain?" rev. of *The Energy of Slaves, The Lakehead Review*, 6, No. 2 (Fall–Winter 1973), 262–65. Later, Frank Davey, in "Leonard Cohen," in *From There to Here: A Guide to English-Canadian Literature since 1960* (Erin, Ont.: Porcépic, 1974), wrote: "Here [in *The Energy of Slaves*] the poetic craftsman of his earlier work becomes another 'beautiful loser,' ridiculing his abilities and mocking his past accomplishments" (p. 71).

41 For example, Tom Wayman attacked Cohen's sexism in "Cohen's Women," rev. of *The Energy of Slaves, Canadian Literature*, No. 60 (Spring 1974), pp. 89–93. The main defence came later in Scobie, p. 158.

42 Michael Estok, "All in the Family: The Metaphysics of Domesticity," rev. of *The Energy of Slaves*, by Leonard Cohen, and six other books, *Dalhousie Review*, 52 (Winter 1972–73), 653–67; and Stephen Scobie, rev. of *The Energy of Slaves*, by Leonard Cohen, *Theme and Variations for Sounding Brass*, by Ralph Gustafson, and *Saying Grace: An Elegy*, by Don Gutteridge, *Humanities Association Review*, 24 (Summer 1973), 240–43.

43 Rick Johnson, rev. of *The Energy of Slaves, Quarry*, 22, No. 2 (Spring 1973), 68; and later, Mandel, "Cohen's Life as a Slave," p. 126.

44 Negative reviews include: Tom Marshall, "Self-Indulgent Cohen," rev. of *Death of a Lady's Man, The Canadian Forum*, Feb. 1979, pp. 33–34; Sean Virgo, rev. of *Death of a Lady's Man, Quill & Quire*, 8 Sept. 1978, p. 11; Bruce Whiteman, "The Tygers of Wrath and the Horses of Instruction," rev. of *Death of a Lady's Man*, by Leonard Cohen, and *Leonard Cohen*, by Stephen Scobie, *Essays on Canadian Writing*, No. 16 (Fall–Winter 1979–80), pp. 243–47; and Al Purdy, "Cohen Has Lost That Special Magic," rev. of *Death of a Lady's Man, The Toronto Star*, 30 Sept. 1978, p. D7. Positive reviews include: Gary Geddes, rev. of *Death of a Lady's Man, The Globe and Mail*, 30 Sept. 1978, p. 27; Sam

Ajzenstat, "The Ploy's the Thing," rev. of *Death of a Lady's Man*, *Books in Canada*, Oct. 1978, pp. 10–11; and Michael Brian Oliver, "Not Much Nourished by Modern Love," rev. of *Death of a Lady's Man*, *The Fiddlehead*, No. 121 (Spring 1979), pp. 143–46.

45 Rowland Smith, "Prayers," rev. of *Book of Mercy*, *Canadian Literature*, No. 104 (Spring 1985), p. 155. All further references to this work appear in the text.

46 Joseph Kertes, "Born Again," rev. of *Book of Mercy*, *Books in Canada*, June–July 1984, p. 22.

47 Ron Graham, "A Book of Common Prayers," rev. of *Book of Mercy*, *Saturday Night*, Aug. 1984, p. 44.

48 Cited in Graham, p. 43.

49 See Jack Batten, "Leonard Cohen: The Poet as Hero: 1," *Saturday Night*, June 1969, pp. 23–26; rev. of *Songs of Leonard Cohen*, *Maclean's*, Feb. 1968, p. 72; and later, Scobie, pp. 129–37. However, for an opposite view, see Juan Rodriguez, "Poet's Progress — To Sainthood and Back," rev. of *Songs from a Room*, *The Montreal Star*, 21 June 1969, pp. 3–4.

50 Arthur Schmidt, rev. of *Songs of Love and Hate*, *Rolling Stone*, 2 Sept. 1971, p. 43.

51 Frank Davey, "Leonard Cohen and Bob Dylan: Poetry and the Popular Song," *Alphabet*, No. 17 (Dec. 1969), pp. 12–29; rpt. (rev.) in Gnarowski, ed., *Leonard Cohen: The Artist and His Critics*, pp. 111–24.

52 Judith Skelton Grant, "Leonard Cohen's Poem-Songs," *Studies in Canadian Literature*, 2 (Winter 1977), 102–07.

53 See Carlotta Valdez, rev. of *Live Songs*, *Rolling Stone*, 19 July 1973, pp. 55–56; Mike Jahn, rev. of *Live Songs*, *High Fidelity/Musical America*, Jan. 1974, p. 110; Barry Wallenstein, rev. of *Live Songs*, *Crawdaddy*, Aug. 1973, p. 69; and "The Voice of Canadian Poetry," rev. of *Live Songs*, *Quill & Quire*, Aug. 1973, p. 10. Noel Coppage disagreed, finding Cohen no better live; see his rev. of *Live Songs*, *Stereo Review*, Nov. 1973, p. 80.

54 See Paul Nelson, "Loners and Other Strangers," rev. of *New Skin for the Old Ceremony*, *Rolling Stone*, 27 Feb. 1975, p. 50; Paul Stuewe, rev. of *New Skin for the Old Ceremony*, *Beetle*, 6, No. 4 (1975), n. pag.; and Noel Coppage, rev. of *New Skin for the Old Ceremony*, *Stereo Review*, April 1975, p. 75. The exception, as always, is Scobie, who finds *New Skin for the Old Ceremony* "a really satisfying and complete accomplishment" (p. 154) and "Cohen's masterpiece of the seventies" (p. 163).

55 See Dean Tudor, "The Record Track," rev. of *Death of a Ladies' Man*, *Ontario Library Review*, 62 (Sept. 1978), 223; and Scobie, p. 155.

56 Janet Maslin, "There's Nothing I Like about It — but It May Be a Classic,"

The New York Times, 6 Nov. 1977, pp. D18, D40.

57 The main exception to this view is Scobie's, for he sees some of the songs, along with *Beautiful Losers*, as Cohen's finest work, offering "an emotional experience which is deeper, more humane, and ultimately more worthy of our attention and respect" (p. 14).

58 *Death of a Lady's Man* (Toronto: McClelland and Stewart, 1978), p. 21. All further references to this work (*DLM*) appear in the text.

59 Woodcock, pp. 95, 97, 100. Frank Davey agrees, in *From There to Here*, p. 69.

60 *Semiotics of Poetry* (Bloomington, Ind.: Indiana Univ. Press, 1978), p. 19. The following discussion is drawn from his early chapters, especially pages 23 and 39. See also his *La Production du texte* (Paris: Seuil, 1979).

61 "As the Mist Leaves No Scar," in *The Spice-Box of Earth* (1961; rpt. Toronto: McClelland and Stewart, 1968), p. 56. All further references to this work (*SBE*) appear in the text.

62 In *Flowers for Hitler* (Toronto: McClelland and Stewart, 1964), pp. 70–72. All further references to this work (*FH*) appear in the text.

63 The term appears to have been coined by Julia Kristeva in *Semeiotike* (Paris: Seuil, 1969), p. 255, and is now widely used, by Riffaterre among others.

64 See my earlier discussions of this in "*Beautiful Losers*: All the Polarities," *Canadian Literature*, No. 59 (Winter 1974), pp. 42–56; and "The Poet as Novelist," *Canadian Literature*, No. 86 (Autumn 1980), pp. 6–14.

65 Scobie discusses this element in several songs in his *Leonard Cohen*, pp. 168, 170.

66 "Ballad [My lady was found mutilated]," in *Let Us Compare Mythologies* (1956; rpt. Toronto: McClelland and Stewart, 1966), p. 46. All further references to this work (*LUCM*) appear in the text.

67 There is one exception to this inversion in *The Spice-Box of Earth* where the poet's recording song may be seen to have a redemptive function: "If it were Spring / and I killed a man, / I would change him to leaves / and hang him from a tree" where "Wind would make him / part of song" ("If It Were Spring," p. 6).

68 The later poem "Why I Happen to Be Free" (*FH*, pp. 59–61) acts as a gloss on this mixing and adds a Buddhist context as well.

69 "Story of Isaac," *Songs from a Room*, Columbia, CS 9767, 1969.

70 Scobie made this point in *Leonard Cohen* (p. 42), but it was already implied in the early poem about Cohen's male family members, entitled "Priests 1957" (*SBE*, p. 70).

71 In *Parasites of Heaven* (Toronto: McClelland and Stewart, 1966), p. 16. All further references to this work (*PH*) appear in the text.

72 See, for example: Davey, *From There to Here*, p. 69; Scobie, p. 35; and

Pacey, "The Phenomenon of Leonard Cohen," p. 8.

73 "Leaving Greensleeves," *New Skin for the Old Ceremony*, Columbia, KC 33167, 1974.

74 "Bird on the Wire," *Live Songs*, Columbia, KC 31724, 1973.

75 "Welcome to these lines," in *The Energy of Slaves* (Toronto: McClelland and Stewart, 1972), p. 9. All further references to this work (*ES*) appear in the text.

76 *Songs of Leonard Cohen*, Columbia, CS 9533, 1968.

77 "The Reason I Write," in *Selected Poems 1956–1968* (Toronto: McClelland and Stewart, 1968), p. 231. All further references to this work (*SP*) appear in the text.

78 Scobie frequently seems to miss the irony, taking Cohen more seriously than the "con" artist himself does (see, for example, pp. 30–31). Ondaatje generally has a better ear for irony (see Ondaatje, p. 19, in comparison).

79 This line was added in the *Selected Poems* version, p. 128.

80 *Beautiful Losers* (Toronto: McClelland and Stewart, 1966), p. 243.

81 Linda Hutcheon, "Leonard Cohen and His Works," in *Canadian Writers and Their Works*, ed. Robert Lecker, Jack David, and Ellen Quigley, Vol. x (Fiction), Toronto: ECW, 1989, pp. 25–65.

82 Ondaatje (p. 39) and Scobie (p. 56) have both seen *Flowers for Hitler* as a preparation for *Beautiful Losers*.

83 *Book of Mercy* (Toronto: McClelland and Stewart, 1984), Nos. 13 and 14. All further references to this work (*BM*) appear in the text.

84 In disagreement with this is Kertes, who sees all Cohen's work as having "an ethic based on selflessness" (p. 21).

85 "Tower of Song," *I'm Your Man*, Columbia, FC 44191, 1988.

SELECTED BIBLIOGRAPHY

Primary Sources

Books

Cohen, Leonard. *Let Us Compare Mythologies.* 1956; rpt. Toronto: McClelland and Stewart, 1966.

_____ . *The Spice-Box of Earth.* 1961; rpt. Toronto: McClelland and Stewart, 1968.

_____ . *Flowers for Hitler.* Toronto: McClelland and Stewart, 1964.

_____ . *Parasites of Heaven.* Toronto: McClelland and Stewart, 1966.

_____ . *Songs of Leonard Cohen.* New York: Amsco Music, 1969.

_____ . *Selected Poems 1956–1968.* Toronto: McClelland and Stewart, 1968.

_____ . *The Energy of Slaves.* Toronto: McClelland and Stewart, 1972.

_____ . *Death of a Lady's Man.* Toronto: McClelland and Stewart, 1978.

_____ . *Book of Mercy.* Toronto: McClelland and Stewart, 1984.

Records

Cohen, Leonard. *Songs of Leonard Cohen.* Columbia, CS 9533, 1968.

_____ . *Songs from a Room.* Columbia, CS 9767, 1969.

_____ . *Songs of Love and Hate.* Columbia, C 30103, 1971.

_____ . *Live Songs.* Columbia, KC 31724, 1973.

_____ . *New Skin for the Old Ceremony.* Columbia, KC 33167, 1974.

_____ . *The Best of Leonard Cohen.* Columbia, ES 90334, 1975.

_____ . *Death of a Ladies' Man.* Columbia, PES 90436, 1977.

_____ . *Recent Songs.* Columbia, JC 36264, 1979.

_____ . *Various Positions.* Columbia, PCC 90728, 1984.

_____ . *I'm Your Man.* Columbia, FC 44191, 1988.

Secondary Sources

Ajzenstat, Sam. "The Ploy's the Thing." Rev. of *Death of a Lady's Man*. *Books in Canada*, Oct. 1978, pp. 10–11.

"Along the Fingertip Trail." Rev. of *The Energy of Slaves*. *Times Literary Supplement*, 5 Jan. 1973, p. 10.

Arnold, A.J. "Leonard Cohen — Disturbing Contrasts." Rev. of *Flowers for Hitler* and *The Spice-Box of Earth*. *Congress Bulletin* [Canadian Jewish Congress], 19, No. 1 (Jan. 1965), 3.

Avison, Margaret. "Poetry Chronicle." Rev. of *Let Us Compare Mythologies*, by Leonard Cohen, and six other books. *The Tamarack Review*, No. 1 (Autumn 1956), pp. 78–85.

Barbour, Douglas. "Canadian Books." Rev. of *Selected Poems 1956–1968*, by Leonard Cohen, and four other books. *Dalhousie Review*, 48 (Winter 1968–69), 566–71.

Batten, Jack. "Leonard Cohen: The Poet as Hero: 1." *Saturday Night*, June 1969, pp. 23–26.

Beattie, Munro. "Poetry: 1950–1960." In *Literary History of Canada: Canadian Literature in English*. Gen. ed. and introd. Carl F. Klinck. Toronto: Univ. of Toronto Press, 1965, pp. 814–16.

Bedient, Calvin. "A Soft Confusion, a Hard Clarity." Rev. of *The Energy of Slaves*, by Leonard Cohen, and *No Jerusalem But This*, by Samuel Menashe. *The New York Times Book Review*, 18 Feb. 1973, pp. 26–27.

Bedingfield, Dolores. "Montrealer's Love Poems Win Praise." Rev. of *The Spice-Box of Earth*. *The Globe and Mail*, 17 June 1961, p. 9.

"Black Romanticism." Rev. of *Selected Poems 1956–1968*. *Time* [Canadian ed.], 13 Sept. 1968, pp. 92, 96, 98.

Bowering, George. "Inside Leonard Cohen." Rev. of *Parasites of Heaven*. *Canadian Literature*, No. 33 (Summer 1967), p. 71.

Bromige, David. "The Lean and the Luscious." Rev. of *The Spice-Box of Earth*. *Canadian Literature*, No. 10 (Autumn 1961), pp. 87–88.

Callaghan, Barry. "Leonard Cohen: Heavy, Heavy, Heavy Hangs His Sense of Evil." Rev. of *Selected Poems 1956–1968*. *The Telegram* [Toronto], 27 July 1968, p. 49.

Coppage, Noel. Rev. of *Live Songs*. *Stereo Review*, Nov. 1973, p. 80.

_____ . Rev. of *New Skin for the Old Ceremony*. *Stereo Review*, April 1975, p. 75.

Davey, Frank. "Leonard Cohen and Bob Dylan: Poetry and the Popular Song." *Alphabet*, No. 17 (Dec. 1969), pp. 12–29. Rpt. (rev.) in *Leonard Cohen: The Artist and His Critics*. Ed. Michael Gnarowski. Critical Views on Canadian

Writers. Toronto: McGraw-Hill Ryerson, 1976, pp. 111–24.

_____. "Leonard Cohen." In *Supplement to the Oxford Companion to Canadian History and Literature*. Ed. William Toye. Toronto: Oxford Univ. Press, 1973, p. 45. Signed: F.D.

_____. "Leonard Cohen." In *From There to Here: A Guide to English-Canadian Literature since 1960*. Erin, Ont.: Porcépic, 1974, pp. 68–73.

Djwa, Sandra. "Leonard Cohen: Black Romantic." *Canadian Literature*, No. 34 (Autumn 1967), pp. 32–42.

Donaldson, Allan. Rev. of *Let Us Compare Mythologies*. *The Fiddlehead*, No. 30 (Nov. 1956), pp. 30–31.

Dudek, Louis. "Three Major Canadian Poets — Three Major Forms of Archaism." Rev. of *The Spice-Box of Earth*, by Leonard Cohen, *The Devil's Picture Book*, by Daryl Hine, and *The Swinging Flesh*, by Irving Layton. *Delta*, No. 16 (Nov. 1961), pp. 23–25.

_____. "Peripatetic Poets Show Their Wares." Rev. of *Flowers for Hitler*, by Leonard Cohen, *The Laughing Rooster*, by Irving Layton, *Near False Creek Mouth*, by Earle Birney, and *Within the Zodiac*, by Phyllis Gotlieb. *Entertainments* [*The Montreal Star*], 31 Oct. 1964, p. 8.

Eakins, Rosemary. "Cohen's Poems Show New Grace and Skill." Rev. of *The Spice-Box of Earth*. *Entertainment and the Arts* [*The Montreal Star*], 3 June 1961, p. 8.

Edinborough, Arnold. Rev. of *The Spice-Box of Earth*. *The Canadian Reader*, 2, No. 9 (July 1961), 5–6.

_____. "Elegant Forms." Rev. of *The Spice-Box of Earth*. *Saturday Night*, 14 Oct. 1961, p. 45.

Estok, Michael. "All in the Family: The Metaphysics of Domesticity." Rev. of *The Energy of Slaves*, by Leonard Cohen, and six other books. *Dalhousie Review*, 52 (Winter 1972–73), 655–58.

Fetherling, Doug. Interview with Leonard Cohen. *Books in Canada*, Aug.–Sept. 1984, pp. 29–30.

Frye, Northrop. Rev. of *Let Us Compare Mythologies*. In "Letters in Canada 1956: Poetry." *University of Toronto Quarterly*, 26 (April 1957), 308–09.

Geddes, Gary. Rev. of *Death of a Lady's Man*. *The Globe and Mail*, 30 Sept. 1978, p. 27.

Gnarowski, Michael, ed. *Leonard Cohen: The Artist and His Critics*. Critical Views on Canadian Writers. Toronto: McGraw-Hill Ryerson, 1976.

Graham, Ron. "A Book of Common Prayers." Rev. of *Book of Mercy*. *Saturday Night*, Aug. 1984, pp. 43–44.

Grant, Judith Skelton. "Leonard Cohen's Poems-Songs." *Studies in Canadian Literature*, 2 (Winter 1977), 102–07.

Harris, Michael. "Leonard Cohen: The Poet as Hero: 2" [interview]. *Saturday Night*, June 1969, pp. 26–31.

Hornyansky, Michael. "Festive Bards." Rev. of *The Spice-Box of Earth*, by Leonard Cohen, and five other books. *The Tamarack Review*, No. 21 (Autumn 1961), pp. 79–86.

_____. Rev. of *The Energy of Slaves*. In "Letters in Canada 1972: Poetry." *University of Toronto Quarterly*, 42 (Summer 1973), 368.

Hutcheon, Linda. "*Beautiful Losers*: All the Polarities." *Canadian Literature*, No. 59 (Winter 1974), pp. 42–56.

_____. "The Poet as Novelist." *Canadian Literature*, No. 86 (Autumn 1980), pp. 6–14.

_____. "The Carnivalesque and Contemporary Narrative: Popular Culture and the Erotic." *University of Ottawa Quarterly*, 53, No. 1 (Jan.–March 1983), 83–96.

_____. "Leonard Cohen and His Works." In *Canadian Writers and Their Works*. Ed. Robert Lecker, Jack David, and Ellen Quigley. Vol. x (Fiction). Toronto: ECW, 1989, pp. 25–65.

Jackson, Marni. "Leonard Cohen: He's Bored, Bitter and Out of Love." Rev. of *The Energy of Slaves*, by Leonard Cohen, *Incisions*, by Robert Flanagan, *Selected Poems*, by Raymond Souster, and *Cannibals*, by Stanley Cooperman. *Toronto Daily Star*, 25 Nov. 1972, p. 64.

Jahn, Mike. Rev. of *Live Songs*. *High Fidelity/Musical America*, Jan. 1974, p. 110.

Johnson, Rick. Rev. of *The Energy of Slaves*. *Quarry*, 22, No. 2 (Spring 1973), 66–68.

Jones, B.W. Rev. of *Flowers for Hitler*, by Leonard Cohen, and four other books. *Queen's Quarterly*, 72 (Winter 1965–66), 695–96.

Kertes, Joseph. "Born Again." Rev. of *Book of Mercy*. *Books in Canada*, June–July 1984, pp. 21–22.

Lehman, David. "Politics." Rev. of *The Energy of Slaves*, by Leonard Cohen, *Monster*, by Robert Morgan, *Debridement*, by Michael S. Harper, and *Burning the Empty Nests*, by Gregory Orr, *Poetry* [Chicago], 123 (Dec. 1973), 173–78.

Levenson, Christopher. Rev. of *The Energy of Slaves*, by Leonard Cohen, and *Driving Home: Poems New and Selected*, by Miriam Waddington. *Queen's Quarterly*, 80 (Autumn 1973), 469–71.

L[ochhead], D.G. Rev. of *Let Us Compare Mythologies*, by Leonard Cohen, *The Bull Calf and Other Poems*, by Irving Layton, and *Even Your Right Eye*, by Phyllis Webb. *Dalhousie Review*, 36 (Winter 1957), 425, 427.

MacCallum, Hugh. Rev. of *Parasites of Heaven*. In "Letters in Canada 1966:

Poetry." *University of Toronto Quarterly*, 36 (July 1967), 361–62.

_____ . Rev. of *Selected Poems 1956–1968*. In "Letters in Canada 1968: Poetry." *University of Toronto Quarterly*, 38 (July 1969), 340.

Macdonald, Ruth. "Leonard Cohen, a Bibliography, 1956–1973." *Bulletin of Bibliography*, 31, No. 3 (July–Sept. 1974), 107–10.

MacSkimming, Roy. " 'New' Leonard Cohen Opens Up His Thoughts." *The Toronto Star*, 22 Jan. 1975, p. E16.

Mandel, Eli. "Turning New Leaves." Rev. of *The Spice-Box of Earth*, by Leonard Cohen, and *The Devil's Picture Book*, by Daryl Hine. *The Canadian Forum*, Sept. 1961, pp. 140–41.

_____ . "Cohen's Life as a Slave." In *Another Time*. Three Solitudes: Contemporary Literary Criticism in Canada, No. 3. Erin, Ont.: Porcépic, 1977, pp. 124–36.

Marshall, Tom. "Self-Indulgent Cohen." Rev. of *Death of a Lady's Man*. *The Canadian Forum*, Feb. 1979, pp. 33–34.

Maslin, Janet. "There's Nothing I Like about It — But It May Be a Classic." *The New York Times*, 6 Nov. 1977, pp. D18, D40.

McCarthy, Brian. "Poetry Chronicle." Rev. of *Flowers for Hitler*, by Leonard Cohen, and seven other books. *The Tamarack Review*, No. 36 (Summer 1965), pp. 64–75.

Morley, Patricia. "Solitary Adventure, or Shared Pain?" Rev. of *The Energy of Slaves*. *The Lakehead University Review*, 6, No. 2 (Fall Winter 1973), 262–65.

Nelson, Paul. "Loners and Other Strangers." Rev. of *New Skin for the Old Ceremony*. *Rolling Stone*, 27 Feb. 1975, p. 50.

Oliver, Michael Brian. "Not Much Nourished by Modern Love." Rev. of *Death of a Lady's Man*. *The Fiddlehead*, No. 121 (Spring 1979), pp. 143–46.

Ondaatje, Michael. *Leonard Cohen*. New Canadian Library, Canadian Writers Series, No. 5. Toronto: McClelland and Stewart, 1970.

Owen, Don, dir. *Ladies and Gentlemen . . . Mr. Leonard Cohen*. National Film Board, 1965.

Pacey, Desmond. "A Group of Seven." Rev. of *Let Us Compare Mythologies*, by Leonard Cohen, and six other books. *Queen's Quarterly*, 63 (Autumn 1956), 438–39.

_____ . *Creative Writing in Canada: A Short History of English-Canadian Literature*. 2nd ed. Toronto: Ryerson, 1961.

_____ . "Three Books of Canadian Verse." Rev. of *Flowers for Hitler*, by Leonard Cohen, *Black and Secret Man*, by Eli Mandel, and *The Colour of the Times*, by Raymond Souster. *The Fiddlehead*, No. 64 (Spring 1965), pp. 71–75.

_____. "The Phenomenon of Leonard Cohen." *Canadian Literature*, No. 34 (Autumn 1967), pp. 5–23.

Pearson, Alan. "Leonard Cohen's New Work." Rev. of *Parasites of Heaven, Entertainments* [*The Montreal Star*], 10 Dec. 1966, p. 8.

Purdy, Al. "Leonard Cohen: A Personal Look." *Canadian Literature*, No. 23 (Winter 1965), pp. 7–16.

_____. "Cohen Has Lost That Special Magic." Rev. of *Death of a Lady's Man. The Toronto Star*, 30 Sept. 1978, p. D7.

Rasky, Harry, dir. *The Song of Leonard Cohen*. Canadian Broadcasting Corporation, 1980.

Rev. of *Flowers for Hitler. Canadian Poetry*, 28, No. 2 (Feb. 1965), 38.

Rev. of *Selected Poems 1956–1968. Maclean's*, Aug. 1968, p. 60.

Rev. of *Selected Poems 1956–1968*, by Leonard Cohen, and four other books. *Times Literary Supplement*, 24 July 1969, p. 828.

Rev. of *Songs of Leonard Cohen. Maclean's*, Feb. 1968, p. 72.

Rodriguez, Juan. "Poet's Progress — To Sainthood and Back." Rev. of *Songs from a Room. The Montreal Star*, 21 June 1969, pp. 3–4.

Ruddy, Jon. "Is the World (or Anybody) Ready for Leonard Cohen?" *Maclean's*, 1 Oct. 1966, pp. 18–19, 33–34.

Schmidt, Arthur. Rev. of *Songs of Love and Hate. Rolling Stone*, 2 Sept. 1971, p. 43.

Scobie, Stephen. Rev. of *The Energy of Slaves*, by Leonard Cohen, *Theme and Variations for Sounding Brass*, by Ralph Gustafson, and *Saying Grace: An Elegy*, by Don Gutteridge. *Humanities Association Review*, 24 (Summer 1973), 240–43.

_____. *Leonard Cohen*. Studies in Canadian Literature, No. 12. Vancouver: Douglas & McIntyre, 1978.

Shain, Merle. "Hurry Marita. Hear the Gathering Volleys of Foreboding." Rev. of *The Energy of Slaves. The Globe and Mail*, 11 Nov. 1972, p. 33.

Smith, Beverly. "By Self Possessed." Rev. of *The Energy of Slaves. Books in Canada*, Nov.–Dec. 1972, pp. 52–53.

Smith, Rowland. "Prayers." Rev. of *Book of Mercy. Canadian Literature*, No. 104 (Spring 1985), pp. 155–56.

Smith, Robert A. Rev. of *Parasites of Heaven. Quarry*, 16, No. 2 (Jan. 1967), 44.

Sparshott, Francis. "Turning New Leaves (1)." Rev. of *Parasites of Heaven. The Canadian Forum*, July 1967, pp. 85–86.

Stevens, Peter, ed. *The McGill Movement*. Critical Views on Canadian Writers. Toronto: Ryerson, 1969.

Stuewe, Paul. Rev. of *New Skin for the Old Ceremony. Beetle*, 6, No. 4 (1975), n. pag.

Tudor, Dean. "The Record Track." Rev. of *Death of a Ladies' Man. Ontario Library Review*, 62 (Sept. 1978), 223.

Valdez, Carlotta. Rev. of *Live Songs. Rolling Stone*, 19 July 1973, pp. 55–56.

Virgo, Sean. Rev. of *Death of a Lady's Man. Quill & Quire*, 8 Sept. 1978, p. 11.

Vizinczey, Stephen. "Leonard Cohen." Rev. of *The Spice-Box of Earth. Exchange*, 1, No. 1 (Nov. 1961), 71–72.

"The Voice of Canadian Poetry." Rev. of *Live Songs. Quill & Quire*, Aug. 1973, p. 10.

Waddington, Miriam. "A Showman in His Images' Grip." Rev. of *Selected Poems 1956–1968. The Globe Magazine* [*The Globe and Mail*], 27 July 1968, p. 13.

Wallenstein, Barry. Rev. of *Live Songs. Crawdaddy*, Aug. 1973, p. 69.

Walsh, Chad. "Poets, Out of Their Shells." Rev. of *Selected Poems 1956–1968*, by Leonard Cohen, and six other books. *Book World* [*The Washington Post*], 28 July 1968, p. 4.

Wayman, Tom. "Cohen's Women." Rev. of *The Energy of Slaves. Canadian Literature*, No. 60 (Spring 1974), pp. 89–93.

Weaver, Robert. "Leonard Cohen's 'Spice-Box' Presents Sombre Vision." *Toronto Daily Star*, 10 June 1961, p. 29.

Whiteman, Bruce. "The Tygers of Wrath and the Horses of Instruction." Rev. of *Death of a Lady's Man*, by Leonard Cohen, and *Leonard Cohen*, by Stephen Scobie. *Essays on Canadian Writing*, No. 16 (Fall–Winter 1979–80), pp. 243–47.

_____ . "Leonard Cohen: An Annotated Bibliography." In *The Annotated Bibliography of Canada's Major Authors*. Ed. Robert Lecker and Jack David. Vol. II. Downsview, Ont.: ECW, 1980, 55–95.

Wilson, Milton. "Turning New Leaves." Rev. of *Let Us Compare Mythologies. The Canadian Forum*, March 1957, pp. 282–84.

_____ . Rev. of *The Spice-Box of Earth*. In "Letters in Canada 1961: Poetry." *University of Toronto Quarterly*, 31 (July 1962), 432–37.

_____ . Rev. of *Flowers for Hitler*. In "Letters in Canada 1964: Poetry." *University of Toronto Quarterly*, 34 (July 1965), 352–54.

Woodcock, George. "The Song of the Sirens: Reflections on Leonard Cohen." In *Odysseus Ever Returning: Essays on Canadian Writers and Writing*. New Canadian Library, No. 71. Toronto: McClelland and Stewart, 1970, pp. 93–110.

_____ . "Poetry." In *Literary History of Canada: Canadian Literature in English*. Gen. ed. and introd. Carl F. Klinck. 2nd ed. Toronto: Univ. of Toronto Press, 1976, III, 284–317.

*Robert Kroetsch
and His Works*

Robert Kroetsch (1927–   )

ANN MUNTON *

Biography

ONE MUST START, as Robert Kroetsch tells us, "with an invocation /
invoke"[1] myth, memory, the muse. Beginnings are crucial and magical for the poet. Roy Kiyooka tells him, "the new myth of beginnings. . . . It's the Western Canadian myth: the artist from the distant
place, from the bookless world." Kroetsch answers, "I'm from a
farm, . . . way hell and gone out in Alberta."[2] The beginnings —
rural, western, fictive, vacant, replete — recur in the writing. Documents are also important. The official ledger recording Kroetsch's
arrival is probably in some obscure room of an Alberta government
building in downtown Edmonton. A more informal recording would
be found in the traces of a farmhouse celebration. And so the story
begins. Some specifics are as follows.

The paternal side of Kroetsch's family ("a widow and her sons, six
or seven"[3]) embarked aboard the *Pauline* on the mythic journey for
the New World, arriving in New York in June 1841.[4] The maternal
side remained in Germany a while longer, where Kroetsch's maternal
great-grandmother, Anna Weller, was born in 1849 (*FN*, p. 65).
From New York the Kroetsch family travelled north and settled close
to Belmore in Bruce County, Ontario, the site for the family sawmill.
Here, in 1856, Kroetsch's grandfather Henry Kroetsch was born,
and in turn Kroetsch's father, Paul Kroetsch, was born in 1893. A
further westering notion overtook the family in the first years of
Alberta's provincial infancy. In 1905 began the movement of the
Kroetsch family to take up farming in rural Alberta. The Wellers
preceded them by four years, via another route. One of Kroetsch's
maternal great-grandfathers fought on the Union side and was
wounded in the American Civil War. Also drawn westward, he
established a homestead in Minnesota, whence his two sons and their

---

* This work is dedicated to Sarah and Don.

families continued on to the district of Alberta in 1901. Kroetsch's mother, Hilda Marie Weller, was born there in 1903 at Spring Lake, a small community in central Alberta. Hilda Weller and Paul Kroetsch were married in 1925 and settled on a farm in Heisler, just a few miles south of Hilda's birthplace.

> [Heisler] was a very small town with only 200 people. It was a shopping centre and there were grain elevators. And there were coal mines nearby. They were little family coal mines on the Battle River. So Heisler was both a farming and coal mining community.[5]

The Kroetsches had five children. Their first child, and only son, was born on 26 June 1927 — the poet, Robert Kroetsch.

Kroetsch grew up in rural Alberta and reportedly was "spoiled rotten from the day of [his] birth."[6] Surrounded by sisters, aunts, uncles, and cousins, he had an immediate sense of the extended family. In fact, farm and family are probably the two most important formative influences on him. The farm was large and worked primarily by horses. "[T]here was a high definition of male and female activity, and lots of hired help working."[7] Prevented from doing the indoor male work because of allergies, and the indoor female work because of the sexual boundaries, Kroetsch spent his time in the solitary, outdoor activities of gardening, fixing fences, and rounding up cattle in the fall. In retrospect, these become tremendously significant pursuits. Planting trees, a reversal of the pioneer norm, and raising a bountiful garden, Kroetsch eagerly received the winter seed catalogues, worked intimately with the earth of his home place, and bridged the traditional male/female divisions. Riding the fence lines or searching out lost cows in Battle River coulees, Kroetsch was free to feed his imagination and dream the beginning stories.

And stories were a crucial aspect of family life. "Women cooking and canning together, visiting. Men working together, drinking together" (Hancock, p. 36). The gossip and tall tales of kitchen and prairie pub provide Kroetsch with an enveloping oral tradition. Stories of the journey to the New World, the first homesteaders and ground-breakers, gave way to stories of immediate surroundings and folk: "That kind of storytelling in a small community is how you invent each other — give each other a character" (MacKinnon, p. 4). Kroetsch tells of being unable to contend in person with his famous storytelling father and thus slipping off upstairs to write (Hancock, p. 36; MacKinnon, p. 6).

These oral stories were Kroetsch's early measure, because the family library consisted of only three or four books: "One of them was on looking after horses. . . . One was on wild flowers. . . . One was on threshing machines" (Hancock, p. 37). He read through the stacks of pulp magazines found in the hired man's room: "*Ten Story Western, Air Aces*. Stories about Doc Savage" ("Taking the Risk," in *RK*, p. 65). He borrowed books from a travelling library and sent off by mail for others, but there was something incongruous about the fiction he found:

> I remember reading voraciously as a boy, and the fictional boys I read about were always doing things I couldn't begin to do, because we didn't have the big oak trees or whatever. And that sense of alienation made me feel that first I had to go see — I didn't really believe you could construct a world without huge wheat fields.[8]

The solution was twofold. First of all, you invent your own stories with wheat fields instead of oak trees. Second, you locate books with resonances deeper than geographic similitude.

Kroetsch attended Heisler Public School, a small school with four grades to a room, from 1932 to 1944. He graduated in 1945 from the Red Deer High School. When only in grade four, he happened by accident on two books which were unlike all the others he had read so far. As he tells it in "Taking the Risk" (*RK*, p. 65), he had exhausted his class's meagre library resources and, upon exploring the wealth of the next room, discovered Joseph Conrad's *The Nigger of the "Narcissus"* and Henry James's *The Turn of the Screw*. The impact, over time, was profound. Another aspect of rural schooling that became significant was the means of transportation. On the long and leisurely horse-and-buggy or horse-and-cutter rides to school, Kroetsch became both an acute observer of the passing scene and seasons and an inventer of complete story worlds. "To this day," he tells us, "I can't walk from my parked car to my office without inventing a story" ("Taking the Risk," in *RK*, p. 66).

Majoring in English and philosophy at the University of Alberta in Edmonton (1945–48), Kroetsch concentrated on nineteenth-century literature, but the stories surrounding him now were those of hardship and bravery told by the returning veterans. Prompted by machismo, and in an attempt to match such daring and discover the experience beyond books necessary for the would-be writer (Hemingway was now the acknowledged exemplar), Kroetsch took off promptly upon graduation for "the North" — that last of Canadian frontiers. He worked first as a labourer on the Fort Smith portage and then for two shipping seasons on the riverboats on the Mackenzie River. In 1951 he briefly worked for a catering company on Hudson Bay, and then from 1951 to 1954 he was the civilian Director of Information and Education for the United States Air Force in Goose Bay, Labrador.

After six years spent primarily in the North, at the age of twenty-seven Kroetsch returned to graduate school. He attended the Bread Loaf School of English at Middlebury College in Vermont during the summer of 1954 and again in 1955 and 1956, completing his M.A. degree there. From 1954 to 1955 he attended McGill University, studying the development of English prose with Hugh MacLennan:

> I'd discovered in six years of not only seeking but finding experience that I had one hell of a lot to learn about literature. About writing. About the experience of fusing of words with experience. ("Taking the Risk," in *RK*, p. 67)

During this time Kroetsch began work on a novel about his experiences on the Mackenzie River, and in 1955 *Maclean's* published his first story of note, "That Yellow Prairie Sky." (His earliest short stories, "The Stragglers" and "The Toughest Mile," were published in *The Montrealer* in 1950.)

While at Middlebury College Kroetsch met Jane Lewis, whom he married in 1956. They have two daughters — Laura Caroline Kroetsch, born in 1964, and Margaret Ann (Meg) Kroetsch, born in 1966. Kroetsch and his wife separated in 1974 and subsequently divorced. From 1956 to 1961 Kroetsch attended the University of Iowa, participating in the Writers' Workshop there, as many Canadian writers have done. Among his professors were George P. Elliott and Harvey Swados. Kroetsch received his Ph.D. in 1961, for the unpublished novel "Coulee Hill," and from 1961 until 1978 he was on the faculty in the English Department at the State University of New York at Binghamton. In 1962 he returned briefly to the Mackenzie to research *But We Are Exiles*, published in 1965 when he was in his late thirties. Primarily a novelist in these first years, Kroetsch next published his "Out West" series of three interrelated novels: *The Words of My Roaring* (1966), *The Studhorse Man* (1969) (which won the Governor-General's Award for fiction), and *Gone Indian* (1973). *Badlands* followed in 1975, *What the Crow Said* in 1978, and most recently *Alibi* in 1983. Experience in a broad sense and the home place continue to be important in these novels, as Kroetsch develops from a realistic approach to fiction to a more fabulist one, exploring, often in a surreal or postmodernist manner, tall tales and myths. These interests are reflected also in Kroetsch's critical activities. In 1974 he founded, with William Spanos, the important critical journal *Boundary 2: A Journal of Postmodern Literature*. A special issue of *Open Letter* (1983) and *The Lovely Treachery of Words: Essays Selected and New* (1989) collect the critical essays that Kroetsch has written since 1971.

Near the end of his sojourn in the United States, Kroetsch again began to feel the pull of the prairies. His early story, "That Yellow Prairie Sky," examined his home place from the perspective of "that western problem that goes back to the homesteaders: do I stay or do I leave?" ("A Conversation with Margaret Laurence," p. 54). Twenty years later, Kroetsch revised this sentiment so that he could embrace both possibilities. He was writer-in-residence at the University of Calgary in the fall of 1975 and at the universities of Lethbridge and Manitoba from 1976 to 1977. In 1978 he returned permanently to the Canadian West as a professor in the English Department at the University of Manitoba in Winnipeg. Kroetsch's daughters remained in the United States with their mother; in 1982 he married writer and teacher Smaro Kamboureli.

Kroetsch's physical return to the West coincides with his beginning to write poetry seriously. Fifteen years intervened between the publication of his first poem and the publication of his first book of poetry, during which time he published five novels and a travel book, *Alberta* (1968), and edited the anthology *creation* (1970). In the years since that first book of poetry, the published work is more evenly divided between poetry and fiction, with the addition of a steady stream of critical essays.

Kroetsch says he wrote his first poem in Iowa at the age of thirty-two, and single pieces began to be published in little magazines in the early 1960s. His first published poem, "Letter to a Friend's Wife," was published in 1961; his first collection of poetry, *The Stone Hammer Poems: 1960–1975*, was not published until 1975. There followed *The Ledger* (1975), *Seed Catalogue* (1977), *The Sad Phoe-*

nician (1979), and *The Criminal Intensities of Love as Paradise* (1981). Then in 1981 Kroetsch published *Field Notes*, the title of which came to designate his ongoing long poem. *Field Notes* consists of the five previously published book-length poems, plus four others. In 1983 he published *Letters to Salonika*. In 1985 he published the five-part *Advice to My Friends*, and in 1986, the ten-part *Excerpts from the Real World*, both continuations of *Field Notes*. In 1986 he also published a reprint of *Seed Catalogue*, which contains further poems for *Field Notes*, and in 1989, *Completed Field Notes: The Long Poems of Robert Kroetsch*.

More clearly autobiographical than his novels, the early poetry is profoundly regionalist in Eli Mandel's sense of focusing on first place:

> ... surely ... the essence of what we mean by a region [is] the overpowering feeling of nostalgia associated with the place we know as the *first* place, the *first* vision of things, the *first* clarity of things.[9]

Kroetsch captures this essence in his absorption with beginnings; memory replaces history as a means to tell the past; the storyteller is revered; and tall tales demonstrate a "humour in the ludicrous." In the most recent poetry, Kroetsch explores the borders of possibility in language, form, and process.

Although the facts with which we can qualify the myth of Robert Kroetsch are those which he himself chooses to reveal, they are nevertheless related to the poems. Shirley Neuman, for instance, examines the actual strategies of autobiography in two articles that I discuss in subsequent pages.[10] Autobiographical aspects have loomed larger in Kroetsch's later works, specifically in the poetry, and are intrinsically associated with major concerns: language, place, doubleness, boundaries. In fact, there are many biographical significances that become apparent in the poetic patterns. Kroetsch's sojourn in the United States, for example, probably allowed him the distance and perspective necessary to tackling the crucial questions of home place and belonging (*nostos*), alienation and exile. In fact, it allowed him to act out the familial westering journey and to embody the doubleness of his parents' geographic sensibilities:

> My father was from Ontario — so he came west [at age 16] with a deep sense of nostalgia for Ontario — he preferred its rich

green, rural landscape. My mother was born in Alberta and its landscape was the world she was used to. I felt that I grew up with a kind of double vision. (MacKinnon, p. 3)

The unique division of labour in the prairie town of Heisler further emphasized the duplicitous view:

> They [the coal miners] lived a strange life and the fact that they went underground contributed to my double vision. The farmers working on the surface would give me a kind of surface metaphor while the coal miners working below the surface would provide the underworld metaphor. (MacKinnon, pp. 3–4)

The doubleness is reinforced by an erotic tension of the sexual boundaries implicit in Kroetsch's childhood world. The ambiguity of the garden space is amplified in the endless ambiguities of Kroetsch's poetry and the continual pushing of boundaries. This doubleness of vision, readily apparent in the poetry, is examined more closely in the section dealing with the poetic works.

The temptation of silence is also constantly present, while, ironically, language is one of Kroetsch's major concerns; and even this doubling of silence and speaking can be related to biography: to the silence of his geographical place, the seductive unspokenness of a primal landscape, and to the death of his mother when he was only thirteen. Kroetsch explains:

> ... I think part of my move to autobiography was daring to say that my mother died when I was so young and I was very close to her: I think some of the female presence in my book [*Badlands*] is almost a parody of the absence which is really what the book is about. . . . [O]ne of the things that I can see happening, in the next few years as I go on writing, is a kind of enunciation. I can feel even my long poem, *Field Notes*, drawing toward that. (*LV*, p. 22)

The enunciation of silence or the voicing of the unvoiced is central to the poetry as both subject and process. There is also Kroetsch's literal silencing as a unilingual citizen of world literature: his parents refused to speak German after the day of his birth.

Autobiographical patterning thus seems to structure the poems:

duplicity, the pull between belonging and leaving, a westering movement, the search for home, absence, loss, the seasonal growth cycle. Patterns of return are found: in *Seed Catalogue*, when a cousin of Kroetsch's returns to Anna Weller's birthplace, first descendant to do so, nearly a century after her birth, he comes carrying death, "a cargo of bombs" (*FN*, p. 65), and meets his own. Kroetsch returns to Germany himself many years later and meets his double in the Frankfurt *Hauptbahnhof*, recorded in the poem of that title. He takes his two American-born daughters to Greece, birthplace of his second wife and home of muses and oracles, recorded in "Delphi: Commentary." He seeks crucial and magical beginnings in "Mile Zero" and "Spending the Morning on the Beach."

Myth, memory, the muse.

Tradition and Milieu

"[T]he Canadian writer is in a very exciting predicament . . . ," Kroetsch has said. "[T]here's a profound sense in which we have nothing to write about. . . ." Far from being paralysed by this notion, Kroetsch concludes, ". . . we come back to writing" (*LV*, p. 145). He expands: "As a child I had that really strong feeling that I was living in a place that had no story to explain it and so I suppose one of the things I wanted to do was tell *that* story of nothing to tell" (*LV*, pp. 186–87). This notion of coming from an unnamed world is very different from the feeling of existing in a literary void that a Canadian poet of the previous century might have held. Kroetsch is both excited by the task of naming his world into existence and haunted by the literary voices that speak around him: ". . . I found this incredible web of story around me which turned me into the hero/jokester: the *one* accident was that blank but the *other* accident was a lot of literary education which told me all those stories" (*LV*, p. 187).

Kroetsch, then, is both a literary nationalist and a literary internationalist. His approach is fundamentally shaped by his childhood experiences in the Canadian West and by his wide reading of other writers' works. His imaginative vision is inexorably that of his time and place: ". . . as a kid, the one science that tempted me was geography" (*LV*, p. 9). Place is much more than a static, physical location; for Kroetsch geography is kinetic: ". . . every journey across

it [geography] or through it is another reading in a way" (*LV*, p. 8).
In *The Crow Journals* he asks, "Is not landscape an event as well as
a setting?" His experience of landscape is constantly related to
writing[11]:

> The western landscape is one without boundaries quite often.
> So you have the experience within a kind of chaos, yet you have
> to order it somehow to survive. I'm particularly interested in the
> kinds of orderings we do on that landscape.[12]

The structural concerns for Kroetsch embrace a finding of form in
the chaos. A landscape viewed in this way frees Kroetsch from
realistic fictionalization and provides an alternative to linear narration. It also paves the way for poetry:

> What has come to interest me right now is . . . the dream of
> origins. Obviously in the prairies, the small town and the farm
> are not merely places, they are remembered places. When they
> were the actuality of our lives, we had realistic fiction, and we
> had almost no poetry at all. Now in this dream condition, as
> dream-time fuses into the kind of narrative we call myth, we
> change the nature of the novel. And we start, with a new and
> terrible energy, to write the poems of the imagined real place.
> ("On Being an Alberta Writer," in *RK*, p. 76)

Kroetsch is very much at the heart of the Prairie's blossoming in
poetry. He figures prominently in anthologies of Prairie writing and
in the many new Prairie journals. He taught for many summers at
the Saskatchewan School of the Arts in the Qu'Appelle Valley, and
his descriptions of the camaraderie shared by the writers there (Ken
Mitchell, Lorna Uher, Rudy Wiebe, Byrna Barclay, Steve Scriver, Eli
Mandel, and others) exemplifies his own warmth and generosity
within the growing Prairie writing community. So the feeling of
coming from an unstoried place or having to find words for the
unboundaried chaos leads not to isolation but to a community of
writers dealing now with a shared experience.

If geography early held a fascination for Kroetsch, then archaeology, a deepening of geography, is the crucial science for Kroetsch the
mature writer. It suggests at once the idea of an underlying text in
the landscape, and also the idea of text as an open site with layers

of prior texts to unhide. Identifying what texts are recovered from the site of a Kroetsch poem, and clarifying Kroetsch's own attitudes towards the tradition they represent, are complicated, but some clues are found in his background, which is both rural and academic. There is a strong sense of an oral tradition and an agricultural tradition, so that some of the uncovered texts are seed catalogues, ledgers, or stories overheard in pub or kitchen. Kroetsch tells us: "The great sub-text of prairie literature is our oral tradition . . . [in which] the visit is the great prairie cultural event. . . . We talk ourselves into existence" ("On Being an Alberta Writer," in *RK*, p. 75). But Kroetsch is also highly educated in a formal sense and has spent many years in universities, as a student and as a professor. Many of the layered texts are thus literary, stretching from Homer's *Odyssey*, through Spenser, to Joseph Conrad, to William Faulkner, to Gabriel Garcia Marquez.

It is necessary, however, to distinguish between the layers of influence that underlie Kroetsch's novels and those that underlie his poetry. Over the years Kroetsch has acknowledged the importance of many writers to his fiction, and traces of them are evident in his work: at first Conrad and Joyce, Lawrence and Woolf, then Faulkner, Beckett, Nabokov, and more recently Borges, Italo Calvino, Julio Cortazar, and Garcia Marquez. Closer to home: F.P. Grove, W.O. Mitchell, Sinclair Ross, Hugh MacLennan, Margaret Laurence, Rudy Wiebe, and Sheila Watson — all, except MacLennan, Western writers. Perhaps because the poetry is more personal, the question of tradition is more difficult to unravel. Crucial to the novels are other novels, and how problems of style and form are handled by other novelists. Crucial to the poems are the patterns of Kroetsch's home place: "the dream of origins," *nostos* and his own return, the presence of absence, and prairie cycles that include germination, growth, harvesting — the magical potency of seed. From a grounding in the greats (Homer, Spenser, Shakespeare, Cervantes), Kroetsch came to be moved by poets who are largely North American and more usually Canadian: sharing an experience of creating a new literature in a new land with an established language. Through his critical readings and his own critical writings Kroetsch has developed poetic solutions to the problems of grammar and language. Immersed in deconstruction theory, Kroetsch writes deconstructive poetry.

For any contemporary writer aware of his literary context, the notion of tradition and influence is one with which to contend. The anxiety that Harold Bloom so clearly articulates[13] must be acknowledged and creatively manipulated, as Kroetsch is aware:

> . . . there is that sense of anxiety — I suppose the root word would be anxiety there — you had better know the tradition and you had better be viewing it as a kind of risk-relationship that you're engaged in. . . . To lose the tradition is fatal but to surrender to it is fatal. (*LV*, pp. 3–4)

The line Kroetsch is drawing for himself to walk is fine indeed. It involves a knowledge and acknowledgement of previous writing without a surrendering to it. Kroetsch makes a crucial distinction between writing and literature. The notion of literature, he contends, can be "overwhelming — there is Homer and Shakespeare and Dante and all those books that I dearly love" (*LV*, p. 3). Loved or not, these greats can be formidable company unless the process of writing is balanced against them. Kroetsch's dualistic response is to appreciate his literary ancestors while foregrounding the language and process of writing itself. His critical grounding in Roland Barthes, Jacques Derrida, Julia Kristeva, and Mikhail Bakhtin among other postmodernist theorists helps provide the structural means. Foregrounding and discontinuity are two relevant postmodernist aspects of Kroetsch's poetry examined in my section on his poetic works.

Prior texts may be embedded in the site of a Kroetsch poem, but the Kroetsch poem is more than an accumulation of stratified, anterior artifacts. The Derridean intertextuality posited places a large responsibility on the reader to unravel the various writings.[14] One of the pleasures of deconstruction theory can be just this uncovering to recover, a practice that connotes both the archaeological model and Kroetsch's "dream of origins" by recapturing processual beginnings. Multiple names for this practice all indicate the attempt to get back to beginnings by removing layers of meanings and conventions: deconstructing, demythologizing, unhiding, unnaming, uninventing. This involves penetrating the encrustations that build up over the years and attach themselves to words, word patterns, myths, so that originality and freshness can be re-instilled and released.

> Deconstruction implies an operation involving the dismantling of something into discrete component parts and suggests the

ever-present possibility of putting the object back together in its
original form [emphasis added]. . . . Deconstruction is really
more of a technique of *de-sedimentation*, . . . a technique of
de-sedimenting the text in order to allow what was *always
already* inscribed in its texture to resurface.[15]

So the poet rehearses previous methodologies, myths, and literatures,
then by turning the tactic against himself, dislocates and finally
deconstructs the system. Kroetsch at once builds on past traditions
and myths (the quest, ledger, seed catalogue, oral tradition, literary
tradition) and deconstructs the position just left. "This operation is
paradoxical in that the deconstructive movement is at the same time
a close reading of texts and a commentary on its own practice of
writing. . . ."[16] "The Ledger" is then a ledger; "Seed Catalogue," a
seed catalogue; and both are poems about writing poetry. The
tradition and the writing remain in balance.

Traces can be found in Kroetsch's poetry from the distant literary
past. The epic qualities of Homer's great quest, so evident in
Kroetsch's novels, are also distinguishable in the poems. Kroetsch
notes the relationship between *The Odyssey* and the long poem, each
being "a kind of travel book" with "its own complex relationship
to the idea of love" ("For Play and Entrance: The Contemporary
Canadian Long Poem," in *RK*, p. 104). These aspects, as well as the
attempt to return home and the endless delays, can be found in
Kroetsch's continuing poem. In the blend of wit and sensuality, there
are also traces of Ovid, the amatory poet and the mythological poet,
who experimented with narrative techniques and structures to
include the disconnected stories of his *Metamorphoses*. Evidence can
also be found of Cervantes's *Don Quixote*, again in the use of the
quest and particularly in the extension of an existing literary form.

In terms of movements Kroetsch has more affinity with the
Romantics than with the Victorians. There is no Arnoldian yearning
for eternal verities or any desire to find an inclusive unity in
Kroetsch's poetry. Rather, he demonstrates his desire to recapture
the language of speech — the prairie subtext of talk — and embraces
a form founded on discontinuities, resisting any sense of ending. The
dialogic nature of his poems and the revolt against convention that
they exemplify further link Kroetsch with Romanticism, as do the
autobiographical aspects and the concern with beginnings rather
than endings — Wordsworth's continuing "Prelude," the growth of

a poet's sensibility. Still, for all the similarities, Kroetsch is resoundingly a "postmodernist" poet, breaking from the Romanticism of Wordsworth and Whitman and the modernism of Eliot. And the influences are as much critical as poetic. He uses myths, but not in the manner of Eliot who used them to structure poems. In the movement from allusion to quotation, Eliot's upfront use of references is alien to Kroetsch. Myths for Kroetsch are part of the process and must be reworked to fit the discontinuous form rather than to provide unity. Modernism is, in fact, a movement that Kroetsch believes was largely bypassed in Canada, thus making the step into postmodernism smoother in this country than in the United States.

To simplify greatly, the most important literary influence on Kroetsch's poetry are twofold: first, there is the influence of American poets, and second, there is the influence of postmodernist critics, largely European. In addition, Kroetsch is part of a strong, contemporary Canadian group of poets who influence and stimulate each other, including Michael Ondaatje, bpNichol, Fred Wah, Eli Mandel, and Daphne Marlatt. Kroetsch's sense of place and his attitude to language and structures have been clearly influenced by exposure to American poetics. First, there is evidence of Whitman's naming into being, the cataloguing of a place and time. (The Walt Whitman Kroetsch would have read is the one who wrote his poems in order to free the American mind to the possibility inherent in the beginning position, to free it from the stultifying effects of outmoded and inappropriate traditions.) Second, there is evidence of the special awareness of language found in the poetry of Wallace Stevens. But central is the influence of William Carlos Williams, who provided the all-important model for Kroetsch. As Kroetsch says, "Williams' poetry is never failed."[17] When he is stuck, Kroetsch turns to "Kora in Hell" or "Spring and All." And then there is the crucial poem, *Paterson*. Here the evidence is in both the subject and the form, Williams' association of person with place and the combination of personal and regional history. Simply, Williams provided a model, and the opening words of *Paterson*, "a local pride," form a motif throughout Kroetsch's own writing. He explains:

The feeling must come from an awareness of the authenticity of our own lives. People who feel invisible try to borrow visibility from those who are visible. To understand others is surely difficult. But to understand ourselves becomes impossible if we do not see images of ourselves in the mirror — be that mirror theatre or literature or historical writing. A local pride does not exclude the rest of the world, or other experiences; rather, it makes them possible. It creates an organizing centre. Or as Williams put it, more radically: the acquiring of a local pride enables us to create our own culture — "by lifting an environment to expression." ("On Being an Alberta Writer," in *RK*, p. 75)

This enabling act is both the part Williams played for Kroetsch and the design of Kroetsch's own poetry. It is important to note Kroetsch's care in emphasizing that this "local pride" is not a parochial regionalism, not a closing in, but an opening up. The poetic voice Kroetsch discovered to lift his "environment to expression" is the talking voice of his prairies and the "dream of origins."

Unlayering once begun, further traces can be found: of Pound, the Black Mountain poets, and Ed Dorn, the releasing dynamics of the spoken word and phrase, allowing for intertextuality; while in *Excerpts from the Real World* Kroetsch is influenced by Noam Chomsky. One obvious connection is between Charles Olson's "composition by field" theory of "projective or open verse"[18] and the title of Kroetsch's ongoing poem, *Field Notes*,[19] but the real influence is again one of freeing up. The Olsonian transfer of energy and concentration on process are clear in the site of a Kroetsch poem. While Olson arrives at the speech power of poetic language through special attention to the breath and Kroetsch arrives at it through an awareness of the oral tradition, both are concerned with the opening of possibility in language and the association of the various elements: "the syllable, the line, as well as the image, the sound, the sense."[20]

The association of form and content for Black Mountain poets has certain similarities to the distinction between signifier and signified as raised by certain postmodern critics who form the second important influence on Kroetsch's poetry. The distinction between actual influence and the recognition of similarities in ideas, however, is a difficult one to draw. After making a strong case for Kroetsch's location in a particular place, then, I would suggest a similar case for his location in a particular time. He is as much a product of a postmodern world as he is of the prairies. Discontinuity rather than unity, collage rather than strict chronology, deferral rather than immediate answers, continuation rather than conclusion — above all, *différance* — mark postmodern writing. Process is foregrounded; meaning is deferred; hierarchy is eschewed. Kroetsch moves from metaphor to metonymy, and thereby "recover[s] distant texts" (*LV*, p. 9).

Kroetsch's years in the United States and his association with William Spanos were undoubtedly crucial. Special issues of *Boundary 2* on Heidegger, Nietzsche, Robert Creeley, Jack Spicer, and "The Problems of Reading in Contemporary American Criticism" indicate the exciting range of this postmodern journal, while the special issue on Canadian literature bears Kroetsch's unmistakable mark. He has also acknowledged the fruitful nature of his interrelationship with Smaro Kamboureli, who has an intimate knowledge of European literary theory.

We can trace in Kroetsch's own writing — novels, poems, and essays — his reading and misreading of theorists: for instance, Roland Barthes's erotics of the written (*The Pleasure of the Text*) is evident in *Alibi*, "The Sad Phoenician," and "For Play and Entrance." Kroetsch's understanding of Julia Kristeva is crucial to his ideas of intertextuality, as demonstrated in his reworking of his early poem "Mile Zero." In *Labyrinths of Voice* he explains:

> I think that what Kristeva says is that we have a number of intertexts that don't have to come together, that it's their not coming together that makes them strong because then all these possibilities can operate at *this* point in time through the codes of the intertexts. (pp. 16–17)

Kroetsch goes on to relate this idea to the structure of "Mile Zero" and the manner of its writing:

> I have a traditional poem, a kind of post-Surreal poem, and footnotes. I use footnotes as intertext . . . footnotes fascinate me as a form of writing. It's the *disjunctions* I use. . . . (p. 17)

Further, Kroetsch's fascination with Bakhtin's notions of violence in literature and what Bakhtin calls "carnivalization" are evident in Kroetsch's essay "Carnival and Violence: A Meditation" (in *RK*, pp. 111–22). This fascination is also evident in his poetry, which incorporates oral discourse in the literary texts and embraces the breakdown of hierarchies and the givens in both literary structure and language itself. Responding to a question about Bakhtin, Kroetsch says:

> Again, it isn't simply recording, it is a transformation that has to take place; I find a *source* in that oral tradition, rather than an answer of any sort. (*LV*, p. 164)

Transformation, then, often becomes a means of impetus in Kroetsch's poems, and it is important to note its association with Bakhtin and the use of oral language. As a poet with a rich sense of the possibilities of language, both oral and literary, of the potential in ambiguities, and of the release inherent in transformations, the unilingual Kroetsch notes that these European critics first write in languages alien to his own:

> . . . in translation you push the language away from you a little bit. I'm sometimes surprised at how many of the books on my shelf are translations. (*LV*, p. 18)

Helping Kroetsch with translations, not merely lingual, are the Canadian writers to whom he is drawn: the risk-takers, those who take risks to find their individual voices. This is Kroetsch's milieu and not so much a matter of "influence." These are the poets with whom he converses, the poets whose work he reads with particular attention, and the poets who read his. These are his friends — other contemporary Canadian poets who are similarly drawn to use and break traditions, to acknowledge and shatter conventions. Kroetsch is drawn to what Ondaatje does with documents and the myth of the land, what Marlatt does with language and her experimentation with compositional units, to bpNichol's meditations on notation, his punning solutions, and the inherently discontinuous structure of, for instance, the chains in Book v of *The Martyrology*. Kroetsch and Mandel share their prairie heritage, which leads both to a double vision, or what Mandel calls "duplicity."[21] Kroetsch and Wah share a search for relief from the burden of the line and keep their readers off-balance with techniques Wah calls "making strange."[22]

What all these poets have in common is a concern for language and the process of poetry. All are also writers of long poems, so Kroetsch has a particular place in the tradition of the long poem form in Canada, always important, but now used with more experimentation, more openness, and certainly much energy, in an attempt to solve structural dilemmas. Crucial as part of a Canadian poetics is the primacy of the long poem which now allows for increased possibilities, such as the "movement away from metaphor and into metonymy" (*LV*, p. 155) and the crucial question of from where the voice is coming. The long poem, then, is a vast project in more than just poetic length. As Kroetsch tells us, "To understand the long poem of our time would be to understand our time" ("For Play and Entrance," in *RK*, p. 107). This is his project in both poem and essay.

Critical Overview and Context

There has been much critical interest in the work of Robert Kroetsch. There are to date two book-length studies, one collection of essays, and numerous individual articles considering his work. This concentration, of course, recognizes the excellence of Kroetsch's writing, and also acknowledges the fact that he is a crucial figure in Canadian literature when studied from a regional, postmodern, or comparative point of view. This wealth of critical material also reflects the diversity of Kroetsch's own writing as novelist, poet, and critic.

The two book-length studies, one written comparatively early and the other more recently, are insightful and well-written. Both were published in particular literary series, yet both generally rise above the limitations such series often impose and incorporate work each critic had done on Kroetsch over the years. Peter Thomas's *Robert Kroetsch* (1980) is part of the *Studies in Canadian Literature* series, while Robert Lecker's *Robert Kroetsch* (1986) appears in Twayne's World Authors Series. Both books concentrate on Kroetsch's fiction, and neither deals with Kroetsch's second volume of *Field Notes*, *Advice to My Friends*, *Excerpts from the Real World* and *Completed Field Notes: The Long Poems of Robert Kroetsch*.

In 1984 *Open Letter* published a collection of essays dealing with Kroetsch's writing. Included are some of Kroetsch's most perceptive critics: in addition to Lecker, the most notable are Ann Mandel, Russell Brown, and Shirley Neuman, all of whom have published a number of essays on Kroetsch.

Significant is the fact that Kroetsch himself is perhaps one of his own most sensitive and intelligent critics. The essays collected in *Open Letter* and in *The Lovely Treachery of Words* clearly have a bearing on his fiction and poetry. Kroetsch's essays dealing with the writing of others reveal insights into his own fiction and poetry, and his writing concerning specific formative or influential moments or movements in Canadian writing is particularly crucial.

In addition to his critical essays, Kroetsch may have more interviews in print than any other Canadian writer, and as a record of his own views about his work and the creative process, these are invaluable. There are at least a dozen individual interviews published and one book-length interview, *Labyrinths of Voice: Conversations with Robert Kroetsch*, by Shirley Neuman and Robert Wilson.

Despite this wealth of critical material about Kroetsch, there is still much work that can usefully be done. Some, of course, must wait until the conclusion of his writing career. An annotated bibliography of work published to 1986 has been published by ECW PRESS, for instance, but we must wait for a final bibliography, a full biography, scholarly editions of correspondence, and a definitive edition of the collected poetry. At present a substantial examination of the poetry is still needed.

Today, the critical reception of Kroetsch's writing is generally positive. He is much in demand at conferences and in classrooms, and his new work, by and large, receives a favourable response. There is, perhaps, a larger audience for his fiction, and his poetry is often seen in terms of the fiction, but in recent years as his long poem lengthens there has been an increasing number of essays dealing with the poetry.

It seems to be more common in Canada for authors who first published poetry to turn to prose, than the reverse. (One thinks of Earle Birney, P.K. Page, Margaret Atwood, George Bowering, bpNichol, and Daphne Marlatt.) Certainly, reviews of Kroetsch's first books of poetry reveal a certain bemused sense of tolerance for such aberrant behaviour by an established novelist. "[T]hough best known as a novelist"[23] is how many of the early reviews begin, while some actually insist that Kroetsch is a storyteller and therefore not a poet at all.[24] On the strength of his first collection, David Carpenter proclaimed that Kroetsch "seems destined to be considered by literary historians as primarily a prose-fiction writer."[25] And Howard Engel's review in *The Canadian Forum* of this same collection concludes:

Robert Kroetsch writes prose of distinction. It would be indeed rare if his poetry were of the same stamp. There are few Thomas

Hardys and few Earle Birneys in any culture. But, having said that, it will be interesting to watch the novelist develop now that we have seen the poet at work in these thirty-five or so prose-flawed poems.[26]

Kroetsch's first books of poetry were generally reviewed either individually by small journals or as part of a collective review including many other volumes in a larger journal. It took a while for reviewers to accept Kroetsch's poetry as more than the recreational activity of a novelist. Once recognized, however, the poetry was quickly seen by many reviewers as central to contemporary poetic practice and theory, and reviews of Kroetsch's poetry began to reveal the interesting debates current in poetic circles. Reviews concentrate on Kroetsch's experimentation and his attempts to structure his poems in new ways. Appreciation of his poetry has much to do with whether or not this experimentation is exciting or upsetting to the reviewer. David S. West, for instance, calls *The Sad Phoenician* an "ambitious undertaking," a "complex poem," but admits to his own difficulties when he claims that it "defies full analysis in the space of a review" and finds the "humour . . . hard to describe."[27] Joseph A. Lipari claims in his review of *Field Notes*, that "Kroetsch is at his best when he works in the tradition of W.C. Williams and Olson, but too often he settles for the merely clever and inventive."[28] Lesley Choyce "found many of the poems [in *Advice to My Friends*] to be little more than stylistic diversions,"[29] yet Bruce Whiteman describes Kroetsch as "a brilliant and innovative poet."[30] Albert Moritz calls *Field Notes* "vivid and important poetry." He continues:

> The selection engagingly displays Kroetsch's wide range as a poet, his supplely shifting tones, his seriousness, humour, and irony, his talent for epigram, lyricism, description, and narrative, his formal inventiveness, his learning, and his deft, unassuming way with an allusion.[31]

Noting the duality in Kroetsch's attempt and achievement, Jon Kertzer sums up:

> . . . *Field Notes* is confusing, vexing, delightful, uneven, and highly entertaining. It mixes depth of feeling and thought with irreverence and even banality. Kroetsch seems to be restlessly

experimental, forever seeking a new idiom which often sounds like fragmentary prose rather than verse.[32]

Again the old genre dilemma, but over the years Kroetsch's poems have earned him much respect and are now reviewed on their own merits, without the need to bolster their author with his novel-writing prowess.

The number, location, and tenor of the reviews do emphasize, however, that poetry is an art with a relatively small audience, and that experimental poetry reaches even fewer readers. Kroetsch deliberately challenges his readers, and when that challenge is accepted by reviewers, the opinions are generally positive. Perhaps Kroetsch's politically affirmative decision to publish his poetry with small, regional publishers affects the distribution of his books and the number of reviews they receive. While his poetry is regularly reviewed in *The Canadian Forum, Books in Canada, Essays on Canadian Writing, The Fiddlehead, CV/II, NeWest Review*, and numerous smaller, particularly Prairie, magazines, only one volume of poetry has been reviewed in *The Dalhousie Review*, none has been considered in *Queen's Quarterly*, and *The University of Toronto Quarterly* only accords them a few paragraphs in its yearly literary roundup. Perhaps most surprising of all, until 1986 only one review of his poetry appeared in *Canadian Literature*, and that a rather uncomprehending review of *The Sad Phoenician*.

A number of reviewers — Douglas Barbour, Louis MacKendrick, and Peter Thomas, for instance — seem to follow Kroetsch's career and review different volumes, often for different journals. Some reviews considered *Field Notes* in conjunction with Thomas's book on Kroetsch. In fact, this book *about* the author has received as much attention from reviewers as have the individual volumes of poetry, and is a good place to begin consideration of extended critical opinion about Kroetsch's poetry.

Although Thomas' book was published in 1980 and therefore does not consider any of the poetry written after "How I Joined the Seal Herd," Thomas does take an interesting approach. Instead of reserving the poetry for the end, as if an afterthought after the novels have been given due consideration, he deals with the poetry first, using the poems as a means of ingress to the fiction. Here, as in his essay "Robert Kroetsch and Silence," Thomas explores the mythic dimensions of Kroetsch's poetry (both Graeco-Roman and North American

Indian) and argues that the poems work out ideas expanded in the novels. Noting that questions of form are raised by the common concerns, Thomas summarizes the recurrences:

> The obsessive search for source and "ground," the "dream of origins"; the persistent duality of perception, understood in mythopoeic terms as the double kingdom of winter/summer, extended to the male/female hegemonies of underworld and vegetation; the Orphic and narcissistic motifs of descent, with their associated notions of entry into chaos or "terror"; the structure and language of shamanistic dream, flight and song; the movement towards an erotic comedy of existence — all are richly present.[33]

After giving primacy of place to his consideration of the poetry, Thomas goes on to give primacy of space to his consideration of the novels. The chapter dealing with the poetry is a very small part of the book, and although it is sensitive and suggestive, it suffers from its truncated nature (considering only a fraction of Kroetsch's poetic output) and leaves much room for deeper study. The fiction is still the true focus of Thomas's book.

Lecker reverses Thomas's order of consideration, by building up to a discussion of Kroetsch's poetry after looking at the fiction up to and including *Alibi*. Again a major shortcoming is that Lecker's single chapter on the poetry does not consider any of the poetry written after the first volume of *Field Notes*. His view of Kroetsch's poetry reaffirms what he establishes in the first chapters as his view of Kroetsch's "aesthetic stance(s)."[34] Again the poetry is seen as a concentration of the concerns elaborated in the novels. In Lecker's work, however, the consideration of the poetry is not made to carry the whole weight of the annunciatory section, and there is more scope for specific elucidation. Lecker describes the recurrence in Kroetsch's work of the idea of the border position; in Kroetsch's words, ". . . Canada is a peculiar kind of border land, and a border land is often the place where things are really happening" (Brown, "Interview," p. 14). Lecker emphasizes Kroetsch's references to the border position as being peculiarly Canadian, a position in which is found "the play of possible meanings."[35] Kroetsch emphasizes his experience as "double" in one interview,[36] and elsewhere argues that Canadians are caught between two balanced and "opposing forces" and that the "dialectic" of this opposition reflects Canadian society.[37] For Lecker, Kroetsch's idea that Canadian literature "is a literature of dangerous middles" (Kroetsch, "Beyond Nationalism: A Prologue," in *RK*, p. 89) is crucial to an understanding of Kroetsch's own writing. Lecker applies this to his study of Kroetsch's fiction and poetry, stressing in his careful analysis of the early poetry the dualities of concern and form: the questions of place, narrative strategy, and tradition.

Lecker emphasizes the dilemma of the critic trying to deal with Kroetsch's work. There is, on the one hand, a desire to locate a central belief, discern a particular development, or discover an overriding unity, while, on the other hand, there is the temptation to respond to Kroetsch's own theorizing and resist categorization, closure, or conclusion. Lecker's own discussion of the ambiguities and doubleness of the pervasive border position neatly synthesizes this dilemma. He is able to posit a recurring metaphor and consider the development of Kroetsch's poetry while at the same time acknowledging the oppositions and contradictions always at play, and with a much fuller analysis of the poems than Thomas achieved.

The shortcomings of both books are those necessarily encountered in writing an overview of such a prolific author. In each case, primacy of space and consideration is given to the fiction, and the poetry criticism thus suffers from the necessary "and also" approach. Specific essays studying individual poems provide the most in-depth looks at the poetry, and, simplifying somewhat, can be divided into roughly three particular approaches: the regional, the autobiographical, and the postmodernist or processual.

A number of essays and interviews concentrate on the regional aspects of Kroetsch's writing, not just on place as subject in the poems but on place as a structuring principle, alternative to narrative. This is the focus of a particularly intelligent interview by Robert Enright and Dennis Cooley in a special issue of *Essays on Canadian Writing* devoted to Prairie poetry. In this interview, questions about the relationship between place and poetics are discussed. The interviewers suggest theories to explain the present proliferation of poetry on the prairies, and Kroetsch directs attention to the formal problems that such stances indicate. In Russell Brown's early interview with Kroetsch in which they discuss landscape and "the kinds of ordering we do on that landscape" (Brown, "Interview," p. 2). Kroetsch talks about the technical aspects of "discovering your landscape" and relating that process to the process of poetry (Brown, "Interview," p. 7). Fourteen years later Brown delivered a paper at the Long-liners conference, "On Not Saying Uncle: Kroetsch and the Place of Place in the Long Poem," in which he investigates more specifically place as a structural device in "Seed Catalogue." Noting the absences of the prairies that relate to the poet, "no history, philosophy, and culture to draw on,"[38] Brown studies how Kroetsch turns these into a strength in his long poems. And my own essay, "The Structural Horizons of Prairie Poetics: The Long Poem, Eli Mandel, Andrew Suknaski, and Robert Kroetsch," associates Kroetsch with these two other Prairie writers and examines the techniques they employ to reflect their place: the structural solutions (for instance, Kroetsch's deconstructive tactics) to get back to beginnings in order to construct a past and a present consonant with their aims and ideals.

The link between place and autobiography in Kroetsch's writing is clear, and a number of interviews seek to uncover Kroetsch's past and the importance of the West to him. For instance, Brian MacKinnon in "The Writer Has Got to Know Where He Lives" directs the conversation to the relationship between the real and the dreamed place, and how this double sense of place structures Kroetsch's imagination. But the clearest examination of autobiographical tactics in Kroetsch's poetry is found in two essays by Shirley Neuman. The first relates formal solutions to the question of autobiography in *Field Notes*, while the second concentrates on the reader's position in the text. In "Allow Self, Portraying Self: Autobiography in *Field Notes*," Neuman looks at what Kroetsch calls the " '*language* problem' of writing autobiography" and examines his notion of "autobiography as freeing us from Self."[39] She questions his language usage and techniques such as fragmentation, the doubled "I," and intertextuality. In "Figuring the Reader, Figuring the Self in *Field Notes*: 'Double or noting,' " Neuman expands the dialogic reading by looking at the reader "encoded" in the text and examining Kroetsch's ideas about the relationship between autobiography, notation, and the reading process.

The critical theories that clearly underlie Neuman's essays are postmodernist and reflect the ideas and vocabulary found in Kroetsch's own essays. Less astute critics than Neuman can be trapped by the topical stance to the extent that they ignore more traditional readings, denying, as Lecker correctly warns, exactly the double sense of "tradition" and "innovation" at the heart of

Kroetsch's poetry. More recent essays provide a wealth of postmodern responses: "poststructural and deconstructionist readings of his early poems, phenomenological rereadings of his long poems, reader-response critiques of his intertextual narratives, talk of fragments, *différance*, and meaning deferred" (Lecker, p. 123). Done well, these critical responses can themselves be fresh and restorative, while done poorly, they can be narrow and inequitable. E.D. Blodgett, in his "The Book, Its Discourse, and the Lyric: Notes on Robert Kroetsch's *Field Notes*," assumes his readers are familiar with postmodernist theory and gives a sophisticated reading of intertextuality in *Field Notes*, arguing that Kroetsch applies to his poetry contemporary theories usually applied to prose, thereby opening up to possibility the "margins" in his long poems. As Kroetsch does, Blodgett expects a lot from his readers, but if they are sympathetic to his critical approach, they will find his essay enlightening. On the other hand, Don McKay seems to fall into the trap of postmodernist criticism. His essay "At Work and Play in *The Ledger*" tries to capture the theory and playfulness of Kroetsch's poem, but sabotages itself. By reflecting the syntactical and grammatical compression of the poetry, McKay's argument is diffused. Talking of structure, he mirrors discontinuity. When he concentrates on tallying the balance of images in "The Ledger," for instance, he is interesting, but overall the style of his essay intrudes into the cogency of his argument. George Bowering's narrative of his reading of the "Stone Hammer Poem" is perhaps the most exciting demonstration of contemporary critical practice, opening up the poem while at the same time *demonstrating* a deconstructionist reading. By example, he explores Kroetsch's process of writing: the puns, the dialogic approach, the techniques of erasure, parody, inversion, ambiguity. Bowering examines the grammar and language (phonology, syntax, inflexions, derivations), even the punctuation. He follows Kroetsch's and his own starts and stops and re-starts, emphasizing the alternative nature of the lines. The story of Bowering's reading is a process and not the final, interpretive product of a New Critical approach, and as such is the best of current criticism.

Individual interviews can also be associated with various approaches taken by the critics, and the most important document in this connection is the book-length interview *Labyrinths of Voice*, which reads almost like the fiction of an interview. Kroetsch got together with Neuman and Robert Wilson over a period of seven months in various places in the Canadian West. They sat down with a tape recorder in Banff, Edmonton, and Winnipeg a number of times between April and November of 1981. There are traces of other speakers, other writers, in the many quotations with which Neuman and Wilson punctuate their text. Tightly edited, *Labyrinths of Voice* organizes the conversations around four subjects: influence, game, myth, and narration.

There are autobiographical aspects to the book, as we are privileged to gain a personal glimpse of Kroetsch: remembering the big farm of his childhood, the garden he grew, the death of his mother. There are also regional aspects, as Kroetsch speaks of the significance for him of Western geography. Most notable are the ways in which the book demonstrates its underlying postmodernist philosophies. On a number of occasions Kroetsch describes his belief in challenging his readers, keeping them off-balance and making them work (or play, as in game theory) hard. Pushing conventions, many of the ideas expressed by the three in *Labyrinths of Voice* challenge the reader in this way, as do many of the quotations, some bereft as they are of contextual signification. The quotations, while resonating with some aspect of the conversation being recorded, are inserted between speeches and, often, in the middle of a developing argument. For the uneducated reader, used to continuity and progression, this can be extremely disruptive and annoying, and the form of the text would perhaps be improved by a binary notation which would illustrate the necessary simultaneous reading. The richness supplied to the text by these quotations is undeniable, and the discontinuity created by the distinct inclusion of the intertexts is a further postmodernist aspect.

Particularly absorbing in *Labyrinths of Voice* are the exchanges about tradition and influence, and about alternatives to narrative. Kroetsch explains that while he resists overriding systems, "I suppose there's an ideological bias in my very interest in language itself as a way to come at literature as opposed to life as a way of coming at literature" (*LV*, pp. 33–34). One strategy to avoid entrapment in the labyrinth that Kroetsch talks of and that *Labyrinths of Voice* demonstrates is the refusal of endings, the deferral of "meaning and other finalities": "Now existing on the circumference rather than in the center excites me. . . . I want to avoid both meaning and conclusiveness. And one way to achieve this is to keep *retelling*, keep transforming the story" (*LV*, p. 130). *Labyrinths of Voice* thus does not end. There is no leave-taking. Other possibilities are opened up.

This labyrinth is transformed with the aid of the archaeological metaphor into a multi-dimensional maze — no longer a single, definitive confrontation, but the continual and continually restated dilemma. *Labyrinths of Voice* is full of such energy and detail, with its wealth of references, that it is invaluable for anyone interested in Kroetsch's writing.

Final judgements are, of course, not possible — nor are they desirable — about an author engaged in writing an ongoing poem. Criticism tends to reflect the diversity of Kroetsch's own writing, often getting tangled in the dangerous borderlands between genres in an attempt to impose labels, or reflecting too facilely the complex theories of Kroetsch's own critical writing. The chapter devoted to poetry in Lecker's book and the individual essays by various critics examining individual poems or particular aspects are the most informative so far. In the future, a book-length study of the poetry, addressing questions of place, autobiography, form, technique, and development, needs to be written, and critics will need to judge Kroetsch's achievements in relation to those of his contemporaries.

Kroetsch's Works

Malcolm Ross calls "the broad design of our unique, inevitable, and precarious cultural pattern" one of "opposites in tension."[40] Northrop Frye details these tensions, first at the level of language, and next at the level of opposing moods: "one romantic, traditional and idealistic, the other shrewd, observant and humorous."[41] Finally, he notes tensions in the culture as a whole, between "the sophisticated" and "the primitive,"[42] between society and the wilderness. A.J.M Smith writes of colonialism and nationalism, the cosmopolitan and the native in Canadian poetry.[43] Hugh MacLennan titles a novel *Two Solitudes*, giving to Canada an enduring name for this tension or duality which seems to be at the heart of the Canadian state and the country's literature. For Robert Kroetsch, "the double experience" (Cameron, p. 84) reflects a very Canadian dialectic of being "almost in stasis . . . between opposing forces," and being "caught between the two" provides the excitement and impetus to write, and particularly the impetus to experiment and find new ways of writing and saying (Enright and Cooley, p. 25). Kroetsch describes as particularly Canadian the double hook. The total ambiguity that is so essentially Canadian: be it in terms of two solitudes, the bush garden, Jungian opposites, or the raw and the cooked binary structures of Levi-Strauss. Behind the multiplying theories of Canadian literature is always the pattern of equally matched opposites.[44]

Robert Lecker, recognizing this tension in Kroetsch's poetry, concludes: "Kroetsch sees Canada as a locus of poetic reference, as a dynamic centre of activity thriving on the tension between extremes" (Lecker, p. 5).

In "Disunity as Unity: A Canadian Strategy," Kroetsch expands his ideas of tension and boundaries as particularly definitive, Canadian aspects, discovering an answer to Canada's ongoing identity question in the double hero, the double hook, the double entry, the double reply. Canada, a marginalized country, thus becomes the epitome of postmodernism for Kroetsch. "The margin, the periphery, the edge, now," he claims, "is the exciting and dangerous boundary where . . . the action is."[45] Definition for Canadians, then, comes in voicing the question, rather than providing any final answers:

All the reality of the story, the speech against the silence, is on the circumference. The margin. We live a life of shifting edges, around an unspoken or unspeakable question. Or, at best, in asking who we are, we are who we are. ("Unity as Disunity," pp. 9–10)

Kroetsch thus transforms the continuing dilemma itself into the solution, as well as discovering an appropriate poetic process along the way.

Transformation becomes a poetic technique for handling the doubleness at the heart of Canada's and Kroetsch's writing, as well as a means of living life on the margins. Transformation, an enabling and amplifying process rather than a diminishing or depleting one, recognizes the concerns already noted: in addition to the doubleness there is the sense of place, intertextuality, the oral tradition, the presence of absence, and the postmodern need to experiment and rebel. Kroetsch explains: "The unnaming allows the naming. The local pride speaks. The oral tradition speaks its tentative nature, its freedom from the authorized text" ("Unity as Disunity," p. 11).

Kroetsch's first important lyric poems thus transform people from the past (all the fathers: "Old Man Stories," "Elegy for Wong Toy," "F.P. Grove: The Finding," "Poem of Albert Johnson," "Meditation on Tom Thomson"), while his first long poems transform artefacts ("Stone Hammer Poem," "The Ledger," "Seed Catalogue"). Next he transforms himself ("How I Joined the Seal Herd"), his language ("The Sad Phoenician"), and his syntax ("The Criminal Intensities of Love as Paradise"). Then he transforms his place ("Postcards from China," "Delphi: Commentary," "The Frankfurt *Hauptbahnhof* "), while finally he transforms his persona (*Excerpts from the Real World*). This most recent metamorphosis is in turn brought about by the crucial transformation of silence, the poetic suppression of his mother's death. There has been a major shift in his poetry from the search for the father to the search for the mother; from the need to speak to the father to the need to speak to the mother; from the desire to understand the father to the desire to understand the mother. Kroetsch's poetry is autobiographical to the extent that it is written towards the confrontation with his mother's death, the final of many absences. As early as "The Ledger," his wife and daughters tell him, "everything you write / . . . is a search   for the dead" (*FN*, p. 25). He has had to learn the process for dealing with silence or suppressed material, what Eli Mandel calls learning how to say "the unsayable."[46] When Kroetsch faces his mother's death, he has also exhausted that autobiographical sense of self in his poetry. Thus he is led to transform his persona. He explains:

> . . . one of the healing acts that we engage in is the *transforma-tional act* — metamorphosis —, the way in which you have to move out of yourself into other possibilities . . . keep it open . . . re/dis/cover. (*LV*, p. 173; emphasis added)

So Kroetsch distils his own notions of autobiography, influence, poetic process, and recurring patterns into an open process/image that is in itself variable. As a "healing act" it suggests the notion of the poet as shaman, reflected in Kroetsch's poetry. His essays also comment on the recent incarnation of poets as shamans, inter-mediaries between humans and the unknown — this unknown including the sacred, the inexplicable in the natural world, and the significance of important rites of passage. The shaman as healer tends to both the physical and spiritual well-being of his people. In a foreshadowing of the Nietzschean definition of the poet, the shaman is the one who, from his own sickness, can cure his society. Kroetsch elaborates:

> [The shaman] uses language and he's the person who attempts to connect heaven (or what we would call heaven) with this world and with the underworld. He's the person who can take the journey and connect these different worlds. And that is what a poet is supposed to do. He's supposed to make that trip and then come back and give us the message, and, in that sense, heal us. (MacKinnon, p. 17)

The poet-shaman restores health after a purgative journey through the abyss, returning with often riddling answers phrased in the images of a particular place,[47] transforming them for us.

Transformation thus provides a link for Kroetsch to the mythic past of his prairies, to his own life, and to the contemporary world of postmodern theory. It is a means of ingress to the Blackfoot Indian legends, the trickster of the early "Old Man Stories," and the later coyote and stone hammer. It allows him to translate his inner silences. It also provides a theoretical basis for the use of sources and a technical means for preventing closure. It allows for the play inherent in Kroetsch's poetry, keeps the reader off-balance, and is closer to metonymy than metaphor. The repeated use of parody can also be seen as a stylistic and structural aspect of transformation.

In the "Tradition and Milieu" section I discussed the embedding of sources in a literary text. This is not simply the inclusion of quotations or echoes from previous writers, but rather the transformation of past writing into the present text. According to Kroetsch this also accounts for the incorporation of oral language in written language: "Again, it isn't simply recording, it is a transformation that has to take place; I find a *source* in that oral tradition, rather than an answer of any sort" (*LV*, p. 164). Of course, a source posits continuation, while an answer would suggest conclusion, and conclusions above all are to be avoided. Again, Kroetsch explains, and in so doing, associates transformation with the border notion, as well as linking it to the inclusion of myths and the deferral of meaning and closure:

> You stay alive by moving around on those edges where you risk meaninglessness all the time. That's one of the risks you have to

97

take on the edge, that it might be just totally meaningless. When you disallow the center, you take that risk. We have sought out the decentering rather than the centering function of myth. There is a paradoxical notion, which shows up in Beckett, that a circle can exist that has no center. All we will know is its circumference. Now existing on the circumference rather than in the center excites me. It is a way to resist entrapment, to resist endings and completion. On the circumference we can defer meaning and other finalities. I want to avoid both meaning and conclusiveness. And one way to achieve this is to keep *retelling*, keep transforming the story. It is the old trick of Proteus or the trickster figure. . . . It is, in a word of Beckett, the unknowable: deliberately staying out of the knowable, being interested in what one doesn't know. So myth can become a very useful notion again. Instead of a fear of myth as closure, and as entrapment, myth can become generative again. But it must be decentered. (*LV*, pp. 130–31)

And it must be transformed.

The "transformational act," then, becomes both a way of looking at Kroetsch's poetry that provides some sense of development and cohesion, as well as a means of embodying the very shifts and endlessness of it. "[I]f transformations are possible, then the world is renewable" (*LV*, p. 98), Kroetsch tells us, and goes on to demonstrate convincingly in his poetry.

Kroetsch's success and reputation as a poet lie in his continuing poem, and certainly his strengths are best demonstrated in the longer form. Still, some of his ongoing concerns can be noted in his first, lyric poems. These apprentice works hint at future patterns in a tentative way; for instance, the compelling nature of narrative and the power of the oral tradition are evident in several poems. "Tidewater Burial" tries to capture the authenticity of a rural interment, but the location and idiom are not natural to Kroetsch. His humour and attempt to play with traditional poetics (here Anglo-Saxon alliteration and kennings) do come through, however, as he demonstrates the validity of fish-wharf mythology:

Thou shalt not eat ice cream after a fish dinner.
. . . .
He dined (mullet, shad, flounder, mackerel, red drum)

98

And did (fudge ripple)
And died.[48]

"Projected Visit" (*SHP*, p. 39) is important as it foreshadows (projects) Kroetsch's return to his prairies in poetry and in actuality, describes the land (the harvest, a graveyard), and suggests the magnetic attraction of his father. In "Spring Harvest" (*SHP*, pp. 40–41) and "October Light" (*SHP*, pp. 42–43) the idiom is his own, as he writes of a spring fire harvesting mice as well as the grain, and captures the yarning voice of the hired man. The sexual tension of his early life, patterning the poetry as in "Seed Catalogue" (*FN*, pp. 46–49), is also suggested here. His aunt is in the kitchen "cooking for threshers" ("Spring Harvest," in *SHP*, p. 40), while outside the hired man shoots at owls and brags of his prodigious feats. This idea of creating a usable past to transform into poetry is further suggested in "Sentence":

Not to recover but
simply to face/ force
the past to discover:

(*SHP*, p. 61)

the relation between time and place, the immediacy of language, and that the poet defines human existence.

In the "Old Man Stories" (*SHP*, pp. 9–23) Kroetsch starts trying to reconstruct his place by transforming what traces he can find into the story of that place; so he creates the possible poetry of the Blackfoot Indians who left tepee rings in the fields later plowed by his father. The first poem on the first page of his first book of poetry is a rewriting of mythology, and at least three lessons seem to be obvious: that his roots in Alberta are important, that the expropriation of traditions is valid, and that form and content could and perhaps should fuse. That is, the "stealing" of the tales (the form) is appropriate to the content (the trickster). Kroetsch's interest in origins is evident in the first poem about creation. He humanizes the mythology he transforms. His tendency to puns and games, to a bawdy appreciation of life, is also clear, while the pattern of descent ("he would go to the bottom of things" [*SHP*, p. 9]) is likewise established at the outset.

The shape-changing transformation of "How I Joined the Seal

99

Herd" (*FN*, pp. 71–74) is partially prefigured in "Winter Birds" (*SHP*, pp. 33–34), which describes the questing poet metamorphosing to a bird-sheltering tree with the promise of spring in winter, and in "Pumpkin: A Love Poem" (*SHP*, pp. 26–27), which playfully describes a garden-view vision of creativity. Using the three-line stanza form of Williams and Stevens[49] to transform the Eden myth, Kroetsch posits his erotic metaphor of poetry, later expanded in "For Play and Entrance: The Contemporary Long Poem." From inside a pumpkin he fashions a Halloween head from which to experience the sensibility of garden and remodels all the senses in the process. Suggesting the contraries of his origins ("my pioneering / ancestors") and "new territory," of time and place, male and female, outside and inside, Kroetsch raises the question of boundaries:

> my recovered ancestry
> of borders   bravely crossed
> ("Pumpkin: A Love Poem," in *SHP*, p. 27)

That he is seeking a poetic means to voice his concerns is indicated by the structural centrality of the pumpkin's "new mouth   the place that / must be" (p. 26), and its sexual connotations. The "new mouth" is both the locus of voice, expression, and the "opening" for creative-sexual gratification.

Both Thomas and Lecker single out the four short "father poems" as the most crucial from this period. In these Kroetsch transforms the paternal model into the Canadian idiom. Thus they reflect loss, longing, and a sense of not belonging. "Begin from loss. The double hook," Kroetsch tells us ("For Play and Entrance," in *RK*, p. 97). "I never liked the paternal models, I never felt easy with the — literally — great paternal figures of writing," he says (*LV*, p. 23). So he claims this "dis-ease" and changes it into the positive acknowledgement of his Canadian paternal models: the Chinese cafe owner, the fugitive, the lying artist, the drowned artist. All are displaced, silenced somehow, yet equally survivors. Kroetsch is fascinated by the mythic qualities of these men's lives and the parallels between them and the larger life of the country. Each reflects the Canadian tension or duality, and each poem is constructed on this principle. The mystery essential to the existence of all four figures captures for Kroetsch the problem at the heart of the Canadian artist: "We live with the exquisite fear that we are invisible men.... For in our very invisibility lies our chance for survival" ("The Canadian Writer and the American Literary Tradition," in *RK*, p. 15). Kroetsch's search for the Canadian paradigm of the artist is fuelled by the desire to recognize the model for understanding out time and place:

> (there are no models)   and always
> (there are only models). . . .
> > ("F.P. Grove: The Finding," in *SHP*, p. 46)

The first model, and the only one from Kroetsch's life, is Wong Toy, proprietor of the Canada Cafe. Twenty years after his death, Kroetsch writes to thank him and acknowledge him as "one of my fathers" ("Elegy for Wong Toy," in *SHP*, p. 44). Wong Toy is a silent, foreign enigma in opposition to the prairie town of his cafe. His banishment from Heisler society emphasizes his silence and helps to create the locus for youthful pleasures and experimentation: "jaw-breakers," "licorice plugs," the "first touch / of Ellen Kiefer's young breasts" (p. 45). In an attempt to get back to origins, Kroetsch acknowledges the importance of Wong Toy as one of his ancestors, associating him with both place and the voicing of place. His "bright showcase" contains the wonder of "a whole childhood" (p. 44), while seasonal imagery helps to explain how this enigmatic man helped fuel Kroetsch's desire to write:

> You were your own enduring
> winter.   You were our spring
> and we . . .
>
> . . . .
> cracked the still dawn alive
> with one ferocious   song.
>
> > (p. 45)

Quite literally, Wong Toy is a mystery man who survived through his invisibility and thereby embodied for Kroetsch the paradox of the Canadian artistic experience. Equally literally this poem is an example of Kroetsch's desire to reinvent his past in his poetry.

In the fifth year of Kroetsch's life, Albert Johnson, "the so-called 'Mad Trapper of Rat River' was hunted to death by a small army of men in the Northwest Territories and the Yukon . . ." ("Poem of Albert Johnson," in *SHP*, p. 49). Spellbound by Johnson's silence,

Kroetsch acknowledges him as an ancestor as well, calling him "the poet of our survival" (p. 49). His perfect refusal to speak to his pursuers and his tactics of evasion raise him to mythic proportions for Kroetsch. He becomes the paradigmatic artist, "confus[ing] the hunters" (p. 48) and escaping "the closing frame," but with "no words betraying   either love or hate" (p. 49). The process of Kroetsch's own poetry-making is evident in his description of the risk-taking Johnson as "the silent man / circling back   to watch them coming / giving new tracks . . ." (p. 48). Significantly, this "recovered ancest[or]" ("Pumpkin: A Love Poem," in *SHP*, p. 27) *has* "made the impossible crossing" (p. 49), but as his resting place is a frozen death, his ultimate silence is not the exemplary one for Kroetsch.

The last two fathers, F.P. Grove and Tom Thomson, are more obviously the artistic models for Kroetsch. They, too, are isolated men (Grove is "alone in the cutter" ["F.P. Grove: The Finding," in *SHP*, p. 47], while Thomson "drowned   all alone" ["Meditation on Tom Thomson," in *SHP*, p. 50]), men who preserve their own mysteries. (The poem to Grove is phrased as a series of questions, while the one to Thomson focuses on the "grave mystery / of [his] genius" [p. 50].) Both also turn their experiences into art. They embody the tension of the Canadian experience (Grove is the epitome of duality: "the name under the name" [p. 47]), and Kroetsch emphasizes the collectiveness of this experience by the use of the first-person plural pronoun: "our survival" ("Poem of Albert Johnson," p. 49), "*our* story" ("Meditation on Tom Thomson," p. 50). Both men are lured by the silence Kroetsch sees as a primary temptation for Canadian artists: "the imperative QUESTION (?)" (p. 50) of the Thomson poem, Grove's "silence of sight   'as if I were not myself / who yet am I' " (p. 47). Any resolving vision must be dual: "Existence and doubt" ("The Canadian Writer and the American Literary Tradition," in *RK*, p. 14). Any recording must become a form of deconstruction: "exfoliating / back to the barren sea" (p. 47). Not surprisingly, Kroetsch is fascinated by the mystery of Grove's origins and the gap between the "imagined" or "invent[ed]" man (p. 46) and the real man: "The more his literal life comes into doubt, the more we find ourselves attracted to the man. As his reality, so to speak, comes into doubt, he comes more and more to represent our own predicament" ("The Canadian Writer . . . ," p. 14). Writing himself into identity by creating his own story,

Grove holds an endless fascination for Kroetsch, "but the archetypal Canadian artist is Tom Thomson":

> He lived between south and north, Toronto and the wilderness. . . .
>   Thomson is the paradigm. Of the man who took the risk, got free, perished. . . . The Tom Thomson Mystery. The Canadian Mystery. ("The Canadian Writer . . . ," p. 14)

The grammar of these poems thus establishes an essential grammar for the following longer ones: the double vision. Tension is embodied in the lines and images. Grove balances invention and reality, silence and sight. Thomson, another to cross "the impassible gap," balances "time and space." For him, "to know light is to know darkness; to surface is to drown" (Lecker, p. 130). His "spring" contains "ice," but can yet light up with the promise of rebirth: "candled into its green rot" (*SHP*, p. 50). These artists, the risk-takers, embody the archetypal Canadian artist for Kroetsch, as these poems clearly demonstrate. Having acknowledged his ancestors, he continues on into the longer form.

Tension is part of the theoretical basis for the longer form as well, effectively articulated in Kroetsch's essay "For Play and Entrance: The Canadian Long Poem." Structured as an extended sexual pun, "For Play and Entrance" outlines a "grammar of delay" (*RK*, p. 91); Kroetsch likens the writing of long poems to lovemaking, once again looking to origins rather than endings:

> Poets [of the twentieth century], like lovers, were driven back to the moment of creation; the question, then: not how to end, but how to begin. Not the quest for ending, but the dwelling at and in the beginning itself. (*RK*, p. 91)

This reflects, of course, Kroetsch's distrust of meaning and the deferral of closure, as well as deferral of orgasm in the erotic equation. "The writing of the long poem becomes an erotic gesture in which fulfilment must be postponed, the reader's ultimate response delayed" (Lecker, p. 134).

Kroetsch examines specific possibilities ("the short long poem," "the book-long poem," and "the life-long poem") and the ramifications of his own attraction to archaeology:

> Poems in which archaeology supplants history; an archaeology
> that challenges the authenticity of history by saying there can be
> no joined story, only abrupt guesswork, juxtaposition, flashes
> of insight. A perpetual delay as we recognize the primacy of the
> forthcoming and as yet unmade discovery. (*RK*, p. 93)

Kroetsch searches for new interpretations of narrative: "The story
as fragment *becomes* the long poem: . . . our interest is in, not story,
but the *act* of telling the story . . ." (*RK*, p. 94). Thus, his own poems
become narratives of writing and investigate the various possibilities
and contradictions. But as seductive as fragmentation and deferral
of meaning are, there is always the desire for coherence: "a long work
that has some kind of (under erasure) unity" (*RK*, p. 92). The
grammar is one of matched opposites: time and place, myths and
maps, births and tombstones, the endless doubles, "the destruction
that allows the new" (*RK*, p. 102), "the long poem as, literally,
rewriting" (*RK*, p. 103), "the sound of sight/site" (*RK*, p. 104), "our
disbelief in belief" (*RK*, p. 92). Kroetsch describes explicitly the
"basic tension . . . in the Canadian long poem" as being between
"the temptation of the documentary" (a ledger, a seed catalogue,
Pausanias' description of Greece, "The Eggplant Poems," *The Missing Book of Cucumbers*) and "the skepticism about history" (the
questions, contradictions, corrections, fabrications, parodies) (*RK*,
p. 93). Kroetsch locates this tension in the very title of his own
continuing poem: "the field notes kept by the archaeologist, by the
finding man, the finding man who is essentially lost" (*RK*, p. 103),
and in turn this tension is clearly evident in the voice, structure, and
lost and found items of the very first poems.

Thus, the first three poems transform into poetry three found
objects from Kroetsch's past: an ancient stone implement which is
now his paperweight, the ledger his grandfather kept while working
the sawmill in Belmore, and a seed catalogue discovered in a base-
ment archive, reminding him of the seasonal seed catalogues of his
youth. There is continuity as well as discontinuity between the
various sections of Kroetsch's continuing poem. A dialogue is set up
among them — references to one section are found embedded in
another — and thus Kroetsch's own poems become part of the
intertext. Movement in part forms the relationship between the early
sections of the ongoing poem: back through memory and invention
into the past of "Stone Hammer Poem" and "The Ledger," then to

the all-inclusive present of creativity in "Seed Catalogue," on to a flight from restrictive time and space in "How I Joined the Seal Herd" and "The Sad Phoenician," and finally to an exploration of the absences and silence beyond language in "The Silent Poet Sequence" and "The Winnipeg Zoo."

"Stone Hammer Poem" begins the backward journey with a stone "old as the last / Ice Age . . ." (*SHP*, p. 56), "a million / years older . . ." (*SHP*, p. 55) than any hand of man functioning with creative intent. The poem deconstructs and then recreates the past of this stone and documents the various transformations through which it has passed. The stone was fashioned into a hammer by an Indian, then bucked the plow of a homesteading farmer, and now weights papers and watches words on the poet's desk. As symbol, the stone leads back to a memoried past — both actual and possible — and inspires the necessary muse of memory and meditation. As Kroetsch says in "Seed Catalogue": "and you have / no memory then / no meditation / no song" (*FN*, p. 56). The stone, with shaping and the addition of rawhide loops, was made more than primordial stone by an Indian ancestor. This is what happened. The stone hammer was then lost in play or use, beneath prairie grass or in buffalo skull. This is what might have happened.

> I have to / I want
> to know (not know)
> ? WHAT HAPPENED
>
> (*SHP*, p. 57)

The binary-system structure and the strategy of deconstruction are evident: actual and possible pasts balance, and knowing through unknowing is impetus. Kroetsch unhides the stone's history and prehistory:

> It is a stone
> old as the last
> Ice Age, the
> retreating/the
> recreating ice,
> the retreating
> buffalo, the
> retreating Indians
>
> (*SHP*, p. 56)

The stone suffers a succession of losses and findings, reflected in the loss of possession and repossession of the land from which it derives. The land has successively and inappropriately (as Kroetsch questions the very notion of "possessing" land) been given by Indian to Queen to CPR to grandfather to father to poet, who in turn sells it "to a young man / (with a growing son)" (*SHP*, p. 57). The stone goes through a similar succession of unlikely ownership and loss until it finally sits on the poet's desk and inspires his poem. The stone's origins and functions as hammer and as poem ("The poem / is the stone" [*SHP*, p. 57]) are similar. Both are "chipped and hammered," transformed into shape. Both chisel and shape, transform material to create new possibilities. Musing on the stone's past, Kroetsch ponders such questions as ownership, belonging, familial relations, and the origins of art.

The techniques he employs are those of ambiguity, contradiction, and erasure: loops, hand, skull — all are "gone." There is also erasure in the grammar, as past and present collide: was/is. Alternatives are constantly balanced without conclusion: this *or* that *or* that. Sentences begun are not always completed. Parenthetical comments interrupt. Questions are announced before they are recorded: "? WHAT HAPPENED" (*SHP*, p. 57). Syntactical ambiguity is evidenced by lines that conclude with a negative and no final punctuation, and which are then followed by a declarative statement:

       this maul
  is the colour
  of bone (no,
  bone is the colour
  of this stone maul).

                    (*SHP*, p. 54)

There is doubling in the very notation, and words do double duty as more than one part of speech. The ambiguity of logic and syntax in turn reflects the poem's central tension. Echoing the father poems, the stone "stands for mystery, yet it also promotes mystery-making as a central aesthetic pursuit" (Lecker, p. 129). Kroetsch now needs to get back to place not to possess it, but to understand it, and this he tries to do in the next sections of his poem.

"The Ledger," an example of Kroetsch's ability to fuse effectively form and intent, goes back to explore the westering notion of his ancestors. The starting point is a ledger Kroetsch's grandfather kept at a mill in Ontario, recording purchases and payments, from which derive the two controlling structures of the poem: Kroetsch orders his lines in the binary accounting form of credits and debits, while through the amplification of six dictionary definitions of "ledger," he explores his family's history, the settling of the new land, his personal involvement, and his artistic shaping. The two structures are exclusive as well as simultaneous. Just as life is unpredictable and understanding is incomplete, so the ledger comes to Kroetsch with "some pages torn out (/ by accident)" (*FN*, p. 24). There are gaps in the record, reflecting Kroetsch's sense of his absence-filled prairies. Here he provides the document of the torn-out pages, while in "Seed Catalogue" he even more clearly makes a presence/poem of the absences.

The first definition of Kroetsch's poem, the ledger as accounting "book of final entry" (*FN*, p. 23), is the obvious record of his ancestors' struggles in the new land, while an exploration of the other definitions of ledger continues this record: ledger as support timber, resident (obs.), nether millstone, flat tombstone, "a book that lies permanently in some place" (*FN*, p. 41). Each section of the poem begins with one of the definitions and enlarges upon it through stories about Kroetsch's ancestors and quotations from the original ledger and other documents. The starting definition is then embedded within the section, having a renewed meaning in relation to Kroetsch's own poetic process, until the final definition coalesces the previous ones. The definitions variously and together become the building of the new life and shelters through hard work, residency and a sense of place, the dangers of the new life, inevitable death, and finally Kroetsch's book itself (in punning paradox — "a book that *lies* permanently *in place*" [emphasis added]). The transformation of the word also emphasizes the magical and metaphoric possibilities of language, particularly poetic language. Kroetsch acknowledges the preeminence of "quest" for his own art and the tendency to see contraries:

EVERYTHING I WRITE
I SAID, IS A SEARCH
(is debit, is credit)

(*FN*, p. 25)

Through ledger entries and definitions, Kroetsch describes the balance of destruction and creation his ancestors struck — they tore down the trees to build their houses:

> To raise a barn;
>
> cut down a forest.
>
> To raise oats and hay;
>
> burn the soil.
>
> To raise cattle and hogs;
>
> (*FN*, p. 26)

kill the wildlife. Deconstruction is both the rhythm of life and the necessary artistic methodology.

As he transforms the ledger, Kroetsch maintains his own ledger about the original one, a poem about his own poem-making. Balancing debits and credits, he also manages to keep his readers off-balance. Ambiguity and tension still structure the lines, which can be read horizontally as well as vertically. The tension between documentation and scepticism is evident. As well as entries from the original ledger and from a dictionary, Kroetsch includes passages from *The Canada Gazette, A Pristine Forest*, the census, and a letter from his aunt. Surprised interjections by the poet provide a sceptical commentary on the documentation: "(I'll be damned. It balances)" (*FN*, p. 27). And: "(I can't believe my eyes)" (*FN*, p. 31), parodying the archetypal Canadian sense of distrust. In succeeding poems, Kroetsch has to relearn to trust his senses, and he directs his readers to do the same.

Weighed against each other are arrivals and departures —

> arrivals: the sailing ship
> arrivals: the axe
> arrivals: the almighty dollar
> > departures: the trout stream
> > departures: the passenger pigeon
> > departures: the pristine forest
> >
> > (*FN*, p. 29)

— and the balance of accents/origins in ancestors:

born in Alsace, she spoke
German with a French accent,
English with a German accent

(*FN*, p. 37)

Old World and New World, East and West, original forest and cultivated field, affirmatives and negatives, narrative and its alternatives, finding and loss, voice and silence, life and death ("Shaping the trees. / Pushing up daisies" [*FN*, p. 28]). Kroetsch's theory of unhiding/deconstructing/uninventing/demythologizing and the concomitant descent to a netherworld preparatory to creation are obvious in the continuity of destruction and creation initiated by the original settlers: "That they might sit down / a forest / had fallen" (*FN*, p. 27). Trees become "shingles," "scantling," "tables and chairs" (*FN*, p. 27), ledger, and this book of poems, which endures. The parallel between ancestors' experiences and Kroetsch's own in writing this poem is clear. Propounding a theory of poetics, Kroetsch suggests deconstructing the settlers' accomplishments:

you must see
the confusion again
the chaos   again
the original forest

(*FN*, p. 34)

Returning to source is crucial. Before the journey up to the light must come the journey down into the darkness. They are opposites which for Kroetsch are necessary to creativity. The trees had to be chopped before the dwellings could be built. The ledger had to be "lost" before Kroetsch could "find" it. And he must uninvent and reinvent the process to fulfil Williams' notion of lifting his "environment to expression." Near the end of "The Ledger" Kroetsch repeats the wisdom gained — "You MUST / marry the terror" (*FN*, p. 39) — and concludes his poem:

REST IN PEACE
You Must Marry the Terror

(*FN*, p. 43)

It balances.
Each definition in "The Ledger" leads to a death of sorts. "*The*

Ledger is a mausoleum of ancestors that is simultaneously a living stage. It signifies an attempt to define life as a consciousness of death. Writing comes alive (speaks) only when it welcomes the horror of the unknown . . ." (Lecker, p. 137). Kroetsch takes death, then, the death of his mother, as germinal to his poetry in the next section of his continuing poem. "The two poems spoke to each other," Kroetsch says. "They changed each other" ("The Continuing Poem," in *RK*, p. 81). But here his mother's death is turned into a poetic absence, which still has to be faced in his more recent poems, specifically those at the end of *Advice to My Friends*.

The renewal proposed in "Seed Catalogue" is one fundamental to Kroetsch's prairie place. "Seed Catalogue" is both a re-vision and a re-voicing of Kroetsch's past and place. In ten parts the poem investigates the significance of the catalogue blooming in a dark prairie January, promising fertility, virtue, singularity, superiority, wonder. Structured on the seed catalogue metaphor, the poem puts the questions: "How do you grow a gardener? . . . a lover? . . . a prairie town? . . . a past? . . . a poet? . . . a garden?" The seedtime/seektime of the poem is the course of the poet's life, from the "terrible symmetry" of "the home place" to the terrible symmetry of his present writings (*FN*, pp. 65, 49). The constant balancing of birth and death is emphasized by the story of cousin Kenneth, first family member to return to Germany, killed while trying to deliver death-dealing bombs (he, the navigator) to the city of his great-grandmother's birth: "a terrible symmetry."

The three most crucial questions that "Seed Catalogue" raises are "How do you grow a prairie town?" (p. 53), "How do you grow a past?" (p. 54), and "How do you grow a poet?" (p. 56). The latter is asked a total of five times, and all three questions are intimately related. The definition of past becomes a catalogue of absences: the lack of history, traditions, philosophy, literature, and culture. The model for place likewise becomes one of disappearance, whether the continually vanishing gopher down his hole, or the hotel fire that destroys the grandmother's chest of transported hope: "satin sheets," "embroidered pillow cases," "English china," and "silver serving spoons" (p. 53). One crucial answer that we have already noted is Kroetsch's solution of turning the very absences into poetry, as he does here.

"The seed catalogue is a shared book in our society," explains Kroetsch:

We have few literary texts approaching that condition. I wanted to write a poetic equivalent to the "speech" of a seed catalogue. The way we read the page and hear its implications. Spring. The plowing, the digging, of the garden. The mapping of the blank, cool earth. The exact placing of the explosive seed. ("The Continuing Poem," in *RK*, p. 82)

Important is both the giving of "form to this land" (*FN*, p. 58) (the father's impulse to fence — possession, story, hunting — in order to sabotage "poetry") and the planting in this land (the mother's impulse to seed — bestowal, song, renewal — in order to promote "poetry"). But this implies an old-fashioned notion of "poetry," just as a literary language used to be essential. Dialect is now possible; the tall tale is now possible. Writing of another Prairie poet, Kroetsch describes the "endless talk" recorded — the listening in to "the laments, the tall-tales, the ironies, the indignation, the resignation, the sentimentality," heard "all together, finally" ("The Discovery of America Continues," in *RK*, p. 30). The double attraction expressed in "Seed Catalogue" of paternal story (the father yarning on in the kitchen's warmth about hunting a badger, shooting a magpie) and maternal song (the mother planting radish seeds and whispering promises of fertility) leads to problems of form. Peter Thomas describes Kroetsch's dilemma: "He continues to construct an elaborate symbolism of story's flight from song, rooted in the primordial female/male duality, bullshit's conflict with love in a deathly game of words."[50] The oral tradition of stories, whether told in farm kitchens or the local pub, is strong on the prairies. To translate this tradition into poetry the only solution is the long poem — the appropriate poetic gallery for the prairie "characters." The structural solution to the dual claims of the oral and lyric traditions is the long poem. In "Seed Catalogue" is the struggle. In "The Criminal Intensities of Love as Paradise" Kroetsch sets up a binary entry form in which the two impulses vie on the page. In "Spending the Morning on the Beach" we begin to see a resolution; hence its publication with a reissue of *Seed Catalogue*.

The tension set up in "Seed Catalogue" between the male and female imaginative impulses is thus partly resolved several long poems later. At first in "Seed Catalogue" the maternal influence seems strongest, as the mother marks out the garden and directs the seeding, but her directions are whispers, and one of the first "happenings" recorded is her wake. As her funeral turns into a story, narrative seems to take over, but Kroetsch is committed to finding alternatives to narrative for his poetry, and this is the story of a story. The solution is not simple and requires the consideration and rejection of the fiction writer's ordering of landscape, the "great black steel lines of fiction" (Rudy Wiebe, quoted in "Seed Catalogue," *FN*, p. 59) which are antithetical to "song." The mother herself at this point in Kroetsch's writing seems oddly absent. The poem concludes, ambiguously, with a storied acknowledgement of the poet's debt to his mother for an intimate and sensual knowledge of place as well as the powerful image of the dark muse "forgetfulness," who feeds "her far children / to ancestral guns," and has blood "on her green thumb" (p. 65). The poet must interpret both the springtime planting of his prairies and the "strange planting" of a cousin (p. 64), seeded in the foreign soil of ancestors, by a self-guided bomb. This becomes a powerful argument for recognizing and releasing the energy of origins. The symmetries of home place and this first return are both "terrible," but as in "The Ledger" the chaos must be faced in order for creativity to follow. As elsewhere in Kroetsch's poetry, we find here not the balance of binaries, but of contraries.

Stone hammer, ledger, seed catalogue: all are transformed into poetry, and all turn out to *be* poetry. The simultaneous function of these controlling metaphors, which thus are also just as clearly metonymical, is suggested on the first page of "Seed Catalogue" when Kroetsch signals the shift from winter to spring with the shift of "storm windows" to "hotbed" covers. The seasonal change is signalled by removing the storm windows and installing them as covers for the hotbeds.

> We took the storm windows/off
> the south side of the house
> and put them on the hotbed.
> Then it was spring. Or, no:
> then winter was ending.
>
> (*FN*, p. 47)

Russell Brown explains:

> These two objects turn out to be the same thing — or, rather, their two names turn out to refer to the same thing (framed panes

of glass), one object transformed in a way that prepares us for the reconsidered opposition and transformation next named, "winter" into "spring," an opposition that was defined out of existence as soon as it is set up.[51]

Here spring is actually defined not by its own presence, but rather by the absence of other, the absence of winter, and this is a technique which is repeated in Kroetsch's later poetry, as is the process of continual correction, the "Or, no:" of revision here in "Seed Catalogue," which was first introduced in "Stone Hammer Poem," and is perfected in the revised "Mile Zero."

The desire to know what happened in "Stone Hammer Poem" is similarly transformed in "Seed Catalogue" into an attempt to explain: "This is what happened:" and again, "You've got to understand this" (FN, p. 47). The autobiographical patterning is clear: the male and female tension, the seasonal growth cycle, the prairie rhythms of germination, the belonging and leaving, and the presence of absence. Kroetsch creates the equation: "The double hook: / the home place" (FN, p. 61), and rereads Sheila Watson's The Double Hook in an attempt to reach a poetic solution. What emerges is the documentation of his time and place, his origins on the prairies, as "the double experience" (Cameron, p. 84). His writing here is substantially and structurally "caught between the two" "opposing forces" (Enright and Cooley, p. 25). The poem is framed by the recognition that "the home place" is "a terrible symmetry" (FN, p. 49), but between is a renewed understanding. As in "The Ledger," there is the tension between document (here entries from a found seed catalogue and letters from prairie gardeners) and scepticism (the questions that also structure the lines: "How do you grow a poet?"). Lines end inconclusively and ambiguously:

a winter proposition, if
spring should come, then,

(FN, p. 48)

The promise is not articulated, and this technique of leaving the line to be completed by the reader, which also recurs in subsequent sections of the continuing poem, ironically here allows the reader the last line/last laugh. "Seed Catalogue" concludes, *"Adam and Eve got drowned — / Who was left?"* (FN, p. 67), and the poet reaches out of his poem to pinch his reader. Here the dialogic relationship between poet and reader, explored in later poems, is clearly established.

"Seed Catalogue" thus ends/refuses to end with a drowning which is not a drowning. Kroetsch returns to his prairie origins and, through his unlucky cousin, to those of his maternal great-grand-mother. The last lines point to the further return proposed in "How I Joined the Seal Herd," as Kroetsch is there reborn in a watery element, suggesting a further regression, to the mythical and evolutionary origins of humans from water. "We must always go back to the shore," says Kroetsch ("The Continuing Poem," in *RK*, p. 81), and does himself in several of his poems.

As central character in his continuing poem, Kroetsch transforms himself into a "bull" seal (not a casual choice of disguise certainly) and later into ". . . a kind of Phoenician, with reference, that is, / to my trading in language, even in, to stretch a point, / ha, my being at sea" ("The Sad Phoenician," in *FN*, p. 79). In "How I Joined the Seal Herd" Kroetsch gives in to the perplexity of "being at sea" and in an ultimate act of deconstruction, unhides his human form and returns to a preliterate animal state in order "to know life before the distortions imposed by language" (Lecker, p. 140). The search for knowledge of his time and place has been for Kroetsch a search for appropriate speech and form. This is one crucial reason why he takes for artefacts, and then practises the form and language of, inherited texts, such as a ledger and seed catalogue, "shared book[s] in our society" ("The Continuing Poem," in *RK*, p. 82). It is one logical way of returning to his prairie origins to simulate the structures of primary documents, but it is not so simple because even these documents carry with them a weight of values and expectations, for instance that the columns must always balance. For Kroetsch, in his continuing poem, of course, equilibrium is to be disturbed. The inherited language and values of the first immigrants are thus out of place in the new world, and although Kroetsch may mourn the absence of "books, journals, daily newspapers," "Sartre and Heidegger," "ballet and opera," and "Aeneas" ("Seed Catalogue," in *FN*, p. 54), there is something restorative about the hotel fire that eradicates the past of possessions. To get further back even than these inherited texts, Kroetsch attempts to decrease the language process by transforming himself into a basically physical creature and submerging himself in ocean. The sea is a transitional and mediating agent between air and earth, life and death, and as such is symbolic of the unconscious world of the imagination. This description of "How I Joined the Seal Herd," however, disguises the fact that the transformation is presented in a highly entertaining manner. Dissatisfied with the expectations of his life, the "I" of the poem is lured by the "snort" and "grunt" of breeding seals beneath his window (*FN*, p. 71). Peeling off his clothes, he learns to lose his control over his world and "undo [his] very standing / crawl." Noticing an attractive young seal cow, he confides, "frankly, I wanted to get laid," and does. Even the corrective technique is amusing here: "men in their forties / . . . are awfully good / in bed (on a sandbank   I corrected myself)" (p. 72). Accepting his new form, he snaps at passing herring, fights off a rival bull, and dances with his cow seal in the "rising tide" (p. 74).

"How I Joined the Seal Herd" begins with a rejection of the intellectual stance — "my head did not please me" (p. 71) emphasizes that his actions are conducted *"without thinking"* — but ends with the realization, "I was still a man, I had to talk" (p. 73). This reconstruction of past is ultimately "too far past everything" (p. 74), but still Kroetsch has hopes for the offspring spawned by his unlikely mating. What he returns to is "words again, / words" with which he describes the underlying, autobiographical nature of his continuing poem:

> I wanted to say / I am
> writing   this poem   with my life
>
> (p. 74)

This affirmation comes immediately after a "song" of the near fatal effects of his sojourn in the United States and his need to return in his writing to "the gone world" (p. 74), the absences of his prairies. In "How I Joined the Seal Herd" Kroetsch experiments with a further regression, concluding with a hope for the renewed integration of the senses, encoded in the ambiguity of the last lines:

> I hope my children
> (ours, I corrected myself)   their ears perfect
> will look   exactly like both of us.
>
> (p. 74)

The wish is that the result of this union will be perfected aural perception and a vision that will join the capabilities of both parents.

The "children" are not to be mimetic reproductions, but rather it is hoped that they will learn to see as both parents do. The concentration on ears in this poem ("the sight / of my ears   was the first / clue" [p. 71]) suggests as well a possible pun in the title, which could read homonymously: "How I Joined the Seal *Heard*."

Regression and a renewed understanding of language are furthered in the sea escapes of the next two sections of Kroetsch's continuing poem, in which the relationship between eye and ear in regard to language is also evident. Language, meaning, mating, and silence are all continued concerns in "The Sad Phoenician" and "The Silent Poet Sequence," but here, as Lecker suggests, ". . . the aesthetic implications of the voyage are easier to identify, in large part because they form the subject matter of these sequential poems" (p. 141). By atomizing language and examining the basic components, Kroetsch deconstructs language and his use of it throughout "The Sad Phoenician," to its logical outcome of silence in "The Silent Poet Sequence." "[P]oetry is the absolute confrontation with language," Kroetsch tells us, demonstrating in "The Sad Phoenician" his poetic answer to the insistence of narrative:

> Nobody looks as hard at language as the poet does, and asks what it is to us, what it does to us, without evasion, with no ulterior motive like the politicians, the military, the advertisers. The poet does not lie in this respect. He has to say, how come? what's going on here?[52]

This probing, then, is part of the evident aesthetic structure of "The Sad Phoenician."

The tension between losing tradition and surrendering to it is equally evident. On the back cover of the first edition of *The Sad Phoenician* Kroetsch directs our reading of both the structure and theory of his poem by explaining the significance of the Phoenicians. They were the traders of ancient times, fetching and carrying across the seas of the then-world. They were also the ones who, traditionally, are credited with originating our form of writing. Being adopted and then adapted by the Greeks, the Phoenician alphabet is the direct ancestor of all Western alphabets. It is thus the origins of writing and the significance of language that Kroetsch explores here. He emphasizes the urge that prompted the great leap forward that the Phoenicians made: moving "writing from the temple, down to the wharf," demystifying it, and freeing "the reader from the wall."[53]

Practically, the Phoenicians needed a transportable alphabet, one "they could learn fast, write fast, send anywhere." "Hey, they [the Phoenicians] said, the ship is leaving." And Kroetsch is not a poet to miss the boat. "Get that cargo sorted and counted, the destinations marked." For this they designed an alphabet that reflected sounds rather than pictorial shapes, and for Kroetsch this is the breakthrough.

> The poem as hubbub. Freed from picture, into the pattern and tumble of sound. Poetry as commotion: a condition of civil unrest. Now listen here.
> The poet, not as priest, but as lover.

The dialogue thus continues: the reader is directed to listen and hear/here. Puns are the order of the poem, as the dialogue also continues through parody and cliché. The tension of the poem, expressed in the structural balance of the lines, is also captured in the "civil unrest" of Kroetsch's directive, as he explains in a conversation with Smaro Kamboureli: "I think that's precisely what language has got to be. To stay alive it must be in a state of civil unrest, the kind of contradiction that's implicit in the yoking of those two words."[54] Once again, the tension of opposites is clearly seen to be generative.

"The Sad Phoenician" is a very visually arresting poem. A series of twenty-six monologues, the poem is headed on each page by a fragmented lower case letter of the alphabet. A type of order is thus imposed, while at the same time it is seen to be in the process of disintegration. References are made directly and by way of puns to the Phoenician, Greek, and Hebrew alphabets, as well as to the development from hieroglyph to our aurally inspired alphabet. Kroetsch goes back to the very origins of language in the source of our alphabet and then deconstructs even that. Before he can propose his own reconstruction, he must examine the tools of his poetic trade, the very language at his disposal. The other thing that a reader notices immediately about this poem is the balance of "and" and "but" on the left-hand margin, the dialogue between connective and corrective. As soon as the poet gives us something, he modifies it or takes it away. The poet as lover, with his "traditional grammar of love" disintegrating through "experience" (Kamboureli, p. 50), begins the archetypal process of renaming his universe, but it is a tentative process. "He ands and buts his names" (Kamboureli, p. 51).

The tension, of course, is not new. It is reflected here in the and/but contradiction, the simultaneous desire for both defiance and civility, the fascination with the Phoenicians' breaking with tradition while at the same time creating something new, and also in the very language and allusions. The poem is structured by resistance. "I live by a kind of resistance" ("The Sad Phoenician," in *FN*, p. 90), Kroetsch tells us. "The poem must resist the poet" (p. 82), but also, "the poet must resist the poem" (p. 85). He must resist tradition while at the same time acknowledging it; Kroetsch therefore encodes enigmatic references to such classic poems as Spenser's *Faerie Queen*.[55] Other literary allusions, for instance to Auden and Shakespeare, are left incomplete, drifting into silence: "the wind has full cheeks, blow, thou" (p. 87). He resists traditional literary language and resorts to the vernacular of oral tradition to recount some of his tales, as well as to cliché, such overworked, automatic phrases that are a further resistance to communication. Some of the clichés are linked to the aesthetics of the poem:

> I have a few tricks up my sleeve myself.
>
> (p. 77)

> I keep my trap shut.
>
> (p. 80)

> I can see where some people might prefer just plain
> outright lies, as did Ms. R[eading].
>
> (p. 82)

> compose yourself.
>
> (p. 92)

> double or nothing.
>
> (p. 94)

> hide what must be hidden.
>
> (p. 98)

> it's a disguise.
>
> (p. 102)

Others are linked to the alphabetic ordering. The monologue for β [Greek *beta*] concludes, "you bet you me" (p. 78), while the monologue for ι [Greek *iota*] includes, "there's all as well as iota" (p. 85).

More predictable are: under *q*, "on the / Q.T." (p. 93); under *s*, "s.o.s. says sink or swim" (p. 95); and under *t*, "fit to a T" (p. 96). Clichés expose the intellectual rites of passage:

> I had my peek into the abyss, my brush with the verities,
> such as they are, my astounding fall from innocence, you
> better believe it
>
> (p. 78)

They are also humorously linked to prairie metaphor ("you can't get blood from a turnip" [p. 93]), as are biblical allusions ("the gopher lay down with the hawk, the cabbage plant / with the cutworm" [p. 97]). Perhaps most telling are the clichés that refuse to be completed by anything but silence: "a bird in the hand, he said, joking" (p. 77), or "a rose by any other name" (p. 81).

The metonymic suggestions of the alphabetic ordering are similarly undercut. C puns on "sea" and the poet's disorientation:

> I am, you
> might say, a kind of Phoenician, with reference, that is,
> to my trading in language, even in, to stretch a point,
> ha, my being at sea
>
> (p. 79)

D suggests development, but also deceit. F discusses artifice, by associating the poet's own shoe-encased foot with the foot "in / the line of poetry" (p. 82). H ironically identifies the poet with the questing hero in search of the holy grail, while I extends the quest to a search for a "pack of illusions" (p. 85). O is full of puns: the shape and sound of the letter suggesting "grief" and happiness, and "oops . . . the right name for accident." The poet comes "full circle" as *o* suggests origins, "the orifice of love, open," as well as its opposite:

> but   ouch my ass is dragging
> and   that means the end can't be far away, ha. . . .
>
> (p. 91)

This monologue concludes with the further paradoxical naming, "I, the anarchist who needed order" (p. 91). R provides a "remonstrance," but "no remedy" (p. 94), of course.

The incomplete or uncompletable clichés and allusions lead logically to a further linguistic breakdown. Near the midpoint of the poem, the poet asserts, "I've sworn off myself" (p. 87), and by the end he claims, he is "ready to call it quits" (p. 99). The poet who earlier found himself returning to "words again, / words" ("How I Joined the Seal Herd," in *FN*, p. 74), now finds himself becoming "a good listener" (p. 97). The first-person accounting transforms to a distanced, third-person on the last pages, as the crucial link between living and language is explained:

>   sir, she said,
>   I'll *take your word*
> but   I should tell you, twisting a few of the rings on her
>   fingers, *you've just*, in that case, wiseacre, *died*
> and *she meant it*
>   (p. 101, emphasis added)

And so does Kroetsch, who takes this absence to the next step, in the next section. The logical progression of these silences leads, then, to the "Silent Poet Sequence," in which Kroetsch attempts to find a new voice, a new way of saying, under erasure. By the conclusion of this first volume of *Field Notes* there is evidence of a definite syntactical shift. The Sad Phoenician's voyaging concludes with "the tree . . . not an inch closer. If it was a tree" (p. 102), and a muse-figure who further deflates the "I" becomes a "him." The light transforms the green of the questionable tree to blue. "Or vice versa" (p. 102). The poet is still "at sea" (p. 79).

In an ultimate poetic deconstruction "The Silent Poet Sequence" allows the poet "to eat his words" ("The Silent Poet Eats His Words," in *FN*, p. 112), but it also allows him to formulate the tension created in a dialogue between self and other, between the Sad Phoenician figure and "a sailor, Earache the Red" ("The Silent Poet Sees Red," in *FN*, p. 105). The continuation from one poem to the next is signalled by the continuing and/but structure, the repetition of clichés, as well as a continuation of the silenced poet. The "good listener" continues to listen ("The Sad Phoenician," in *FN*, p. 97), and we the readers, of course, are enjoined to be good listeners also. But Kroetsch does not make it easy for us. "I turn signs around, I point / all travelers in the wrong direction," he warns ("The Silent Poet Craves Immortality," in *FN*, p. 111).

As in "The Sad Phoenician," there are at least two levels to "The Silent Poet Sequence." On the one level there is the ongoing drama of the speaker, while on another level there is a discussion of aesthetics, the possible options for poetry. The persona of both poems is at once a writer and a lover, and the problems he encounters in both roles are linked. As a lover he is melodramatic and long-suffering, both self-assured and self-conscious. The poetic "resistances" are sexual as well, and the female/male dichotomy is explored further. Kroetsch delivered the following to a conference at the same time he began work on "The Sad Phoenician"[56]:

> How do you make love in a new country? . . .
> In a paradoxical way, stories — more literally, books — contain the answer. How do you establish any sort of *close* relationship in a landscape — in a physical situation — whose primary characteristic is *distance*? The telling of story — more literally, the literal closedness of a book — might be made to (paradoxically again) contain space.
> Already the metaphor of sex, uneasily, intrudes. We conceive of external space as male, internal space as female. More precisely, the penis: external, expandable, expendable; the vagina: internal, eternal. The maleness verges on mere absence. The femaleness verges on mystery: it is a space that is not a space. External space is the silence that needs to speak, or that needs to be spoken. It is male. The having spoken is the book. It is female. It is closed. // How do you make love in a new country? ("The Fear of Women in Prairie Fiction: An Erotics of Space," in *RK*, p. 47)

"Not the having written, but the *writing*" ("The Continuing Poem," in *RK*, p. 81). The question of writing and the question of making love, then, become synonymous, the difficult sexual relations becoming metaphors for difficulties in writing ("touch your typewriter, poet, she whispered, then I can / sleep in the morning" [*FN*, p. 112]). But this sexual refusal leads to "another failure" with words (p. 112).

The persona in "The Silent Poet Sequence" is packing up to return to his prairies, and the absences Kroetsch catalogues in "Seed Catalogue" to answer "*How do you grow a past? / to live in*" (essential absences of prairie place — bases of foreign economies, historical and cultural figures or sites, books, particulars) become the postmodern absences of communication that the borderland "literature of exhaustion" exhibits, here and in the next poem "The Winnipeg Zoo." If the poet is still "at sea" in "The Silent Poet Sequence," then the trader figure has become an explorer, with a concomitant shift from Mediterranean to Northern waters, from the Old World to the New. A trader may be at home everywhere and at home nowhere, while an explorer at least is searching for a possible home. The rival figure against whom Kroetsch talks in "The Silent Poet Sequence" is named "Earache the Red." The name refers to ears again and to the importance of renewed hearing, but this pompous character also suggests Eric the Red, who has a place of some importance in Kroetsch's mythology. He "is very much a part of our culture . . . , an alternate to the Columbus story. He was on the edge of being an outlaw. He made explorations and discoveries that were forgotten" (Kamboureli, p. 51). If Columbus' voyage provides the archetypal American story — searching for a quick get-rich route to the Orient, arriving in the New World instead, thinking first he has discovered paradise, and then realizing the potential in exploiting the native people — then Eric the Red's voyage, for Kroetsch, provides the archetypal Canadian story. Just as in the father poems, we have a borderline figure, escaping from as much as searching for. According to the *Saga of Eric the Red*, Eric spent three years of outlawry exploring the coast of Greenland, but his son, Leif Ericsson, is now credited with establishing the first European settlements in North America. It is only recently that notice has been taken of the accomplishments of either father or son.

Earache, however, only "*thinks* he's a sailor" (*FN*, p. 105; emphasis added), while the persona of this poem is also an explorer of sorts. He "watch[es] for a light in the west, occidents will happen, ho" (p. 105). Perhaps he is remembering Columbus' accidental discovery of North America rather than the Orient. In bed he "stud[ies] maps," but once again, the track fragments: "I look for rivers that trail off into / dotted lines," he says (p. 111). Furthering the link between geography and creativity, he adds: "I peruse a linguistic atlas" (p. 111). We recall that in the first sequence he was called "the guardian of ought / but that's [his] loss" (p. 105). Once again, loss and finding. In the second sequence, while packing to move and questioning the "function of objects" (p. 106), he discovers he is unable to get rid of anything, however apparently trivial or outmoded. There is a relatedness somehow, and we are reminded of the dense interrelatedness of the image of "The Sad Phoenician," the obsessions of all the women: fires, submarines, doorknobs, adverbs, clams, and so on. Here the list of objects concludes with the simple line, "this rock" (p. 107). As this is a list of office objects, it suggests the paperweight rock, the stone hammer that was transformed in the first poem of *Field Notes*, "Stone Hammer Poem." It also suggests the technique of Kroetsch's continuing poem at this point, the cataloguing of fragments in an attempt to tell the story and discover the means. Kroetsch tells us:

> . . . I think of the field notes kept . . . by the finding man, the finding man who is essentially lost. . . . It is as if we spend our lives finding clues, fragments, shards, leading or misleading details, chipped tablets written over in a forgotten language. . . .
> Perhaps we tell a blurred story because the story is blurred. ("For Play and Entrance," in *RK*, p. 103)

The final sequence is titled "The Silent Poet Eats His Words," which is, on the one hand, the ultimate form of correction, the erasure of the poet's words. We begin to recognize the pattern, though, because this image also suggests sustenance and continuity. The poet lives by and on language — a diet of words as it were. Once again we discover the possibility of presence in absence, and this sense provides what hope there is in the failure framing the next section of *Field Notes*.

The poet who is packing in "The Silent Poet Sequence" is "arriving" in "The Winnipeg Zoo," but the journey back has been "exhaust[ing]." The poet feels he is without his usual resources: "yes, I am here," he affirms, but he is "exhausted, a wreck, unable / to imagine the act of writing. . . ." (*FN*, p. 117). He is not, however, "unable to imagine," which is the reading of some critics. This is a "breathless" poem, that is, strictly speaking it should be read with no intake of breath and no pauses; therefore, the lines should be carried on, with no break, to read:

unable to imagine

I am here, it is quiet, I am exhausted from
moving, we must take care of our stories

the moving is a story, we must take care, I am
here, I shall arrive, I am arriving. . . .

(p. 117)

So, his difficulty is with imagining he is "here," not with imagining per se, and he actually, by the sheer act of carrying the thought on and not pausing, begins to write himself into an acceptance of the "here," which is so powerful for Kroetsch. Stories, or narrative, must be cared for, and new ways of handling them must be discovered. The westering movement is, of course, a magical, mythical movement, and the arrival must now be handled anew. Kroetsch tells us in an interview: ". . . the 'going' has been everything for so much writing, but that denies the experience of arrival." And he warns: "There is a danger in that model of never living where you are. The going is not everything, the being there is something, the being here" (Keeney Smith, p. 29). And this is the new emphasis in "The Winnipeg Zoo." Kroetsch has left previously, and now he is arriving back, the resolution of the dilemma proposed in his earliest story. Now it must be turned into poetry, the transformation he attempts in "The Winnipeg Zoo." Although he calls it a "failed" poem (LV, p. 166), it is successful to the extent that he can conclude, with some repetition, but now with affirmation:

> we must take care of our stories, I am ex-
> hausted from moving, it is quiet, I am here
>
> (FN, p. 119)

The exhaustion is split up, and the poem comes to rest with the positive acceptance of being, and particularly of being "here." The Sad Phoenician, who has been "searching or longing for home," is now arriving, albeit "with the awareness that home is not a final place, not a fixed place" (Kamboureli, p. 48). Stasis is surely not the desired goal, and thus in "The Winnipeg Zoo" the verbal form of "arriving" suggests continuation. In fact, defeat in "The Winnipeg Zoo" seems to come in the form of inaction or fixation. The succession of abandoned lovers is described as immobile: "the standing boy" (p. 117), "the farmer" who "does not move" (p. 118). The animals are also catalogued in this way: the stationary flamingoes "have no names," while the "polar bear dives deep." We are enjoined not to follow the owl, the "master of sleep" (p. 118). Repeated often is the observation, "the man at the gate is not counting" (p. 118). The lawyer, "cracking sunflower seeds," "cannot quite imagine // the artist" (p. 119). The central action revolves around an imposter figure, Audubon, who attempts to "fix" the scene in the sights of his gun. This reversal of the naturalist as predator underscores the falseness of his position. Such action as his provides narrative, but it also ultimately provides conclusion: "the ducks in the duck pond / cannot fly" (p. 119). This observation Kroetsch counters with his repetition throughout the poem of the need to "take care of our stories," and his affirmation of the "quiet . . . here." This repeated phrase, "it is quiet," also suggests regeneration, for this could be a positive silence that will assist creativity. The poet must "hear" the sound of the quiet, and he enjoins us to do likewise: "it is quiet, reader, listen" (p. 118), and again, "reader, listen, be careful" (p. 117). The "hubbub" is stilled, and the clichés are silenced. Once again, it is a fruitful absence.

Kroetsch's claim that "The Winnipeg Zoo" is a "failed" poem must be balanced against his assertion that it is still an "important failure" (LV, p. 166). In his previous poems he transformed documents, "non-literary verbal things" (LV, p. 166), and then he looked more closely at the very components of language. In "The Sad Phoenician" he used the alphabetic sequence to create an ordered listing. It is comprehensiveness that he apparently sought in "The Winnipeg Zoo": "There's an encyclopedic quality to a zoo that's very fascinating. I just haven't found a way to get from my impulse to a form" (LV, pp. 166–67). His attempt in "The Winnipeg Zoo" is a sort of surrealistic condensation of a day at the zoo, in which tension again provides a clue:

> There is, in much Canadian writing, a tension between, on the one hand, the desperate need to count, to list, to catalogue — as Whitman did for America in the 19th century — and, on the other hand, the terrible modern suspicion that the counting is being done in a slightly mad dream. ("The Canadian Writer . . . ," in RK, p. 14)

This perhaps accounts for the "slightly mad" surreal aspect of "The Winnipeg Zoo."

The next poem describes the arrived poet comfortably at home, engaged in a specifically domestic situation. There is a progression. "Sketches of a Lemon" is just that, twelve sketches, short takes that meditate, with pauses, on the objectness of a lemon and transform it into a poem, albeit a slight one. These are not twelve portraits, concluded and polished. Kroetsch approaches the object from the usual physical and philosophical positions, describing its shape, which significantly is a nonshape, its similarities to other like objects, again definition by absence, or what it is not. One begins to wonder whether Kroetsch is perhaps parodying Kroetsch in this poem. We even find him puckering "to kiss a lemon" (*FN*, p. 125), making incomplete (incompletable?) puns: "I bought a second-hand car — / Okay, okay" (p. 126). The first sketches are generally concluded with a distancing "so much for that" (pp. 123, 125), but the ninth, which suggests ". . . a lemon is shaped / exactly like an hour," ends parenthetically: "(Now we're getting somewhere)" (p. 126). The tenth and eleventh are similarly positive, ending with Kroetsch's faith in continuation rather than conclusion. After a recipe for the "lemon cure," he says: "Repeat as necessary" (p. 126). After a litany of "see, what did I tell you, see," advice to the "child who has just bit into" a lemon, he says, "One could, of course, go on" (p. 127). Kroetsch does go on in the next section, "The Criminal Intensities of Love as Paradise," but he brings this type of exercise to a close by eating the lemon in the twelfth section, a fitting "close," which, of course, contributes to renewal.

The final poem of the first volume of *Field Notes* continues the search for a form. The need in "The Winnipeg Zoo" to "take care of our stories" (p. 117) is resolved somewhat in "The Criminal Intensities of Love as Paradise" by the dialogic handling of story and a surreal sequence. The tension between the narrative and the lyric impulses that was embodied in the autobiographical intertext of "Seed Catalogues" finds an interesting resolution here. As in "The Sad Phoenician," the visual impression of the poem is strong. Divided into twelve sections, the poem is a balance of two voices. On the right-hand side is a straightforward recounting of a camping holiday two lovers take in the Canadian Rockies. Rather prosaically it documents their waking in their tent at night and hearing a bear, quarrelling over who will get up "to kindle / a fire" (p. 132), going for a walk, making love, eating lunch, shopping in town, swimming "in the buff" (p. 140), returning to their sleeping bags, and finally dreaming. This is presented in the unembellished language of the surface life, while the longer, left-hand text is written in the image-laden language of the unconscious. Lecker explains that this version "transform[s] through metaphor, dream, and imagination" (p. 145) the plot synopsis on the right. The only image found in the right-hand text is in the last lines, as the couple significantly slip into their dreams. Neither poem is sufficient on its own; in fact, both seem to be exaggerations of their mode, the narrative just too prosaic, and the surreal transformation just too abstract. Taken together they suggest an interesting, dialogic solution, and Neuman rightly locates the poem's "fulfillment" (after all, the poem's "subject" is two lovers, and the title is, in part, "Love as Paradise")

> in the gap between the conscious and the unconscious, between language as system and language as subversive of that system. That is, it lies in the white space, the silent center, on the page where the poet and the reader encounter the impact, the edge of both languages and make the leap between them. . . . the space in which movement, transformation can take place. ("Figuring," p. 183)

And once again we encounter transformation as structure and text of the poem. Here it provides a means of handling the dialectic between "opposing forces" which at the beginning of this section we noted Kroetsch and others recognize as a dialectic that reflects Canadian society (Enright and Cooley, p. 25), and literally here being "caught between the two" is the fulfilment of the poem. Ending his essay "For Play and Entrance," Kroetsch could be talking about his own poem: "The gap between language and narrative . . . generates new possibilities, new long poems" (RK, p. 108).

The title "The Criminal Intensities of Love as Paradise," as well as continuing the parallel between lover and poet, suggests a subversion of the Edenic myth. "Criminal" further suggests the fugitive nature of the exercise, once again the model of the risk-taker or outlaw. Kroetsch is breaking the so-called rules of the art and forging new possibilities. The associative images so noticeable in "The Sad Phoenician" provide the ambiguous, syntactical progression of the left-hand text. Here the linkages are etymological, alliterative, homonymous, synonymous, figurative, and punning. Kroetsch begins his poem by explaining:

> etymologies
> of sun or
> stone of ear
> and listening

the bent of
birth on edge
the chrysalis
and parting bone

old as old as
time as time

(*FN*, p. 131)

As well as hinting at the mode of association here by providing some of the metonymical possibilities "of ear / and listening" and "etymologies," Kroetsch demonstrates by providing a reference to the "birth" of sorts of his own continuing poem. "Stone," "bone," and "old as old" provide clear echoes of the developmental progression of "Stone Hammer Poem," while the emphasis on "ear" and "listening" suggests the concern most evident from "How I Joined the Seal Herd" on. The new kind of associations here link "stone" to "bone" through rhyme and poetic reference as well as to "ear," "stone-deaf" being the death of this kind of poetry, as opposed to "birth on edge," the actual mode of this poem, newly released in the whiteness between the colliding "edge[s]" of the two texts. A new form is born as from a "chrysalis," a form unlike that which went into it. "Bent" is also interesting, as it suggests, when linked to the earlier "listening," the curve of intense concentration. The earliest sense of bend is, however, "to bind or constrain," just the release, through a new birth for which Kroetsch is striving here. And he finds a new "bent" so to say, "ripe as rite" (p. 131). Ripe as a cognate of "reap" here suggests, of course, that the poet will once again reap what he sows in the poetic ritual. Further references to earlier sections of *Field Notes* are again embedded in the text, and thus we also find a "lodgepole" (p. 131), suggestive of the second definition of "ledger."

This kind of multiple reading of the left-hand text can be sustained throughout the twelve sections of the poem. On the last page, under the title "And Dreamers, Even Then, If Dreaming," Kroetsch suggests the dream quality of the images, which come not from the consciousness, wide awake, but rather from the expansiveness of "wide / as sleep" (p. 144). As he suggested on the first page of "The Criminal Intensities of Love as Paradise," the "dreamers [are] / dreaming / feet or foot" (p. 131), of bear or poetry. The result has been the "extricat[ion]" of the "called / grammarian" (p. 144), the disentanglement of chatter, the stilling of the "hubbub." A "calling" is also a vocation, and to "call out" is, etymologically, a challenge, which is what Kroetsch seems ever willing to accept. Here a "storm / commencing seed" (p. 144) suggests once again the tempestuous nature of such issue. Kroetsch accepts the challenge of not ending, as he provides the promise of further creation in the last words of the first volume of *Field Notes*:

> the closed eye
> listen &
> O nesting tongue
> hatch the world
>
> (p. 144)

Birds are always important in Kroetsch's image systems, and here the eagle, which spread its wings over the opening of this page, is resolved into an image of fecundity that suggests ". . . the new mouth the place that / must be . . ." of "Pumpkin: A Love Poem" (*SHP*, p. 26). Here closure, as would be expected, promises continuation. The "nesting tongue" in "the new mouth" promises birth and regeneration.

"The Criminal Intensities of Love as Paradise" is at once the evident progression of the earlier sections of *Field Notes*, symbolized by the embedded references, and also the promise of new possibilities to come. The growth of a poet is evident. "How do you grow a poet?" Kroetsch asks in "Seed Catalogue" and then demonstrates. He has to deconstruct himself back to nothingness and then put himself back together. He begins by transforming actual artefacts from his extended past. Then the artefact becomes himself and his language. He has to free himself from all definitions: of poet, of human, of language. After "How I Joined the Seal Herd," everything is breaking down, even the language. The letters are fragmented in "The Sad Phoenician." The breakdown, the absence, is confronted in "The Silent Poet Sequence" and "The Winnipeg Zoo." A new form/model is required, and there seems to be a new syntactical coming together in "The Criminal Intensities of Love as Paradise." The syntactical shift is evident from the associative patterning of "The Sad Phoenician" to its refinement in the left-hand text of "The Criminal Intensities of Love as Paradise." Kroetsch has discovered an appropriate form to capture the very tension of "the double experience."

In the next volume of *Field Notes*, *Advice to My Friends*, he continues to explore the poetic possibilities of this experience, most clearly in "The Frankfurt *Hauptbahnhof*." And here he specifies one formal/structural resolution:

> Notation, in *Field Notes*, Barry, is the reader in the text. The narrator, always, fears his/her own tyranny. The notation in the poem occasions the dialogic response that is the reader's articulation of his/her presence (the ecstatic now of recognition? the longer, if not always enduring, experience of transformational vision?). (*AMF*, p. 124)

From that first reaching out of poet to reader in the lingering "pinch" of "Seed Catalogue"'s last lines, to the more obvious inclusion of the "Dear Reader" in the later poems, Kroetsch has endeavoured to engage his reader in a dialogue, and the play of voices, as in "The Criminal Intensities of Love as Paradise," can provide structure and solution. The reader, pushed to work at the poems too, can participate through the "experience of transformational vision." With the notational form of the reader in the text, Kroetsch thus encodes the balanced forces. He experiments with dialogue, as a form of notation, in several of the further sections of his continuing poem. The shift from *Field Notes* to *Advice to My Friends* is signalled by the very titles. In the title sequence of the second volume, Kroetsch addresses twenty sonnet-variations to friends, all of whom seem present in the lines, while other sections of this life-long poem take the form of letters or postcards to his life partner or his daughters, ever a dialogue with another.

"Advice to My Friends" is an obvious playing against convention, here the traditional sonnet sequence. While some are addressed to his wife/lover, the conventional addressee is modified. As the title tells us, these "sonnets" are written to friends, not a lover, and when two do include Smaro Kamboureli, she is not the elusive ideal, but present in the poet's arms and bed. In more ways than this, however, these are not conventional sonnets. Most obvious, all except two are longer than the accepted fourteen lines. The majority contain eighteen lines, either divided into three stanzas of four lines each plus two stanzas of three lines, or four stanzas of four lines each plus a couplet, loosely reflecting the Italian and English forms respectively.

Kroetsch gives his game away and pokes fun at himself in the very first "Advice" poem:

> but you take now your piecemeal sonnet
> wow, certain of these here poets,
> these chokermen can't even count to fourteen
> ("Advice to My Friends," in *AMF*, p. 9)

We would not expect Kroetsch's sonnets to be written in iambic pentameter either, nor are they. They rely more heavily on prose rhythms in fact, as Kroetsch seems to have broken up the breath line with which he experimented so exhaustively[57] in "The Winnipeg Zoo." Here he is moving towards the sentence, which becomes the important unit of his most recent poems. "[I]f we could just get a hold of it, / catch aholt, some kind of a line," he muses, wishing to stack the lines and rhyming words like wood, "holt," "behind the kitchen stove" (p. 9). But the traditional rhymes and rhythms no longer suffice, and the replacement breath-line is beginning to fail also. Kroetsch exposes the humour in the "kiss and tell" kind of sonnet as well: "but (now and then) you've got to tell *some*body / and a reader has I guess, in spite of all, ears" (p. 9), which he has been advising us to use all along.

These sonnet variations, then, demonstrate the need, as always, to break from tradition, while at the same time recognizing it. One variation, significantly titled "I find myself reading the old guys now: December 6, 1983," is a fourteen-line poem, even ending with a rhyming couplet. Kroetsch runs through some of the clichéd formulas, but this sailing leaves him "clinging to the moon, seasick" (*AMF*, p. 22). It is, after all, a strange world, an unsettling sea. Kroetsch's playing off the sonnet form can be compared to Phyllis Webb's use of the Persian ghazal in her *Water and Light: Ghazals and Anti Ghazals* and bpNichol's use of the Japanese utanikki or poetic diary as a formal model in *The Martyrology*.[58] In this light, the poems of "Advice to My Friends" can be seen as "anti-sonnets"; not that they are subversively *against* the form, but rather, as with Webb's and Nichol's poems, they break up the traditional form to create it anew. References to Webb and Nichol, supporting this idea, are embedded in the poems: "a menagerist / enters the parlor, accompanied by thirteen // ghazals" ("The Bridegroom Rises to Speak," in *AMF*, p. 15). And Nichol arrives "in the company of a Mr. Basho of Japan"

("Reading It in the [Comic] Papers: for bp," in *AMF*, p. 14), a master of the Japanese utanikki. Most of the Canadian poets who were identified in the "Tradition and Milieu" section as being influential on Kroetsch or mutually stimulating are mentioned or addressed in this sequence: those with whom a dialogue would be fruitful. So in addition to the references to Webb and Nichol, we have poems for Eli Mandel, Fred Wah, Michael Ondaatje, Doug Jones, George Bowering, and Roy Kiyooka, as well as for some less established poets, and two poems to critic and friend Laurie Ricou. The dialogic nature of the poems is important because they are as much *seeking* advice from friends, reviewing what is stimulating poetically about them, as they are giving advice.

These poems, then, are about influence and demonstrate inter-textuality — the marriage of contraries, the dance of affinities. A series of five poems celebrates the unlikely wedding of hockey player Howie Morenz and painter Emily Carr. The first is addressed to Ondaatje and perhaps suggests his similarly subversive way of handling history, playing with it and making it serve his own purposes, faking the record of historical characters. The significance of the hockey model is explained in the epigraph to the following section of *Advice to My Friends*. In the words of author and hockey player Ken Dryden,

> . . . hockey is a *transition game*: offence to defence, defence to offence, one team to another. Hundreds of tiny fragments of action, some leading somewhere, most going nowhere. Only one thing is clear. Grand designs don't work. (Quoted in *AMF*, p. 29)

There are, of course, obvious parallels to Kroetsch's own poetry: the balanced opposites, the fragmentation, and the refusal of closure and "grand designs." In the first of the wedding poems, Kroetsch suggests further similarities, the discontinuity, the "moving / and stopping," and the use of "masks" to further the game; "The goalie's mask in the goal's mouth" ("Listening to the Radio: For Michael Ondaatje," in *AMF*, p. 13). Nichol and Webb attend the wedding reception, and Nichol's advice for the newly wed hockey player is "Work on your line." "Keep it edgy, // Mr. Morenz replies, scoring a point" (p. 14). Mr. Basho addresses the assembled guests with his own advice about language foregrounded and sensitized through the doubling of models: "When we both talk, . . . / the words are listening" (p. 14), he says, and Bowering demonstrates with a two-step: "George / (which George?) is dancing, with Gertrude Stein" (p. 16). Kroetsch suggests that such a "dance is the first decoding" (p. 16). "Roy Kiyooka arrives by balloon," his own "Fontainebleau Dream Machine," and his poems provide an example of a way out of closure and dead ends:

> He is the only person who brings
> an escape plan as a gift. It is a collage
> of 1,243 pages, in code, with maps and diagrams

(p. 16)

And no wedding would be complete without photographs, taken here logically by Ondaatje[59] and suggesting the "temptation of the documentary" to balance the scepticism, here "the ecstatic / document, in arrest" (p. 16).

Not surprisingly, the poets included are generally poets of the long poem, and the advice they give and receive has to do directly with the possibilities inherent in that form. In addition to questions about models and intertextuality, documentation, the fictionalization of the real, the foregrounding of language, and "borderland" solutions, Kroetsch introduces the ironic fruitfulness of absence, the encounter with the double, and the moment of arrival in the New World. One of the most successful of the poems, "to the Wahs, on the Kootenay River," includes the wisdom:

> Lao Tzu was right about these matters.
> I forget what he said — the way concealed
> in its namelessness, or something like it.

(p. 11)

This demonstrates both the correct respect/disrespect for sources, as well as Kroetsch's creative sense of coming from an unnamed world. "Call[ing] / down to [his] own absence," he then receives the following answer:

> Poet, ... Let the chips fall.
> Think of yourself there [in a bathroom under construction] as your
>   own shadow.
> Consider submission.   Forget desire.

(p. 11)

The terrible juxtaposition is again introduced in two poems explaining Columbus' discovery of America. The "bodies run[ning] naked down to the beach / to embrace our arrival" ("For Doug Jones: The Explanation," in *AMF*, p. 23) are compared with the waste and havoc wreaked on the environment subsequent to this arrival. One of the last poems reproduces the image patterns of "The Criminal Intensities of Love as Paradise" — dream, bear, and blackness — and perhaps recounts a "version" of its inception. The poet wakes up "hollering" from a dream of a "bear . . . blacker than the night." Instead of turning tail, the poet runs to embrace the bear, his fate. He tells Smaro:

> I have begun the poem
> of my country, you are present
> at the moment of conception,
> I wish that John Cabot could be with us,
> and Champlain, and maybe Susanna Moodie,
> here in our bed, in Winnipeg.
> ("Seeing the Bear," in *AMF*, p. 24)

And, of course, in a way, all the previous explorers/discoverers/divided models[60] are "in at the birth."

The next section of Kroetsch's continuing poem demonstrates a similar idea of poetic generation, as in both birth and intertextuality. Kroetsch takes an earlier poem, the six-part "Mile Zero" that appeared in *The Stone Hammer Poems* and in a journal as early as 1969,[61] and adds footnotes and bracketed, arrow-directed insertions, which pierce the original. There is a balance/imbalance between a narrative poem and a post-surreal sequence similar to the tension found in "The Criminal Intensities of Love as Paradise." And as that poem presented a subversion of the Edenic myth, this one presents a subversion of the creation story, for the six parts represent six nights of a journey west to the life-spawning ocean. There is a demonstration of the creative process ("the story of the poem / become / the poem of the story / become" [*AMF*, p. 41]), as Kroetsch comments on underlying concerns in his poem, changes he has made in this one, and describes, in the third person, the occasion of the writing. As Neuman suggests, ". . . reading enacts that writing" ("Figuring," p. 185).

The original poem plus the additions and commentary become a dialogue between two Kroetschian poetic voices: "a voice that in the sixties insisted on a source that was at once oral and local" and a voice that in the eighties insists on disjunction, intertext, and "post-surreal niceties" (*AMF*, p. 38). The sixties voice speaks the original poem, "being some account of a journey through / western Canada in the dead of six nights" (p. 30). This journey, searching for "the mansource of the man" (p. 38), replicates the mythic westering journey so crucial to Kroetsch. Obvious is the association of an exploration of that movement and his own home place with the genesis of poetry. This journey, searching for "the mansource of the man" (p. 38), replicates the mythic westering journey so crucial to Kroetsch. Obvious is the association of an exploration of that movement and his own home place with the genesis of poetry. The road taken west finally reaches the furthest point on the coast, Mile Zero. "The road ended // but it did not end" (p. 40), Kroetsch tells us, for he has really reached the shore. ("We must always go back to the shore," he says in "The Continuing Poem" [*RK*, p. 81], as he does continually in his poetry.) End is thus again source, and "Mile Zero," or Mile O, suggests the having "come full circle" or the generative "orifice of love" of "The Sad Phoenician," the last line of *Field Notes*, providing the beginning of the rest of the continuing poem: "O nesting tongue / hatch the world" ("The Criminal Intensities of Love as Paradise," in *FN*, p. 144).

The first part of the original "Mile Zero" even provides the model for the later additions and alterations. Parenthetically, the poet suggests we partake in the process, and he provides three possible stanzas for us to "try." Significantly, we take over as the poet "look[s] around the horizon" (p. 30). Possibly fearing his erasure, he ends this first poem by asserting his presence and vocation, but typically he asserts not only his presence but the possibility of erasure as well:

I AM A SIMPLE POET
I wrote in the dust
on the police car hood.

(p. 30)

The post-surreal pairing to the original poem contains a version of the westering journey "(*ouest* / or quest or)" (p. 35) as well as "the poet's equal fascination with the visit to the land of the dead (in search of?) — " (p. 38). "Death is a live / issue" (p. 41), Kroetsch says, but there is always the return journey, "summer and / a scent" (p. 35), the shaman returning to "give us the message, and, in that sense, heal us" (MacKinnon, p. 17). The journey is one of self-discovery as well:

> westering is
> madrona,[62] west
>
> the wooden shore
> to look inland
>
> (p. 31)

When you arrive at the furthest reach of the land there is the sea or the re-doubled journey back "in land," and inside the poet too. There are also references to the mode of Kroetsch's poetry: intertextuality ("allot illusion as / is necessary to" [p. 35]); autobiography ("allow // self, portraying / self" [p. 39]); defamiliarization ("and every way and / which, confuse" [p. 33]); and deferral:

> wrong or alone
> we live, in delay's body
>
> bone, altering
> bone
>
> after the word (after
> which there can be no after)
>
> (p. 37)

For this would be silence, but typically Kroetsch does encounter silence. One of the explanatory footnotes tells us that the original poem failed; the poet hesitated "to write the longish poem the occasion dictate[d]" (p. 38). Thus, he explains the original lines, "Despair is   not writing the poem / say what you will about despair" (p. 38). Only now (the 1981 of the additions and rewriting) does he realize the lost poem, but concludes that his later voice does not "weld" into the earlier one (p. 38), so that he cannot at this point provide the missing lines. The voices may not "weld," but the *dialogue* of voices does become the now poem.

And dialogue with self again becomes dialogue with others in the following sections of *Advice to My Friends*, as journeys continue. "Letters to Salonika" is in the form of a correspondence to his lover, away from "home," in her "homeland" of Greece. The poet next becomes traveller himself, and sends home "Postcards from China" to his two daughters in America. "Delphi: Commentary" links these two poems, as the poet journeys to Greece in the company of his daughters.

Nostos, the longing for home, the westering journey and its reverse, and the quest all figure in these poems, and all are in some way subverted. In "Postcards from China" Kroetsch continues the westward journey past the western edge of Canada into the alien "west" of the Far East, while in "The Frankfurt *Hauptbahnhof* " he retraces the family's westering trip from Germany back to its source. In "Letters to Salonika," the trip is displaced from the text, as the poet writes to the other who has made the trip instead of him. And the longing is also displaced, from the longing for home, to the longing for the loved one, who is now in her original home place; but this displacement causes further disjunction. The home these two share is "made different" by her absence. It is now unfamiliar, and this absence, of course in true Kroetsch fashion inspires the poem. He writes, ". . . your absence that fills this apartment fills my mind at this hour" (*AMF*, p. 45), and fills the poem. He even learns "to dream emptiness" (p. 46), and when he fails to receive replies, he turns the letters into "the poem about you [the beloved] and your silence" (p. 53). Once again it is a poem about loss and finding, and the poet transforms himself into Columbus:

I am a Columbus trying to sail away and forget the finding. Columbus, who could not sail back to Europe, because he had made his own Europe cease to exist. (p. 46)

Kroetsch expands the metaphor of poet as explorer to include the lover as explorer.

This series of twenty-seven "letters" of varying lengths constitutes a prose poem that resembles a poetic journal in form, with chronological, dated, nearly daily entries. The journal has been a popular model for recent poets of the long poem in Canada, and these creators of contemporary poetic journals have much in common.[63] They share a renewed sense of their roots, and their travel often takes them back in their own and their ancestors' pasts. Relationship to a parent is often crucial. Patterns are important, and the parallels outside of chronology are often more significant than any purely sequential ordering in time. The journal form is, of course, self-reflexive, and the division between writer and written is no longer rigid. Valuing synchronicity, writers now assume the fictive nature of reality. Experimentation is key, with the relationship to language perhaps the most common bond between these writers. Kroetsch's subversion of the journal form here includes his own situation and the encoded other. He is not the one travelling and experiencing new places or re-experiencing original ones. Neither is he keeping a diary record for his own eyes or for an anonymous readership. These entries encode a specific reader and stay rooted at "home" with the poet or imaginatively follow the recipient in her travels. When the poet does travel himself (to a cottage north of Winnipeg, to a poetry festival in Ontario, to Calgary), there is a brief interruption in the daily recording. And the trip to China, which is alluded to several times during the correspondence, closes this sequence with Kroetsch's departure and opens the next sequence, "Postcards from China."

In "Letters to Salonika" the model of the quest, used recurrently in Kroetsch's poetry and fiction, is also subverted. In "For Play and Entrance" he tells us,

> The long poem, since the time of *The Odyssey*, has been a kind of travel book. Since its beginning, you might say. The travel book as poem *contains* aversion of narrative. The travel poem has, traditionally, a specific (if not clear) sense of goal. Of ending (eschatology), if you will.
>
> Further, the long poem as travel poem elaborates its own complex relationship to the idea of love. Separation and delay and fulfillment are elements in the grammar. Surprise and temptation take the traveler away from and towards. (*RK*, p. 104)

It is clear that in "Letters to Salonika" Kroetsch is at once using and breaking from this tradition. In his version, Odysseus stays at home, while Penelope goes off travelling. Speaking to the beloved, Kroetsch says, "You on your quest, me here at home" (*AMF*, p. 63). But, "Loneliness is a fire" (p. 63), and the separation kindles poetry. In the version of geography which emphasizes "Its emptiness. / Its spaces":

Penelope was the artist, in that story. Odysseus, only the dumb and silent one, approaching and being unravelled and approaching again. Odysseus, unravelled, approaching. Penelope gave the story to herself. She did not give the story to Odysseus. (p. 56)

Here the poet remains at home unweaving and re-weaving, deconstructing and reconstructing, making from the silences his poem. With the reversal of roles, the embedded "version of narrative" is displaced, and the goal or ending is disaffirmed. Even the to-be-expected ending for this reversal, the reunion of the lovers, is delayed — postponed by the poet's own departure; and this, in turn, serves to prolong the grammar of "separation and delay and fulfillment."

It is particularly significant that the beloved is from Greece, classical home of the Muses, direct progenitor of our alphabet, and story-source for Kroetsch. In addition to the archetypal quest story, he says, "In Greece I found a maze and stories of mazes that became, I now see, metonymous with my own life" (p. 60). So the beloved makes her quest back to her own homeland, to Greece, but in terms of Kroetsch's own writing, she makes the journey for him, that he later makes himself in "Delphi: Commentary," to one of his potent beginning places. Kroetsch recognizes this as well as the dissimilarities between their origins:

Yours is a complex ritual of place and culture. I come from huge silences. Strange, that I so long ago borrowed the sound of Greece. I always heard the biblical stories as something a little bit bizarre, grotesque. Even that version of the garden story, for all my obsession with stories of the garden. But the Greek stories, for all their passion and violence, spoke *exactly* to me. I could find no mismatching between me and them. Except for the distance. The actual place of those stories was distant. Except that you erased that distance. (p. 60)

One tension of the poem, then, is the discord between this celebration of the erasure of distance with the complaint against the reestablishment of the distance.

As the grammar of the poem is established by the patterns of journey and separation, so many of the correspondences of this correspondence have to do with the process of Kroetsch's poetry. In preparation for his imminent trip to China, he reads "Chinese poems

. . . many of them about travel and separation" (p. 71). Not only does he record his reading and his writing/not writing, but also there is a duality to his journal-entry speculations. Speaking of "living together," Kroetsch implies much about the process of his poem-making:

> Part of living together is the allowing for repetition. The nuance, the change, the exploration. The making strange. The discovery within the known of what was known and what was unknown and what is mystery. (p. 52)

Suggesting Wah's concept of "making strange,"[64] Kroetsch is not only talking here about the unfolding of a relationship, but also about the poetic form of defamiliarization. Similarly, when he begins his last letter before his own leave-taking, he captures both the tension of extremes and the deferral of meaning that he desires:

> By meaning we mean something that means
> but, in the process, means its opposite.
>
> (p. 72)

In "the process" of Kroetsch's poetry, he "means" the dialectic of opposites. And echoing the lines from "Seed Catalogue," "we silence words / by writing them down" (*FN*, p. 63), Kroetsch ambiguously reaffirms:

> We write books to avoid
> writing books.
>
> (p. 72)

Then he "concludes" this section and opens the next with a multi-level recognition of the influences at work in his lines. "From you, from Pound, from the Chinese" ("Postcards from China," in *AMF*, p. 72), he writes before quoting, as Neuman explains, "three lines of Modern Greek, apt for the situation. They translate, 'Please let me know beforehand, // And I will come out to meet you, // As far as the Cho-fu-Sa.' Apt, because the intertext here is Seferis's translation into Greek of Ezra Pound's translation into English of LiPo's 'The River Merchant's Wife'" ("Figuring," p. 184). A few pages previous, Kroetsch mentions reading Seferis and LiPo and TuFu, "those contrary poets" ("Letters to Salonika," p. 63), while a few pages further on, now journeying himself, he describes an "encounter" with TuFu.

"Postcards from China" thus becomes a continuation of the journal, more conventional here only in so far as the poet is travelling now and recording his sensations. The beloved is still on her quest, while Kroetsch now sets out on his own. The sequence, addressed to his daughters, is a journal of sorts, recording his nine days in China with six other Canadian writers. Theirs is a question complete with guides:

> You must have a guide when you go on a journey to a mysterious, unknown place; that's one of the rules of literature, and maybe of life also. As it happens, we have three guides, and that makes it even better. ("Postcards from China," p. 77)

The "journey to a mysterious, unknown place" suggests the mythic journey to the underworld found previously in Kroetsch's writing, and this idea is strengthened by the fact that Kroetsch emphasizes his arrival in China as one of descent. His first view of China is from the air, and his opening lines describe the significantly labyrinthine aspect of the Chinese landscape when viewed from the air: "It was a web of water below us, the Chinese land" (p. 75). His last entry takes him by train through the maze of canals in "this landscape of hope" (p. 91), and so out of China. The poet of "Seed Catalogue" is fascinated with the "garden world" (p. 90) of China and its bounty, and the poet whose life is metonymous with stories of mazes finds them in Peking and Xi'an. "China is a garden and a maze" (p. 81), he says. And then later:

> . . . I saw an old man, walking. In a garden. In a garden that to me seemed to be a maze, a pattern of hedges and paths; one of those gardens designed especially to tease us out of our habitual ways. Like the Forbidden City, in Peking, that unfolds and contradicts and confuses with impossible repetitions. He was following paths, the old man, making turns, pleasing himself with surprise and mystery. Himself stopping, now and then; he watched those about him, doing tai chi, while I watched him watching. (p. 88)

And we watch Kroetsch watching him watching, and are ourselves "tease[d] . . . out of our habitual ways" by the poetry that "unfolds and contradicts and confuses / with impossible repetitions," such as those about meaning and writing at the end of the previous section. The grammar of a Kroetsch poem is always one of "surprises and / mystery."

In addition to recording his journey in the Orient, significantly perhaps finding the land for which Columbus was searching when he mistakenly found America, demonstrating the process of his poetry, Kroetsch also records his encounter with a literary father. As no biological father of his can be found in such a landscape, as is the purpose of many of the poetic journals written today in Canada, Kroetsch finds a literary one: "Joseph Conrad at a crowded table in the rooftop restaurant of the Friendship Hotel" (p. 81). As these journeys are often an exorcism of sorts, Conrad, who is "showing his age" (p. 82), is no longer there when Kroetsch returns with a beer for him. The early hold of Conrad's narratives is evidently modified here.

The enunciation of silence or the voicing of the unvoiced which is central to Kroetsch's poetry, as both subject and process, is here crucial. The unilingual poet finds he is "in China without a language" (p. 76), and this absence of speech is the ultimate deconstruction for the poet who in "How I Joined the Seal Herd" kept coming back to words. His first vision of China is faulty; things are not what they seem. The maze that from the air seemed like a road system begins to distinguish itself as "the irrigation system" — "roads that weren't roads," but "in a sense they were roads" (p. 76). And in Peking a fine rain blurs the vision: "we could and we couldn't see what we were seeing" (p. 81). "I was lost and I was trying to find a post office," he says (p. 88). Of course, the post office is necessary to the poem of postcards, and the loss and finding is crucial to the grammar of the text.

His senses sharpen in this alien land in which he needs a translator. Kroetsch is warned even before he leaves Canada by a man he meets in the Vancouver Airport, who announces solemnly, "I am a man with no language" (p. 75). Kroetsch explains: ". . . he was the son of a Japanese soldier stationed in Korea during the Second World War. His mother was Korean. He had not quite learned Japanese. He had not quite learned Korean. He had come to Canada and had not quite learned either English or French" (p. 76). This sense of language alienation haunts Kroetsch. Living through translation in China, he lives metonymically. Each small act or communication becomes subject to another naming. The poets try musically to translate their emotions by singing to a growing crowd in an unknown section of Peking. "We sang the surprise of ourselves, we writers, to the astonished audience. To our own ears. Country & Western" (p. 86). There is a wonderful sense of release or enlightenment when the poet meets a young, Chinese man with whom he can communicate. The young man has been studying English theoretically for a few years, never having been able to test his proficiency, doubting his ability to communicate. When Kroetsch actually understands him, he is ecstatic, and "proof" is sought: "we embraced and had ourselves photographed, because he was studying photography" (p. 87). This is one possibility, but the poem, in exploring the need for translation, asserts the multiplicity of possibilities. In the Forbidden City there are nine thousand rooms, and Kroetsch has "been into ten of them" (p. 78).

Seeking an answer to the significance of dragons that are everywhere in Kroetsch's China and everywhere in Kroetsch's poem about China, he asks his guides: ". . . each guide gives me a different explanation. Finally, I begin to understand," he says (p. 83). The dragon comes to represent the similarities and the differences, the disparities or tension, for the dragon can be the intermediary between extremes.

> Broadly speaking, present-day psychology defines the dragon-symbol as 'something terrible to overcome,' for only he who conquers the dragon becomes a hero. Jung goes as far as to say that the dragon is a mother-image (that is, a mirror of the maternal principle or of the unconscious) and that it expresses the individual's repugnance towards incest and the fear of committing it. . . . [65]

If we accept this, then this poem indeed becomes a station on the way to the last poem of this volume that finally confronts Kroetsch's attraction to his absent mother, the confrontation that transforms his poetry substantially. And the dragon is a symbol of transformation, as well: the flying dragon, to which Kroetsch is attracted ("I knew, secretly, that if I tried I could fly like a dragon . . ." [p. 80]), is an image that can transform the "dark unconscious forces into triumphant creative forces."[66] The lotus flower, which Kroetsch sees blossoming in a pond, is also a potent symbol of transformation. Because it grows out of water and not land, it is a primeval plant, symbolic of rebirth or enlightenment. Thus, Kroetsch's journey to China again has to do with origins. The "dream of origins" is critical to the continuation of the poem; this origin pre-dates even the Greek genesis: poems in China were "put together about 600 B.C. Before Plato and Socrates had their confabs" (p. 83). "Finally, I begin to understand," he says. "I have come to China to read the future" (p. 83). As he said in "Letters to Salonika," "Like Liebhaber [in *What the Crow Said*], I begin to remember forward" (p. 47).

Kroetsch expands this notion of divination into the very notation and process of the next sections of his continuing poem. In "Delphi: Commentary" he travels to Greece himself in the company of his daughters, seeking further enlightenment from the oracle at Delphi. His concern with translation is furthered in the weaving of four voices, one an actual translation, another a critical translation, and two versions of his own voice. On one level, the poem is a journal of the journey to Delphi by Kroetsch and his daughters. On a second level, the poem is a weaving of voices demonstrating the processes of intertextuality and discontinuity. On a further level, the poem is a statement about origins.

Kroetsch and his daughters, in the land of the loved one, language, and the Muses, travel from Athens to Delphi, trying to compose a question with which to confront the oracle. One voice in the poem is Kroetsch's voice commenting on their journey. A second voice is that of Pausanias, speaking in translation from the second century A.D., also commenting on travels through this area. Pausanias was, according to Sir James Frazer, the "ordinary traveler" who explained the "labyrinth" of Greek ruins and provided the "answer" to their "riddle" ("Delphi: Commentary," in *AMF*, p. 99) and is thus an appropriate guide on this journey through the labyrinth for answers. Frazer's voice, translating and in turn explaining Pausanias, becomes the third voice in Kroetsch's poem. The fourth voice is supplied by Kroetsch himself in the fragmented form of an "abandoned poem" series (p. 101), "The Eggplant Poems." Visually, the voices speak to one another, as well as to us, across the page. The first pages begin with one or two lines from "The Eggplant Poems" in regular type. The poet's present-journey voice is also presented in regular type, and it often nearly surrounds, or is set up in binary opposition to, the italics of Pausanias' voice or Frazer's voice. Sometimes the pages

ROBERT KROETSCH

typographically reflect the images of the lines. For instance, one page
is set up to reflect the "letter 'S' in reverse," which is the form of the
path up "the Sacred Way" (p. 102) that Kroetsch and his daughters
are ascending. As in "Mile Zero" and "Postcards from China," there
is an ascent, and again there is a guide. Another page reflects the
"Rock of / Sibyl" "rising above the ground" (p. 109), as the poet's
own words rise in a narrow column from the "ground" of Pausanias'
words across the bottom of the page. Almost encircled, Kroetsch's
next words warn, "beware / any trick of / the eye" (p. 109).

The poem proceeds by parallels and disjunctions between the pasts
of Pausanias and Frazer, the present of Kroetsch's journey, and the
future possibility of his writing. All are journeying/have journeyed
to Delphi, for Pausanias and Frazer make the trip again with
Kroetsch. It is an appropriate quest for the poet, to seek the oracle
who made her home on the south slopes of Mount Parnassus, seat
of Apollo and the Muses, and thus an inspiring source of poetry. The
spot where the oracle delivered her answers was believed to be the
"center of the whole earth," and the poet and his daughters photograph themselves in various combinations beside the marble
"omphalos," or navel (p. 104). On the way, they have been trying
out suitable questions to elicit a desired answer, and so this journey
for answers begins as a search for the appropriate question. Thus, it
is only right that at the end, the answer sought comes in the form of
a question, and by a suitable reversal, the voice that provides the
question-answer is not female, but male, the poet's own father.
Throughout there has been an appropriate confusion:

The answer   (or was it the question?):

                        mislaid?
                        stolen?
                        revised?
                        erased?
                        forgotten?
                        denied?
                        concealed?
                        replaced?
                        remembered?
                        laughed out
                        of court?

> supposed
> to be
> sacrilegious?
>
> (p. 105)

And so Kroetsch also provides a gloss on his own poetic processes.

The meeting between father and son is prepared for by the earlier reminder that "on the dangerous road to Delphi," at "The Cleft Way," the difficult point of choices, Oedipus previously met his father (p. 101). But he did not recognize him and thus killed him, fulfilling the oracle's prediction. Kroetsch deconstructs this past meeting by casting his father in the role of oracle, supplying questions that provide an answer, and directing his way at the crucial point.

> What are you doing here?
> my father said.
> Did I teach you nothing?
>
> (p. 111)

So he questions the direction of Kroetsch's search for origins.

> It was the long trip
> rewarded and
> recalled.
>
> (p. 111)

His trip is "rewarded" because he receives an answer, but the answer is also literally a "recall[ing]." The return for his trip to Delphi proves to be just that — the injunction to return to his origins in his West. With these questions in mind, Kroetsch overrules his daughters' suggestion that they stay in Delphi. "It was I who said, We've got to go," he repeats twice for emphasis (p. 113), drawing the poem to a temporary close. His father has reminded him that he has to return to his West for his writing, that he cannot remain at Delphi. Earlier he had said, parenthetically:

> (Sometimes,
> high on a mountain,
> one hears the lost poem.)
>
> (p. 108)

And on this mountain, through his father's voice, Kroetsch does hear "the lost poem," in the sense that he receives a direction that would allow the possibility of recovering the lost poem. This at once refers to Homer's lost poem, *Margites*, "that comic poem / with a fool for its hero" (p. 108), about which Kroetsch has just been speaking, but it also suggests his own lost "The Eggplant Poems." On the previous page he asked his daughters the crucial question, "is / there a difference between / a Greek poem which is lost / and a poem of mine which I / haven't been able to, for / whatever reasons, complete?" (p. 107). Although his daughters claim there is, Kroetsch continues by providing the references they require. "As for the poem itself . . . ," he says, and the ellipsis tells it all. The poem exists in its absence. The fragments which have referred to "the holes in the cheese [which] contain the cheese" (p. 100) explain the significance and refer twice to "silence." The lost poem could be recovered, that is, the absence can speak, if the poet returns to his West, as his father, "high on a mountain," directs him. And this, in fact, is what does happen. "The Eggplant Poems" could theoretically be recovered by a return; but here their eloquence is in their silence. "Delphi: Commentary" provides Kroetsch's own "answer" to the "labyrinth" of these fragments, just as Pausanias before him provided an "answer" to the "labyrinth" of the fragments of Greek ruins. Kroetsch transforms the fragments of poem and of archaeological site alike just as he transformed the artefacts in the first sections of *Field Notes*. In his continuing poem Kroetsch, after one more section searching for his European roots, does return to his Western origins and confronts the major absence that he has so far avoided, his mother's death. This is the "real" lost poem, the poem of his mother's death that he returns to recover, and the confrontation alters *Field Notes* significantly, bringing to a type of close (one that is also a beginning) this stage of *Field Notes*.

Before this generative completion, though, Kroetsch makes another journey, a quest to divine the future from past patterns, and explores further the sense of doubling so evident in "Delphi: Commentary." As Neuman explains, there is a dialogue between sections of the continuing poems: ". . . 'Delphi: Commentary,' in which the travels of Pausanias and Frazer double and differ from the poet's own journey to the oracle, finds its response in "The Frankfurt *Hauptbahnhof*" in which the double is self, other, and the poem" ("Figuring," p. 186). The specific "Reader" of "The Frankfurt

Hauptbahnhof," encoded in the text, is fellow-poet bpNichol. Kroetsch is responding to a question put particularly by Nichol and in general by *Open Letter* about poetic notation. Two volumes of *Open Letter* were devoted specifically to this question, with replies from such poets as Fred Wah, Daphne Marlatt, George Bowering, Frank Davey, and Nichol.[67] In the next volume of *Open Letter*, which was devoted to essays about Kroetsch, Kroetsch recorded his own reply, the first publication of the poem "The Frankfurt *Hauptbahnhof*."

As well as being a dialogue with Nichol about poetic notation, it also, by the very fact that it is a dialogue with a reader, enacts the process of notation that it advocates: "Notation, in *Field Notes*, Barry, is the reader in the text" ("The Frankfurt *Hauptbahnhof*," in *AMF*, p. 124). Moreover, "The Frankfurt *Hauptbahnhof*" is a travel journal recording Kroetsch's return to his ancestors' homeland and his meeting with his double. Thus, several additional important Kroetschian poetic processes are enacted as well.

The journey that the poem records takes the poet by plane from West Berlin to Frankfurt, by taxi from the airport to the train station, and by train from Frankfurt to Trier, having transferred at Koblenz. In Trier he gives a talk on Canadian writing at the university, but there is another purpose: "I expected to see the birthplace of one of my ancestors" (p. 119). From here he goes by train to Vienna and from thence into Switzerland and back to the Frankfurt *Hauptbahnhof*, to catch a train to the airport. The poem focuses on three happenings (which Kroetsch links up) during all this moving around. First is his meeting with his double during his first passage through the Frankfurt *Hauptbahnhof*; his double acts as guide, directing the lost Kroetsch to the right train for his journey. Second is his discovery in Trier, instead of traces of his great-grandmother, of "a plaque marking the birthplace of Karl Marx" and the ruins of "a Roman spa" (p. 119). Third is his vision of swarming crows in the skies above Schönbrunn Palace and Park in Vienna. The poem knits up these three occasions, and Kroetsch demonstrates, through his reading of them together, the process of his poems and how we should read them.

By subject and demonstration, then, the poem is about notation, providing the answer to Nichol's question, and, in addition to the poet's movements, the poem is structured, as was "The Ledger," by a series of definitions. Kroetsch defines and redefines notation and provides examples of the process. In addition to the encoding of the reader in the text and the subsequent dialogic process, notation, Kroetsch says, is also "prediction" (p. 117) and instruction.

Notation is a set
of instructions for
reading (in) the
future.

(p. 123)

It is also "what happens in the margin" or "silence" (p. 119), the double experience: "The double of the poem" (p. 125), "transformational vision" (p. 124), "flying," fragmentation ("broken / [the remaining] / lines" [p. 125]), and deconstruction.

Kroetsch begins his poem by addressing us directly and introducing the subject of the double, which is clearly both himself and other, and the double experience of *nostos* in his family history:

keep an eye peeled
for an ancestor,
me, in *das alte* country.

(p. 117)

The "old country" is the original country from which his ancestors began the westering journey, but perhaps also the other country of the underworld or the unconscious double of our conscious world. At any rate, we the readers, have to be on the lookout. The first page concludes:

notation is
(what is   notation   (horse
Barry says (in *Field Notes*))   (hero
                                   (eros
prediction,   (roses
a saying (assaying) of
what will be said: (or so
                                   (the
aerie (*prae-dic-ere*) and   (story
eagle,   (goes
both

	Ladies and gentlemen,
me, flying,	as you realize, we are
West Berlin to Frankfurt	in an area of turbulence.
Pan American FLUG NR. 641	Please remain seated.

(p. 117)

Several different notational systems are clearly evident in just this short section: poetic language, cliché, quotation (of a fellow poet and a flight attendant), definition, etymology, parenthesis, airline ticket, and word transformation. The binary positioning on the page also suggests the marginal frame, the doubled reading, and the dialogue that takes place in the space between.

In "Postcards from China" and "Delphi: Commentary" we noted the inclusion of divination, and these last poems of *Advice to My Friends* all point towards and "predict" the enunciation of the remaining two sections. They become an "assaying," or attempt to determine "what will be said." The continuity of the poem is emphasized by the dialogue between the various sections that is encoded here and elsewhere. Each section is, in a sense, predicted by the ones which preceded it, could not exist without the ones before. So Kroetsch, while examining the etymology of prediction, suggests the homonym "aerie," a natural jump to a nest, place of origin, home place. This suggests eagle here and on the last page of "The Criminal Intensities of Love as Paradise," where the eagle, associated with risk and flight, is associated through "eerie & enter" to the final, generative "nesting tongue" which is to "hatch the world" and the following poems. Here Kroetsch and eagle are both flying, taking the risk and encountering "turbulence." This in turn suggests both the disjunction of Kroetsch's poetry and the necessary danger. "You Must Marry the Terror" ("The Ledger," in *FN*, p. 43). The left-hand poem moves metonymically by way of definition, etymology, and homonym, as well as by references to previous poems, similar actions (flying), and similar journeys (westward/ return). The right-hand poem, by transforming "horse" to "roses," also encodes the transformation in Kroetsch's poems. The horse on which he was seated in "Seed Catalogue" leads into "hero," or the poet's position in the following quest poems, particularly "How I Joined the Seal Herd." "Eros," of course, watches over "The Sad Phoenician" and "The Silent Poet Sequence," while "roses" perhaps represents convention, the usual metaphoric comparative, which Kroetsch continually subverts, as in "The Sad Phoenician" when he suggests the cliché "a rose by any other name" (*FN*, p. 81) and leaves it incomplete. "Or so / the / story / goes" suggests the narrative impulse of his poetry, as well as the inclusion of cliché. This, in turn, provides a commentary on the previous lines, as a compression of the western story, the hero-lover on horseback. Such density is typical of Kroetsch's image-laden lines, and the final words, typically, are subversive. "Please remain seated," the airline passenger-poet is told, but going back to the horse: the point was that Kroetsch could *not* remain seated, even though "the horse was standing still" ("Seed Catalogue," in *FN*, p. 49). The turbulence must be experienced.

If Kroetsch's poems are not immediately understandable to the reader, that is because the "turbulence" serves to keep us off-balance as well. The "story" in this poem tells of Kroetsch's own difficulty in understanding. He is lost when he first enters the Frankfurt *Hauptbahnhof* and does not appreciate the significance of his meeting with the double who guides him on his way. His experiences in Trier and Vienna serve to provide the significance for him and for us. You look for one thing and find another. Kroetsch looks for evidence of his great-grandmother and finds no trace of her, but the silence is significant: ". . . notation / is a system of _____ / written down against / the _____ " (p. 119). What he finds instead is "a plaque where Marx's mother changed his diapers (and the world)" and some Roman ruins: "those sites, those ruins, as notation" (p. 123). Reading the past, as Kroetsch does in "Delphi: Commentary" and "Postcards from China," is also a form of notation. Neuman explains: "Delphi, as Kroetsch figures it, is its commentaries, the intersection of all the past and all the future readings of the site, and of their differences" ("Figuring," pp. 187–88). So at Trier Kroetsch provides a future reading by recalling a story about his great-grandmother after she had left Germany:

> . . . she was famous for having shied* a stick of wood clean across a large kitchen, through an open window, and into direct contact with her fleeing husband's skinny ass. And so the story goes. (p. 123)[68]

In Vienna, Kroetsch is struck by the movements of thousands of whirling crows. An interesting side point is that these crows, a guide tells Kroetsch, come from Russia to winter, the reversal of Marx's journey from his birthplace in Trier to his destiny in Russia. The crows, however, provide a more important parallel, as their flight inscription, black against the sky, provides a notation by which Kroetsch can "read" his encounter with his double.

> notation divination augury
>
> (p. 121)

Again, as in "Delphi: Commentary," an unusual mediator provides the "answer." "In Frankfurt," Kroetsch says, "when I couldn't read the schedule and find the track my train was on. I was close to despair" (p. 121). His inability to decipher, divine the schedule, because of the silence imposed by his unilingual condition and his sense of defamiliarization, is translated by the double. In turn, the significance of this meeting with his double, which he at first is not able to "read" either, is then translated by his encounter with the crows: the "double or nothing" of "The Sad Phoenician" (p. 94) becomes here "Double or / noting / My / doppelgänger" (p. 121).

> It was the crows'
> notations that
> told me
> how to meet
>
> the gone stranger.
>
> (p. 121)

"Because of its black colour, the crow is associated with the idea of beginning (as expressed in such symbols as the maternal night, primigenial darkness, the fertilizing earth). Because it is also associated with the atmosphere, it is a symbol for creative, demiurgic power and for spiritual strength. Because of its flight, it is considered a messenger" (Cirlot, p. 71). A study of the significance of birds in Kroetsch's writing might be worthwhile, and the crow has particular meaning. As a symbol of origins and creativity it has obvious importance, as well as being a riddling double for Kroetsch himself (crow sounds like Kroetsch, and he wrote *The Crow Journals*). In "The Frankfurt *Hauptbahnhof*" crows serve in their role as messengers, providing "the necessary / transfer" or translation of the meeting with the double, and providing the "beginning" of Kroetsch's and our reading of the encounter:

the gone stranger
the mysterious text
the necessary
transfer
the stick (or
chunk) of
wood

somehow
taking both

flight and
it would seem

aim

(p. 124)

Neuman reads these lines perceptively: they repeat, she explains,
"the 'story' of the poem, giving us the double ('the gone stranger');
the inability of the poet and reader to understand the encounter ('the
mysterious text'); and the 'crows' // notations' ('the necessary //
transfer') which told the baffled poet/reader 'how to meet // the gone
stranger.' . . . The flight or necessary transfer is further glossed by
the chunk of wood: notation is an aimed flight from 'poem' to its
'poet' and 'reader' " ("Figuring," p. 179). That this is a solution both
to Kroetsch's dilemma and to the reader's is emphasized by the
juxtaposition of these lines with Kroetsch's explanation of the
reader's response that is occasioned by the poem's notation: "the
reader's articulation of his/her presence (the ecstatic now of recognition? the longer, if not always enduring, experience of transformational vision?)" (p. 124). Kroetsch demonstrates just how this
"transformational vision" operates, and goes on to link his experience with the reader's:

> Notation is the double of the poem. Or: we are the poem, and
> cannot hear except by indirection. We can only guess the poem
> by encountering (by being surprised by) its double. The notation
> announces the poem to the poem. (p. 125)

Being "surprised" by his double provides Kroetsch with his poem,
and the indirect reading he supplies is the disjunctive process of the

writing and the understanding. The reader is included in the very process of the poem-making. "The Frankfurt *Hauptbahnhof* " thus becomes one of Kroetsch's most articulate statements about the "double experience" of life and writing in Canada. Early on he explained that as Canadians we are involved in "the *doppelgänger* thing. You meet yourself in another form . . ." ("A Conversation with Margaret Laurence," in *creation*, p. 59). Here he does, and captures both the experience and the ambivalence of the process in his lines. Just as the double was like himself and different from himself, so this poem is like the others and different from them, and likewise our experiences as readers are similar and different. But this is what helps to keep the poem in "flight": "The notation / keeps it moving" (p. 127), Kroetsch says in his closing lines, to demonstrate that the poem has no conclusion:

> Perhaps every poem is a poem lost (in the poet, in the reader), and can only find itself in the
>
> broken
> (the remaining)
> lines

(p. 125)

A version of the lost poem that was refused in "Mile Zero," given a direction in "Delphi: Commentary," and provided with a notational process in "The Frankfurt *Hauptbahnhof* " is finally written down in "(the remaining) / lines" of *Advice to My Friends*. In "Mile Zero" Kroetsch claims that the fascinating journey is "turned entirely into implication without adequate substance (i.e., ground)" (*AMF*, p. 38). He notes the removal of the line "(her breasts were paradigms)," going on to explain the "long family history of losses," which began for him with his mother's death when he was young. He questions, "is not the mother figure the figure at once most present in and most absent from this poet's work?" ("Mile Zero," p. 36). So in two poem sequences, "Sounding the Name" (*AMF*, pp. 131–36) and "The Poet's Mother" (*AMF*, pp. 139–43), he finally confronts this absence, gives it ground, and writes his mother and his own loss into his lines. Linking her death and the "concern with *nostos*" in his writing, by way of his family's first trip from Germany, Kroetsch elides the century separating the two "un-homing[s]."

"Both quest and goal become paradigmatic" ("Mile Zero," p. 36), he says. So before the lost poem can be articulated, he must return to the original home in Germany and then to his own Western home, place of his mother's death and direction of his father's voice at Delphi. After "The Frankfurt *Hauptbahnhof*," he accepts the message of his father's voice and finds his own voice for his original loss.

Kroetsch tells us that these sequences were initiated by his response to a photograph of his mother as a young woman. He goes on to write a deconstruction of his mother's death and then its reconstruction, with the attendant darkness and nothingness. This is the "enunciation" towards which he felt *Field Notes* "drawing." In an interview done before these poems were written, he describes the generative experience:

I told you about finding a picture of my mother when she was sixteen years old and about how my erotic relationship to this woman has shocked me — my sense of desiring the woman in that photograph — which I'm going to have to write about. It denounced all my silence to me. It spoke the time. (*LV*, p. 22)

In "Sounding the Name" and "The Poet's Mother," he accepts the time and speaks the silence. The repressed material finds expression.

Kroetsch places himself in the snapshot with his young mother: in "the empty chair" beside which she is standing, "in the house" in front of which she is standing, and "in the yard" which is reflected in the window "To her / right, and behind the chair." By entering the picture, Kroetsch also enters his mother. This is both genetic appropriation of physical attributes ("Her waiting eyes contain my eyes. / Her mouth, almost smiling, contains mine") and sexual appropriation ("I become her approaching lover"). Kroetsch seeks to know, in all its connotations, his mother, who is also his double: "In this poem I rehearse my mother" ("Sounding the Name," p. 132).

In poem and dream he returns to "the garden" — metaphoric place of origin, scene of prelapsarian pleasures, and mother's domain. As he grows older himself, "Death begins to seem a friend that one has almost / forgotten, then remembers again" (p. 133). And in rehearsing his mother, Kroetsch must also rehearse her death. In the title poem of "Sounding the Name," Kroetsch brings his mother back to life, thereby deconstructing her death: "In this poem my mother is not dead" (p. 134). He recalls all the things that happened on the day of his mother's death as not happening. The annunciatory phone call does not come, and Kroetsch places his mother back in the kitchen, "finishing the October / canning." He himself is then sent on a quest:

> . . . My mother asks me
> to go pick some dill. The ducks are migrating.
> I forget to close the garden gate.
>
> (p. 134)

He leaves the garden, the first garden, and as those two before him, he cannot return. Closure is foreign to him, and the ducks are leaving on their seasonal journey. Traditionally, the duck is "associated with the Great Mother and with the 'descent into hell'. . . . It is linked with destiny . . . representing the dangers and fortunes of existence, prior to the return to the maternal bosom" (Cirlot, p. 120). And Kroetsch goes on to enunciate the "descent to hell," the darkness and nothingness that he has largely suppressed until now, now that he returns to the absent maternal bosom. He repeats: "nothing // but // nothing / but / darkness / outside my / window" (p. 135). Inside the picture of his mother behind the window, he hides, but there is only "darkness." Now that he is "getting old," outside the window is "nothing." But recognizing this terrible emptiness leads to "the shape of / water" (p. 135) and the origins of life, his debt to his mother. The final "sonnet" of this sequence, in addressing his daughters, indicates continuity. Poet and mother stand by the window. The water is prairie "sloughs," and the poet's mother demonstrates the primal naming by giving names to all the ducks. The phone call announcing her death does not come, so mother and poet stand together.

> There are mallards and
> pintails, in the dark.
> My mother, listening,
> names their talking.
>
> (p. 136)

This is her gift, "in the dark." The ducks are wild, not domesticated, and are "part of the weather" on their migratory journey (p. 136), and as with the crows, they provide a notation, a reading in the listening for how to "sound" the long-suppressed name.

The final sequence, "The Poet's Mother," describes the poet's reordering of his world and senses in the light/dark of her death. "In the death of my mother," he begins seven two-line stanzas, and goes on to link it to augury ("I read the empty sky") and to concealment, hell, and the womb ("I enter the cave"). In her death, as they are in some way doubles, Kroetsch says, "I say good-bye to myself," but it also leads to a full enunciation, "I recite my name" (p. 139). The second poem lists all the ways in which the poet's life has been patterned by the absence of his mother. He has "sought" her, he says, in travel, literature, drink, philosophy, other women, and writing. Now, in silence, and through his "transformational vision," he finds her and himself:

> These are the scars
> that make us whole.
>
> These are the scars
> that empty us
> into our lives.
>
> (p. 142)

Kroetsch is delivered "into" himself and has delivered himself to us in his poems. In the sense in which we have already discussed, that this continuing poem is autobiographical, the end to which it has been drawing has been this confrontation with the mother figure, "at once most present in and most absent from the poet's work" ("Mile Zero," in *AMF*, p. 36). We noted that as early as "The Ledger," Kroetsch's wife and daughters warned him: "everything you write . . . is a search   for the dead" (*FN*, p. 25). Now he has "found" what he has been searching for. This enunciation, then, brings the exploration of the literal sense of self to an end. The persona as the poet's self is exhausted. Thus, we find on the last pages of *Advice to My Friends* an "envoi"; but these parting remarks do not conclude the continuing poem, they serve as an entry to the next volume. The full title of the end poem is actually "envoi (to begin with)," and Kroetsch relishes the apparent opposition and provides the title and movement for the next volume. The "scars" of the previous page are transformed into "stars":

There is no real
world, my friends.
Why not, then,
let the stars
shine in our bones?

(p. 143)

The dialogic "my friends" of this volume's title is encoded along with the title of the next one, in the claim that there is "no real / world." The world of the continuing poem so far, the poet's life, is exhausted as poetic subject. The big delaying tactic, the refusal to face the darkness surrounding his mother's death, is finally overcome. The poem which began with the bone of "Stone Hammer Poem" has reached a point of critical change. The persona must now undergo a transformation if the poem is to continue. So Kroetsch creates a double, a new persona, to communicate the vision from the "real world," which here he claims does not exist.

Excerpts from the Real World thus continues the poem, but with a radical shift. Kroetsch creates a fictitious persona, a narrator who resists narrative patterns and fakes the record. He continues the tension between documentation and scepticism by creating a persona who writes faked journal entries, complete with sequential date headings. The impulse to document is balanced by the impulse to tamper with the record, and here Kroetsch tampers with the persona of the journal's author as well. The journal, which has entries from January to December of 1985, takes the author from Manitoba to North Dakota, Scotland, Holland, a Greek Island, and Iraq. Kroetsch drew on his own travels for these locations, but altered the dates somewhat. Some entries were apparently written before the date given,[69] indicating his continuing resistance to authority and systems. But when systems collapse, he goes on to ask, "How do we rejoice in this sense of fragmentariness?" As is indicated by the answers in *Open Letter* to the question about notation, the line has lost a lot of its energy for a number of poets. Many of them begin writing prose poems, and Kroetsch, in his subtitle, calls *Excerpts from the Real World* "a prose poem in ten parts." The sentence, which has "taken a beating and broken down," begins to take over for Kroetsch, and he creates a surreal poem by placing unlikely sentences end-to-end. Grammatically, the writing is correct, but the multiple possible meanings are often unusual. Kroetsch continues to

158

keep his readers off-balance:

> I want to explain. Words surface from inside, bringing with them vinegar and whales. Your eyes grow darker when you eat figs or when you flirt with other men. Owls pick up mice. Sky burial, you might call it.[70]

The language is foregrounded, as signifier is prized over signified: "In the switchblade of your tongue, the fish hawk studies mayhem" (p. 15). Taking Noam Chomsky's deep sentence structures as a pattern, Kroetsch slots in his own words, substituting anything he wants to get the desired effect. He found he had to resist short sentences and rewriting his own patterns of sentences, and the effect produced with this new method captures the continual sense of surprise so crucial to Kroetsch. By assuming formalized grammatical concepts and then slotting in words with little regard to conventions of logic, Kroetsch tests the creativity of language. Interestingly, this is the opposite of clichéd writing, which Kroetsch so often parodies, because he takes the generative aspect of Chomsky's theories of grammatical structures, that is, that there is an infinite number of possible sentences which often occur only once. It is the deep structures (or underlying or, significantly, "initial" structures) rather than the surface structures in which Kroetsch is interested. Significantly, the rules that convert deep structures to surface structures are called "transformations." "[A]rguments for transformations can be viewed as arguments for two levels of representation within syntax,"[71] with which Kroetsch is playing here. His sentences can be considered grammatical; that is, they abide by the rules of generative grammar, and the deep structures are correct, but the logical meanings are subverted. Still, Kroetsch resists absurdity, and there is a sense of continuity between this book and previous sections of the continuing poem.

After transforming artefacts and nonliterary texts in earlier sections, Kroetsch here takes a subliterary text and creates a narrator who is a country and western figure. In "Postcards from China," country and western expression similarly created surprise. Parody of this form, as well as of the journal, creates as narrator a "big strong man crying in his beer about some woman who has done him wrong."[72] The revision of sexual stereotyping fascinates Kroetsch here, the contradiction of the toughest man in the world who nevertheless cries a lot. Some of the journal entries are actually written as verse parodies of a country and western song, while others contain the trappings of country and western mythology. The narrator talks of his "pain" (p. 12) and of his woman's infidelities, which are, of course, linked:

That role of barbed wire you put in my bed. Don't you realize I could have hurt myself, mistaking it for you? (p. 20)

Later he muses, "Mr. Bad is a lady" (p. 49). She plays the guitar, composes songs, drinks straight liquor, and "once broke horses" (p. 46). One section, titled "You Are My Country & Western, Lullaby," contains images of predators in a barren landscape. "There's a law against shade in that country. Trees are considered improper. Sometimes the cattle graze, for a whole week, in a mirage" (p. 49). The landscape as well as the lady are out to wound the narrator: "camouflaged button cactus" just waits for "the bare foot," while "barbed wire fences" wait to ensnare other parts of the anatomy (p. 49). Gophers are tracked by hawks; grasshoppers are flattened by the windshield; the narrator is victimized by the lady. He parodies his vulnerability: "a Greyhound bus, three half-tons, two galloping horses, a motorcycle gang and a woman in a convertible began to converge on the spot where I was standing with my back to the road" (p. 51). Comparing the lady to a hawk, he asks her about the tortures she inflicts: "Do your lovers dislike being staked to the ground, naked, that way?" (p. 52). The eighth entry of the section parodies the "Does your mama know?" country and western refrain, while the fifth entry is a "Cowboy's lament" about losing his lady. Earlier she jotted the names of her "truckdriver-lovers" (p. 16) on the narrator's paper plate, and he is attracted/seduced by this cruelty:

I want to explain why I like the country & western songs you compose in your sleep. She's a cheatin lyin woman / with a cheatin lyin song. / She's a cheatin lyin woman, / so I know we'll get along. (p. 57)

In *Excerpts from the Real World* one main intertext is thus the lyrics of country and western songs. "I can't forget you" (p. 55), he vows, and later, with perhaps the toughest of all country and western heroines in mind, he says: "Stockings like yours aren't made for walking" (p. 57). One reference interestingly also suggests the incomplete allusions in "The Sad Phoenician." One week he echoes, " 'But most of all I luv you cuz yr you' " (p. 29), while the next he merely says, "But most of all I love you" (p. 31). What is omitted here significantly is the sense of identity.

There are references to other sections of the continuing poem embedded here as well, and the sense of dialogue between the parts continues. "Everything recurs (more or less)" (p. 35), Kroetsch reminds us, and suggests both "The Winnipeg Zoo" and "Sounding the Name" when he says, "Once, years ago, watching a flock of ducks feeding in a slough, I fired my 12-gauge shotgun into a passing rainbow" (p. 22). During the deconstruction of his mother's death, which initiates the later sequence, the poet stands with his mother at a window, watching and naming ducks in a slough. That seems like "years ago" (p. 22) because the naming has altered so markedly, but it was a crucial moment of instruction. The moment in "The Winnipeg Zoo" when Audubon raises his gun to still the ducks is similarly illuminating, as the poet learns a sense of affirmation in the silence of his place. We also find in *Excerpts from the Real World* another silence and another lost poem:

> I go through the secondhand bookstores of Amsterdam, looking for a single remaining copy of my first book, the book I never wrote. It was a study of the silence of cucumbers. (p. 36)

Kroetsch still reads the sky, or tries to, as a form of notation, but is aware of the disjunction between *Excerpts from the Real World* and "The Frankfurt *Hauptbahnhof*": "These great flocks of birds, even now, practising their migration, must be a sign" (p. 52). Words continue to be broken up by line endings, and there is a lack of certainty: "Premonitions are, I would imagine, a form of hindsight" (p. 52). Divination, as in Kroetsch's previous poems and in Margaret Laurence's novel with a similar title, is still a future reading of the past:

> This is a poem I didn't write. And not because I wasn't writing. And not because it isn't a poem. I'm beside myself, purely as a way to anticipate the past. Endings have stems and blossoms. (p. 24)

The last line reminds us that Kroetsch's "endings" are generative and lead to new seedtimes/seektimes, fresh growth. The ambiguity of the cliché, "I'm beside myself," suggests the doubling nature of the persona shift, which is explained here as also being an attempt to find a notational form, as in "The Frankfurt *Hauptbahnhof*," which will in turn provide a reading for both the author and us. Kroetsch emphasizes the displacement of the narrator because it is so crucial: "*L'autre*. The author. I'm not myself today" (p. 15). Encountering one form of the double and being guided by him in "The Frankfurt *Hauptbahnhof*," the author stands by and observes here as another double takes over the writing. The previous autobiographical impetus is, at least for now, silenced: "I hadn't noticed the margin. . . . I fell off the page" (p. 21).

Enjoining us to read Lacan,[73] the poet reminds us of his concern with poetic delay, so eloquently linked to lovemaking in "For Play and Entrance": "Desire is that which stands outside the boundaries of satisfaction" (*ERW*, p. 15). In *Excerpts from the Real World* he continues the metaphorical link between poet and lover, as well as his "meta-poetic" concern with reflecting process in his lines. Fascinated by all the possibilities, all the rooms of the palace in Peking's Forbidden City left unexplored, all the possible word combinations left unuttered, Kroetsch recognizes that each sentence committed to paper lessens the number of possibilities remaining, and this is both alarming and reassuring: "Each entry, by its coming into existence, excludes itself from the potential of the poem. The spending lover both creates and fears the growing silence" (p. 13). We recall the poet of "Seed Catalogue" saying, "We silence words by writing them down" (*FN*, p. 63). And he here practises the various names for silence: "a goose egg," "zero," "naught" (p. 58). The labyrinth also manages to capture possibilities and is for Kroetsch a paradoxical way of making connections: "The net, too, is a container of sorts" (p. 14). As he has learned time and again, place is crucial to the naming. "Let place do the signing for us" (p. 39), he says. But he pokes fun at meaningless conventions as well:

> The hawk on the telephone pole, folding its wings like an angel at rest, is planning a gopher's visit to the blue sky. The grass-hoppers hit our windshield like hail. You raise your head from my lap, asking what the sound is. This is called writing a landscape poem. (p. 50)

While the major subliterary text in this book may be the country and western mode, others also surface. Kroetsch parodies the clichéd conventions of the Harlequin romance (p. 44) and quotes a "Gimli Proverb" (p. 45). The "awe-ful" punning continues here also: "Praxis makes perfect, you tell me. But I'm Dedalus on my feet" (p. 45).

As in previous sections of the continuing poem, there is a dense patterning of recurring images: strawberries, hooks, hawks, rainbows, and butterflies. Doors and gates also recur, for they can shut off possibilities or open them up. You go through doors to move to other places: "Doors, in a manner of speaking, are descriptive. Otherwise we wouldn't be here now" (p. 13). Doors capture both contradiction and musical refrain: "Close the door and let me in" (p. 39), the poet demands. "Gates are inclined to swing both ways" (p. 45), he reminds us, relishing the ambiguity encoded in the image, as well as the possibility for disjunction: "The gate is off its hinges" (p. 78), he later says. The poem is also structured as a search for a unicorn. The first pages are full of references. "My life is a portrait of the woman who deceived me into hunting for the unicorn" (p. 12), he declares. And again: "I should not have sought the unicorn beside the sea" (p. 13). Perhaps as a mythical beast, the unicorn should be sought in mythical places, and this proves true. The unicorn has ambivalent implications, both good and evil. Despite the suggestiveness of its single horn, it represents chastity and "inner creative power in contrast with the phallus" (Chetwynd, p. 412). The unicorn is also associated with the repeated rainbows, as it is either white or many-coloured: "It is the principle which unites the spectrum . . . all the colours of the rainbow" (Chetwynd, p. 412). From a psychological point of view, the lady and the unicorn represent

> . . . the relationship between the feminine soul, or Anima, of man, and the spirit or self. As the story goes, the soul cannot capture the essence of life, or realize its inner unity, by running hectically from activity to activity, but only by sitting quietly, which is how the lady Anima catches the unicorn. This refers to what can only be achieved by passiveness, openness, receptivity in the inner world. (Chetwynd, p. 413)

Openness and receptivity, if not passivity, are the way of a Kroetsch poem. On his search the poet discovers a significant painting in the

"Rijksmuseum. 'Wild man on a unicorn with a bird.'" This he recognizes as a "self portrait with still life" (p. 36). The poem closes with a shadowed sighting of the unicorn. Earlier he tells his lady, "yours are the unicorn's buttocks. I recognized that, the first time you knelt to my whisper" (p. 21). On the last pages, in the suitably mythical setting of Babylon, the poet confronts Ishtar in her lair and echoes these images with an interesting reversal. In the Baghdad bazaar copper-smiths pound metal "into the roundness of your buttocks" (p. 77), while the next day in Babylon the poet finds a "bas-relief" of Ishtar and says, "I put my mouth to your bum" (p. 78). But he is now the one who kneels:

> . . . I went down onto my knees. You put your hand to the back of my neck. The water buffalo, grazing at the edge of the river, lifting its head to your long moan, looked vaguely like a unicorn. (p. 78)

As we shall see, this confrontation with Ishtar and the sighting of the unicorn bring the search and the poem to another change. Earlier the poet had wondered, "What if, for instance, we replaced the unicorn with the common mallard or the garter snake?" (p. 14). This would be turning the search into one for something familiar, of his own place. The "common mallard" is one of the ducks his mother taught him to name, while the garter snake is the familiar form of the serpent, related to woman and her temptation of man.[74] And this search began as a deception of the poet by woman. It is fitting that the search succeeds through the intervention of a mother goddess and through the transformation of an animal symbolizing here submissiveness, patience, and labour.

Ishtar is, ironically, associated with another repeated image: the angels that hover over the pages of *Excerpts from the Real World* that Kroetsch says he borrowed from Rilke,[75] as did Bowering in his *Kerrisdale Elegies*.[76] There are angels on the frozen prairies (p. 19), "becoming scarcer" "with the loss of their natural habitat" (p. 28). Hawks are likened to angels (p. 50), and so are country and western singers and solitaries: "Country singers and misanthropes get to sit on the clouds" (p. 66). The angel of the *Duino Elegies*, as Rilke explained, "is that creature in whom the transformation of the visible into the invisible . . . appears as already accomplished."[77] Significantly, in relation to the "crying" persona of *Excerpts from the Real*

World, Rilke's elegies begin, "Who, if I cried, would hear me from the order / of Angels?"[78] But the angel for Rilke "brings terror,"[79] and contact would destroy the individual. "The 'angel' of the elegies," Rilke has said, "has nothing to do with the angel of the Christian heaven (more perhaps with the angel figures of Islam). . . ."[80] Perhaps in Kroetsch's interpretation the angel has something to do with an earlier female deity of the same area, who in *Excerpts from the Real World* does "destroy" the persona by bringing the poem to an "end."

The meeting with Ishtar in the last pages closes the poem, as there is no way for the poet to get past her. One is led to speculate that meetings with powerful female forces, here, as in "Sounding the Name" and "The Poet's Mother," force Kroetsch's poem to pause. Earlier in *Excerpts from the Real World*, Kroetsch parodied Hammurabi, the Babylonian king who codified laws allegedly given to him by the god, Shamash. In Kroetsch's poem Hammurabi appears as a used car salesman on the "Pembina strip" in Winnipeg, "Hammer Happy" or "the Shyster King of Babble On" (p. 35) In this the fourth part of his "prose poem in ten parts," Kroetsch makes fiction out of Babylonian lore, while in the tenth part the real world actually intrudes and cuts off the excerpts. Kroetsch and his persona go to Iraq, and they visit the remains of Hammurabi's Babylon, but it is Ishtar's city of Babylon that they discover. The world plays a trick on the poet, and he discovers that Ishtar is a presence with whom to reckon. She was a "fertility and mother goddess who represented the planet Venus personified. Her symbol was a star."[81] Thus, in more ways than those already noted, the "envoi (to begin with)" from the last page of *Advice to My Friends* is prophetic. It divines Ishtar and the close of the next book, when it states: "Why not, then, / let the stars / shine in our bones?" ("The Poet's Mother," in *AMF*, p. 143). Ishtar's star *does* shine in the last pages of *Excerpts from the Real World*. Legend also relates that when Ishtar was spurned by Gilgamesh, she sent a bull against him. The poet was perhaps lucky that all he meets here is a "water buffalo . . . [that] looked vaguely like a unicorn" (p. 78). Still, it does defeat him in a way, for he cannot continue this poetic line. *Excerpts from the Real World* is dedicated, in part, to Ishtar, and the epigraphic lines from *The Missing Book of Cucumbers* reveal what happens with the poet's mother and with Ishtar: "Perhaps if I call you forever you'll hear me toward the end" (p. [7]). As his poems are a calling after his mother and here a drawing towards the "mother goddess," when they hear him, it is "toward the end," and the poem must change.

A clue to the next direction the continuing poem will take is found in another of the recurring image patterns of *Excerpts from the Real World*, the shoreline sea creatures. In the first part, the lady cooks dinner for the narrator — scallops. Her hair in lovemaking "spills down [her] back . . . like seaweed in the Bay of Fundy" (p. 13). In the third part, they eat oysters "on the coast" and make love "in the seaweed on the shore of [her] bed" (p. 27). The poet is prompted to muse, "Your body is so smooth when you sleep, lobsters, moving along the ocean floor, bruise the water to a rougher sheen" (p. 27). And in the second to last part, they again eat scallops. Two aspects are significant here, the nature of the creatures (shellfish) and their habitat (the meeting place of land and sea). Shells have several symbolic meanings. They are associated with water and fertility, related to woman in general and Venus in particular. They are also the symbolic attribute of the pilgrim, and this "idea is cognate with that of the labyrinth: to go on a pilgrimage is to come to understand the nature of the labyrinth . . ." (Cirlot, p. 255). "The shell is [also] the mystic symbol of the prosperity of one generation rising out of the death of the preceding generation" (Cirlot, p. 294), as Kroetsch's poetic creativity rises out of, or circles around, the death of his mother.

The sea is also a significant location, as was apparent in "How I Joined the Seal Herd." "The waters of the oceans are . . . seen not only as the source of life but also as its goal. 'To return to the sea' is 'to return to the mother' . . ." (Cirlot, p. 281) — the return that for Kroetsch signalled a new direction after *Advice to My Friends*. But Kroetsch always seeks to acknowledge sources without giving in to them completely, so he explores here the boundary world of the shoreline, where opposites meet, the place where the exciting work/creation is going on. In an attempt to work out the difficult confrontation with the strong female figure, mother or Ishtar, and discover the next direction of his continuing poem, he seeks the tension the shoreline offers. It is the contradictions again which excite, not the balance of binaries.

"Spending the Morning on the Beach — Ten Related Lyrics" was first published along with a 1986 reissue of "Seed Catalogue."[82] It is, on the one hand, a furthering of the exploration of origins, here the primary one, where our species came from; while on the other hand, it is a furthering of the exploration of the borderland, here the marginal world of the beach. It is a "morning" reverie, a new start, but it is also a continuation of the "lifelong poem." Because of the relatedness here (of the lyrics themselves, of man to source, and of poet to reader), the poet is able to step back and consider his poem. He acknowledges the end to which *Excerpts from the Real World* came, when the real world intruded and prevented a furthering of the fictional: "I can no longer keep a journal" (*SC*, p. 31), he explains before beginning the most recent section of the continuing poem. "My life erases everything I write" (p. 31). He is at a crucial point. The autobiographical thrust is written out. The journal of the fictional persona reaches erasure. Where should he turn now? "Realizing the poem for him has lost its expectancy" (p. 33), he sets out on a pilgrimage, a quest, further west, but now also further south. He establishes a new relationship (relatedness) with the reader, aligning himself with us to observe the poem. He quotes from George Bowering's *Burning Water* to explain:

> We all live in the same world's sea. We cannot tell a story that leaves us outside, and when I say we, I include you. But in order to include you, I feel that I cannot spend these pages saying *I* to a second person. Therefore let us say *he*, and stand together looking at them. (p. 31)

So instead of the earlier encoding of the reader as you, the persona becomes "he," while poet and reader become the concomitant "we."

As well as signifying the origins of man (the beach) and the origins of the day (morning), this new section also suggests Kroetsch's poetic origins (the lyric). One answer after Kroetsch has written of his mother's death and confronted the "mother goddess" is a return to the lyric impetus, the maternal song of "Seed Catalogue," and hence the publication of "Spending the Morning on the Beach" with a reissue of "Seed Catalogue." The lyric impulse can be explored now that the poet has found the words to express the unsayable. "Seed Catalogue" ended with a drowning, and so it is also appropriate that "Spending the Morning on the Beach" should return to the shoreline. One previous problem with the lyric, found in "Seed Catalogue" and articulated in "For Play and Entrance," was the lyric's "ferocious principles of closure" (*RK*, p. 92). The solution here is in "relating" the lyrics to delay or prevent closure. And "relatedness" also suggests the poetic questions that are explored in this section of the lifelong poem. How does poetry relate to the world? What is the relation of word to world, signifier to signified? Not a one-to-one relationship, surely. Think of the contraries always in Kroetsch's poetry, the doubling, punning, parodying, intertextuality. Think of what Mandel calls "duplicity": poets as "divided men seeking to make themselves whole" ("Writing West: On the Road to Wood Mountain," in *AT*, p. 77).

"Spending the Morning on the Beach" consists of ten lyrics, related by their common beach locations and their titles, which all refer to places from Kroetsch's trip to Australia and New Zealand: "Fiji," "Brisbane," "Geelong, Victoria," "Rotorua," and so on. Travel becomes a metaphor for writing and the problems encountered:

> Somewhere in his recent flying is a lost day. Words are like that.
> Once upon a time he was a gardener of the possible fruition.
> (p. 33)

Poems, as we have seen, can be "lost," in their refusal to be written, or the poet's refusal to write them. But the loss, or silence, can also lead to further expression, as here the loss of one day can be made up on the return journey with "doubled" hours. The reference to the poet as "gardener" further serves to link this opening lyric of "Spending the Morning on the Beach" with the preceding reprint of "Seed Catalogue." Throughout these lyrics the poet seeks to experience the exotic vegetation as a means of understanding his situation: ". . . he drinks the juice of passion fruit, he eats papaya and a thin slice of fresh pineapple . . ." (p. 33). He "visit[s] an avocado farm," "breaks in two a custard apple" to examine and eat the seeds, and observes the growth cycle of bananas. He "hike[s] into the native forest" (p. 35). In a garden he notes "fig, lemon, peach, pomegranate, pear, apricot, lime, apple, kiwi, passion fruit and feijoa" (p. 37), an abundance of actual fruition against which is balanced the poet's difficulties. He is "beached," so to speak, "high and dry" (p. 41).

The lyrics are even related at the grammatical level, by a syntactical repetition, similar to that found in "Seed Catalogue." In the earlier poem, the lines were linked by the repeated "How do you grow . . . ?" question, which began the poetic quest and led to the shoreline transformation of "How I Joined the Seal Herd." In the most recent lyrics, the poet is once again at the shoreline, and the lyrics repeat a series of "realizations" expressed as participial constructions:

Realizing the poem for him has lost its expectancy, he heads directly for Fiji. (p. 33)

Realizing he's no longer obliged by the ache in his body to write poems, he watches the grasstrees burning free of their dead leaves. (p. 34)

Realizing the poem is the tormentor of his sleep, he strangles it by his refusal, in the hot sunlight, to close his eyes. (p. 35)

Realizing *poetry* is a mousetrap on the tongue, he calls ashore for water. (p. 36)

Realizing he cannot foil his own inertia, he steals a pomegranate. (p. 37)

Realizing that light, not dark, is the poet's affliction, he gives himself the Governor General's Award For Not Writing Poetry for the year 1999. (p. 38)

Realizing he is done with poetry, he goes to a museum to see a reconstruction of an extinct New Zealand bird, a bird that was flightless, huge, possibly the largest bird (height to 12 feet) that ever lived, the Giant Moa. Now how's that for self-pity? (p. 40)

Realizing that poetry is a hospital for the sane, he watches the Maoris building their replica village. (p. 41)

Realizing the poem is a cruising shark, he curls his toes in the mud. (p. 43)

There are two syntactical exceptions to this rule of "realizing." In the fifth lyric, Kroetsch clearly associates realization with the creating of poetry. As in "The Winnipeg Zoo," he suggests that he can write himself into an understanding of his "inertia": "Realizing the poem. Talking the poem onto the page or writing the poem onto the tongue" (p. 37). This precedes the passage savouring the variety of fruit that can also be experienced by the poet's tongue. The lyric "ends": "Spitting out the seeds, into the water, is half the fun" (p. 37), a planting of the possibilities in the imagination. The other syntactical exception is in the second to last lyric, in which the poet and a friend find themselves locked in a park after closing. The keeper, an old woman, challenges them: "You didn't read the sign, did you?" To which the poet acknowledges: "I realize that" (p. 42). The signs given (whether they be a flock of crows or an oracle's voice) must be read in order to prevent closure. Here the poet "realizes" the implications.

Reading the related syntactical structure, we find that, with no immediate poetic prospects, the poet "heads directly" for the beach. Paradoxically, when he is "at sea," he "calls ashore for water," or imaginative inspiration. During his voyage he encounters a doubling experience, a "replica village." (A replica always presupposes an original, an-other.) In the last lyric, "he curls his toes in the mud," in ancient myth the source of man. Here, the willingness to experience the childish pleasures of mud oozing between the toes suggests at least a partial victory over the earlier "inertia." Mud is

> the basic material which life moulds and shapes to its requirements. Inertia, transformed into the VESSEL.

> The great secret of Nature, and therefore the great search of man is to discover the relationship of life and matter. Which within the psyche is the attempt to relate Intuition, and the highest FUNCTIONS of the mind, with the senses . . . . Mud is the malleable substance of our being, full of potential for growth and TRANSFORMATION. (Chetwynd, p. 273)

Thus, mud again signals a new genesis at the "end" of a section. The actual final words are, "Sighting two dolphins, just out from shore, rising and gracefully diving, he hurries into the water" (p. 43). Once again, he plunges into the watery world of the imagination, promising a continuation from this exploration. Significantly, the dolphin "is the womb animal of the sea" (Chetwynd, p. 19), and as such can represent rebirth. "The dolphin . . . is an allegory of salvation, . . . the friend of man" (Cirlot, p. 85). Such is the propitious closing of the penultimate section of the ongoing poem.

Before reaching this point, however, the lyrics reflect the working out of the poetic and aesthetic problems engendered by the "endings" of *Advice to My Friends* and *Excerpts from the Real World*. Kroetsch reviews some of the possibilities:

The poem as evasion.
The poem as resignation.
The poem as a net
that drowns fish.
The poem as a postcard
sent directly to the sun.
The poem as POET TREE.

(p. 40)

The ambivalent tree that remained distant at the end of "The Sad Phoenician" is here rooted and waiting for poet and reader. As Earle Birney suggests, "poettrees . . just need me   & maybe you."[83] In Kroetsch's poem, poet and reader stand together. The "tree" bears fruit.

But the first lyric of the series finds the poet in a state of eclipse: "Nadi is dark to his landing" (p. 33). Travelling to the southern hemisphere unbalances his expectations, but such defamiliarization has in the past proved fruitful: "The Southern Cross signals the upset world. Even westward is lost in east. We are not where we were" (p. 33). "It is early winter, a morning in May" (p. 36). He begins by tasting the fruit and recalling "Odysseus, somewhere on a beach, hiding his nakedness yet keeping it available" (p. 34). Nakedness becomes a metaphor for poetic readiness and the poet heads for a nude beach. His companion, another poet (Douglas Barbour), "learns the semiotics of nakedness," while Kroetsch here demonstrates:

It's a matter of knowing when to look and when not to look.

The mathematics of the gaze; angle and tangent and the theory of the line. (p. 36)

The line here in the lyric paradoxically becomes the prose line, and the spaces on the page dramatically set off these lines. The sentence is still the generative, compositional unit. The poet begins to formulate an aesthetic regarding the "signified" as well, for the question has now become not only "*how* do you write?" but also "*what* do you write about?" There are conventions about subject matter, just as there are conventions about style and language. "The slide (the sly) of metonymy" (p. 36) provides a "how," while the poet writes himself into the "what." In his essay "On Being an Alberta Writer," he says, ". . . we talk ourselves into existence" (*RK*, p. 75); in his poetry he often writes himself and his poem into existence. The beach here provides a sign for the poet to read: "Brian foretells the future by riding a surfboard along the edge of a hurricane" (p. 37). There is a certain danger that is stimulating. "There are sharks in these waters, . . . but not so many as on land" (p. 43). Again, the divination of the possible future is found in the notation of surroundings: "Each surfer is a small miracle of stillness and motion. Each surfer slips down a rising wave, then disappears into a bed of foam" (p. 35). Poetically, Kroetsch must also experience this tension, the contraries of "stillness and motion," to clarify his vision: "He is somewhere under the failed wave. The sand scours his eyes. He hardly bothers to hold his breath" (p. 36). Surfacing, the poet continues his search: at an "art show, ORIGINS ORIGINALITY + BEYOND" (p. 38), at the already-mentioned museum in New Zealand, and at a Maori building display. As did the gallery in *Excerpts from the Real World*, the gallery here provides a significant reading for the poet, but whereas at the Rijksmuseum the poet discovered a painting that served as a mirror for his condition, here he encodes his own work in the catalogue: "Anon, Canada, 1927, SELF-PORTRAIT OF POET or / THROWING IN THE TOWEL, EH?" (p. 39). Several of the paintings on display are suggestive: "TIME TO CHANGE THE GREEK HERO," "MEMORIES OF COLUMBUS' FRIEND," "THE SIXTY-THREE RICE MEALS FOR A STONE," "DEUTSCHER MANN SUCHT WAS," "(LOOKING AT ONESELF IN A HEAVENLY MIRROR)," "THE BOOK'S PARTHENON," and "YOUNG MAN WITH FRUITS." As the show's title suggests, these pictures take the poet "beyond" origins.

Birds again serve as messengers in "Spending the Morning on the Beach" and begin to provide a way "to see" these pictures:

Orpheus, nothing, says the parakeet.

Orifice.

If the carved boat floats in a sheltered pool, and the iconic face bites its defiant tongue, then we have come to see the picture. (p. 41)

Suggesting previous models, previous poems, previous notations, previous forms, the poet does begin to resolve his vision of the "self portrait . . . [the] found object, given a name by another" (p. 36). The double leads to the naming, while the silence is again revelatory. The "new mouth" ("Pumpkin: A Love Poem," in *SHP*, p. 27), "the orifice of love, open" ("The Sad Phoenician," in *FN*, p. 91), and the "nesting tongue" ("The Criminal Intensities of Love as Paradise," in *FN*, p. 144), with the clichéd suggestion, learn again the possibility of quiet and the promise of future lines. What follows is the realization of the need to read signs, the experience of the mud, and the plunge "into the water" (*SC*, p. 43).

The exploration of "the imagined real place" ("The Continuing Poem," in *RK*, p. 81), which first fuelled the move to poetry for Kroetsch and was perhaps best exemplified in "Seed Catalogue," is expanded here in the awareness of place, and the "dream of origins" gathers a renewed importance through the multiple levels of relatedness at work (or play) in the poem. There is a return to the autobiographical mode as well, but again from a renewed perspective. "The self-portrait is a found object, signed by yours truly . . ." (*SC*, p. 36). The "realizations" note the personal aesthetic concerns, here applied to an area outside the personal mythology of the poet. He is beginning to travel in and taste new and more exotic regions. Previously there has been a displacement of form and language, now the displacement of the poet is emphasized. Wah, in his "Making Strange Poetics," quotes from Viktor Shklovsky:

> And art exists that one may recover the sensation of life; it exists to make one feel things, to make the stone *stony*. The purpose of art is to impart the sensation of things as they are perceived and not as they are known. The technique of art is to make objects "unfamiliar," to make forms difficult, to increase the difficulty and length of perception because the process of perception is an aesthetic end in itself and must be prolonged. Art is a way of experiencing the artfulness of an object; the object is not important.[84]

So, by recording the phenomena of his sensual perception of his surroundings, particularly symbolized by the tongue's awareness of fruit and seeds, the poet "recover[s] the sensation of life." The tongue, bitten, does prolong the experience and also suggests the difficulties of a Kroetsch poem, the work to which the reader is put. The next section of the continuing poem, then, would be, as well as a continuation, a further expansion. The loss of "expectancy," because it is unsettling and unfamiliar, is exciting and excites. This is one more deconstruction, one more silence, to transform.

And transformation thus continues to signify both the necessary open-endedness and the continuity of Kroetsch's poem. It is a variable image in itself, suggesting the processes Kroetsch explores (fragmentation, disjunction, duplicity, parody, play, intertextuality), as well as reflecting Kroetsch's ideas of autobiography, influence, and recurring patterns. It satisfies the desire to discover growth and continuity in Kroetsch's work, while at the same time recognizing his own resistance to categorization, closure, or conclusion. He provides the solution himself when he suggests that one way "to avoid both meaning and conclusiveness" is to "keep transforming the story" (*LV*, p. 130), as we have seen he does from one section of his continuing poem to another. "It is the old trick of Proteus or the trickster figure" (*LV*, pp. 130–31), he suggests in conversation, and demonstrates in his poetry: Proteus — the archetypal transformational symbol, the prophetic old man of the sea who tended the sea god's flocks of seals. Hovering on the borders of sea and land, he could slip from one world to the other. Owning the gift of divination, he was supposed to prophesy the future for any who could catch him asleep in the rocky shade of the shore. As soon as one reached out for him, however, he would repeatedly transform himself to escape the necessity of prophecy. Upon realizing he could not escape, he would assume his usual form and speak the future, truthfully. Not only is this a parable for the poet in "How I Joined the Seal Herd," acting out the transformation from seal-tender to seal, but it suggests the practice of the continuing poem: the slippery poet not often caught dozing, shifting shape at will, encoding the signs of futurity for himself and us, providing a way of reading, but no final answers. Speaking, above all, when held and read carefully, the truth.

And the truth Kroetsch presents leads to a renewed understanding. As he says, ". . . to understand ourselves becomes impossible if we do not see images of ourselves in the mirror . . ." ("On Being an Alberta Writer," in *RK*, p. 75), as he does in the opening of "How I Joined the Seal Herd," thus discovering "the first / clue" (*FN*, p. 71), and later in the art galleries included in *Excerpts from the Real World* and "Spending the Morning on the Beach." The "mirror" for Kroetsch can mirror "theatre or literature or historical writing" ("On Being . . . ," p. 75) or the continuing poem written by himself, which presents images, images of self and other, through which *we* can also begin to know ourselves. And images of Kroetsch are images of the poet searching "for home and therefore [searching] for the self," as well as for his poetic form and language:

> According to Levi-Strauss, the image keeps a future place open for ideas not yet present. It exists then in the realm of possibilities. Perhaps that is why the artist always moves between the end toward which he is impelled and the beginning where all was foretold. (Mandel, "Images of Prairie Man," in *AT*, p. 52)

Perhaps that is why a poet like Kroetsch transforms the primary, the nonliterary, documents of his place and the subliterary documents of his time, and wanders the world seeking his roots in life and art, acting out the patterns of his people. Perhaps that is why Kroetsch explores and embodies tension and doubleness throughout. If definition for Canadians comes in voicing the question rather than providing any final answers as Kroetsch suggests, then his poetry lives out the "life of shifting edges" and begins to frame the "unspoken or unspeakable question" in the incomplete or uncompletable lines ("Disunity as Unity," pp. 9–10), the biting of the "defiant tongue" ("Spending the Morning on the Beach," in *SC*, p. 41). The strength of Kroetsch's poetry is evident in his sensitivity to the possibilities inherent in language, form, process. The dialogue continues: poet to family, poet to reader, poet to other poets, and poem to poem. Once again hovering on the borders of land and sea, the poet "hurries into the water," ready to shoulder the foam and plunge beneath the waves to surface again with possible lines.

Thus, it is false to "conclude" a consideration of Kroetsch's poetry at this stage. Not only is closure alien to his writing, but also as I write these last words of mine here, and as you, *my* reader, read them, further words of Kroetsch's continuing poem are being imagined, written, published, for us, *his* readers, to read.

And so it continues . . .

NOTES

* This manuscript was completed and submitted in 1986. Ann Munton died in September 1990, before she was able to read and revise the proofs. Carole Gerson and Laurie Ricou, who read the page proofs, have decided that the absence of commentary on the last section of *Completed Field Notes*, "After Paradise," which Ann was not able to include, should stand.

¹ "Seed Catalogue," in *Field Notes 1–8: A Continuing Poem* (Don Mills, Ont.: General, 1981), p. 56. All further references to this work (*FN*) appear in the text.

² Robert Kroetsch, "Taking the Risk," in *Robert Kroetsch: Essays*, ed. Frank Davey and bpNichol [*Open Letter*, 5th ser., No. 4 (Spring 1983)], p. 65. All further references to this collection (*RK*) appear in the text.

³ Robert Kroetsch, *The Crow Journals* (Edmonton: NeWest, 1980), p. 37.

⁴ Robert Kroetsch, "Mile Zero," in *Advice to My Friends* (Don Mills, Ont.: Stoddart, 1985), p. 36. All further references to this work (*AMF*) appear in the text.

⁵ Brian MacKinnon, " 'The Writer Has Got to Know Where He Lives': An Interview with Robert Kroetsch," *Writers News Manitoba*, 4, No. 1 (Feb. 1982), p. 3. All further references to this work (MacKinnon) appear in the text.

⁶ Geoff Hancock, "An Interview with Robert Kroetsch," *Canadian Fiction Magazine*, Nos. 24–25 (Spring–Summer 1977), p. 36. All further references to this work (Hancock) appear in the text.

⁷ Shirley Neuman and Robert Wilson, *Labyrinths of Voice: Conversations with Robert Kroetsch* (Edmonton: NeWest, 1982), p. 21. All further references to this work (*LV*) appear in the text.

⁸ Robert Kroetsch, "A Conversation with Margaret Laurence," in Robert Kroetsch, James Bacque, and Pierre Gravel, *creation*, ed. Robert Kroetsch (Toronto: new, 1970), p. 62. All further references to this work ("A Conversation . . .") appear in the text.

⁹ Eli Mandel, "Images of Prairie Man," in *Another Time*, Three Solitudes: Contemporary Literary Criticism in Canada, III (Erin, Ont.: Porcépic, 1977), p. 50. All further references to this work (*AT*) appear in the text.

¹⁰ Shirley Neuman, "Allow Self, Portraying Self: Autobiography in *Field Notes*," *Line*, No. 2 (Fall 1983), pp. 104–21; "Figuring the Reader, Figuring the Self in *Field Notes*: 'Double or Noting,' " *Open Letter* [Robert Kroetsch: Reflections], 5th ser., Nos. 8–9 (Summer–Fall 1984), pp. 176–94. All further references to the latter work ("Figuring") appear in the text.

¹¹ Kroetsch, *The Crow Journals*, p. 56.

¹² Russell M. Brown, "An Interview with Robert Kroetsch," *University of*

Windsor Review, 7, No. 2 (Spring 1972), 2. All further references to this work (Brown, "Interview") appear in the text.

[13] Harold Bloom, *The Anxiety of Influence: A Theory of Poetry* (New York: Oxford Univ. Press, 1973).

[14] Julia Kristeva, French feminist philosopher and critic, is generally recognized as having pioneered the concept of intertextuality. Jonathan Culler defines intertextuality in a way that sheds light on Kroetsch's poetry:

"Intertextuality" . . . has a double focus. On the one hand, it calls our attention to the importance of prior texts, insisting that the autonomy of texts is a misleading notion and that a work has the meaning it does only because certain things have previously been written. Yet in so far as it focuses on intelligibility, on meaning, "intertextuality" leads us to consider prior texts as contributions to a code which makes possible the various effects of signification. Intertextuality thus becomes less a name for a work's relation to particular prior texts than a designation of its participation in the discursive space of a culture: the relationship between a text and the various languages or signifying practices of a culture and its relation to those texts which articulate for it the possibilities of that culture. (*The Pursuit of Signs: Semiotics, Literature, Deconstruction* [Ithaca, N.Y.: Cornell Univ. Press, 1981], p. 103)

[15] Josué V. Harari, "Critical Factions/Critical Fictions," in *Textual Strategies: Perspectives in Post-Structuralist Criticism*, ed. Josué V. Harari (Ithaca, N.Y.: Cornell Univ. Press, 1979), pp. 36–37.

[16] Harari, p. 36.

[17] Statement at a reading in Vancouver, 8 July 1986.

[18] Charles Olson, "Projective Verse," in *Human Universe and Other Essays*, ed. Donald Allen (New York: Grove, 1967), pp. 52, 51.

[19] This is only one obvious meaning of the title; others are discussed in the "Works" section.

[20] Olson, p. 56.

[21] Throughout *Another Time*, for example, Mandel uses "duplicity" in his definition of the "state of mind" that defines the Western writer, a state of mind that "has a good deal to do with a tension between place and culture, a doubleness or duplicity, that makes the writer a man not so much in place, as out of place and so one endlessly trying to get back, to find his way home, to return, to write himself into existence, writing west" (p. 69).

[22] See Fred Wah, "Music at the Heart of Thinking," *Open Letter*, 5th ser., No. 7 (Spring 1984), 33–39; "Making Strange Poetics," *Open Letter* [Long-Liners Conference Issue], 6th ser., Nos. 2–3 (Summer–Fall 1985), 213–21.

[23] Douglas Barbour, rev. of *Seed Catalogue*, in "Poetry Chronicle v," *Dalhousie Review*, 58 (Spring 1978), 164.

[24] Beth Popham, rev. of *Seed Catalogue*, by Robert Kroetsch, and three other books, *Quarry*, 27, No. 2 (Spring 1978), 87.

[25] David Carpenter, "Stone Chipped and Hammered," rev. of *The Stone Hammer Poems: 1960–1975*, CV/II, 2, No. 2 (May 1976), 39.

[26] Howard Engel, "Prose-flawed Poems," rev. of *The Stone Hammer Poems: 1960–1975*, *The Canadian Forum*, Oct. 1976, p. 33.

[27] David S. West, "Wrestling the Alpha-Bet Beast," rev. of *The Sad Phoenician*, *Canadian Literature*, No. 91 (Winter 1981), p. 124.

[28] Joseph A. Lipari, rev. of *Field Notes*, *Library Journal*, 1 Oct. 1981, p. 1930.

[29] Lesley Choyce, "From Bath to Verse," rev. of *Advice to My Friends*, *Books in Canada*, Jan. 1986, p. 30.

[30] Bruce Whiteman, "Some Books of Canadian Poetry in 1981," rev. of *Field Notes*, by Robert Kroetsch, and five other books, *Journal of Canadian Studies*, 17, No. 2 (Summer 1982), 152.

[31] Albert Moritz, "Scaffolds in Chaos," rev. of *Field Notes*, *Books in Canada*, Dec. 1981, p. 21.

[32] Jon Kertzer, rev. of *Field Notes*, by Robert Kroetsch, and *Robert Kroetsch*, by Peter Thomas, *The Fiddlehead*, No. 132 (April 1982), p. 116.

[33] Peter Thomas, *Robert Kroetsch*, Studies in Canadian Literature, No. 13 (Vancouver: Douglas & McIntyre, 1980), pp. 31–32.

[34] Robert Lecker, *Robert Kroetsch*, Twayne's World Authors Series, No. 768 (Boston: Twayne, 1986), p. 4. All further references to this work (Lecker) appear in the text.

[35] Diane Bessai, "Death Is a Happy Ending: A Dialogue in Thirteen Parts," in *Figures in a Ground: Canadian Essays on Modern Literature Collected in Honor of Sheila Watson*, ed. Diane Bessai and David Jackel (Saskatoon: Western Producer Prairie Books, 1978), p. 208.

[36] Donald Cameron, "Robert Kroetsch: The American Experience and the Canadian Voice," in *Conversations with Canadian Novelists* (Toronto: Macmillan, 1973), p. 84. All further references to this work (Cameron) appear in the text.

[37] Robert Enright and Dennis Cooley, "Uncovering Our Dream World: An Interview with Robert Kroetsch," *Essays on Canadian Writing*, Nos. 18–19 (Summer–Fall 1980), p. 25. All further references to this work (Enright and Cooley) appear in the text.

[38] *Open Letter* [Long-Liners Conference Issue], 6th ser., Nos. 2–3 (Summer–Fall 1985), 261.

[39] Neuman, "Allow Self, Portraying Self," p. 107.

[40] Introd., *Poets of the Confederation*, ed. Malcolm Ross (Toronto: McClelland and Stewart, 1960), p. xi.

[41] Northrop Frye, "Conclusion to a *Literary History of Canada*," in *The Bush Garden* (Toronto: House of Anansi, 1971), p. 218.

[42] Frye, p. 219.

[43] A.J.M. Smith, *Towards a View of Canadian Letters: Selected Critical Essays, 1928–1971* (Vancouver: Univ. of British Columbia Press, 1973).

[44] Bessai, p. 215.

[45] "Disunity as Unity: A Canadian Strategy," in *Canadian Story and History 1885–1985*, ed. Colin Nicholson and Peter Easingwood (Edinburgh: Edinburgh Univ. Centre of Canadian Studies [1985]), p. 3. All further references to this work appear in the text.

[46] Eli Mandel, "Auschwitz and Poetry," in *The Family Romance* (Winnipeg: Turnstone, 1986), p. 3.

[47] See Thomas, *Robert Kroetsch*, pp. 16–32, for a further discussion of this image pattern in Kroetsch's poetry.

[48] In *The Stone Hammer Poems: 1960–1975*, 2nd ed. (Lantzville, B.C.: Oolichan, 1976), p. 31. All further references to this work (*SHP*) appear in the text.

[49] Kroetsch, who has experimented with the possibilities of the three-line stanza, credits Williams and Stevens:

When they got to the three-line stanza they made incredible changes in their work. I'll offend some of my friends when I say the three-line stanza changed them. They want it to be life that changed people. That's not true, it's the three-line stanza that did it. In something as simple as letting go of your left-hand margin the implications for what is ultimately vision are just staggering, they really are. (Enright and Cooley, p. 27)

[50] Thomas, *Robert Kroetsch*, p. 28.

[51] Russell Brown, "Seeds and Stones: Unhiding in Kroetsch's Poetry," in *Open Letter* [Robert Kroetsch: Reflections], 5th ser., Nos. 8–9 (Summer–Fall 1984), 162.

[52] Patricia Keeney Smith, "WQ Interview with Robert Kroetsch," *Cross-Canada Writers' Quarterly*, 6, No. 3 (1984), 5. All further references to this work (Keeney Smith) appear in the text.

[53] These and the following quotations are taken from the back cover of the original edition of *The Sad Phoenician* (Toronto: Coach House, 1979).

[54] Smaro Kamboureli, "A Poem *out of* Love: An Interview with Robert Kroetsch on *The Sad Phoenician*," *Open Letter* [Robert Kroetsch: Reflections], 5th ser., Nos. 8–9 (Summer–Fall 1984), 47. All further references to this work

(Kamboureli) appear in the text.

55 Spenser, as the author of the longest major poem in English, is an obvious poet for Kroetsch to play off against here. Like Kroetsch, Spenser was aware of past traditions and used them (in Spenser's case, for example, the epic form and Chaucer's language) but was also innovative and exploited traditional forms for new possibilities. He was a playful poet with words, as is Kroetsch, inventing new words, making puns, posing riddles, and using ambiguous syntax. He turned back to the classics for language and then reinvented it. The quest motif, important in Kroetsch's work, is also central to the *Faerie Queen*. The question of conduct is crucial to both; for Spenser, the conduct of the gentleman, while for Kroetsch, the conduct of the lover and poet. Kroetsch acknowledges, "I actually used Spenser when I wrote *The Sad Phoenician*. There are a couple of hidden references to Spenser" (*LV*, p. 101). Perhaps Kroetsch is referring to Una and her dwarf in the *Faerie Queen* when he says, "I am a dwarf to her needments, I lug / them, after, uphill" (*FN*, p. 87). This echoes Spenser:

> Behind her farre away a Dwarfe did lag,
> That lasie seemd in being ever last,
> Or wearied with bearing of her bag
> Of needments at his backe. . . .
>
> (1.i.6)

And when Kroetsch says, ". . . walk away from rather than toward, spell / pig backwards" (*FN*, p. 88), perhaps he is thinking of the end of Book II of the *Faerie Queen* (II.xii.87) when the men who would not give up fleshly pleasure are turned into hogs. "Even in dark places. See Henry, / I beg your pardon, Henri" (*FN*, p. 94) could refer to Henri Burbon (v.xi). Other, more general references might be: to Spenser's view, "virtue will out" (*FN*, p. 79); to the seeking of illusions, particularly in Book III (". . . hiking over the hills after a / pack of illusions . . ." [*FN*, p. 85]); to the basic Renaissance view of the cosmos, "the chain of being" (*FN*, p. 87).

56 The conference was held in April of 1978, while an entry in *The Crow Journals* for April 1978 (p. 80) says Kroetsch then started "The Sad Phoenician."

57 "Exhaustive" is the correct word here, because reading "The Winnipeg Zoo" without taking a breath is exhausting.

58 Nichol acknowledges the utanikki as his "retroactively recognized formal model" ("some words on the martyrology march 12 1979," in *The Long Poem Anthology*, ed. Michael Ondaatje [Toronto: Coach House, 1979], p. 336). See also my article "The Long Poem as Poetic Diary," *Open Letter* [Long-Liners

Conference Issue], 6th ser., Nos. 2–3 (Summer–Fall 1985), 93–106.

59 Ondaatje is, as well as a poet, a professional photographer and has made a number of films.

60 John Cabot and Samuel de Champlain were, of course, early discoverers and explorers of Canada, one sailing for England, the other for France. Susanna Moodie, the English gentlewoman who recorded her impressions of early life in Canada in her celebrated *Roughing It in the Bush* and *Life in the Clearings*, is seen in Margaret Atwood's equally significant *The Journals of Susanna Moodie* as reflecting the tension of the country, which Atwood calls "a violent duality." She says, "Mrs. Moodie is divided down the middle," and goes on to describe Moodie's particular doubleness (Afterword, in *The Journals of Susanna Moodie* [Toronto: Oxford Univ. Press, 1970], p. 62).

61 *Alphabet*, No. 17 (Dec. 1969), pp. 54–56.

62 The madrona is an evergreen tree, indigenous to the west coast. It is part of the arbutus family, so that the bark continually peels to reveal the inner tree.

63 Other Canadian poets who have recently used the form of the poetic journal include Roy Kiyooka, Douglas Lochhead, Eli Mandel, Daphne Marlatt, bp Nichol, and Fred Wah.

64 See above, note 22.

65 J.E. Cirlot, *A Dictionary of Symbols*, 2nd ed. (London: Routledge and Kegan Paul, 1971), p. 88. All further references to this work (Cirlot) appear in the text.

66 Tom Chetwynd, *A Dictionary of Symbols* (London: Granada, 1982), p. 126. All further references to this work (Chetwynd) appear in the text.

67 Frank Davey and bpNichol wrote the essay which opened the first of a series of issues of *Open Letter* addressing the question of notation. "Our intent in this essay is to describe the notation that we take for granted in both our writing and reading of contemporary open form poetry" ("The Prosody of Open Verse," *Open Letter*, 5th ser., No. 2 [Spring 1982], 5). They refer to Kroetsch's poetry in their essay.

68 A footnote provides sixteen alternative "verbal attitude[s]" for the word *shied*, as well as being a further example of Kroetsch's elaborative notational form.

69 From a talk given at an informal reception at the Kootenay School of Writing, Vancouver, 8 July 1986. Many of the ideas in my discussion of Kroetsch's process in writing *Excerpts from the Real World* are taken from this talk.

70 *Excerpts from the Real World* (Lantzville, B.C.: Oolichan, 1986), p. 14. All further references to this work (*ERW*) appear in the text.

71 Neil Smith and Deirdre Wilson, *Modern Linguistics: The Results of*

Chomsky's Revolution (Bloomington: Indiana Univ. Press, 1979), p. 289.

[72] Kootenay School of Writing, 8 July 1986.

[73] "Ask your friend, the mounted policeman, to read Lacan. Identity, he should realize, is at once impossible and unavoidable" (*ERW*, p. 15). Again, the contradiction. Jacques Lacan, a French psychoanalyst, claims psychoanalysis is the ultimate truth of language and explores in some of his critical work the "dialectic of identification" encoded in the very language the poet chooses. For an informed discussion of this subject in relation to Kroetsch's earlier poetry, see Neuman's "Allow Self, Portraying Self: Autobiography in *Field Notes*."

[74] This myth is prevalent throughout the Mediterranean world, not just in Judeo-Christian lore.

[75] Kootenay School of Writing, 8 July 1986.

[76] Kroetsch dedicated *Excerpts from the Real World*, in part, to Bowering.

[77] Quoted in Egon Schwarz, *Poetry and Politics in the Works of Rainer Maria Rilke*, trans. David E. Wellbery (New York: Ungar, 1981), p. 90.

[78] *The Duino Elegies*, trans. Stephen Garmey and Jay Wilson (New York: Harper and Row, 1972), p. 35.

[79] *The Duino Elegies*, p. 35.

[80] Letter from Rilke to Witold von Hulewics, 13 Feb. 1925, in *Briefe aus Muzot* (Leipzig: Insel Verleg, 1935), p. 337; quoted in Schwarz, p. 146.

[81] Rhoda Hendricks, *Mythologies of the World* (New York: McGraw Hill, 1979), p. 95.

[82] *Seed Catalogue* (Winnipeg: Turnstone, 1986), n. pag. All further references to this work (*SC*) appear in the text. As suggested in a note at the beginning of this volume, Kroetsch's "lifelong poem," *Field Notes*, continues with Volume III, *Country and Western* (incorporating *Excerpts from the Real World*, "Spending the Morning on the Beach," and "After Paradise"): see *Completed Field Notes: The Long Poems of Robert Kroetsch* (Toronto: McClelland and Stewart, 1989). Kroetsch points up the irony of his using "the dread 'c' word of postmodernism — completed" by ending his "Author's Note" with a comment on the book's "incompleteness" (p. 270).

[83] "Poet-tree 2," in *The Collected Poems of Earle Birney*, III (Toronto: McClelland and Stewart, 1975), p. 145.

[84] Viktor Shlovsky, "Art as Technique," quoted in Wah, "Making Strange Poetics," p. 213.

SELECTED BIBLIOGRAPHY

Primary Sources

Kroetsch, Robert, James Bacque, and Pierre Gravel. *creation*. Ed. and introd. Robert Kroetsch. Toronto: new, 1970.

Kroetsch, Robert. *The Stone Hammer Poems: 1960–1975*. Lantzville, B.C.: Oolichan, 1975. 2nd ed. 1976.

———. *The Ledger*. London, Ont.: Applegarth Follies, 1975.

———. *Seed Catalogue*. 1977; rpt. Winnipeg: Turnstone, 1986.

———. *The Sad Phoenician*. Toronto: Coach House, 1979.

———. *The Crow Journals*. Edmonton: NeWest, 1980.

———. *Sketches of a Lemon*. Toronto: League of Canadian Poets, 1980.

———. *The Criminal Intensities of Love as Paradise*. Lantzville, B.C.: Oolichan, 1981.

———. *Field Notes 1–8: A Continuing Poem. The Collected Poetry of Robert Kroetsch*. Don Mills, Ont.: General, 1981.

———. *Letters to Salonika*. Toronto: Grand Union, 1983.

———. *Robert Kroetsch: Essays*. Ed. Frank Davey and bpNichol. [*Open Letter*, 5th ser., No. 4 (Spring 1983).]

———. *Advice to My Friends: A Continuing Poem*. Vol. II of *Field Notes*. Don Mills, Ont.: Stoddart, 1985.

———. "Disunity as Unity: A Canadian Strategy." In *Canadian Story and History 1885–1985*. Ed. Colin Nicholson and Peter Easingwood. Edinburgh: Edinburgh Univ. Centre of Canadian Studies [1985], pp. 1–11.

———. *Excerpts from the Real World*. Lantzville, B.C.: Oolichan, 1986.

———. *Completed Field Notes: The Long Poems of Robert Kroetsch*. Toronto: McClelland and Stewart, 1989.

———. *The Lovely Treachery of Words: Essays Selected and New*. Toronto: Oxford Univ. Press, 1989.

Secondary Sources

Barbour, Douglas. Rev. of *Seed Catalogue*. In "Poetry Chronicle v." *Dalhousie Review*, 58 (Spring 1978), 164–65.

Bessai, Diane. "Death Is a Happy Ending: A Dialogue in Thirteen Parts." In *Figures in a Ground: Essays on Modern Literature Collected in Honor of Sheila Watson*. Ed. Diane Bessai and David Jackel. Saskatoon: Western Producer Prairie Books, 1978, pp. 206–15.

Blodgett, E.D. "The Book, Its Discourse, and the Lyric: Notes on Robert Kroetsch's *Field Notes*." *Open Letter* [Robert Kroetsch: Reflections], 5th ser., Nos. 8–9 (Summer–Fall 1984), pp. 195–205.

Bowering, George. "Stone Hammer Narrative." *Open Letter* [Long-Liners Conference Issue], 6th ser., Nos. 2–3 (Summer–Fall 1985), pp. 131–44.

Brown, Russell M. "An Interview with Robert Kroetsch." *University of Windsor Review*, 7, No. 2 (Spring 1972), 1–18.

———. "Seeds and Stones: Unhiding in Kroetsch's Poetry." *Open Letter* [Robert Kroetsch: Reflections], 5th ser., Nos. 8–9 (Summer–Fall 1984), pp. 154–75.

———. "On Not Saying Uncle: Kroetsch and the Place of Place in the Long Poem." *Open Letter* [Long-Liners Conference Issue], 6th ser., Nos. 2–3 (Summer–Fall 1985), pp. 257–66.

Cameron, Donald. "Robert Kroetsch: The American Experience and the Canadian Voice." In *Conversations with Canadian Novelists*. Toronto: Macmillan, 1973, pp. 81–95.

Carpenter, David. "Stone Chipped and Hammered." Rev. of *The Stone Hammer Poems: 1960–1975*. *CV/II*, 2, No. 2 (May 1976), 38–39.

Chetwynd, Tom. *A Dictionary of Symbols*. London: Granada, 1982.

Choyce, Lesley. "From Bath to Verse." Rev. of *Advice to My Friends*. *Books in Canada*, Jan. 1986, pp. 30–31.

Cirlot, J.E. *A Dictionary of Symbols*. 2nd ed. Trans. Jack Sage. London: Routledge and Kegan Paul, 1971.

Culler, Jonathan. *The Pursuit of Signs: Semiotics, Literature, Deconstruction*. Ithaca, N.Y.: Cornell Univ. Press, 1981.

Davey, Frank, and bpNichol. "The Prosody of Open Verse." *Open Letter*, 5th ser., No. 2 (Spring 1982), pp. 5–13.

Engel, Howard. "Prose-Flawed Poems." Rev. of *The Stone Hammer Poems: 1960–1975*. *The Canadian Forum*, Oct. 1976, p. 33.

Enright, Robert, and Dennis Cooley. "Uncovering Our Dream World: An Interview with Robert Kroetsch." *Essays on Canadian Writing*, Nos. 18–19 (Summer–Fall 1980), pp. 21–32.

Hancock, Geoff. "An Interview with Robert Kroetsch." *Canadian Fiction Magazine*, Nos. 24–25 (Spring–Summer 1977), pp. 33–52.

Harari, Josué V. "Critical Factions/Critical Fictions." In *Textual Strategies: Perspectives in Post-Structuralist Criticism*. Ed. Josué V. Harari. Ithaca, N.Y.:

ROBERT KROETSCH

Cornell Univ. Press, 1979, pp. 17–72.

Kamboureli, Smaro. "A Poem *out of* Love: An Interview with Robert Kroetsch on *The Sad Phoenician.*" *Open Letter* [Robert Kroetsch: Reflections], 5th ser., Nos. 8–9 (Summer–Fall 1984), pp. 47–52.

Keeney Smith, Patricia. "WQ Interview with Robert Kroetsch." *Cross-Canada Writers' Quarterly*, 6, No. 3 (1984), 3–5, 29.

Kertzer, Jon. Rev. of *Field Notes*, by Robert Kroetsch, and *Robert Kroetsch*, by Peter Thomas. *The Fiddlehead*, No. 132 (April 1982), pp. 116–18.

Lecker, Robert. *Robert Kroetsch.* Twayne's World Authors Series, No. 768. Boston: Twayne, 1986.

———. "Robert Kroetsch: An Annotated Bibliography." In *The Annotated Bibliography of Canada's Major Authors.* Ed. Robert Lecker and Jack David. Vol. VII. Toronto: ECW, 1987, 271–402.

Lipari, Joseph A. Rev. of *Field Notes. Library Journal*, 1 Oct. 1981, p. 1930.

MacKinnon, Brian. " 'The Writer Has Got to Know Where He Lives': An Interview with Robert Kroetsch." *Writers News Manitoba*, 4, No. 1 (Feb. 1982), 3–18.

Mandel, Eli. *Another Time.* Three Solitudes: Contemporary Literary Criticism in Canada. Vol. III. Erin, Ont.: Porcépic, 1977.

———. *The Family Romance.* Winnipeg: Turnstone, 1986.

McKay, Don. "At Work and Play in *The Ledger.*" *Open Letter* [Robert Kroetsch: Reflections], 5th ser., Nos. 8–9 (Summer–Fall 1984), pp. 146–53.

Moritz, Albert. "Scaffolds in Chaos." Rev. of *Field Notes. Books in Canada*, Dec. 1981, pp. 21–22.

Munton, Ann. "The Structural Horizons of Prairie Poetics: The Long Poem, Eli Mandel, Andrew Suknaski, and Robert Kroetsch." *Dalhousie Review*, 63 (Spring 1983), 69–97.

———. "The Long Poem as Poetic Diary." *Open Letter* [Long-Liners Conference Issue], 6th ser., Nos. 2–3 (Summer–Fall 1985), pp. 93–106.

Neuman, Shirley, and Robert Wilson. *Labyrinths of Voice: Conversations with Robert Kroetsch.* Western Canadian Literary Documents. Vol. III. Edmonton: NeWest, 1982.

Neuman, Shirley. "Allow Self, Portraying Self: Autobiography in *Field Notes.*" *Line*, No. 2 (Fall 1983), pp. 104–21.

———. "Figuring the Reader, Figuring the Self in *Field Notes*: 'Double or Noting.' " *Open Letter* [Robert Kroetsch: Reflections], 5th ser., Nos. 8–9 (Summer–Fall 1984), pp. 176–94.

Olson, Charles. "Projective Verse." In *Human Universe and Other Essays.* Ed. Donald Allen. New York: Grove, 1967, pp. 51–61.

Popham, Beth. Rev. of *Seed Catalogue*, by Robert Kroetsch, and three other

185

books. *Quarry*, 27, No. 2 (Spring 1978), 84–88.

Smith, Neil, and Deirdre Wilson. *Modern Linguistics: The Results of Chomsky's Revolution.* Bloomington: Indiana Univ. Press, 1979.

Thomas, Peter. *Robert Kroetsch.* Studies in Canadian Literature, No. 13. Vancouver: Douglas & McIntyre, 1980.

_____. "Robert Kroetsch and Silence." *Essays on Canadian Writing*, Nos. 18–19 (Summer–Fall 1980), pp. 33–53.

Wah, Fred. "Music at the Heart of Thinking." *Open Letter*, 5th ser., No. 7 (Spring 1984), pp. 33–39.

_____. "Making Strange Poetics." *Open Letter* [Long-Liners Conference Issue], 6th ser., Nos. 2–3 (Summer–Fall 1985), pp. 213–21.

West, David S. "Wrestling the Alpha-Bet Beast." Rev. of *The Sad Phoenician. Canadian Literature*, No. 91 (Winter 1981), pp. 122–24.

Whiteman, Bruce. "Some Books of Canadian Poetry in 1981." Rev. of *Field Notes*, by Robert Kroetsch, and five other books. *Journal of Canadian Studies*, 17, No. 2 (Summer 1982), 150–54.

*Eli Mandel
and His Works*

Eli Mandel (1922–   )

DENNIS COOLEY

Biography

ELI MANDEL WAS BORN in Estevan, Saskatchewan, on 3 December 1922, to parents who had emigrated from Ukraine in their early teens, his father from Kiev and his mother from Odessa. His father, a grocer in Estevan, struggled to survive in a marginal economy that soon turned to disaster during the Dirty Thirties. The family lived in what Mandel remembers as "just a ramshackle part of town" (Cooley 1982) on the edge of the Souris Valley, riddled with abandoned mines and tunnels. The valley has come to figure prominently is some of his more recent work, notably *Out of Place* in 1977, but it appears covertly from the outset in his first book publication in *Trio*, where the cave, a major symbol, recurs in the next two books, as source of oracular powers and sexual mysteries. "That was a magical part of my childhood, the valley," Mandel remembers. "It was cowboy country . . . it was mythic country." The edge of the valley represented "a definite break" between the town and a symbolic space "which I don't understand. I really don't . . . . It's a haunting image that remains powerful for me" (Cooley 1982). The valley also contained, at Roche Percee, southeast of Estevan, an outcropping of rocks in which Indians had once carved petroglyphs, which in Mandel's childhood and, later, adulthood spoke strangely and strongly to him.

Much of his childhood was filled with reading adventure stories about Tarzan and Doc Savage and with all the fantasies, taboos, and fevered sexuality that infuse such childhood. Mandel's boyhood life was informed, too, by

the whole panoply of 19th century versification ranging as it does from the impossibly sublime to the intense[ly] inane. . . . In that poor shabby house surrounded by the devastated land and indeed in very peril of our lives, the high-minded sentimentality of those words moved across my mind like a vision of real human possibility. (*AT*, p. 72)

Mandel recalls those days when in the midst of a rough prairie his imagination began to take on literary contours that would turn him away from the place:

> . . . living in Estevan I didn't even know I lived there. The life of the mind and the life of the body had been radically separated, compartmentalized. Mentally, I was being brought up as a genteel Victorian boy, with a quaint though serious touch of middle-European Yiddish gentility to boot. (*AT*, p. 73)

In 1935 Mandel's family moved to Regina where his father reestablished himself in the grocery business and Eli finished the last grade of public school before going to Central Collegiate. In high school he was influenced by one of his teachers, Mr. Fife — "Great God, I liked him very much" (Cooley 1982) — who introduced him to the Romantics, and who encouraged bright young students to write and to read Canadian literature.

After graduation Mandel worked in a Regina pharmacy for two years. Then his parents, free from debt, and feeling an enormous respect for learning, were able to send Mandel to Regina College to study pharmacy. But he didn't enjoy the technical work and in 1943, after his first year, left to join the army. He arrived overseas on his twenty-first birthday and served in the Royal Army Medical Corps and in supply command, with a short, wild stint in a motorcycle training unit.

When the war ended, Mandel enrolled for six months in Khaki College in England. It was a heady experience for him: he took four courses and began to publish poetry in the school paper. At the time, he began reading recent British literature — MacNeice, Eliot, Yeats, Joyce — and, what proved to be just as important, continental writers — Dostoevsky, Mann, and above all Kafka. This opened an influence that figured prominently at the time in his writing and that has continued in abated ways since.

He was deeply affected by war, too, particularly the appalling death on a spectacular scale, and the personal loss of friends and relatives. Heartsick, he made his way back to Saskatchewan in June 1946 to pick up his life: "I was going back to talk to my aunt about

her son [his cousin, Jack Mandel, who died in the war] and realized
the revulsion I felt. It was looking at those [graves] that I got sick
... in seeing all the dead and then having to talk about the dead"
(Lowey). The terrible sense of cultural and personal desolation he
felt figures in the early poem "Estevan, Saskatchewan" and, together
with the influence of his European literary models, gives rise to the
black romanticism that characterizes the first stage of his writing, in
which the poet presents himself as tormented outsider who would
heal a sick world.

Mandel enrolled in the fall of 1946 at the University of Saskatchewan, from which he received a B.A. in 1949 and a M.A. in 1950.
While there he was strongly influenced by Carlyle King, "a great
fighter for Canadian literature" (Cooley 1982), by the novelist
Edward McCourt, and by John Lothian, a Shakespeare scholar and
another Scotsman who, like Mr. Fife, championed Canadian literature. When Mandel did come across modern Canadian poetry he
was ecstatic:

I think that my writing Canadian poetry, that is writing poetry
in Canada, became possible when I realized that people were
doing it, and doing it well. When I came back from Europe ...
I was reading Auden, Hopkins, Yeats, I was reading Eliot and
so on and terribly excited by it and believing I could do something. I remember in the library at Regina coming across a book
called Go to Sleep World by Raymond Souster ... and I read it
and I said, "Wow this is the real stuff." That meant a great deal
to me. (Fee, pp. 7–8)

In 1949 Mandel married Miriam Minovitch, who came from
Moose Jaw and who was herself studying at the University of
Saskatchewan. After Mandel completed his Master's degree in the
next year, they left for a three-year stay at the University of Toronto
where, in his own words, Mandel was "very erratic and very high
strung" as a Ph.D. student (Cooley 1982). He excelled nevertheless
and began to publish poems in literary journals, the first, "Train
Wreck," in Northern Review. He soon published a batch of poems
in Contact at Raymond Souster's invitation and, on further invitation, a larger group in Trio (which included Gael Turnbull and Phyllis
Webb) in 1954. His career as a poet was well underway.

In the fall of 1953 he took a position at Collège Militaire, Royal
de Saint-Jean, where until 1957 he taught, worked on his dissertation

on Christopher Smart, and wrote poetry, and where in 1955 his daughter Evie was born. In 1957 he completed his doctorate and that fall moved to the University of Alberta in Edmonton where, with one year's interruption, he held an academic appointment until 1967. At first he found it "rather dreary" (Cooley 1982), perhaps because he had become accustomed in the East to the company of Irving Layton, Phyllis Webb, F.R. Scott, Louis Dudek, Leonard Cohen, and James Reaney, and he took some time to establish new literary connections in Edmonton. He soon, however, struck up a fine and fertile relationship with the novelist Henry Kreisel, whom he greatly values. While he was at Edmonton, Mandel's academic and literary life blossomed. In response to an enquiry from Roy Daniells, a poet and professor at the University of British Columbia, he put together a new manuscript, *Fuseli Poems*, for which he received a Canada Foundation Fellowship in Writing, and which in 1960 appeared to favourable reviews and to a near miss in the awarding of the Governor General's medal.

After spending 1963–64 at York University, Mandel returned to Edmonton for another three years, where he continued to work productively. *Black and Secret Man*, which was not as well received as *Fuseli*, came out in 1964, and in 1966 his *Criticism: The Silent-Speaking Words*, based on a series of CBC Radio talks and distilling his current thinking on poetry, appeared. The book illustrated a dimension to Mandel's literary life which has been constant, and that is the active interplay of poetry, criticism, and literary theory, his criticism being especially concerned with the value and meaning of poetry in the twentieth century.

In 1967 Mandel divorced his first wife, married Ann Hardy, and returned to York. His swaying between Toronto and Edmonton, the forays east and the returns west — often sporadic but by the mid-1970s increasingly sustained — marked something more than the occasions of an academic's life. They signified and perhaps intensified Mandel's vacillation between two cultural worlds: one which in a sense he was born into; another which since the end of the war, during the first years of studying and then teaching in the East, he had been moving more and more into.

In the same year that he moved east, he published *An Idiot Joy* (1967), a major accomplishment for which he received the Governor General's Award, one of those fine occasions when jurors identify a crucial book. His inclusion in Gary Geddes' influential Oxford anthology *15 Canadian Poets* in 1970 gave his work greater impetus, for it provided added visibility and access to readers. Those opportunities Mandel soon put to good use. One of his first projects as critic was to publish in the Coles Canadian Writers and Their Works series, edited by William French of *The Globe and Mail*, a book on Irving Layton, a poet for whom Mandel has always had a great admiration. Another important consequence of his new contacts came in the form of a series of poetry anthologies he edited and co-edited in the late 1960s and the early 1970s. Mandel's astute knowledge of contemporary poetry, his openness to the new, his knack for recognizing talent, and his generosity in celebrating it led him to produce several breakthrough anthologies, among them *Five Modern Canadian Poets* (1969) and (with Ann Mandel) *Eight More Canadian Poets* (1972).

In 1973 Mandel began to consolidate some of his writing with the publication of *Crusoe: Poems Selected and New*. He also moved into new territory during the 1970s by drawing on memories and dreams of the prairies. Margery Fee at the time asked him, "Do you think of yourself as a Canadian poet?" His reply pointed to an archaeological drive to origins, however mediated:

> Not particularly. I think of myself now as a prairie poet, a writer whose being was formed by the experience of living on the prairies as a boy. I think the first six to ten years are absolutely essential. There's no way of escaping that. (Fee, p. 8)

He added that *Stony Plain* (1973) "is right because this is a book that's going back to roots, towards the prairies" (Fee, p. 8). In his own poetry this rethinking led in 1977 to a striking long poem, *Out of Place*, about his literal and his spiritual return to birthplace, to Estevan in particular and to the prairies in general. His turning back to his origins almost certainly was related to an enabling poetics he began to develop in the 1960s. In "Writing West: On the Road to Wood Mountain," an essay central to understanding his shifts, he speaks — this is 1977 — of the muse of Estevan and of "divided men seeking to make themselves whole" (*AT*, p. 77) by imaginatively recovering their lost selves. The way back to the authentic, Mandel was coming to believe, might lie through a more direct and simple language. In this view the writer is "not so much in place, as out of place and so one endlessly trying to get back, to find his way home, to return, to write himself into existence, writing West" (*AT*, p. 69).

Signs of that redirection emerged elsewhere in *Another Time*, a collection of essays published in 1977. The collection was divided into three parts: "Reflections," "Writing West," and "Writers and Writing." The relative strengths of the sections provide a good indication of the new centres Mandel was arriving at. The first part, "Reflections," contains the essays that are most "European" in their subjects and procedures, and it is the weakest. Compared to other essays in the collection these ones tend to be vague, stylistically tortured, semantically dull — as if the intellectual basis that lay beneath his earliest writing had lost its power and could no longer command his best thinking. The third part, "Writers and Writing," presents a variety of essays, the most interesting of them in what they reveal about Mandel's own practice being "Modern Canadian Poetry," "Ecological Heroes and Visionary Politics," and "Banff: The Magic Mountain." The second section, "Writing West," is the strongest and includes the fine essay I've already mentioned, "Writing West: On the Road to Wood Mountain," which meditates on his own prairie childhood, explores the poetic example of Andy Suknaski, and speculates on moving into an aesthetics that is more vernacular and immediate.

More recently Mandel has travelled abroad, as scholar and as poet, to read and lecture. And in his writing he has begun to draw on those experiences and to find new forms adequate to them. *Life Sentence* (1981) combines in intriguing ways excerpts from his travel journals together with poems the occasions gave rise to. In 1981 Mandel published a second and updated selected, *Dreaming Backwards*, in the new Spectrum series begun by General Publishing. The Yeatsian title, which for years he had intended to use, declares his continued respect for an earlier rhetoric and for literature as an institution.

Although Mandel has long been an important and esteemed academic, he has become, from the mid 1970s, roughly, more and more involved in the literary community in Canada, and less and less active in the internal structures of the university. Teaching can be, he has found, an impediment to writing because ". . . real teaching is a drain . . . [and] you end up having used up that creative energy which would have gone into your writing" (Fee, p. 2).

Nevertheless, Mandel has led a productive life and has worked on many fronts. As teacher, editor, critic, lecturer (in person and on the radio), anthologist, workshopper, conversationalist, reviewer, writer-in-residence (City of Regina during 1978–79, University of

Rome in 1983), visiting professor (University of Victoria during 1979–80, University of Calgary during 1984–85), correspondent, fan, he has shaped the literature he himself has contributed to, so much so that it might be most accurate to describe his role in Canadian literature as being, in the best sense of the term, that of a man of letters.

In 1986 he published a new collection of his essays, *The Family Romance*. Many of its pieces derive from talks he has given in recent years. The new role as public figure is somewhat surprising because in the past Mandel never cultivated a public personality. Nor for many years did he cultivate relationships with other poets, thinking ". . . it doesn't matter to me very much to see and talk to other writers. On the whole I don't like it" (Fee, p. 7). He has until recently been so withdrawn that he has known two of his esteemed colleagues at York — Miriam Waddington and Frank Davey — primarily through their appearances in print. In many ways a shy man, one who never could feel comfortable promoting his own work, Mandel has mainly gone his own way, working privately and attending to friends on private occasions. He reads intently, alone with his thoughts until he presents them in some public forum. Even so Mandel has become increasingly conspicuous as a literary guru. He is especially prominent and instrumental as lecturer at conferences, where invariably he gives a compelling address or reading. Never one to rest with approved texts, suspicious of their authority and the status that has been thrust upon them, he courts the new, seeks to mediate our collective writing, but always in the light of the old.

Mandel until his recent retirement has served as Professor of English and Humanities at York University. He has three children, two by his first marriage — Evie and Charles — and one from his second — Sara.

Tradition and Milieu

Eli Mandel was born into a family whose parents had very little formal education and who came to Canada without being able to speak English. His father, however, spoke "about six languages. Dad could speak Ukrainian, Russian, Polish, everything. It was just astonishing." That experience "reflects itself especially in . . . my syntax and prose," Mandel muses. And he recognizes, too, despite (or perhaps because of) the overwhelming preference of his cousins for careers in medicine and law, "this enormous respect for education, which is part of the Jewish background" (Cooley 1982). The same holds for the importance of intelligence, to this day a supreme necessity to Mandel: "I think that one of the deficiencies in Canadian criticism and one of the deficiencies in Canadian reviewing, and even in Canadian poetry, is a lack of intelligence" (Arnason, p. 73).

Late in his career, after leaving his family roots, Mandel would return to them. Although his memory is vague on just when he assimilated Jewish culture, he does recall "reading the Old Testament in Hebrew" (Cooley 1982). As a result, his immediate and extended family inculcated in him a profound sense that knowledge should be put to an ethical purpose. It is tempting to see Mandel's literary life in that way. Certainly his poetry, his criticism, his conversation is full of references to taboo, secrecy, mysteries, obligations, transgression. As he writes later in *Criticism: The Silent-Speaking Words*, "To be a spy of God . . . is to move feelingly and alive among and through *things*, to come into the realm of being out of the mad realm of appearance and delusions" (p. 52). Although the consequences in guilt and a sense of criminality are felt most powerfully in the first three books, Mandel's primary belief in the poet's calling abides to this day. So Mandel can still say the writer is "at the centre of a culture. He's the point of articulateness in a culture and therefore he's the best hope of that culture" (Arnason, p. 75). And so we read his essays in *Criticism* with an inescapable awareness that Mandel is always and deeply shaken by questions of value and reality:

How often have we heard this defence: it may be offensive, it may be disturbing to the casual or ordinary reader, but it is an honest work and it is, you must admit, well-written. Since it is well-written you really ought not to say that it is wicked. Well, this defence, I submit, is specious. All aesthetic judgments seem to me to be moral judgments in disguise, and I cannot understand how it is possible to say that good writing is good writing without invoking some moral notion. It may be honesty, or sincerity, or complexity, or compassion, or purity, but whatever it is it will in fact involve a morality of one kind or another. And I fail to see why a dishonest, insincere, simple-minded, and cruel writer might not be one who delights us or compels us. (pp. 48–49)

That belief has never left Mandel, whatever other shifts he has gone through as poet or thinker.

In his regard for value, perhaps he enters a more general Canadian role. As man of letters engaged in literature as an act of deeply human and humanizing significance, he compares to figures like George Woodcock, Northrop Frye, Desmond Pacey, Malcolm Ross, Lorne Pierce, Alan Crawley, or Fred Cogswell. Unlike them, however, he migrated toward the grotesque and the macabre, at least at first. His vision is at once bleaker and more bizarre than is theirs. In finding the world bedeviled with nightmarish horror he may be Hebraic, but the perspective certainly derives in large part from "literary" sources: "the line is European, it is surrealistic" (Cooley 1982). When Mandel returned as a young man to Saskatchewan from the carnage of World War II, his nausea found a cultural rationale in continental writers, whom he found, like himself, to be rubbed by the monstrous:

> . . . I had a Nietzschean view of the poet's role [soon enhanced by the example and the solicitation of Irving Layton] and a Thomas Mann view of the poet's role. He's the sick person who makes the society well. . . . It was *the price that I paid* as a creative person *to serve in my society* or something like that. (Fee, p. 3; emphasis added)

In this view the writer, or at least the projected artist, was a "superman" free from the fears and inhibitions that entrapped others. Attractive as this view was to the young Mandel, he had some problems with it ethically. Years later, in a CBC conversation with Irving Layton, who was beating the tub for supermen, Mandel protested: "No consequences, though, no consequences! Does one really face up to that?" In that same exchange he says, ". . . I'm still very much disturbed by the relationship between that radical freedom and its consequences on the one hand and its relationship to suffering on the other" (Irving Layton and Eli Mandel, 1972, p. 26). Nevertheless, given what seems to be his sense of the poet as prophet, his own exposure to exotic fantasies in his childhood reading, and the trauma he underwent in the war — there may well be other and better explanations — he was drawn to a version of the artist's work as " 'biological blasphemy' " or " 'criminal perception' " (*Criticism*, p. 26). In fact, he was quite prepared when he began writing to identify with what he has since called "the savage":

Like the child in literature, the savage or the clown or the fool is a symbol. He is, at least in some of his manifestations, what Leslie Fiedler would call an Id figure. He appears as the image of all that is irrational in the human being: revelry and misrule, gluttony and mischief, folly and trickery, cunning and simple-mindedness. . . . But if there is any sense at all in which art is an expression of irrational urges, the desire of man, it follows that the civilized or cultivated approach to art will invariably either turn it into an illusion or into an intellectual structure. As the language of the body, anarchic, grotesque, ludicrous, art remains an illusion to the intellect and a threat to the intellect and to the ordering powers of man. (*Criticism*, p. 70)

It is essential to keep these derivations before us — particularly the European, whose impact is evident well into the 1950s — if we are going to avoid a common but somewhat misleading identification of Mandel as Frygian acolyte. The claim has an obvious appeal, since several poets were mining the mythopoeic lode at the time. But they never met on a regular basis, or corresponded. (For years Mandel's strongest personal connections were with writers based in Mon-treal.) And Mandel, at least, first tapped into mythopoesis quite independently of Frye. His succession ran from Yeats and Eliot.

It would, however, be correct to say that until the mid-1960s Mandel had no great quarrel with Frye. The first cracks, Mandel argues (Miki, p. 34), show up in *Black and Secret Man* in 1964 but that book seems more a continuance than a change in poetics. The breakthrough came shortly after with *An Idiot Joy* in 1967. The first signs actually appeared in *Criticism: The Silent-Speaking Words*, published the year before:

The literature to which the new criticism paid its allegiance and for which it provided a rationale is now passing. The meta-physical or closed lyric, peculiarly suited to its methods, and the elaborately symbolic novel, to which it could apply its tech-niques, are no longer the dominant literary forms. They have been succeeded by the open poems of Creeley, Duncan, and Olson in America, by the deliberately flat and low-keyed poetry of the "group" in England, by the black-humour novel, and the non-novel, by the theatre of the absurd and the theatre of cruelty. (p. 33)

The signs of change reverberate in Mandel's essay "Modern Canadian Poetry," first published in 1969, and find their way in a poetics of locality and immediacy, based in Charles Olson's insistence on "getting rid of the lyrical interference of the individual as ego" (AT, p. 87). When the poet abandons a high rhetoric, such as Layton's "dramatic and flamboyant assertiveness,"

> the laconic comes to be favoured over the elaborated structure; the unemphatic tone seems more precise than the singing voice in dramatic or ironic lyrics; the poem as experience, apparently extemporized, is preferable to the poem as literature, a structure set apart for contemplation. (AT, p. 87)

The connection with these sources of contemporary poetics began a few years earlier when Mandel was introduced to the Williams-Olson sense of poetry. And the gates were opened to a drastic shift in his writing. For the first decade he had enlisted in an aesthetic of overriding structures, heavy symbolic import, and grand rhetoric. Mandel now moved into more modest measures in which the poet or his surrogate no longer acted as supreme maker, apart from and superior to society. We could think of the move as a shift from modernism to postmodernism, although Mandel continues to be attracted by modernist practices.

In any case, the alteration continued to inform his writing, including the new poems that appeared in Crusoe and Stony Plain, both issued in 1973. Within a few years the premises he had recently adopted took him further, providing another and more personal access to the prairies of his childhood, till then largely shut off to him by the poetics of high modernism he had observed. In the 1980s, he was struck by the terrible rightness of Wallace Stegner's Wolf Willow, and he speaks of knowing that he himself "was very much possessed by that sense of things that were lost, lost towns, the town was a lost town to me" and believing (instructed by contemporary French theory) that "poetry is written out of some sort of loss or something you don't have" (Cooley 1982). Mandel saw that if he were going to regain the original world, he would, like Andy Suknaski, have to find an adequate "sense of dialect, of voice" (AT, p. 76). The writing in the mid-1970s, then, turns more towards document and the edges of vernacular. Yet, it never enters the free-wheeling idiom of Robert Kroetsch or the fine ear for the colloquial in Prairie poets like Glen Sorestad, David Arnason, or Lorna Crozier (Uher).

Out of his now more contemporary position, which prized situation and looked to region, to what was at hand, as a base for processural writing, Mandel found a way of rethinking and or repudiating Frye, at least the Frye of *Anatomy of Criticism* and *The Bush Garden*. The results were brilliant. No longer subscribing to universalist or purely visionary views of literature, and no longer quite so ahistorical (if not anti-historical) as once he was, Mandel was in a position to read Frye's arguments about the garrison, about the North, and above all about the informing myths of "Canadian" literature as terribly wanting because limited to part of our history and part of our geography. Mandel has written in many places about Frye's reading of Canadian literature, and he has sought to work out quite a different understanding of our culture and our history, one that would pay attention to its peculiarities. In fact, he has for some time now played a minority (but not solitary) role in articulating a counter-reading and maybe even a counter-tradition for our literature. The point is doubly worth stressing, since it underlines Mandel's initial independence of Frye.

Later work, notably *Life Sentence*, shows how Mandel has continued to probe and move intellectually. He prides himself on not settling into a position or a style. In *Life Sentence* he also shows — more signs of locating himself in the contingent — an overt commitment to politics that began as early as *An Idiot Joy* and *Crusoe* and that continues prominently into *Stony Plain*, which he was at one time thinking of calling *The Secret Life of Pierre Elliott Trudeau* or the *Trudeau Papers* and then *War Measures* (Fee, p. 8). The alteration he has undergone from his Nietzschean days he explains with typical insight in 1974:

Poetry is energy, poetry is delight, poetry is power. And politics is power, and it's the tension between two kinds of power which really, really concerns me. Now it's been said many times . . . that writers form a second government. That's something like Shelley's "unacknowledged legislators," and I just can't imagine a poetry which in some sense or another is apolitical. Merely to turn your back on politics is in fact to make a political statement of a certain kind. So while I began in one sense in the Nietzschean romantic tradition of the poet as concerned with a kind of sacred private experience which is necessary for the health of the tribe, I've developed from that I think a much more public position where I consciously concern myself with political issues. (Fee, p. 4)

The claim here is astute and heads off some of the objections that are sometimes raised against poetry that does not vehemently and directly involve itself with politics. It contains the implicit recognition which holds for all Mandel's work: his literary life has been cast in an oppositional model — art set against life — and privileging art as a means of knowing and making. In the past, until the mid to late 1960s say, the model has been largely synchronic for Mandel and has simply put the two realms into some sort of suspended tension. Since then, Mandel has come closer and closer to making the opposition diachronic, that is, located in history and subject to various kinds of interchange and alteration. One consequence of this adjustment can be located in his beginning to entertain what he has called "sociological" views of literature that would locate its origins not only in literature itself, but in the larger world as well. Having lost faith in some eternal realm of canons in which the verities abide forever, he came to think of literature as being contingent — of giving rise to our lives, yes, but now also deriving from the rest of our lives, and never separated off in some ideal realm from which it gained authority and from which it issued instructions. That perception enabled him to write *Out of Place*, a record of his return to Estevan to tap the local muse. Mandel's vision of literature and of its role in life became more complex and more dialectical, then, by the mid-1970s. A Yeatsian vision of eternity in artifice lost its hold on him for many reasons, one of them undoubtedly being his interest in postmodernism, another perhaps being the dismay in contemporary circles about the consequences of perpetuating certain aesthetics and texts. He began to realize, as did others, that such a superstructure is imperialist to the core and always locates literature in other times, in other places. And in somebody else's terms.

Freed from the presuppositions that informed his career at the start, Mandel also found a way to work with texts that for the longest time were unavailable to him as a poet. As late as 1974 he told Margery Fee that some poets he greatly admired and knew intimately did not, because they could not, enter his own work:

Contrary to what people might say, Smart and Blake were not influences. . . . Smart couldn't be an influence. I once tried to do something with all the work I had done with Smart. He couldn't be an influence because of the particular mode he was working in, the high ode, the exalted Biblical approach and that's just not possible now. And Blake because I never fully assimilated Blake. And you really have to assimilate a writer. Somehow his voice has to speak through you. (Fee, p. 13)

But in 1979 he brought out an oratorical poem/play, *Mary Midnight*, in the Coach House MS Editions series. The text, in its first 1963 version published in James Reaney's *Alphabet* magazine, bears signs of earlier writing in *Black and Secret Man*. It in some ways resembles Robert Duncan's work in this mode, and includes among its characters Blake, Shape, Fuseli, Christopher Smart, Crowd, Mary Midnight (an alias of the historical Smart), and Author (Eli Mandel as "Eli Mandel"). Of that play Mandel has recently spoken:

It is not a play really, but rather it is a poem and a version of street theatre. I think it touches on certain aspects of Smart which most people aren't aware of — the transvestism, the street-theatre aspects, the wildness of Smart and his grotesqueness. That's the kind of poetry of his that wasn't very well known at all compared to his high odes. (Meyer and O'Riordan, p. 117)

Mandel's intellectual flexibility — his reading in continental literary theory and its domesticated versions, and his own restless experiments — has brought him more fully into a fluid, personal criticism, one which might in accordance with his own preference be called phenomenological. He has been working out an aesthetic of contemporary literature and of contemporary poetry. In fulfilment of that project, his collection of essays, *The Family Romance*, confirms his life-long willingness to set off in new directions.

Critical Overview and Context

"One day I intend to write an essay . . . called 'The Treason of the Clerks.' This is the essay that has to be written, about the betrayal of intelligence and the betrayal of integrity in criticism" (Arnason,

p. 74). This is what Mandel said in 1978 and there's no reason to believe he has changed his mind since. The comments should not be seen as referring particularly to Mandel's own reception (he is thinking more generally of the state of Canadian letters), but to a degree they can be. He has suffered no more than most writers in this country; arguably, he has fared better. Nevertheless, to this day there is only a handful of substantial pieces on him. There are many reviews, however, and they are on the whole commending.

It is possible to discern some patterns in the criticism on him. The earliest pieces on *Trio* and *Fuseli* were positive and in some cases enthusiastic. R.D. McMaster wrote a long and detailed review of *Fuseli Poems*, Milton Wilson described the same book as "rich, coherent, assured, exciting" (1961, p. 387), and an anonymous reviewer in *Alphabet* spoke of "brilliant confrontations of seemingly unrelated things" and of "a recognizably individual voice . . . saying something well" (p. 41). In 1961 Desmond Pacey said Mandel had "found a distinctive voice of his own" (p. 242), and Alden Nowlan in the next year observed that ". . . Mr. Mandel is one of the most interesting members of the newer generation of Canadian poets" and "displays sincerity, compassion and technical skill" (pp. 59–60). Collectively, readers spoke of Mandel's craft, noticed his attempts (successes, in most reviews) to localize myth and seek prophecy, appreciated his dramatic personae and mix of voicings, reported on what several enthusiasts called his "musical" phrasing, and — what is quite startling — claimed to have found horrific shock and deep emotion. In phrases typical of that response, James Reaney noted "such a granary of disturbing and powerful images" (p. 704), and Pacey reported "concentrated agony" in the poems (1961, p. 242).

With the appearance of *Black and Secret Man*, the reviews began to wobble. Pacey complained about its obscurity and mythopoeic contortion (1965, p. 74). Wilson found the new book "a disappointment" (1965, p. 354), and Brian McCarthy complained that Mandel had failed to write convincingly of horror (p. 73). Douglas Barbour was more severe: Mandel "tries too hard, and the strain shows in the somewhat baroque mannerisms of some of the poems" (1966, p. 46). On the other side, Fred Cogswell wrote of it favourably, noting its complexity, its allusiveness, and its technical skill (p. 14). Others, such as H.W. Sonthoff and B.W. Jones, admired Mandel's new work, though even Sonthoff feared that the structure in several poems "doesn't work emotionally" (1965, p. 68).

We well might take these to be the doubts of reviewers who had passed the excitement of discovering a new talent and who had now come to look for something more. But the restrained and even dismissive criticism continued and grew with the appearance of *An Idiot Joy*. Putting aside lukewarm or non-committal receptions, we still have Pacey's estimation that the book is (once more) disappointing and "needs the restraining force of intellectual discipline and moral vision" (1968, p. 92). Gregory M. Cook launched a moralistic attack on the book for what he took to be its despair, its decorative style, and its lack of certainty (p. 147). Kenneth Gibson, writing in *Quarry*, found only five poems from the book worthy of respect, and Norman Simms, in *The Far Point*, concluded that despite virtues *An Idiot Joy* was too often "heavy-handed and distastefully cute" (p. 63), banal, uncontrolled, or tedious. Barbour said the book was a "backward step." In the strongest condemnation found in any of the reviews, he argued the work was anarchic, loose, unfocused, and slovenly (1968, p. 119). Scattered through the reviews are complaints about the insignificance of many new poems.

Most of the complaints seem to have been based on a desire for a high Yeatsian rhetoric and to have been oblivious to the mode Mandel was moving into. A young poet, George Bowering, was among the few at the time who saw and liked what Mandel was starting to do. In a shrewd analysis Bowering praised the new Mandel poems "that seek to strip away anything of rhetoric or metaphor in order to arrive at pure honest disclosure, of emotions, of ideas, of the poet's condition" (p. 74). The argument was soon to become almost commonplace in Mandel criticism.

Several years later, picking up on Bowering's lead, A. Barry Cameron in a review of *Crusoe* and *Stony Plain* identified Mandel's aesthetic of silence and spareness of language. The Bowering and Cameron readings found confirmation and consolidation in Frank Davey's entry on Mandel for the 1973 *Supplement to the Oxford Companion to Canadian History and Literature* (virtually the same entry occurs in the updated *Oxford Companion to Canadian Literature* in 1983), where Davey put Mandel's career into perspective:

In style, Mandel is intellectual and meditative — an ironic poet rather than an angry one. A central feature of his work is a deliberate lack of emotion. . . . His early work is exceedingly complex in its syntax, formal in its prosody, and literary in its references. . . . Mandel sees ancient myths and literary stories alive in contemporary actuality, but in this poetry the mythic often obscures the actual and personal. . . . However, beginning with the poetry of *Black and Secret Man*, Mandel enriches his work through the introduction of open verse-forms, spare but colloquial language, simplified syntax, and reportorial detail. (p. 228)

But Davey's was not the first overview of Mandel. John Ower in 1969 wrote an article, "Black and Secret Poet: Notes on Eli Mandel," which located Mandel in a biblical tradition and in a romantic tradition. In those bases, Ower argued, Mandel sought symbols and narratives of spiritual transformation located in the unconscious. Ower further discerned in *An Idiot Joy* a release from a narrowness of tone and focus that beset his earlier work. From Ower, Cameron, and Davey on, and with the spate of Mandel books in the late 1960s and early 1970s, including especially the selected *Crusoe*, we get criticism which, with a sizeable body of work before it, responded more widely. Christopher Levenson's "Magpies and Nightingales" offered such a view by sketching in the history of Mandel's work up to his open poetics that carried well into the 1960s and by identifying an important move by Mandel into political writing by the early 1970s.

In 1974 two significant pieces appeared: an informative interview conducted by Margery Fee and another shrewd entry from Davey in his book *From There to Here: A Guide to English-Canadian Literature since 1960*. The new edition of the *Literary History of Canada*, issued in 1976, was skimpy on Mandel, although it did pick up one essential quality, the Mandel persona, as "a diffident and sardonic creature, with a sharply developed sense of the ironic and the grotesque" (II, p. 306), a figure Milton Wilson had first noticed way back in 1961: "One of Mr. Mandel's favourite *personae* is a shabby hero with a querulous, defensive, ineffectual tone of voice, who moves through a commonplace world of local landmarks and petty officials, of next door gossip and tall tales" (p. 386). The entry in the *Literary History* nevertheless took more satisfaction in the elegant that the irreverent:

. . . he can scarcely be bettered in his command of a middle style of discourse. However phantasmagoric his subject-matter, his

choice and order of words are almost unfailingly precise, deco-
rous, civilized, touched with wit, and with a sure feeling for the
placing of the single telling word or image. Occasionally . . . he
slips beyond the colloquial into the slovenly . . . or he forsakes
his comely syntax to whore after modish perversities . . . but his
writing in general provides again and again the peculiar delight
of hearing the elusive thing phrased with grace and clarity. (II,
p. 306)

Another spate of responses were set off with the simultaneous
publication of *Out of Place* and *Another Time* in 1977. I acknowledged a lyrical strength but supposed Mandel never realized the
potential of vernacular or document in *Out of Place*. Peter Stevens
in "Poet as Critic as Prairie Poet" similarly commented on "Mandel's
inability to evoke in his poems any detailed sense of the people in
the Hoffer colony, his refusal (conscious or unconscious) to try to
use the terrible authenticity of voice he finds in the poetry of
[Andrew] Suknaski" (p. 57). Stevens' essay appeared in a special
Prairie poetry issue of *Essays on Canadian Writing* that includes an
interview with Mandel, mostly on contemporary poetry and prairie
poetry. Suknaski himself, in long impressionistic "letters," wrote
very personal responses to Mandel, especially on his concerns with
guilt and doubles.

Dreaming Backwards and Life Sentence also occasioned several
reviews, generally favourable and, as we would expect in the case of
the "selected" *Dreaming Backwards*, several of them retrospective.
Those brief surveys generally spoke of the changes in Mandel's
career, much as earlier critics had diagnosed them. There was some
attempt, however, to find continuity in the body of writing. Jon
Kertzer wrote that Mandel has always regarded poetry "as a means
of intellectual and emotional scrutiny" (p. 41), and John Bemrose
said the "seriousness and complexity of Mandel's attack on moral
issues is always impressive" (p. 41). Recent years have also seen a
positive review of those same two books by Douglas Barbour, who
stressed the authentic power of Mandel's political poetry; a thoughtful interview with Roy Miki in the magazine *Line*; and an excellent
study of the "preface:" in *Out of Place* by Smaro Kamboureli.

The body of criticism is still small. Its patterns are apparent, but
so are its limitations. What is needed is some detailed, wide-ranging,
and thorough response. Except for the Kamboureli article, and

possibly two or three other publications, there are few minute discussions of texts, comments being confined, by the size of reviews and the limited body of scholarship, to brief generalities. All the same, there are reasons to be hopeful. The basis is there and several studies are significant. The journal *Essays on Canadian Writing* is bringing out a special issue on Mandel, several dissertations have recently appeared or are under way, the University of Guelph and Wilfrid Laurier University cosponsored a conference on Mandel, and scholarship will benefit from the placing of the Mandel papers in the Department of Archives and Special Collections at the University of Manitoba.

Mandel's Works

There are several qualities that run through Mandel's life work. From time to time some of them ebb or take on qualifications, but never to the point of disappearance. Always there is an acute sense of poetry as crucial activity. The poet speaks unpleasant but necessary truths in pain of otherwise betraying his calling. For Mandel it is a calling, since he thinks of the act as essentially religious, one that is marked by reverence and awe. For the most part the poet bases his vision in a textual universe, where texts derive from texts, and enter the body of writing or, in religious terminology, the scripture of which they are a part. Whether texts are literary and European, or visual and Amerindian, they remain texts nevertheless. From *An Idiot Joy* on, Mandel came to modify that position, but it keeps reappearing. Always there is a formal aestheticism alongside the prophetic role — the two reconciled in the belief that the poet, forced in our society to the margins where he plays an adversarial role, orders the world according to the word. In virtually everything Mandel has written he displays a profound sense that literature invents life and invests it with meaning. Such a poet would serve his tribe by all the erudition and care he can muster, although he need not, as Mandel came to understand, display his learning. Nevertheless, he is a dealer in secrets — either (as Mandel was to begin with) as occluder of them, one who would keep esoteric knowledge hidden or obscured, or (as Mandel came to be) as revealer of it. Either way, he acted as secret/ary — one who keeps and records secrets, who deals in them.

Closely related to prophecy in Mandel's writing are the quest and the double. His personae go forever in search of themselves, in narratives which recently have led to travel books, including *Out of Place*, based on his return to the town of his childhood. But that town, like almost all the subjects Mandel chooses, he insists on viewing as fictive, preferring in his most typical statements to view writing as pre-eminently inventive. Although he softened that view in mid-career, he never let it get far away.

It will be evident from the following pages that I take Mandel to be most skilled in the hesitant lyric and in certain satiric pieces. He is extremely accomplished at a minimal style and in a meditative mode, a virtuosity that has not yet been accorded its due. His facility in satire chiefly takes the form of self-mockery in which the speaker bungles life with comical bravado, and of technically adventurous parodies of official public voices, most of them political. Mandel also has a flair for closed poems on the theme of entrapment.

Trio (1954)

I am a prodigious pun
to hide and show myself between these walls

Enrolled as a Ph.D. student, and immersed in modern poetry, the 32-year-old Eli Mandel saw his first book publication into print in 1954. The poems show intellectual sophistication and an ear for flexible rhyme. They are also loaded with erudition (mainly of the sort that figures in influences like Eliot). They freight in biblical and classical myths, often by naming figures — Job, Orpheus, Mary, Abel, Theseus, Icarus, Cain, Leda — and they verbally echo modern writers such as Dylan Thomas (in "Fair in Town"), Auden, and Yeats.

The poems — nineteen in all, counting the individual pieces in the two major sequences, the "Minotaur Poems" (six poems) and "Val Marie" (four poems) — not only refer to exotic sources, they in many ways defer to them. Full of weighty allusions and grand rhetoric, the poems enter the tradition of high modernism, mainly as it derives through Yeats. They speak a language of uncertain pronoun references and wobbling syntax: "Stiff-necked, double-towered and red, once shone / [She] Who was so lovely in her pride [but] now like a brute / [She] Moved and chewed in the land."

They also reach towards climax and closure. There are several sonnets, for example. As if further to reinforce the autonomy of the form, Mandel chooses the Elizabethan, the tighter of the two, with its self-contained three stanzas and couplet to clinch the poem by summary or revelation. The final two lines also work visually because set off as an intact unit, and prosodically with end rhymes that close the poem like a screen door slamming shut. Each of the four parts of "Val Marie" is in fact a sonnet, the least successful of which, "II," puts the lexical in servitude to the structural. Unstable in its pronoun references, in the cohesion of its syntax, in its connections between subject and predicate, the poem is extremely difficult to understand. The first two stanzas will give an idea of the difficulties:

> What he was skulled in and built, the frame of,
> The grain and shelter of his house and place,
> Bone's trust of jointure and contract, all claims have
> Yielded in him who is separate and vagrant in flesh and place.

> Now only the priestly policing of animal and bird
> Sketches his plan in a snowed, in a sealed land,
> The inform of his track, their stencil and care of a bared
> And feared skill, his being unseen, that power gained

Reading here consists largely of an effort to locate grammatic markers, a struggle that is heightened, as is so typical of these early poems, by opaque references. The extent to which meaning is lost to form (as much as we can allow the criticism, heuristically) is one indication of the damage caused by Mandel's allegiance to a high rhetoric.

Other poems build to climax. We read in "Train Wreck" the delays of inverted syntax:

> down the shocked bridge
> Rode the gleaming cars, accoutrements
> Fell, fell away, over the trestled edge;

And:

> still on the topless waves forever
> Where she crested the waves, would the young
> Name she called in the broken car save her?

The delayed completion of the sentence in both cases speaks a rhetoric determined to withhold its end. It shows a speaker studying effects and arranging his words to build toward some point. In the second example, Mandel marshals a Yeatsian combination of rhetorical question and periodic sentence to declare both a grand theme and a dramatic suspension.

It would be well to think of these poems as dramas — not in the most obvious and overt ways, but in the citational stance they assume, especially the "Minotaur Poems." It is this mode — *"the* sun people," *"those* same fields," "There were *those* crowds," *"the* pipes and hammered arteries of *the* place" — that inserts a dramatic quality, for the definite articles and demonstrative pronouns declare the presence of a speaker (perhaps more in Auden's than in Yeats's style) and — this is important — his appeal to some audience, perhaps to us ourselves: oh, yeah, *those* people; sure, the *pipes*, of course.

The speaker further declares his presence and purpose in the indices of parable: "It has been," "I came upon," "They chose among us in the fall of the year," "Within these walls I am to look for light." These expressions mark the "Minotaur Poems," whose speakers are engaged in some kind of quest, usually for understanding. The first poem in the sequence stresses a vocabulary of labyrinth. In it we find numerous references to doors, rooms, sashes, stairways, floors. We have an architecture of mystery — what is contained, excluded, covered, separated, whatever exists at threshold. (One poem, later in the book, "Erie County," makes much of "broader country" and "crossing frontiers," and many others deal with threshold experiences of transformation or of a profane world receiving the sacred.)

Even the waste baskets into which the janitors dump the bones and brains they sweep up (a grotesque allusion to the war? concentration camps?) enlarge their category, from the macabre to a secondary set in which they figure as objects of secrecy and revelation. So, too — and we see Mandel's hand as lover of paranomasia in these early poems — the speaker comes to a discovery "after several *stories*," the movement towards illumination, however gruesome, being facilitated *and* hindered by the architectural stories and the verbal stories through which he must pass.

The mythic allusions are so evident it is commonplace to speak of Mandel's mythopoesis, and in recent years, as the dominant aesthetic has come to change in Canada, to disparage that style. I myself have mixed feelings about the early poems, seeing their weaknesses as deriving largely from their mythopoesis. The problem is perhaps not because they are mythic but because they choose as their base the proper nouns of an exotic mythology. In a sense they haven't fully localized the myths and depend too much on invoking the *names* of other places and other times, so that the myths' claims upon us are more nominal that actual.

Even so, the poems seek to domesticate the myths in two major ways. For one thing they mix a grand or at least a measured voice, one that speaks in serious tones, together with an off-hand, at times even slangy voice. The combination removes the myths from the deadliness of high-minded speech and confers on them the snap of the colloquial, a sign that they *are* available in something other than the sanctified and elevated language of the priestly, the learned, and the bookish, where they are in danger of seeming not to be available at all. The poems also seek to articulate a contemporaneity by including references to what appears to be an ordinary and up-to-date world. We can take the disarming mention of the janitors in the first "Minotaur" poem for example. Or "Orpheus," the last of the "Minotaur" poems and the only one of them which is entitled, where Mandel represents Orpheus as a Welsh miner — a good idea, but one that is hardly realized because the language defers so heavily to literary texts that only a minimal sense of Orpheus as an actual coal miner emerges. Much the same problem besets, say, "Leda and the Swan" and the better known "Estevan, Saskatchewan." At every turn the language prefers Leda to Estevan, the Swan to Saskatchewan. We get more a homage to Yeats than a bringing forth of felt reality or of myths alive and embodied *in* their supposed setting. We could describe the weakness as the result of wanting to place words within the reflexive operations of a literary system *far* more than inside any referential operations that would snag the tangibles our bodies pass through and that would invest the myths therefore with a *sense* of immediacy and authenticity.

Two of the finest poems — "Minotaur" II and "Val Marie" IV — succeed very well in putting flesh on old skeletons. In both instances, the language becomes less obviously reflexive and acts in a more referential way to name a local habitation. It injects enough idiom to remove the occasion from the high-blown abstraction that weakens some of the other poems. Here is the second stanza of the "Val Marie" poem:

Out of God knows where and beached against these shoals,
The ridge of Mary's valley. A gull screams
Looking for water over these bones and shells,
North to the lake behind the damned and rotting streams.

How refreshing — how convincing — it is to hear the street voice
"Out of God knows where," its witty pun, irreverence mixed with
reverence, for in the special vocabulary of these mythopoeic poems
God *does* know. My main point, however, is the effect of the voice
in implying that it speaks vitally of tangible things, things that really
matter. And how telling is the language that would simply name the
things at hand: "A gull screams / Looking for water over these bones
and shells." The words, escaped from inflation, more readily convince that the numinous is at hand, right there, immanently. The
simple translation — "Val Marie" to "Mary's Valley" — by working
so modestly and so inconspicuously, also serves to locate the mythic
as if it were in fact incarnate.

In a thoughtful review, which covers a wide range of poetry with
typical insight and generosity, Mandel explores the relationship
between poetry that would seek the "powerful liberalizing effects"
of myth (1960, p. 291) and poetry "concerned with coming to terms
with experience" by providing us with the feel of "the fierce, physical
grip of language" (p. 292). The former favours the reflexive qualities
of language in literature as a self-contained and self-referring system,
and the latter insists on the lexical or semantic properties of words
as they might point to a larger world outside their own existence and
prior to it. Mandel here supposes there is no escaping "the general
rule that since mythic poetry depends for its effect on coherence of
pattern and a general, rather than a particular, relationship to
experience, its usual appearance is stylized and formal" (p. 288). But
he goes further. Later, in an essay called "Lapwing You Are. Lapwing
He — A Note on Icarus in Myth and Poetry" he points in quite a
different direction: ". . . Breughel shows us, in an unforgettable
image, how the extraordinary enters the temporal order and relates
to (indeed, *is*) ordinary experience . . ." (1962, p. 59). Elaborate and
a priori structure, *and* description of the phenomenal world — he
seeks them both. It is difficult to realize both, not to lose the weight
of experience in such passion for structuring.

In *Trio* Mandel is not always successful at naturalizing myth, as
I've tried to suggest, often preferring the myths to "experience." But

in "Minotaur" II he tellingly locates myth in a tangible world:

My father was always out in the garage
building a shining wing, a wing
that curved and flew alone the edge of blue air
in that streamed and sunlit room
that smelled of oil and engines
and crankcase grease, and especially
the lemon smell of polish and cedar.
Outside there were sharp rocks, and trees,
cold air where birds fell like rocks
and screams, hawks, kites, and cranes.
The air was filled with a buzzing and flying
and the invisible hum of a bee's wings was honey
in my father's framed and engined mind.
Last Saturday we saw him at the horizon
screaming like a hawk as he fell into the sun.

Perhaps the example of Auden's "Musée des Beaux Arts" has helped Mandel here, in finding ways to body forth the idea (as perhaps Mandel's poem itself gave occasion to Margaret Atwood's Circe poems). The "Minotaur" poem places the Icarus myth squarely in the body — in smells (of oil and grease, of polish and cedar), in numerous images of light (shining, blue air, sunlit room, birds and rocks), in sounds (buzzing, hum, screaming). We get even a sense of touch ("sharp rocks," "streamed," and "the edge of blue air") and heft (in the "filled" air and in that wonderful line "cold air where birds fell like rocks"). But more, the high finds nomination in unassuming or "unpoetic" things — garages, crankcases, bees' wings, cranes — and in casual phrasings ("My father was always out in the garage") of a speaker who again adopts a citational mode ("the garage," "the edge," "the smell," "in that streamed and sunlit room") that enlists our identification and our sympathy. Although the speaker is emotionally detached, like other speakers in these poems, he is by no means effaced.

Mandel's mythopoesis soon aligns him with wonder and magic, most notably in the superb poem "Fair in Town" (misprinted in Trio where its last two stanzas are wrongly added — they belong to a different poem). It seems to me badly overlooked: it is not even included in either of Mandel's selecteds, though "Estevan, Saskatchewan," a much weaker poem from the same period, is. We can observe in "Fair in Town" Mandel's belief in the transforming power of imagination, his celebration of the artist figure, here in the guise of circus performers, and his lyrical expression of awe: "clouds tumbled and sang like cherubs / In their rags and noise of light." We also find Mandel's celebration of release into magic, into peoples' best repressed selves: the town that "lost itself" and "became itself." This is a carnival, a carnal place of permission and transgression, but in it Mandel locates divinity. Its sanctity figures in the multiple meanings Mandel milks out of "rose up in mass," "aghast," and the whole set of words referring to breath and spirit — spired, breathing, breathless, in the new spirit. It jostles through the kinesthetics of "Shock" and "shivering," and "staggered," the phonemic play on "alert" and "altered" that consolidates our connection of those states. A sense of wonder declares itself in the nasal resonance of "pennants furled and sang" and "time sang." It emerges, full blown, in "A maze" of entertainers, performers, tricksters — simply amazing, we wandering, in wonder, wondering where we are in the maze. Lost in wonder.

Fuseli Poems (1960)

Certain themes that Mandel touches on in *Trio* emerge more emphatically in his first single-author book. One of them, vaguely Oedipal, had appeared in "my father's framed and engined mind" ("Minotaur," II), in the incest theme of "Joy of Conquest," in "Estevan, Saskatchewan," and probably in the telling references to eyes that watch so vigilantly in the earlier poems. A counter to the father makes its way into those first poems, too. There is Mary of the "Val Marie" poem, Mary with her valley which contains all life, and there is in the first of "Val Marie" sonnets a female principle rather like the terrible or devouring mother of ancient mythology. Here she is likened in a somewhat strained conceit (so typical of Mandel's early rhetoric) to a threshing machine taking into herself the body of a farmer. That female principle also realized itself in "the furrow's lip, the mouth's murmur" in a terrain so identified with her power that she surrounds and swallows the man: "And over him she leans like love forever / Poised in her grief, her mechanical hover." The struggle of mothers and fathers for the poet's allegiance continues unabated in *Fuseli*. On the whole the poems that concern themselves with Oedipal themes migrate toward the mother, and they take on both an erotic and a prophetic bent.

"Notes from the Underground" (pp. 18–19) gives us a woman who presides over a cave that is "out of town" and full of "rusting texts" and springs. It is to that cave, rife with hints of sexual transgression, the poet is drawn. The caves in the Souris Valley south of Estevan, Mandel told me, "were often used as places where boys took girls to have sex with them, and I must have had a powerful reaction to that, because clearly the caves had become symbols to me, of some kind, and often symbols of a kind of sybil figure" (Cooley 1982). The female principle serves then as muse and gives voice to the poet who would speak as oracle and as prophet.

The opposition between forbidding patriarch in the present and potentially emancipating matriarch in the past brings to a close a strange piece, "Fuseli: Girl Combing Her Hair, Watched by a Young Man." The final section, part three, describes several authority figures, usually male — a principal, an officer, and a batch of "moralists." Significantly it confronts us: "You will ask how . . . the university could tolerate me, / what night it was I hung from the rock / and whether my father knew" (p. 17). And then, against these indications of institutional, cerebral, and male supremacy, Mandel ends with another reference to the fertility and nurturing of women ensconced in concavities, ripe with the language of their fullness:

You will understand how much of this is description,
how in the valley mothers would gather, the river
swollen, the mustard milky and sticky, breasted plant,
and how icy sons blossomed like crystal.

(p. 17)

In "In the Caves of My City" we find, as in so many other poems in the collection, right from the start, the mouth. The word is so recurrent in Mandel it borders on the obsessional. Or at least the central. Little wonder, since it is the source of voices, the organ of speech, of giving testimony and of calling into being. From it we hear voice, with it we issue sounds that in Mandel's poetics might reconstitute the world, and with it we make love. Loving words, we speak them — the loving words. For Mandel would hear the voices:

When there are no more voices
and yet you hear voices singing
   in the hot street

(p. 19)

the zeal of ducks for noise
(touching this question of fire)
is not the music that I hoped to hear
(Isaiah's coal, the final choir)

(p. 23)

And he would speak to them, have them rearrange the world, answerable to his speaking, amenable to his vision: "Who, with his mouth, will stop / this cold blood or put his root / or seed into this vain wound" (p. 51).

This inclination to speak, to hear, to read the world, gives rise to many metaphors of a life which is already written and which needs therefore a discerning mind to recognize and to decipher it. That stance puts Mandel into some opposition with his belief that we constitute our world and that the poet as prophet plays a central role in its making. Reading or recognizing implies that realities are already *there* and that it is our job to detect them or to take them in. The visions can, however, be reconciled by thinking of them reciprocally. For so they surely are seen in the Jewish tradition upon which Mandel is in part drawing. In that tradition the world is a text and we at our best are people of letters, learned, who read it. This is no small feat, for the texts are often occluded and become tests to our skills and perseverance because they are written over like palimpsests, partially erased, or subtended/extended into the margins as glosses. Their being known in any time or any place requires elaborate preparation and attention.

The belief in a lettered world informs "Ceremony for Rosh Hashonah." The first five stanzas locate the poem and raise the theme of failed believers, the poet included (especially him — nervous, distracted, querulous, wordly, maybe even fraudulent, by all odds fallen away). But the scroll, with The Word, brings forth its leaves, to close the breaches and to replace "profit" with "prophet." When it speaks through its "mouth," those in attendance turn over a new leaf, move out of their spiritual winter and into responsive song:

A mouth,
a moth, the scroll unrolls and rolls
the year into a scroll, binds up the year
of law and prophet.

The breach in nature closes.
On waves of Hebrew breath
the ark is steady and the scroll,
a golden leaf, is carried by the rabbi
through the singing Hebrew crowd.

(p. 39)

It is well to remark on this influence, which emphasizes learning
and effort, since it reinforces the impact of modernism in Mandel's
work.

I was brought up twenty-five years ago on the notion that poetry
was obscure, necessarily, and that poetry would also have a
limited audience because the demands of the art were demands
of obscurity. Only a refined person could dare to be so obscure.
Like Ashberry now, eh . . . . So I always worked privately. I also
believed that poetry was about a secret. I still believe that, by
the way. I think it's a confession about something you can't
confess. (Arnason, p. 84)

Modernism, with its respect for erudition, high allusion, and metaphoric ingenuity, nicely coincided with Mandel's Jewish inscriptions.
The response was probably inevitable. How else to read these texts?
Modernism put in place poems as intellectual puzzles, dense in their
resistance to understanding and to satisfaction in felt life. In
Mandel's case the inclination was so heightened it presented what
must have been terrible temptation to obscurity. The effects were
demonstrated, sometime damagingly I think, in the first three books,
but also in references and symbols that have persisted in his writing.
We have already touched on one consequence (the caves), but the
symbol belongs in Mandel to a huge category of words that refer to
occlusion and discovery. A hermeneutic world is one that is not open
or apparent to our understanding. It is informed by secrecy, special
codes, spatial images, and — to use a favourite Mandel word —
duplicity.

It can come as no surprise, then, that many of these poems challenge their audience. Some of them are satirical and briskly ridicule the inanities of our world:

THE GOLD BUG

a poisonous bee burst his pod
in the palm of my hand
                   his venom

flowed over my hand like honey

now honoured among men
I gesture with my golden hand
and speak with the language of money

"The Gold Bug" takes us in by apparently using the language, so common to the book, of the black romantic. The potent and dangerous power the speaker receives, the religious overtones ("the palm of my hand"), the hint of magic (alchemical? medical, as in having the touch?), the invoking of a "golden" hand, with its hints of extraordinary or pure or god-like qualities, the emphasis upon transformation (a bee burst . . . now I) that would seem to draw on the conventions of epiphany or change, the culmination in the metalinguistics of "gesture," "speak," and "language" that seem to move into a category of enlarged significance — all these enlist the poem, in the light of the other poems, in celebration of its own twisted prophet. But no, there is the sudden undermining with that very last word, the language of . . . money, and the whole reading collapses. Perhaps we might have noticed that "gesture" could point in another direction; after the fact we certainly do. The realization transposes the poem into a different understanding. The sudden discovery of a word that violates the apparent decorum, compounded in the shocking collusion of "honey" with "money," delivers us out of romantic admiration and into ironic ridicule.

In quite a few poems, especially ones that feature self-mockery, Mandel speaks *to* an audience. "It had to be a speaking voice. And it had to be a clear dramatic situation," he has said. "People often don't see that, they think it's mysterious" (Cooley, 1982). The voice is affective in its awareness of audience and its seeking to act upon

it. It manifests itself in questions and imperatives, but it occurs too
in Mandel as an instructing voice:

> For blue men do not speak
> the way you speak, or cry
> hail and farewell.
>
> They squeak
> like heels on ice
>
> or needles on a gramophone.
>
> (p. 15)

Though strictly speaking the voice here provides information and
seems therefore to be referential, it does so in order to benefit an
audience, to bring them around to preferred knowledge — insight
that would promote appreciation of the prophet/poet and that would
obviate the banality of phatic utterance ("hail and farewell").
(Though even here we note the care with which Mandel webs his
language in an internal system, rhyming "squeak," "heels," and
"needles.")

More often the voice is comical in its desperation, its self-doubt,
aware of its own outrageousness. We see signs of that in "Entomology" and then in "The Professor as Bridegroom" (p. 47), which
is full of self-ridicule and mounts to a hilarious ending. Absurdity
virtually takes over "Two Part Exercise on a Single Image" (pp.
32–33). The first part, which neatly sets up the second, speaks
seriously and lyrically of vision and of the danger that the visionary
will be forever betrayed and sentenced — hanged, actually, as in so
many *Fuseli* poems — by the world he inhabits *and* by the world he
invents. Part II answers in marvellous language, one that presents to
us a figure who suspiciously resembles Mandel himself, bad speller
hunched inside surreal dreams:

> You think it is easy? A matter of words?
> And wonder that I'm a poor speller?
> Let me tell you that this has nothing to do
> With teaching or even the love of poetry.
> It is the calamity of an eyesore, a stye,
> A social disaster. Look for once
> At the real, ridiculous humped self

Crouched in the unexplained interior.
See it looming in the light
Of exploding volcanoes and dark fig trees
Like the hunched white question mark
Of a polar bear.
Oh my friend, I too like company
And have ambitions in business.

(pp. 32–33)

The strategy figures with great effect in a number of poems. In them the Mandel persona is a driven man, urgent, a bit angry. Frustrated and defiant, he greets us with comical confessions and challenges. More Woody Allen than Isaiah, he is prepared apparently to reveal his own chagrin and ineptitude. But because his fumblings are so ridiculous, so in keeping with his deepest desires and the brute incapacity of life to confirm them, precisely because he becomes so vulnerable in his exhortations and admissions, we find him both disarming and endearing. His appeals ("Oh my friend, I too") come not from aristocratic prerogative but from personal need, from weakness, a shared humanity, and take us in, standing under that knowledge, understanding. They move us, comical conspirators, into the ludicrously unexpected, that madly out-of-place confession: "I too like company / And have ambitions in business." And we wonder then, in retrospection: in what sense is this preposterous prophet a "poor speller"? Does he fail, in the zany pun, not simply as orthographer but as prophet too, inept in casting spells?

Here is the register of a speaker who is *present* to us, actively involved, and wrestling with his angels / his demons. There are other modes in which Mandel excels. The lyrical for one. In 1978 Mandel said "I happen to think that I'm a very good lyric poet and that few people really understand that. There's a lot more lyricism in my poetry than people recognize" (Arnason, p. 83). Mandel is right, his touch has *not* received its due. Although a lyrical grace becomes conspicuous from *An Idiot Joy* on, it is apparent as early as *Fuseli*. Take for example the beautiful "Hallowe'en by St. Mary's Convent":

Streetlights blossom on their stems.
Like honeybees in lust of bloom
small Spirits hum through meadows of the dark
toward the petalled homes, the flowered rooms.

And out of the Revelation, Angels swarm
to feed on spiritual sweet food,
globed fruit, round nut, and jelly bean.

Such occult cheerfulness the swarm
exudes from sticky maiche of skull
and sheeted ghost, gusty with laugh,
as makes them guest, forgives the child
his candle in the skull, forgives
his blinded eye, his idiotic grin,
all ills of flesh unmasked by mask on flesh.

(p. 34)

A great and chilling image, that — "his candle in the skull." (It is
hard not to identify Mandel with his Hallowe'en children here, with
their aberrant looks, their deranged minds, let loose in the permissions of ceremony — harvest rituals that take on dimensions of a
mildly comical apocalypse.) Actually Mandel can write so well in
this mode it is a wonder he didn't choose to cultivate it from the
start. Certainly the possibility did occur to him early on. How could
it not, with his intelligence?

I think about my past and try to change
Into a singing metaphor a silent heart,
A frail red parrot perched within its cage
Repeating what it hears and cackling without change
All that ear hears and tongue speaks. I form in thought
The singing form that forms the silent heart.

(p. 57)

The lines bear the markings of Yeats in their removal of articles (not:
the ear, but: ear; not: the tongue, but: tongue), in their concentration
on one major metaphor become symbol, in their mention of heart
as cultural symbol, in their homage to eternity in art. But they *are*
lyrical, and they demonstrate Mandel's capacity to move in that
direction.

There are other signs in *Fuseli* that Mandel was beginning to depart
from a high rhetoric. "Death of a Poet" (p. 52) deals explicitly with
the possibility. "The Wind at Djemila" (p. 46) breaks up the horizontal trajectory of the poetic line by introducing two vertical

221

columns in such a way that the syntax becomes almost hypnagogic, especially if read conventionally from left to right and top to bottom, across the columns. "Ironist" (p. 63) toys with freeing up words by breaking them into syllables across lines, and "Poetic Process" (p. 21) risks a folksy simile in place of a grand trope.

It would be wrong to suppose that closed forms can no longer work, or that Mandel cannot make them work. As we noted in *Trio*, he has shown great skill in handling the sonnet, clicking those sonnets shut with ingenuity. And one of the most astonishing pieces in *Fuseli*, one of the most accomplished Mandel has ever written in fact, is an Audenesque villanelle, "City Park Merry-Go-Round":

> Freedom is seldom what you now believe,
> Mostly you circle round and round the park:
> Night follows day, these horses never leave.
>
> Like children, love whatever you conceive,
> See then your world as lights whirled in the dark.
> Freedom is seldom what you now believe.
>
> Your world moves up and down or seems to weave.
> And still you pass and pass that same old mark.
> Night follows day, these horses never leave.
>
> You thought your past was here, you might retrieve
> That wild illusion whirling in the dark.
> Freedom is seldom what you now believe.
>
> Sick on that circle you begin to grieve.
> You wish the ride would end and you could park.
> Night follows day, these horses never leave.
>
> Mostly you circle round and round the park.
> You'd give your life now to be free to leave.
> Freedom is seldom what you now believe.
> Night follows day, these horses never leave.

(p. 40)

"City Park" is brilliantly realized. The extremely closed form of the villanelle finds its perfect subject in the theme of human entrapment and lost innocence. Measured out in precise iambic pentametre (there are several trochees, especially at the beginnings of lines, for variety and emphasis), the villanelle contains itself in five perfect triplets and a quatrain, all turning on two end-rhymes. Unvaried and unrelieved by any departures, the set stanzas, the emphatic rhythm, and the severely restricted rhyme all intensify the sense of acute enclosure. Formally, the words as semantic markers are reigned back again and again to the claims of prosody. It seems as though the words themselves cannot escape centripetal forces that centre the poem, as if they were pulled back by some nucleus that would not permit their free trajectory. The lines, true to the root of "verse," turn back on themselves, again and again.

Even the voice in which the narrator construes the park seems to hold the rider forever. In its summary and epigrammatic qualities it too creates an effect of defining: this is what you *are*. When the speaker says "Night follows day" there seems no escaping, no quarrelling with his truth. Distilling, firming up, confident in claims, he is virtually invisible, hidden in sayings, and unquestionable in his authority. For his impact seems to derive from some impersonal source beyond challenge: this is the way things are.

Black and Secret Man (1964)

Mandel has said this was a breakthrough book for him and in many ways it is. A small sign of change comes in the author's name (it is now the more personal "Eli" Mandel, not the high modernist "E.W." Mandel of the first two books). And the new book carries a personal dedication, "This book is for Evie and Charles," his then young children. For the most part, however, these poems are not very personal, although some of them — "Thief Hanging in Baptist Halls" (p. 14), "To My Children" (p. 32), "Charles Isaac Mandel" (p. 3), "David" (p. 10), "Among These Beings Not This at Least" (pp. 31–32) — appear to derive from quite personal experiences. As a whole the poems still enter the world in formal dress and persist in distanced personae of the wounded outsider, though Mandel takes his personae further into poses that can best be described as comically theatrical.

Black and Secret Man to a degree perpetuates Mandel's initial concern with what is hidden and maybe even unknowable — a belief

attendant upon the hermeneutic criticism of the 1950s. We noted in
the earlier work frequent references to caves, dungeons, labyrinths,
boxes, and so on. Objects of containment and concealment, they
stood as symbols of the poem and the world of poetry as being in
some special sense smeared with mystery and therefore available
only to someone in the know. The title poem of his new book, "Black
and Secret Man" (p. 1), continues that belief. It is replete, as its title
might lead us to expect, with occult references to murders, hangings,
and dark secrets. Its language and procedures are quite in keeping:
exotic diction ("choughs and rooks"); unidentified pronouns; high-
blown rhetoric ("temple-haunting martlet"); rapid discourse time
(which suggests fable); echoes of the book's *Macbeth* epigraph; a
closing stanza in the mode of riddle or chant. We are introduced to
a world of fantasy, but one full of darkness, risk, threat, even
grotesque death. There are no sugar plum fairies in Mandel's world,
certainly not in the first three books where, as in the title poem, "A
black and secret man of blood walks / In the garden."

The poem raises a theme which we saw earlier and which emerges
more centrally in this book. The expression "man of blood" may in
some vague way alert us to it, or at least confirm our suspicions, for
in "Black and Secret Man" the mother seems responsible for the
father's death. She may even be the agent of other deaths. It is hard
to tell, the poem is so dense and so evasive. In any case, "Black and
Secret Man" does serve in its prominence as both title poem and lead
poem to establish certain qualities. When the unidentified speaker
says in the very first lines, "These are the pictures that I took," we
are quite prepared in deference to the conventions of placement and
title to project the reference beyond the introductory poem and into
subsequent pieces; much as we in part assign the remarkably similar
first words in Michael Ondaatje's *The Collected Works of Billy the
Kid*, "I send you a picture of Billy . . . ," to a structural role in the
book, serving proleptically to activate a series of later "pictures."

We find confirmation for the strategy in *Black and Secret Man*
when in the penultimate poem, "To My Children" (p. 32), the black
and poisonous flower that appeared earlier in the book (p. 4) has
given way to a rose, and the dead (grand)father in "Charles Isaac
Mandel" (p. 3) has been replaced by a third generation. The poems
serve to frame the book in several other ways, including Mandel's
fuller projection of his Jewish heritage into the poems. In "To My
Children" he writes of the fulfilment of the law as the unfolding of

narrative. Here, specifically, that means each generation recapitulates the struggle to find itself. The repetition seems particularly just, and difficult, because though each new generation is associated with flowers of love and passion, they find it hard to blossom in the "stony and brittle" desert of their parents. The rhythm of succession lies, apparently, in eternity, the almost epigrammatic quality of the assertion "The rabbis are ancient and wise" serving to enlist the stability of their vision. We read other lines, too, so parabolic in their brevity, so firm in inviting us to fill in the unsaid and to generalize the poem's meaning, as if they were immutable. They seem beyond doubt because cast in the indicative mood and in such brevity, such end-stopped, half-rhymed lines — so intact in their assertion — bearing the weight of gnomic wisdom.

Many of these poems contain overt reference to Jewish life. Moses, Ezekiel, Jacob, David, Samson, Samuel, and Job all figure in the book. Several poems refer to Jewish belief, among them "Hebraism" (p. 16), the lovely and faintly metaphysical poem "Day of Atonement: Standing" (p. 9), and the poem about Mandel's father (p. 3). The moments also invoke the claims that faith puts upon its members. In "Hebraism," the more facetious and slighter of the two father poems, the point is made explicit: "The law is the law and is / terribly Hebrew," but it is there in "Charles Isaac Mandel," which involves a certain commitment on the speaker's part. He rejects a bright world of irony and, in a manner so provisional and so understated it becomes poignant, dedicates himself to the emblems of his father and, by extension, of his own: "I gather the few relics of my father: / his soiled Tallis, his Tefillin, / the strict black leather of his dark faith."

For the law *is* strict, it is strong. Mosaic, it sheds the erosions of time, commands the fulfilment of its narrative. Mandel, wrestling with his own parentage, fastens upon those who in the Old Testament are put into troubled relationships with stone. That includes David the psalmist with a sling-shot, and Jacob who dreams on stone: two poets who contend with stone and dream of a more fluid order. David in Mandel's excellent poem of the same name (pp. 10–11) strays uneasily through a world where the king his father insists "my poetry must stop" and where the doctors, evidently in homage to conventional wisdom, solicitously ask about David's sling-shot arm. But David himself prefers poetry to sling-shots and is horrified at small murders and great murders, the killing of gophers and the killing of people. His summary of his people's preference lays bare his dismay, however comical in its mocking:

> murder will end murder
> the saying goes, someone must
> do something about the rodents
> and poems do not:

The language attests to a certain obduracy in David's people, one which borders on stupidity. In their obeisance to "sayings," the already said, the previously written, they endorse that narrative and subscribe to its coercions. Such contracts are not without value. They are of immense advantage in perpetuating a culture, but in another economy (and it is this that preoccupies us here) they can be seen not to continue a vital way of life, but to negate the vagaries, the renewals or re-writings or re-visions, every culture needs if it is to survive.

We have, then, David's vision of a world indentured to murder. It is not for him something easily to be excused in the dictates of saying; it is a world bathed in gopher-blood, of bodies or selves being so taken over by murderous thoughts they are themselves turned into weapons ("my shadow hanging / like a slingshot"), of the cosmos itself altered by the mindless projection so that in the powerful ending "the world turns like a murderous stone / my forehead aching with stars" (p. 11). It may well be that the semantic connection between David as stone-bearer and the cosmos as stone makes him complicit in the murders, but we find for the most part, I think, an artist trying to escape the king's stony law and the granite brains of citizens who hold poems in so little regard.

We recognize in "David" several of Mandel's perennial themes — the poet as outsider and the conflict of generations, the two appearing often, as here, in a single situation. In a number of the pieces in *Black and Secret Man* the father, the stonyman, stands as obstructor in the way of creativity. That figure is relatively recent in Mandel. Its satellites are not. In opposition to the patriarch, we commonly find some grand mother, as we seem to have detected in the title poem. We can find her in the third poem in the collection, "Mary Midnight's Prologue" (pp. 2–3), where she is remarkably reminiscent of the cave women in *Fuseli*. In "Mary Midnight" we find, in comical tones, a woman of prodigious fecundity. As encompassing female principle she is the source and end of all things. She emerges, embraces, swallows, and joins — joins even in the enfolding prosody of the poem. Of Mary's lines, all but the last of them link to each other as couplets, if only in half rhyme. She is labyrinthine / labiarinthine (with her "vulvular mouth"), yes. But she is not, and her poem is not, subject to the tortured intellectualism of the earlier labyrinth pieces.

"Mary Midnight's Prologue" stands for those mothers who elsewhere in the book symbolize the creative potential of "unseen water," "besides the dry reeds of the lakeless fields" (p. 20) and who provoke the question, "How can we turn aside from the mother" (p. 21). The female muse also appears, just barely emerging, in the gently satiric "February Thaw" (p. 28) and, of course, in "Cassandra" (p. 28), which presents the tranced world of the prophet, presided over by Cassandra, bodied forth in contemporary life by women when they have emerged "bright-eyed" as if emulating "an image out of sleep." So transformed by powers "we [men: the gender is forced inescapably upon us] dare not think about":

> They walk
> as if I had dwindled, looking past me
> toward unreasonable parliaments
> crouching beside senatorial hills.
>
> (p. 28)

Once more the wisdom beyond the reach of ordinary "male" understanding dwarfs and shames its smallness. Queasy with inadequacy, the poet courts the muse, aware of the ridiculous figure he cuts: "I have been practising this poetry in secret. / Also I have made advances toward pregnant / women." But he does so with limited results, as the mock-heroic ending makes clear.

He realizes, nevertheless, that if he is going to shake off the necessities of law, he will have to take terrible chances and he will have to break the stone letters that weight him inertly to the past. He will have to observe not the letter but the spirit of the law, serve not as grammarian or scribe who would enforce the law, but as prophet who would in observing break it. In such a reciprocity the law as it is written *is* irrevocable, but it is at the same time susceptible to amplification. One who would endorse the law does so in glossing it, in working the margins, possibly in one version of service acting as black and secret man. In attendance upon a matriarch who predates and would antedate those letters, he would be in a position to find within her matrix no such written language or, better, to find there a more encompassing language. Either way, the poet could find in "Mary Midnight" a promise of emancipation in her "magazine before catalogue and doom [a parody of the Old Testament narrative?] / Where I unpage the universal heart / Of continental tears and provinces of hurt" (p. 3). We have here not quite an unwriting of the wor(l)d. It is more a prior writing, an original script that will surface if we scrape off the language written over it, the damaging palimpsest of patriarchy.

Whatever distance there may be between any poem and Mandel's Jewishness, they do connect in at least one other respect. The creative man of letters walks through an unappreciative world scarcely capable of knowing, much less appreciating, what he offers. In "Carleton University: January 1961" that world hardly surpasses the mineral. In one poem the poet as crazed outsider comes down with "a strange disease" so that "he no longer knows that numbers are / nor understands the language spoken here [in Ottawa]" (p. 24). In other poems voices report of the threat from the "normal" world. One, in the jump of street language, says "I don't like evasion any more than you do / but to speak out at this time / is more dangerous than you might think" (p. 10). In another the speaker talks uneasily of punishment and beaten animals, and of standing beside the maternal waters where "hands have been held out to me / I dare not touch . . ." (p. 20). In a poem addressed to a "Yonge Street Minstrel," a broken-down boxer, Mandel transforms a Sousterish subject (the poem is dedicated to Raymond Souster) into a symbol of the violated visionary, one who is a black and secret man:

> don't you know they will get you
>   in the ring or in some alley
>   that they will break your mouth
> that even the best go blind
>   hear unevident birds
>
> or do you care, thinking of brutes
>   buckled and crushed
>   the great roar
> and the white centre blind with light?

(p. 15)

Many of the poems refer to a hanged and sometimes hunchbacked man. The most sustained expression of this symbol appears in "Thief Hanging in Baptist Halls" (p. 14) where the poet impishly identifies with a dark, hirsute, and distinctly sexual Christ. The poem plays more than one possibility, including the sexual and political (the hung man a puppet in servitude), off the word "hung" and its variations.

Judging from what I have said so far, readers may suppose that Mandel has hit upon a new strategy in handling mythic themes. And so he has. Gone — well, reduced — are the rotund phrase, the dense and esoteric allusion, the abstract language, the high seriousness. The Orpheus who enters the *Black and Secret* poems is more fully and more comically domesticated that he once was. Although he pops up by implication in a number of poems (in "Aesop," pp. 1–2, for example), he has two whole poems to himself, in the first of which, "Orpheus and Eurydice" (p. 16), somebody with few literary pretensions but some real verve idiomatically retells the Orpheus story. Mandel starts him off on what would seem to be solemnity, then quickly undermines the opening with idiom. He then proceeds whimsically to body Orpheus forth as this guy who gets off the odd song when Eurydice turns him on, and ends with a comical undercutting that at the same time honours Orpheus by making him tangible:

> The girls got him with disease
> and watched him fall away
>   in parts
> like some old tree with warts,
> or tree god rotting on the vine.
>
>   (p. 16)

A number of the visionary poems end on a strong lyrical note, frequently in images of fire or light and in rhythms of more stylized regularity. The ending of "Death By Fire" best represents this quality:

> Never this night of gasoline
> these unbearable fumes
> this prayer that for itself consumes
> all that man's own resinous heart had fed
> and all that in his veins runs like the fire red.
>
>   (p. 25)

The book ends with an impressive sequence of poems. Apart from a few I have already mentioned, I would single out "The Mayor's Papers," "The Comedians," "Rapunzel," and "There Is No One Here Except Us Comedians" as being exceptionally strong. The last three work in a similar mode, so it is possible though hardly ideal to speak of them together. They are sonorous (this is most true of "The Comedians") and slightly regular in their stanzas and lines (particularly "Rapunzel" which, though it is the most energetically colloquial in spots, also is the closest to song). They all use simple, concrete words, they all are elegantly structured, and they all end on powerful images and rhythms.

"There Is No One Here" beautifully develops the theme of visionary release. It refreshingly mixes the colloquial and the elevated. And it points always to secrets and prisons. The poem is loaded with masks, doors, dreams, wheels within wheels (shades of Ezekiel), fairs, gates, rolling balls, thoughts of flight, and so on. What would seem to contain the poet, "towering fathers," finds its counterpart in another muse, "a 29-year-old smiling girl" on the other side of the door and the symbolic possibilities that the wheels seem to connote. Certainly it is within these wheels, within a fairground, within "what we *call* dreams" (my emphasis) that the speaker is transformed ("turned into" is his phrase, with its lovely catch of the physical turning on a ride at a fair and an inward turning) into a freed person without parents and without gender.

I am struck by a profound adjustment in Mandel's vision from here on. Whereas once he sought the distant and the hidden, and revelled in a closed world, he now wants to be in a wheat field, symbol of what is local and open. Redeemed in humour and "low" life, he now would be a lock-picker, "my bird feet tinkling at keyholes" and "whispering blasphemies," likely against the fathers. The end seems to me a triumph in its fit of sound and sense:

> I want you to know I am innocent
> I want you to open the last door
> into the field of orphan wheat
> the orient grain the green golden corn

(p. 30)

Although the words here are induced by phonetic resemblances — "door" begetting "orphan," "orient," and "corn," "grain" minting "green" and "golden"; the final "n" in all those words calling into being their like elsewhere — they are appropriate lexically. We hear echoes of Ruth in exile (and surely one trait of Mandel's writers in the first three books is their feeling of exile), of a paradisal world, the satisfying attention in the word "corn" to the exotic (as in the British name for cereal crops, entered into the St. James Bible) and the local (as in maize or Indian corn).

Finally, *Black and Secret Man* opens a new vein of zany political satire. One of the most interesting examples is "The Mayor's Papers" (p. 26). The poem builds upon a collision between the speaker and those who oppose him. The conflict involves a struggle between the speaker, who articulates his sense of ecological crisis, and the others, who try to dismiss his charges or to silence him. The poem progresses by lurching suddenly and elliptically between opposed sections, the narrator bringing a visionary awareness of disaster ("saw . . . told") and the need for a special discourse ("am short of metaphors," "desperate need for / metaphors") to bear witness. The urgency registers all the more in his language of repeated effort: "tried the one / that goes . . . ," "tried," "only hope now the one about. . . ." What is especially striking about the poem as it enters Mandel's oeuvre is its startling mix of language. The speaker struggles towards a discourse adequate to his experience. He recognizes at once, in his need for metaphor, that only poetry can serve him.

Towards the end, the speaker's testimony erupts in run-on or compound words and a construction which, in using parentheses inside words, pries out double words and drastically foregrounds language in what for Mandel is a new way:

> tried:
>   riverunto (ps) oil
>   wild scene (courtroom cleared
>   heads rolling
>   headlines)

Throughout the drama, the authorities have by insisting upon their own discourse imprisoned themselves within it. What they need most of all is a capacity to enter the very language the speaker offers them, but they cannot go past their own to free new meaning. So the bizarre word "riverunto (ps) oil" remains simply scandalous, intolerable to them, and they make no attempt to understand it. They refuse to place themselves in submission to it and the prophetic illumination it represents. They see only nonsense where the poet speaks of the terrible pollution of oil in water, topsoil in water, of river befouled with oil and soil, of a river running to oil. (The combinations go on in a wonderful semantic melding that in its very confusion so clearly enunciates the contamination.)

The poem closes on another note — one that resembles the prophetic voice as it has appeared elsewhere in Mandel up until now:

> only hope now the one about the girls
>   something about harlotry
>   something about Lot's wife
>   something . . . .

(p. 26)

The heavy allusions establish the intense focus of the speaker, dwelling on an epiphany whose edges he brushes (something, something, something) and they lay before us a note of ceremony on the heels of a pell-mell give and take. The speaker, haunted by his half-realization, seems determined to say but gropes to know what must be said. The elliptical closure, voice trailing off in "something . . . ," eloquently reveals his heightened sense of uncertainty and incompletion. The poem, in polyphony and modest closure, points to Mandel's next and perhaps best book where he comes out fully from under the law.

An Idiot Joy (1967)

This certainly is a breakthrough book for Mandel, although it contains many pieces which individually are slight. The relative unimportance of those pieces has something to do with a new aesthetic Mandel has adopted. He journeyed in the mid-1960s into a contemporary poetics of process and locus which for him took its source partly in Robert Creeley. By extension it derived from a wider tradition that originated mainly with William Carlos Williams and entered contemporary practice through Charles Olson.

With that big adjustment in thinking, Mandel turns himself in *An Idiot Joy* to a new reverence for what is "now" and "here." In that conversion (it is tempting to think of the break in religious terms) he moves, much as Margaret Atwood's Susanna Moodie moves, from alignment to an other world to respect for what is at hand. The shift in itself does not necessarily make for better writing, nor as we have seen does high rhetoric preclude strong writing. I would argue, nevertheless, that the new rhetoric — and it too *is* rhetoric — enables Mandel to write several pieces which *at least* in their cumulative effect surpass the best of his early writing.

Mandel does include in *An Idiot Joy* several poems in an earlier mode, some of them effective, but overwhelmingly the contents of this book reveal an opening. His speakers now drop into history and into geography. By this I do not mean they demonstrate formidable knowledge of what we commonly understand by these terms. Mandel never seeks a professional or academic competence in such matters. Rather, he locates himself more intimately and immediately in *his* place and *his* time. A sudden increase in references to contemporary places (Edmonton) and politics (the war in Vietnam, especially), enters the book. Newly attendant on the near and the now, he finds that his allegiances to a timeless realm exempt from the blips of existence virtually collapse. That means he no longer enjoins us to take in big truths, already constituted and, precisely because they *are* prior, properly able to override the small measures of our lives as they are presently and locally realized. No longer dis eased and in thrall to the Essential, he now is at home in the world and pays a new attention to it. He does not overlook as unworthy, as once he did, what was under his nose all along.

The new position means that the speakers no longer issue directives out of respect for the Truth they already know; now they go, genuinely, in search of knowledge, never supposing they have the answer or that it is finally available. They speak in modesty of the experience whose knowing, whose very registering, they grope towards. We recognize those takes in the physical smallness of the new poems and the shortness of their lines, the relative chariness of their metaphor, the stripped-down punctuation, the rhythms of speakers in the act of finding language. We appreciate the tones of supplication and of willingness to be instructed, as the power shifts from poet as inventor and director to poet as attendant and receiver.

In *An Idiot Joy* there is no self-regard. Questions are no longer rhetorical, they are posed out of a desire to know something, as in "Statue in the House" (p. 25). Or they convey overtones of regret or lament, as in the endings of "The Madness of Our Polity" (p. 35) and "Song" (p. 59), or troubled dismay, as in parts of "Pictures in an Institution": "Why would he put his Jewishness aside? / Because there was no bread?" (p. 45).

Everywhere poems speak in phrases of a provisional knowing: "some say," "no i cant / say for certain / why / we, love, sometimes / smile," "remote, I think, / isn't the word" (pp. 71–72); "somewhere, I'm told," "anyhow," "they say" (p. 19); "since I don't know" (p. 75); "I suppose," "I wonder" (but don't pretend to know) (p. 25); "You think there'd be" (p. 58). How appropriate the casual nature of these expressions is. They refuse large knowledge, because acknowledging only personal authority, and abandon a rhetoric of insistence for one of acceptance. The professions when they do come are gentle and far apart, though they quicken in moments of renunciation.

Hesitant though Mandel may be in other parts of the book, he is vigorous in dispossessing himself of the old. We find, in fact, a vehemence in these occasion. "Psalm 24" (p. 14), which so far as I can tell has nothing specific to do with Psalm 24 in the Bible, puts behind Mandel the role of tormented visionary:

> I no longer want to see
> those terrible corrections
> underlined with the red-ink
> of crab-apples bleeding on the lawn.
>
> Take away your Talmudic trees
> commenting on the stone Torah of our streets.
>
> Isn't it enough that I've failed?
> Do you have to indulge in this melodrama
> of snowstorms and black poppies?
>
> What did you expect?
> You, who drove me to mad alphabets
> and taught me all the wrong words.
>
> It's your scripture. You read it.

(p. 14)

The voice is madly self-remonstrative and in keeping with a style Mandel developed before this point. If it is more ferocious than others in *An Idiot Joy*, it is effectively and necessarily so, for the abnegation involves some real struggle. The comical idiom serves to reduce the pain, but we must not overlook what is at issue here.

Mandel relinquishes his literary past and its high modernism, yes, but he at the same time casts aside his cultural ancestry or, if nothing else, its institutions. Here, in seeming ease of colloquial jest, Mandel reconstitutes himself. He remakes himself as a poet and — I'm guessing, but this must be true, Mandel so identifies his personal self with his poetic self — as a person.

Mandel's redefinition takes him towards oral discourse. He had long used the vocative voice and a dramatic structure, but his rhythms were never so casual nor so idiomatic as in *An Idiot Joy* they start to become. The language Mandel gives up came preeminently from other texts, which is to say language composed for the page. There are in "Psalm 24" conspicuous references to the Talmud and the Torah, storehouses of Jewish wisdom, but the category extends into the mention of "mad alphabets," the "wrong words," and "melodrama." It appears first in the cryptic reference to "those terrible corrections / underlined with the red-ink / of crab-apples. . . ." In the metaphor we identify the practice of relating to the world as text, and one which therefore is already written. We read the final line — "It's your scripture. You read it." — in this light, as dismissive reference to faith and to texts that are written and read, and that are in an important sense therefore finished.

I am supposing that *An Idiot Joy* as a whole migrates towards oral models and that in it the ear begins to replace the eye. As it does, it removes the writing from a criticism (mainly hermeneutic) that would spatialize it and make its constituents simultaneously available for scrutiny, as though their sequence or duration were of little consequence. The new model inserts the poems into a category whose members must each be read in time and whose effects are largely dependent upon observing that decorum. Reread the first line of "Psalm 24" and see (see!) if that isn't the case. In the poetics Mandel is now developing the line sits there all by itself, forming a separate unit of meaning, whatever other meanings it may open or complete in the poem: "I no longer want to see," it says simply. When for the moment we read the line as intact, the infinitive "to see" stands as intransitive and we understand the speaker to say he simply does not want to see, period. But it is possible (the implication is there, since each word contains its implied alternatives): I want to hear, I no longer want to see but I *do* want to hear. Though the word "see" also acts transitively as we move into the next line, the point remains. It gains confirmation in colloquial phrases such as "I tell you" (p. 33) and in poems such as "Letter To Be Opened Later" (p. 68) where the vocabulary of knowing appeals to oral transmission: "Tell them," "If they ask," "I've told," and "Listen."

One other feature of "Letter to Be Opened Later" is its confessional manner. That note enters other poems as well, such as "Pictures in an Institution" (pp. 44–46). "I speak of what I know" (p. 44), Mandel writes, and he apparently tells the most private details of his parents' lives. The fourth section will illustrate how Mandel puts aside massive symbol-making and rhetoric:

> These names I rehearse:
> > Eva, Isaac,
> Charley, Yetta, Max
> > now dead
> or dying or beyond my lies
>
> till I reeling with messages
> and sick to hold again their bitter lives
> put them, with shame, into my poetry.
>
> > > (p. 46)

The poem reveals a vulnerable figure, one who is prepared to forego the protection of metaphor, who in fact is happy to "defy / your taste in metaphor" as are speakers elsewhere in the *Idiot* poems. "It is metaphor I distrust" (p. 43) we read blankly in one poem. In another the speaker complains about "strangling metaphor" (p. 33). In still others Mandel will choose the less assertive simile or simple expressions, "as" and "as if." "Marina" (p. 76) provides good examples. "Streetlights" (p. 18) shows how the tropes enter gently, almost by denial: "they're not sunflowers / yet they burn on their stems / like the golden eyes of those other plants." So too when Mandel writes, "I suppose memory is like this african idol" (p. 25), we understand the comparison to come from new modesty: I'm not saying this *is* that, I'm only saying it is *like* that. The claim is doubly attenuated in its use of a less insistent trope, and in its admission to uncertainty even then (supposing but not dictating).

The same goes for symbols in many of these poems. Mandel begins to locate them in what he finds around him and then to develop their import more metonymically than metaphorically. "Statue in the House" (p. 25) begins unassumingly, "I suppose memory is like this african idol," and slides into a related reflection, "I wonder that he reads / so intently." It ends strongly by speculating all the more on the statue and by deriving secondary significance from details of it: "what bright substance could have charred / his tight fists / his small clenched eyes?" The same fierce eyes of the visionary come into the poems, but they appear only after we are situated in the very material presence of those objects that body them forth.

Mandel's greater acceptance of the small and the immediate is borne out in a drastic reduction of classical and high references and, in much the same instances, the removal or erosion of the upper case, which when it appears is almost intimidating because it declares importance and insists on its weight. When the upper case accompanies classical or literary allusions it can be especially insistent, for it acts citationally and inserts the power of high-minded authority. Mandel writes more modestly now. His diction becomes more concrete, monosyllabic, and less exotic, indicating more care for the near and the felt. The accommodation includes mundane prose: "Reading Warnock: *Ethics since 1900* / in my 42nd year" (p. 20). It extends even to the found. Discourses which in their original locations showed no literary ambitions Mandel learns to appreciate and by appropriation put to new purposes, as in the horrific poem "Manner of Suicide" (pp. 55–56), where he effectively juxtaposes for shocking effect material he has taken over. Attentive, receptive, he doesn't insist on being the heroic maker who thinks things are not good enough for him and should be subject to his improvement.

The attitude results in a drastic shift in voicing. *An Idiot Joy*, at least in its breakthrough poems, goes in fear of eloquence and values the most minute measures. "Eloquence," like its cognate "fluent," originally meant simply the ability to speak out or to express oneself, and conveyed much of what the root meaning of "to utter" does. But it took on in its more sinister associations some sense of falseness, and it sometimes came to be thought of as forceful or glib speaking that either misrepresents the speaker, manipulates the unwary listener, or both. It is to this suspicion Mandel implicitly comes in the mid-1960s. In poems such as "The Silences" (pp. 48–50) he rejects "nimble" or "noble" speech (p. 50). (The section in which these words occur Mandel excises in his later selected, *Dreaming Back-*

237

wards, on the grounds, I would assume, that this stretch itself defers
to an earlier rhetoric.) You can get a good idea of how far Mandel
has turned things around when you see how he prizes the unspoken
and the unwritten and how tellingly he comes back again and again
in the poem to speak of the "possible." Commonly on the verge of
speech, the words on the tip of his tongue, the poet places them not
in some anterior world as once he did, but in some present and
imminent moment coming, just now, into language, almost yet to
come. He no longer conceives of the poet's action as plundering
cultural storehouses but as emerging in wonder. He begins in the
repeated word of "The Silences," *"before"* writing, in a position
prior to knowing.

One consequence of Mandel's newfound aesthetic is the use of
much smaller lines and the surrender of the left margin from its
traditional status as inalterable base. The overall visual effect of such
lining suggests someone operating in a sprinkling of glimpses or
sounds, whereas before we had an extending and asserting speaker
who stands behind the long and relatively unwavering line. Respecting the barely discernible beginnings of speech, new poems such as
"The Silences" (and there are a lot like it, mostly toward the end of
the book), introduce a new measure. Susceptible to possibilities, the
speaker works his way through experience in such a way that it seems
to come into being in the moment of finding words. In the delicacy
of Mandel's short line he begins to discover subtle ambiguities he
can open up syntactically:

>   you've no
>   way of knowing what
>   I might say
>   think
>   what whispers
>   before any word spoken

(p. 48)

"I might say" attaches itself to both of the lines that surround it,
completing the first *and* beginning the second. We read as one
grammatical unit "knowing what / I might say," and "I might say [:]
/ think / what whispers" as another. The sparsity of punctuation
depicts a rhetorical nakedness; it also allows lines to attach and
reattach themselves in ways they could not if they were confined by

238

punctuation to one trajectory within the syntax. It is worth adding that these ambiguities are no longer based in intellectual ingenuity that operates in *semantic* instability. The ambiguities between lines come from quite a different source. Out of submission to uncertainty, scored in the provisional nature of the lines, the poet foregoes "control" and permits both language and reader, in time, to find the multiplicities, as he himself comes to find them. Double-jointed.

"We are struck dumb" "The Silences" tells us (p. 50). And Mandel's figures, once loud and loquacious, become intimately aligned with some meditativeness in him, begin to listen. And to respond in informal speech. We have in the stripped-down diction, the parenthetical rhythms, the frequent pauses, the respect for an oral syntax that places prepositions at the ends of sentences — "or what shore she will set her foot upon" (p. 76) — a powerful expression of wonder. Far more than grand histrionics ever could lead him, Mandel's sensitivity to the unuttered and the unutterable takes him into a language commensurate with his awe. Here is what may be the best poem in the book and by all means one of the finest among the many excellent in small measures:

Listen, the sea

yes what is
I'm learning

by your leave
leaving
        rising
to leave
        return
and turn
        we
deliberate
by the waves
rhythm casual
move
        tidal
as
        traffic
as
        the sea-women

neither are they
certain uncertain
but with us
           withal
within
      their song
here
    oh hear
it is

(p. 74)

Consider where the speaker stands. Drastically altered from those times when, learned, he was on the outside, in charge, and imposing structures, he now speaks in different terms, in different times, from "within" experience. He puts himself in a position to learn and is carried by the occasion. He finds someone to guide or to instruct him. But this guide is not some grand symbol; she is far too near and personal for that.

A humility is apparent in the title where the verb "Listen" points more to the speaker himself than to any audience. In this construction the verb is not pragmatic. It is neither command nor admonition: not "you better pay attention," but "ah, the sea!" It is expressive, as the poet, recognition falling upon him, declares his sudden awareness. It also is phatic and solicits connections — know that I exist, acknowledge I am speaking to you — and as such, speaks in intimacy, which the rhetoric of those first poems precluded. It invokes a world made known by sound, in the ear. As the poem ends, it echoes its first astonishment in the simple line "oh hear." In that phrase Mandel risks being sentimental or melodramatic. But he carries the day, I think, in sheer delicacy of language. The minute register, the hair's breadth nuance of his saying, bespeaks appreciation for the moment that comes only with an exceptional power of caring and taking care in what he says. The awareness resides in the broken lines. Not clumsy: articulate. At the joints, where they articulate.

And how simply perfect, how perfectly simple are the lines that open and close "Listen, the sea": "yes what is" and "it is." They could hardly be more poignant. In overwhelming humility they say yes to what is. In the love that nestles in that final last line, they modestly affirm "it is." There is nothing more to say. Evidently here, the poet hears; for really to be here *is* to hear. To be near, to get a hearing. And he enters an intimate circuit of communication once inaccessible to him.

The connection comes through the female, always through her liquid life. Invariably it evokes in the speaker a powerful response, for these are love poems. It is arguable that all poems are love poems. It is certainly possible to suppose that all Mandel's are love poems. In this new rhetoric he shows such a personal willingness to embrace what he now takes to be fellow creatures, that we irrefutably enter love poetry. Women are no longer the "other" that looms large as symbols to excite or trouble. In the affection of fine measures they flood luminous into the poetry, their mysteries made almost unbearably intimate. The ending of "The Moon in All Her Phases" shows what I mean:

> we grope toward each other
> hands fumble among clothes
>
> I cant remember:
>   did your eyes
> your body glow?
>   I cant remember
> the difficult lovely words.
>
>   (p. 70)

There are any number of other poems worth notice. One of them in particular we should mention. "Houdini" continues in certain respects Mandel's ongoing fascination with tricksters, strange figures, and the forbidden terrain they occupy. In form and structure it also preserves some of his most successful earlier practices. It articulates what we can conceive of as his earliest and perhaps, despite what I've said in this chapter, a continuing poetics. That poetics speaks of a perpetual binding and freeing of the artist within some clear or simple structure. As metapoem (Mandel is fond of including at least one metapoem conspicuously late in each book) it could be read diachronically as symbol of the new Mandel locked in a struggle with his former and formal self. The poem would seem to honour a containing that *An Idiot Joy* largely shakes off, though "Houdini"'s possible atypicality at this point in Mandel's work does not make it less:

I suspect he knew that trunks are metaphors,
could distinguish between the finest rhythms
unrolled on rope or singing in a chain
and knew the metrics of the deepest pools

I think of him listening to the words
spoken by manacles, cells, handcuffs,
chests, hampers, roll-top desks, vaults,
especially the deep words spoken by coffins

escape, escape: quaint Harry in his suit
his chains, his desk, attached to all attachments
how he'd sweat in that precise struggle
with those binding words, wrapped around him
like that mannered style, his formal suit

and spoken when? by whom? What thing first said
"there's no way out?"; so that he'd free himself,
leap, squirm, no matter how, to chain himself again
once more jump out of the deep alive
with all his chains singing around his feet
like the bound crowds who sigh, who sigh.

(p. 31)

The deftness of reference and whimsy enable Mandel to use elaborate sustained metaphor, in keeping with what he had done in the past. The penultimate line, "with all his chains singing around his feet," moves us virtually into the stylized rhythms of blank verse (only the middle foot is not iambic) and the lyricism of singing chains. Mandel's slightly facetious phase "quaint Harry," in offering us an adjective without a previous article but followed by a proper noun, encodes in its high-mindedness a pattern of exemplary reference. That structure occurs in earlier poems: "Madman Smart" (*Fuseli*, p. 60) and "Modest Locke" (*Fuseli*, p. 44). So did the "mannered style" Mandel now attributes to Houdini, including the repetitions that draw attention to themselves. And so did the mockery embodied in the words of Houdini's possessiveness: "*his* chains, *his* desk, attached to all attachments" (and imprisoned to his art). So did the play on words we find in "metrics" and "around his feet," with their references to the physical world as it is measured or wandered, and

242

the literary world as it is measured by trickster poets. And so we observe the old prosody that closes in on itself and confirms the theme, and the comical references to audience who, poignant in admiration and despair, respond as they must: "who sigh, who sigh." We have in "Houdini" one version of the poetics of freedom in submission.

There are differences, too, from what once we saw. There is a casual, almost folksy voice ("I suspect he knew," "I think of him listening," "how he'd sweat") that in an endearing way seeks to disarm our reserve and win our assent. There is an acute sense of listening, for this is a world of sound — singing, rhythms, speaking, sighing. And there is a perpetual attempt to escape.

There is, too, what always is central to Mandel, what will emerge more explicitly in the books yet to come: his enchantment with magic and doubles.

Stony Plain (1973)

Stony Plain is a scattered book. The poems vary considerably in theme, style, and power. Between an *Idiot Joy* and the time *Stony Plain* appeared six years had passed, and in that interim Mandel seems to have been struggling to find direction. The assortment in the new book creates an effect not so much of audacity or richness, as we might expect from a poet working in confidence, but something closer to what we might find in a writer who knows he is engaged in forays of mixed success. Quite a few of these pieces seem to me to be treading water, competent but desultory. A number, such as "The Death of Don Quixote," lapse into cryptic or vague language in spots, although there are solid pieces in a more extravagant style ("Snake Charmers" is especially good). In poems reminiscent of an earlier style, we have once again vivid passages on visionary possession, lines which Mandel is more than capable of producing and which he prefers to locate at ends of poems where they gain more weight. Here is a bit from "Don Quixote Writes to His Priest":

yet each night someone pours smoking
dreams into my ears and nostrils

when my mouth opens
only arabic scribbles emerge

who turns my folded thoughts
back and forth like
the pages of an unreliable book?

(p. 43)

Quite a few of the poems, though, do not sustain themselves or manage to articulate a strong experience. This lack is conspicuous in the poems dedicated to artists or about artists, and in many of the political poems which are so common in the book.

"Envoi," which really *is* the last poem in the book, brings together a political theme of repression, a religious theme of the scapegoat, and an aesthetic theme of the therapeutic artist. To a great extent it continues Mandel's belief in adversarial art, especially his version of the tormented artist set against a sick society. But that vision can languish in melodrama and fail to address a contemporary world in ways we might recognize or care about. In "Envoi" Mandel moves the myth of the opposed artist into the contemporary Canada of the War Measures Act (which crucially informs several parts of *Stony Plain*), where he speaks of "my country," of "politics [that] pierce my heart," of a manacled Montreal, and most simply, where he reflects "it must be cold in prison, in québec":

a sick bride
a murderous bridegroom
                that wedding
whose children will be colder killers
than the words of this or any other song

(p. 96)

That disturbing note is sounded in other poems. "Ottawa October 70" (pp. 88–89) puts the creative forces of a Michael Snow film, a child, dream, and "our words" into opposition against the Cabinet, the law, blindness, prisons ("back and forth / back and forth / . . . back and forth"). The collection prefers things that curve or wind or circle, rejects forms of entrapment. The opposition finds its most succinct and most telling expression in the lines

      the law
the iron law
holds us as iron holds tongues

244

as iron holds ice as iron is
iron law we have come again to
iron-time

We are reminded of children with tongues stuck to barrels, door-knobs, railway tracks. But the tongues are stuck to the iron. Struck dumb in law. Locked up in the heavy recursions that beset the poem (there is iron and iron and again iron), the creative forces seem able to find (are permitted to find?) only numbed reiteration. Those repetitions, with their wonderful register of enclosure — again and again, encircled and encircling — convey a reality beyond the language of explanation.

"Ottawa October 70" is rapidly and intricately associational. The structuring device is one which Mandel has been developing for a number of years. He takes it to greater lengths in one of his strongest works, "On the 25th Anniversary of the Liberation of Auschwitz" (pp. 66–69). The poem did not come easily. For years Mandel was paralyzed by the arguments of George Steiner and Theodor Adorno, who said any words would profane the meaning of the concentration camps, that the only response in the face of so massive obscenity is silence. But Mandel did want to speak, eventually. The story of that struggle he tells in an excellent essay "Auschwitz: Poetry of Alien-ation." The result we have before us, in *Stony Plain*, shows substan-tial revision from its earlier published form.

The poem mingles Mandel's memories of an Estevan childhood watching cowboy movies in the Orpheum Theatre with his experi-ence at a memorial service in Toronto many years later, using the structuring convention of then / now and recalled / observed to shape the poem. Stripped down and impressionistic, the rhetoric eradicates most signs of discursive language. Once more Mandel senses, as perhaps Steiner thought, that explanation would be inappropriate. The fillers that go with such language (this is, there was, after they), and the studied voice of distance would in such a poem engender the very triviality Mandel so wished to avoid. His strategy is to move through a series of voices, several of them in halting repetition, some inward, some overheard, some descriptive, but many of them frantic and all of them rapidly giving way to one another. He creates a drama of changing voices, but, in what has to be an astonishing adjustment, however he happened upon it, he soon jumbles the voices together by joining the lines much as we splice tape. The effect is one of horrified immediacy and in the end, when "then" virtually coincides with "now" in syntax and reference, of hinting at some sort of complicity in the atrocities. In interview Mandel has explained what he had in mind:

> I had begun to think that Auden is right when he says every poem represents a resolution to a technical problem. The Auschwitz poem . . . is the most satisfactory solution I've ever had to a technical problem. . . . I wanted to solve the problem of creating in a poem an ambiguity so absolute that it could never be resolved but that would be totally authentic. That poem is not about . . . the memorial service. It's about what happened to me at that memorial service. At one point I got confused about what I was watching, whether it was my childhood memories of violence, the cowboy story, or these things that I was seeing. And when the lights come on in that poem toward the end, you can't tell whether they're coming on in the Orpheum Theatre in Estevan or in the YMHA at Bloor and Spadina. You can't tell and the incoherence of the poem is resolved at that moment. (Arnason, p. 79)

The poem is too long to quote in full and too intricate to discuss in detail here, but it is possible to illustrate its procedures. The language associated with the service itself frequently crumbles into jerks and stutters. It expresses what, if it were to come in the fluency of ease, could only seem glib if not obscene. Here is a section from the middle of the poem:

```
                        walked
    with the others toward the screen
    toward the picture
                    SLIDES
            this is mother
            this is father
            this is
                    the one who is
    waving her arms like that
    is the one who
                    like
```

I mean running with her breasts bound
ing
   running
             with her hands here and there
with her here and
           there
hands
that   that is
the poem becoming the body
becoming the faint hunger
ing body
       prowling
            through
words the words words the words
opening mouth ovens

                         (pp. 67–68)

To begin the voice is calm. It is deliberate, methodical, instructive: "this is . . . / this is . . . / this is." It is brief, to the point of being clinical, certainly inured to the emotional and moral implications of what it points out. We may choose to read this voice as that of someone just barely holding on and able to face the scenes it captions only by resorting to drastic excision. However we assign the lines, all the more benumbed by their perfect visual, semantic, and grammatical symmetry, we almost immediately lose their effect as another voice breaks in upon them in a rush of confusion. Its frantic repetitions and its broken syntax suddenly remove distance and we are brought up against a language that will not allow us to gaze with impunity.

Almost at the outset we meet this stutter of horror: "the gut guttural throat / y scream yell ing open / voice mouth growl." The breakage within words, the syllables snapped off or wedged away, say in ways that only they could say what the experience is. The primal cries precede reflective speech, the howls are pre-lexical. Or post-lexical. Either way, they are not informational, not *just* informational. The lines are not designed simply to pass on involved knowledge, but are there to express the body's noises when it is in distress. We witness the terrible inadequacy of normative syntax, of available diction, of intact units of speech — with their formal assurance that we can depend on those structures of discourse, that we have sufficient ways of knowing and making known. Everywhere Mandel finds means to explode that unperturbed language. He violates the lexical solidity of the dictionary, the solidarity of grammar books. In his poem words lose their integrity, their morphemic unity, and their grammatical standing. How do we understand that line "voice of mouth growl" without resorting to some system of linguistic violation? Whatever we came up with, we would try to incorporate these three words into some convention of language and literature. The main challenge here, we come to realize, is not thematic (we can so readily subsume the line referentially we hardly give it a thought) but syntactic and grammatical.

The same goes for the torrent of negatives in the line that soon follows:

> framed by the name
> looking away from /pretending not there
> no name no not name no

We are struck with the denial, the utterly horrified denial, whosever it is. Someone who has just found his/her name on a Nazi death list? One feature of this poem is its refusal to identify sources or to give us many explicit directions (some appear in Mandel's "Auschwitz" essay), because such action would imply a narrator uninvolved in the occasion. The reaction finds telling form in the manic repetitions, the collapsed syntax, and in the gasping silences that sit in the visual holes.

When in mid-poem we read of the running woman (reference to Krzysztof Pendericki's "Wrath of God"?), we find a slightly altered rhythm and a somewhat altered effect. The jerky rhythms simulate the movement of her running, we might suppose; that, and the effects of early cinema with a film speed that in modern projectors hiccough bodies across the screen. But the lurch and stutter must situate Mandel too as he goes through the trauma, shaken and then regrouping in language, so we can understand the rhythm to belong both to what he sees and to how he responds. The double locating is especially appropriate for the "Auschwitz" poem because its major drama resides in the poet's process of actively dealing with his personal perception, thoughts, and memories.

The heaves and breakage we find in the "Auschwitz" poem become a major part of Mandel's political poetry. In some of them they take on very odd shapes that parody computer language and officialese. "Reading Room: Periodicals" (p. 25) cleverly narrates the unsuccessful attempts of someone trying to get something out of a reading room. The title helps us to gain some footing, but the poem itself doesn't identify the speaker or the subject very sharply. It almost certainly is a fantasy based upon a whimsical projection of certain technologies and mentalities. The dominant voice, asyntactic and disembodied, is curt in its judgements and chary in its willingness to accommodate a blind person.

Mandel exploits the parody of public or political language to great effect in such poems as "Simulation" (p. 24) where the voice involves pointing, directing, and labelling and where the structure, returning to the word "live" as a base, jars loose the claims of a technological world to be presented "live" or in "living colour." Its world is not alive, the poem insinuates, by sheer redundancy calling the claim into question (as Mark Anthony manages to turn "honourable" into its opposite by dint of calculated insistence). The world may well be diseased. Or so the references to cancer incline us to believe, and so the reinvested idiom "real/live" would suggest in the "real/live melanoma" on a biochemist's cheek.

Mandel's willingness to use collapsed syntax, gobbledegook, and computer language for satiric effect takes him in "From 'The Pentagon Papers'" (pp. 85–86) into extreme lexical and syntactic violence. The second part, more amenable to normal reading conventions, bears all the marks of bureaucratese. Its sections are subject to the organizing powers of numbers, letters, and colons. They mark a discourse of rational order with systematic points and categories. As we soon discover, however, the discourse is not rational and it certainly is not humane. We are appalled to see how self-regarding the discourse is, how oblivious it is to the realities it ostensibly regards. It reduces complex matters of politics and ethics into the anaesthetizing structures of the scientific report, replete with initials, passive constructions, missing verbs, and latinate diction.

The passive voice conveniently removes agency and hence responsibility for the actions here contemplated and thus seeks to exonerate those in charge. The same constructions tacitly admit that the real power in the struggle belongs psychologically to the Vietnamese who figure as "the other" in the papers Mandel pillories. It is significant that American actions are located by the anonymous author(s) (they aren't going to take responsibility either) in the relative safety of nouns at points where we might well expect verbs. American forces do not *attack* the North Vietnamese, nor do they strike them or at them, they merely noun their way there: "a. Will-breaking strikes on the North." (Note the reference to geography instead of occupants.) Nor do they deploy troops: "b. Large U.S. troop deployments." The grammar would have us believe, in its structures of evasion, that the war, or at least the American part in it, is more a condition of *being* and of being there — in place, solidly and immutably as nouns — than it is of *doing* something for which you would have to take responsibility.

In earlier publications Mandel got on to the use of found material, but nowhere before has he used it so powerfully or to such devastating ends. Here he brings forward what he has discovered and lets it speak under the intense scrutiny that the institution of poetry in which it is now located would ask of us. Mandel selects and presents the rhetoric, perhaps scandalizing those who believe that "work" and invention are the major constituents of poetry: here it is, give a listen, let it speak for itself. But of course it never does, quite. *We* as readers make it speak.

In *An Idiot Joy* Mandel began to write in a quiet concrete voice. He continues that style in *Stony Plain* and invokes it as a way to encounter retreats into abstraction that once beset and that now and then still beset his own writing. Now, in the gathering of Mandel's political understanding, the abstract is more sharply connected to failed politicians, such as the man in "Plaza Mayor" who laments: "agony / whatever I might chose to say / remains / abstract" (p. 37). In another of the excellent political poems, "On the Renewal of Bombing in VietNam December, 1972," the poet wants to "cry out / that the dead are no less real / for falling into pictures of ruined cities." Believing that in this poem he speaks in a disembodied voice that loses power he quietly admonishes himself in regret and helplessness. Although he would testify, he finds his response inadequate:

> I do not mean to speak as a prophet
> that cherished tone now detached
> as if voice itself could be flung into space
> without body

> (p. 87)

The chastisement emphasizes the need for bodily experience and a personal expression of it. In *Another Time* Mandel writes, quoting

Norman O. Brown, " 'The true meanings of words are bodily meanings, carnal knowledge; and the bodily meanings are the unspoken meanings. What is always speaking silently is the body' " (*AT*, p. 39). And so, now, they are — the body words are speaking.

Mandel's interest in a stripped-down rhetoric derives in part from William Carlos Williams, as the poem "Desert Words" (an echo of Williams' "Desert Music") makes clear (p. 38). The new style, first opened in *An Idiot Joy*, leads Mandel away from the grandiloquent and the poets (Eliot, Yeats, Auden) who once had such a strong influence on him. Searching for forms that would answer to a new vision, one which we might call ecological, Mandel surrenders his old belief in imposed shapes. He comes to see the poet as one who "opens himself to the language of objects and their secrets" (*AT*, p. 87) and who submits himself to a poetry that involves reciprocity between the experience that moves through the poet and the world he moves through. The ideal is one of immediacy, of in a sense accepting "what is there."

It is interesting that whereas Charles Olson, one of the new models, makes his way into expansiveness, Mandel turns towards minimalism. In several poems at the beginning of *Stony Plain* and in such exquisite pieces as "Narrative Poem" (p. 53) and "Sea Things" (*See Things?*) (pp. 70–71) Mandel stands in silence and writes his small lines. The first section of "Sea Things," which describes shellfish extruding into the world, finds a perfect subject, for the poem itself moves off small mental probings. It sets down the rhythms of tenuous movement through the world, of small takes on things to the point of ending lines on prepositions. This lining, relatively new for Mandel, suggests the mind's momentary hesitation as it hangs, seeking but not forcing completion. The words do not speed onward impelled by certainty or insistence, they wait on a rhythm of patient attention. The words — simple, brief, common — seem largely to set aside the "great tradition" and to direct us towards the tangible world.

The second section of "Sea Things" brings the poetics to bear on romantic love. Mandel builds off the most personal but understandable associations between John Cage in America and his beloved in Spain. The whiteness of the page open up holes of silence so the words drop, clear and distinct, clean as pebbles into a well. They speak in delicate, almost breathless, lines. In observance of love's exactions (loving *words*, *loving* words), the poem is short and hesitant. It is particular in its refusal to sweep through language or to lend itself to large public utterance.

By the time Mandel hits *Stony Plain* he has long left behind him his belief in the poet as grotesque hero. No longer a freak who utters inscrutable truths from beyond, he speaks modestly from within a culture. He lowers his voice and in sympathy enters the world around him. "Wabamun" (pp. 10–17) consists of eight very brief sections, each of them short-lined, monosyllabic, and concrete. They do not focus on the perceiver as grand rhetorician so much as the subject, and in that regard they have become less dramatic and more referential. Some of them, the first in particular, risk a child-like naming. Because Mandel now holds that true meanings are carnal and barely spoken, the sections concentrate — and "concentrate" is the word — on the poet's response to things.

Other selections, say part 4 of "Wabamun," sustain sufficient levels of generality to permit viewing them as metapoems. Mainly "Wabamun"'s appeal is in the newness of its lining, and that is something which, even as the words tend to disappear as signifying system, draws attention to the poems as made things. The prosody is situated in the page as a visual space where the rhythms avail themselves of that space. They wait in patience, and in service — giving weight to the words and to the world they incarnate:

7

```
to have come to this
simplicity
            to know
only
    the absolute
calm
    lake
    before
    night
```

(p. 16)

It is crucial not to speed over these lines in hunger for semantics. Despite the simple referentiality of the "Wabamun" series, it too takes on meaning in its lining and the sequence it dances us through. Each line allows the words to resonate equally, allows them their weight, without hurrying on: it is "lake," "the absolute," "only / the absolute," these things in their own right, as they are, uninvested with massive literary importance. Tenuous, the lines score the tenderness with which they are drawn.

The lines also free up syntax. Some of them actually insinuate whole new understandings. Consider the following: "to have come to this," words spoken in wonder, the stress fallen in the speech rhythm gently on "this"; and then "to have come to this / simplicity" where "this" moves from nominative to possessive, and where "simplicity" sits there all alone, in all its simplicity. Or this: "simplicity / to know," where we detect inverted syntax (to know simplicity), that is why we have come; and then the lovely "correction," the second thought — "to know / only," and "to know / only / the absolute." And so on. As the syntax wavers we see lines vacillating between referential and expressive modes. We come to know the absolute, but we come to know too, and then to realize, with amazement, and quietly to exclaim "only the absolute!"

If in Mandel's poem, read as epiphany, we abide the split-second completions that these lines ask us to observe, we put ourselves on an altogether different footing. We appreciate that if we were to insist only on the lexical properties of these words, as we would, say, in setting them as one quick prose sentence, the poem would lose a major source of its power and almost certainly lapse into banality.

Appalled by pomposity, Mandel risks understatement. That is why he bounces between his minimalist meditations and his satiric pieces. "First Political Speech" (p. 64) with great and hilarious effect unlocks meanings that never could have occurred to the original compiler of the list Mandel appropriates and remotivates in one brilliant stroke by naming it as he does. The entire poem consists of "stanzas," each of which delineates a series of rhetorical transitions, all laid out in a chronology that implies narrative if not progression. But — and this is *the* point — all we have are transitions. The substance is missing, embarrassingly telling in the white that nests between stanzas. The effect is powerful. We get a parody of logical structure and of weighty deliberation: all form and no substance. Obeisant only to conventions, the speech proves utterly vacuous. Or: worthy only in the slightness of its transitions, the rest of the speech is even worse, so bad it is not worth recording.

Even as Mandel published these poems in *Stony Plain*, he was struggling to write "a book which is concerned at least in a general way with Estevan, with the Jewish colonies, with the prairies" (Fee, p. 11). We can see the beginnings of that book in *Stony Plain* — in "Narrative Poem" (p. 53), in "Earthworms Eat Earthworms and Learn" (pp. 54–55), the "Auschwitz" poem, "Cabinet Secrets" (p. 83), in the Williams poem, "Desert Words," and covertly, long-ingly, in "Two Dream Songs for John Berryman" (pp. 29–30) where the poet sits "here on the coast of Spain, / heartsick like you / and hurt too / by burning poems that will not write / themselves" (p. 29). The first poem in *Stony Plain*, "Estevan, 1934," is exquisite and opens the flood of poems that four years later give Mandel his most coherent and most personal book.

Out of Place (1977)

"We are here and not here."

(Life Sentence, p. 62)

Mandel's relationship with home has always been ambivalent: home where your preoccupations were laid down, that were to haunt you like a dream; home where there wasn't much room for you — fervent, mystical, intellectual, poetic Jew. Mandel in exile, in Toronto, all those years:

. . . I was a bit uneasy about presenting myself as a *Western writer*. Ten years in Toronto, it seemed to me, hardly qualifies one as a poet of the prairies. But if Wilson can be taken seriously, it is not place alone that matters but a direction, an attraction — something like the movement of a compass needle; not where it is, but where it points matters. My image for the prairie writer then . . . is not necessarily the one who is in the west, or who stays here, but the one who returns, who moves, who points in this direction. (*AT*, p. 69)

That quest "makes the writer a man not so much in place, as out of place and so one endlessly trying to get back, to find his way home, to return, to write himself into existence, writing west" (*AT*, p. 69).

And so in 1977 Mandel writes himself home. In the wasted landscape of his childhood, the abandoned towns and farms that once were Jewish settlements, and in the haunting petroglyphs from earlier Indian habitation, he tries to read the stories of his place. "the return:," the first and the major section of the book, depicts that quest. Gone is the heavy rhetoric of "Estevan, Saskatchewan," one of Mandel's first poems. In its place are simple words, quiet in their reverence, as in the finely tuned "estevan, 1934:" (the poem had appeared earlier in *Stony Plain*). Here is the last part of it:

> how
> seldom they spoke and
> they touched one another
> even when the sun killed
> cattle and rabbis
> even
> in poisoned slow air
> like hunters
> like lizards
> they touched   stone
> they touched
> earth

(p. 29)

A simple and personal present now preempts a bookish and distant past. Like many sections of *Stony Plain*, the poem no longer resides in assertion, it lets things be or, more accurately, gives signs of that abiding. The pacing indicated by the visual configuration is meant to convey the Roques's silence, but it is meant to convey Mandel's too, for neither he nor they are busy with noise. The silence demonstrates their reverence and, in the specific weight of each word as it is laid upon the page, a hovering, on edge, waiting for the precise realization: "they touched" . . . [what?]: "stone"; "they touched" . . . [yes? what? a longer pause, across the line . . . ah]: "earth." But even as we observe that rhythm, we see too that "stone" and "earth" draw together (old friends) out of visual and grammatical symmetry — each set off to the right and each a noun, a common concrete noun, completing the exact same subject and predicate. As the poem leads into these terminations, it foregrounds the elemental words and asks that we give them special hearing. As well we might, for through the rest of the book the world of stone emerges like rocks in spring.

The Roque poem is typical of many in the first section. Its language is almost realist and the poems do appeal on that level. In fact, they appeal as descriptions, assume that words do hook onto things and that they then can invoke things. We have at the beginning of "estevan, 1934:" several graphic words that readily act in a referential way. But the syntax and the rhythms of this poem, in the final lines, are so stylized that we can hear them surely as ceremonial too. The same holds for other poems. The overture, "the return:," comes to these remarkable, remarkably simple phrases:

> in the synagogue
>   of the valley
> in the covenant
>   of coal mines
> in these pictures
>   of estevan

(p. 13)

The preposition that inaugurates each line and the noun that closes it — six of each, one phrasal unit to a line — create an effect that is characteristic of Mandel's poetry. The connections that the device induces by means of syntax and rhythm are enhanced by the three-word lines, broken only in modulation in the last line with its two perfect iambs. (We note too the familiarity certain words gain from one another, as "synagogue," "covenant," and "pictures" line up with each other [objects of "in"], and as "valley," "mines," and "estevan" are put into similar positions by virtue of the prepositions they share. "estevan" then enters a category of primal "other" set alongside a category of [especially] Jewish culture which, as we shall see, becomes a central theme in this book of doubles and of a poet who is "out of place.")

The serene rhythm and tone of "the return:" fit the occasion beautifully, for "the ghostly jews / of estevan" float speechlessly ("saying no words") through the poet's dreams and memories, memories he honours in meditative style. The return is two-fold: it is his return in some complex way, it is theirs as they return, as they come to mind. They pass through a mental landscape like one of those early self-developing photographs which when it failed was smeared with light. There too is Ann in the dream, "pale as a flower / in the white sun." There is the memory of returning from war to "floors gleaming in the white frame house" (p. 31), the "last light wheeling / over the land" (p. 34), and the perception of a fat man by

a 7-Up cooler "in the fourth store across a line / light moving back
and forth defines" (p. 27). Everywhere we find that — a landscape
suffused with light, sometimes violent:

> watching the sun
> watching the sun's wheel
> great slow metaphors
> wheel toward me out of the sun
>
> they take my eyes from my head
> they place my eyes on rocks
> they take my crying tongue
> they wheel back toward the sun
>
> . . . .
>   I remember
> the sun   his arms flailing
> wheat and skin . . . .

$$(p. 33)$$

The light, pale or intense, introduces to, induces us into, a visionary
landscape, one that is known by the mind's eye.

There are other indications that the home Mandel enters or
re-enters is largely of his own making and that it belongs in a
visionary circuit. Take those lines about the sun wheels. As emphatic
tropes they declare their intercession. Distinct echoes of Ezekiel, they
all the more command a reading whose basis of appeal will be more
to other texts than physical existence. As if in confirmation of the
point, the sun wheel poem, "petroglyphs at st. victor:," goes on
explicitly to mention metaphor, "the five figures / of discourse," and
"the seventy / names of rhetoric and tree / alphabets" (p. 33).

For this is a textual universe. A long list of texts is scattered through
Mandel's. To mention only ones that appear in "the return:," we find
several sets of names (pp. 41, 32, 30, 35) — "we drive through
names" he says (p. 35). We find Edward McCourt's *Saskatchewan*
(p. 38); writers Aldous Huxley, Rudy Wiebe, William Blake, Christopher Smart, and David Thompson (p. 15); letters (pp. 36, 37);
petroglyphs (p. 35); copies of Tarzan (p. 27); omens, glyphs, signs,
graffiti, and "Latin heroes in the hills" (p. 14). There are references
to Hebraic texts (p. 30); "the book of years" (pp. 17, 23) in which
"you were written" (p. 23); the Old Testament, often (especially

p. 17). Mandel mentions other texts of Estevan, in particular *Estevan the Power Centre* (p. 25). The vocabulary of textuality goes on and on. This is a world stuffed with signs, a world already written, its messages sealed in stone and consecrated in a scribal belief that the letter institutes the world. The poet is not in the wilderness and wanting a sign, any sign. Signs are bursting out all over, there are inscriptions everywhere. Mandel's trouble is not to find but to read them: how to decipher an enciphered world. In such an economy the poet acts as cryptographer. Impelled by a story in which he is already positioned by pre-diction, Mandel tells himself "I read the land for records now" (p. 23), troubled about how we should "understand / prophecies and miracles" (p. 38).

Many messages are predicated in stone. They appear everywhere, these letters and icons painted on stone, incised in rock. Mostly they are images of gods painted as petroglyphs, their inscriptions contaminated by a later language, a palimpsest of graffiti (p. 14); or they figure as "barred hebrew syntax" (p. 17) or "the Hebrew alphabet" (p. 14) that puzzles Mandel as at the Jewish cemetery near Hirsch he bends over "the still houses of the dead," "the stone trees" beneath which voices sleep, "the stone unmoved" (p. 20). But always life comes in code, as "languages" — native and Hebrew — between which Mandel vacillates in fascination. He imagines "my uncle standing / among rocks with Israel / both Jews proud and successful" (p. 38), but he also warns himself against an alien iconography:

> avoid heroism and gods
> nearly in stone
> past moonscape and river
> they are not yours
>
> (p. 26)

In the poem, though, they do become his, speak to him in "rhetoric of stone its bluntness" (p. 35), as, in "estevan, 1934:" the Roques in homonym touch stone, touch him with the basic authenticity of their lives. One poem, "the crooked gods:," speaks in compelling brevity of those intimations

> do they mean anything?
> I ask Ann
>   parkland
> rolling below sandstone

silent
    she turns
the camera
      here

there
    I kneel
before the crooked gods

last light wheeling
over the land
their handprints
their great feet
their stone faces
move
     turning
we leave
take with us
photographs
silent
   as
their open mouths

(p. 34)

Mandel's disposition, registered in kneeling (a reversal of Jewish practice), exacts its measure in the deposition of words on the page. Writing is to the page, Roland Barthes argues, as voice is to silence — a matter of entrance and timing (p. 254). Pacing coincides with placing. Mandel, responsive as a seismograph to little tremors in time, to wisps that flicker at the edges of consciousness, gropes towards an enunciation that would insert words, provisionally, into that silence, would place them with extreme delicacy on the page. The words as markers or footprints on the page measure the dance, so that Mandel's step through the poem is a matter of being in place.

The rhythms of the slow and the tentative, which could easily be mistaken for what is wary or irresolute, are perhaps more diffident than anything. They are also lingering and regretful. The poem of witnessing, "the crooked gods:," resounds with loss. In the "last night" the Mandels "leave" in silence. Many pages speak of concealment, disappearance, withdrawal, diminishing the "treachery" of memory (p. 19), scattering and dispersal (p. 21), ruins and relics.

One major impulse of the book is to counter that dispersal through re-collection. The poet gathers his thoughts, triggered by return, and he in return hopes "to name / remember and recite" (p. 14). Mnemosyne as mother of the muses. Forgetfulness as spiritual amnesia, as in "petroglyphs at st. victor:" the poet struggles but can only "forget the signals" (p. 33). Dumb, he fumbles for what is hidden, for what remains.

We trace through "the return:" (does it refer to the gods, longingly, as well as to himself in his physical and mental journey?) the figure of Mandel listening, watching prayerfully before the mute mouths, eyes big with messages that remain locked in skulls. There is a kind of listening, writes Roland Barthes, which

> is to adopt an attitude of decoding what is obscure, blurred, or mute, in order to make available to consciousness the "underside" of meaning. . . . The communication implied by this . . . listening is religious: it *ligatures* the listening subject to the hidden word of the gods, who, as everyone knows, speak a language of which only a few enigmatic fragments reach men, though it is vital — cruelly enough — for them to understand this language. (p. 249)

Being able to "read" or to write the language, as Ann Mandel points out in her marvellous book on Robert Creeley, with its frequent and precise parallels to Eli Mandel's work, means putting oneself in a position of "care, concern, prayer" (p. 35). What "care" means she points out by tracing its origins and cognates: anxiety, sorrow, what is dear, carrying, bearing, and touching gently, exactly, as in a caress (p. 27). Having put oneself in such a position, ". . . one may be visited by the numens of the local and particular, and the response to such visitation can only be one of reverence and ceremony" (p. 8). And so Mandel comes again and again before the icons, puzzled and supplicating, in petition and re-petition. That means, Ann instructs us, respecting ways of "greeting what comes, of accepting what must happen, of realizing the place around one as it becomes present: . . . of allowing things to come together in a life or a poem with no diminution of their energies" (p. 21). (Julian Jaynes has argued, "To hear is actually a kind of obedience. Indeed, both words come from the same root and therefore were probably the same word originally" [p. 97].) Thought of in these terms,

Mandel's actions show reverence as well as regret. He says nothing; what is there to say? In a position of divination, care-ful, prayer-ful, Mandel is turned inward on himself. The first poem acknowledges, as if in foresight, omens and "windows / facing inward" (p. 14). Once religion is internalized, writes Barthes, "what is plumbed by listening is intimacy, the heart's secret" (p. 250). Generically the interior is the site of lyric, especially the meditative lyric that forms so large and important a part of "the return:." Mandel moves inland to reflection and the movement of thought. We read in the second poem, "doors of perception:," that the poet and his companion-guide follow great "swooops" of road and make a "sweep" through the terrain. We learn, too, in that same poem, that "time curves" and "our history is in motion curved" (p. 15). The book picks up these or related terms in a number of spots, emphasizing the nature of a life that wheels by, curls in our brain, swirls our minds. Hence, in the superb "birthmark:" Mandel writes, "I carry the Souris [river of my childhood] / on my brow / the river / in my head" (p. 16). The resonance deepens when we learn that Souris rhymes with *Tsouris*, the Jewish word for sorrow, a connection Mandel pointed out in interview (Arnason, p. 82). Hence the treachery of memory and the impossibility of laying down the past (much less the present) on the pages of a book, in the interiors of our skulls.

In the contemplative mode, Mandel moves on eerie silence, in an uncanny still, through the terrain of southern Saskatchewan. His is an eye world, unremittingly iconic. The eye takes strength in the play of text with photograph — Eli Mandel's "silent" poems, his reticence and restraint, Ann Mandel's photographs (as in the retreat from the petroglyph) which do not speak a word. The interplays are intricate and would command a lengthy discussion. I will focus upon only one passage. Before the "text proper" begins we read an exquisite "preface:," written by Ann and describing how in their journey she and Eli discovered and then deciphered various papers they found scattered in a vault. Among them they found "a diary or fiction of a kind" about "the pilgrimage west of a man and wife from the east to the place of his birth, home of his ancestors, a search for a lost home." Then, on the following page, there it is: a full-page photograph of the (a?) vault. Smaro Kamboureli has written a brilliant essay, "Locality as Writing: A Preface to the 'Preface' of *Out of Place*," in which she explores the vault as symbol and origin. It is an occult place of fiction, as depository of secrets, storehouse of stories, the crypt is cryptic, yes. I would add simply it is also in one of its derivations a pile of stones and in that capacity one more of the iconic stones whose strange letters speak to an uneasy Mandel as he writes, Hebraically, (heroically?), aboriginally, his meditation on stone(s). In that act he discloses and amplifies those texts he reads by drawing out the implications of what remains unsaid.

So, divided man, Mandel is there and not there. The double remains for him an irrational source of power. He tells the story of meeting his own double in Banff in the summer of 1975 at the time he was working on *Out of Place* (Meyer and O'Riordan, p. 121). At about the same time he hit upon Jorge Luis Borges' writing on the double:

> In the cultures of all people the double is an omen of death. It is a demonic omen. But Borges said it is an omen of death to all cultures except [the text reads "expect"] the Jews. For Jews, the double in an omen of the immediate onset of prophetic powers. It was when I read that that I understood then that the onset of prophetic powers had something to do with the book I was writing. I felt I had to work the double into my book. . . . My mind was structurally working out a problem, that poetically it was trying to solve . . . . The answer was being granted to me by my own mind. But my own mind was saying that what you have to do it split yourself in two. I decided I had to do an anatomy of the double in order to understand what "out of place" meant. (Meyer and O'Riordan, p. 122)

In "The Double" he explores all sorts of doubles, figures who are grotesquely out of place. Two of the poems deal directly with the doppelganger. The first, "the doppelganger:," is mocking, extravagant, and plays off parody of literary conventions (the speaker pretends to be present when of course, and this is the point, he cannot be) and off incongruities in long shambling lists. As a fine comical touch, the poem ends with the double having so replaced the "you" that he completely takes over his life: "where shall I say you have gone?" (p. 47). The second poem, called "the doppelganger (2):" — what a mad series of doubles in the two titles, back to back — lays out the body as narrative text through which move in sombre lyricism various phylogenies of human evolution: "whatever fish you were / . . . is no longer you" (p. 48). Another, "the cause of doubles:," ludicrously speculates on the sources of the mitotic self who has "crossed the zone" in various guises as "Paul upon the road to the / Alberta faculty club," David Bowie in a film, Houdini, Doc Savage, Christopher Smart, and Prospero — the whole panoply of Mandel's culture. The doubling is neatly arranged in the visual separation of the two *you*'s on either side of a virgule. The section gets zanier and zanier, as if Mandel were released into some comic frenzy (p. 51). At moments "The Double" darkens and disturbs us, just when we are feeling immune and enjoying the playful self lacerations. The absurd performances and confessions of the poet serve to transgress powers that lie elsewhere, in institutions whose officers assume it is their prerogative to call the aberrant to account.

Some poems in the doubles section, such as "the double world:" (p. 53), are quiet and reflective. Some, such as "instructions:" (p. 55), are expansive and solemn, though happy to slide into snappy idiom at surprising moments. The last, "various kinds of doubles:," unwinds a long list whose seriousness it mocks in the intermittent insertions of the effectively vague word "Others," and whose own mirror double it replicates on the left-hand page (pp. 57, 56), a script that would be utterly unreadable without our receiving the mirrored page iconically.

The third section, "A Suite for Ann" (pp. 59–64), picks up the qualities of "The Return" and "preface:" and reinserts the attendant figure of the beloved and the muse. The final section, "Epilogue" (pp. 65–73), enters a series of drastically varied pieces — memories, letters, political parody, photographs — and ends with the bizarre "Picture in an Institution." Almost none of these can be easily reconciled with the rest of the book. We do have a savage sense of defying custom and of saying the unsayable, however, especially in "Institution." That poem alternates the officious voice of disapproval and censorship, mad in its banalities and disparities, directed in its final edict most specifically against poetry, with the tabooed confessions that the institutional voice contains. It would be tempting to see the antagonism as one between some Superego and Id. The admissions, nudging into truculence, focus on the body, its insides — stomach, cunts, ruptures, bowels — signifying shameful inner secrets Mandel is prepared to reveal. Whatever guilt or betrayal may be involved, the poem is also a naked personal tribute, setting aside massive rhetoric so that Mandel simply rehearses in ceremony of naming the names of his family.

Out of Place perhaps finds its continuities in several references to crossing. The word obviously stresses connections; it also hints of transformations (crossings-over) and confusions or betrayals (crossings-up). The term as well as any other subsumes the major concerns in the book: reading the icons, doubles, the slipperiness of language, threshold experiences, the poet as sacrificial figure, the entangled curvatures of mind. If at times the book lurches through tones and rhythms, stumbles into wild fantasy, bewilders with its range, it lays down an emotional centre in that long and accomplished first section, one that in Mandel's next book he manages to reclaim from out of deep malaise in sudden and visionary mood.

Life Sentence (1981)

"The questions are their own kinds of grief."

(LS, p. 126)

In that part of *Life Sentence* which is a journal, Eli Mandel writes:

December 3. Toronto,

Today, two books completed — finally. *Out of Place* will be designed by Ann, *Another Time* in Dave's [David Godfrey's] hands [at Press Porcépic]. . . . It's out of my hands now, but almost at once, for God knows what stupid reason, I begin to play about with the idea of another book. No sense of how or where or why to go. But I know, given the way my life works itself out, soon enough I will be struggling to make or allow new poems to take a special shape. I have always been ambitious. (p. 93)

This very book, *Life Sentence*, in which these words appear, a book about the writing of itself, itself gropes towards shape. And an odd shape it is. It combines a large section of reconstructed journals based on notes Mandel took during his travels. He claims on the "Acknowledgements" page that in composing his journals — interesting collision there, between expressive theories of directing and inventing, and generic presuppositions of describing what is there —

he sees "no need for an accurate rendition of reality" but prefers "to retain an accurate rendition of his notes." Typical Mandel. We allow for calculated shock, but here, as usual, he prefers theories that put literature under the constraints of craft and self-containment, and turns away from terms that would most readily suggest themselves, namely mimetic theories of reference or embodiment. Most of his life he has made that choice. In some stages of his career (notably the mid to late 1960s) he flirted with ideas of description, and the strain never disappears from his work, certainly not in *Life Sentence*. But here again he goes out of his way to stress literature as a self-regarding act.

The journals which, even as we treat them generically, even as they seem to assert "lived" and personal experience, Mandel alters when he puts them up against a set of poems, mainly in a first section that interplays with language in the journals. The effect is in part to direct our thoughts to the very act of *making*.

The book may well be read as an examination of creative life. In that light it becomes a travel book only secondarily, concerned with its ostensible subjects insofar as they contribute to the poet's life as poet. It is obvious enough that *Life Sentence* — and what manner of book is it anyway in its lumpy sections, in such different modes? — looks to language and literature as its measure of things. It includes something like a dozen mentions of *Out of Place*, some overt, some not. At one point the journal discusses the writing of several poems that appear in the front of the book.

But we may better read *Life Sentence* as yet another Mandel quest, perhaps religious, certainly psychological. Beset with anxiety, the Mandel persona listlessly wanders a terrain which even as it occasions his reflections brings him no joy. There is a terrible disquiet in him. He feels at loose ends and at odds with people, including his friends. The signs are everywhere. Externally they can be found in an over-two-year hiatus in publication, a significant (discreet?) reduction in the journal entries. Internally, the book admits to alternation: ". . . I reconstruct these journals," Mandel tells us (p. 56). Repeatedly the writing turns to its author's apprehension. "I don't know who I am or where I am," he writes in India. "Why this extraordinary lack of security?" (pp. 99–100). Mandel itchy with anxieties and suspicions, "pretend[ing] to be, want[ing] to be" what he is not (p. 63), "while somewhere the other side of me lurks and whispers" (p. 64) disconcerting secrets. The feeling runs without let-up through the journals: ". . . I am oddly remote, moved and unmoved" (p. 79), "I feel a chill of strangeness" (p. 74), "I find myself sullen and withdrawn" (p. 95), "I feel alone, semite, poor . . . " (p. 103), "Bill is a natural teacher: entertaining, witty, clever. I feel a plodder, uncertain of tone. I think I'm unprepared" (p. 100), "I can't escape my loneliness despite the good friends I am with" (p. 108). And so it goes. Mandel goes in search of himself, a lost self, an other self, ventriloquist "wondering where I have gone" (p. 32).

The acute inner desolation finds its correspondence in a landscape of human sickness and suffering, but overwhelmingly the entries, for all their awareness, dwell on the author's malaise. In the journals he does seem to find a way out. Following the passage about "an odd surge of ecstasy amid the ruins of time and the lost languages of stone" (p. 122), when the writing quickens and he hits renewed lyricism, he arrives at a profoundly moving reassessment of his life:

> I think about desire, aspiration, hope, its mystery. What aim, what intent, what satisfaction? The meeting with the deepest unknown questions of one's life. Once I thought they would appear in the figures of art, figures of history, patterns. But everything glances off everything else. The large patterns shatter, the personal defects from its centrality. Ego becomes the history of them all. What shall I do? How shall I live? The questions are their own kinds of grief. Who is free of his past? And how far back does that really go? We have come to a border: France/Spain. The border between past and present, there and here, this place that time. Who knows the right tense? (p. 126)

Asking questions, questing. Heart-sick and on the outs in South America, in Europe, in Asia, he longs for home and finds himself there, suddenly, in his mind, off the primal coast of Spain, completing his pilgrimage and comforting him.

In the poems the anxiety comes through on a more domestic note. "So many wars of man and woman," he writes cryptically in a Banff entry (p. 64). The poetry refers to betrayal and hurt, to violence and anger between men and women, between self and spouse. "Once his heart sang, once he knew bright places, / nothing was impossible, not even love itself," he writes. "What will you say now to his sick heart?" (p. 49). He cries out in "Poem as Person as Place as Words" (rhetorically a far cry from "Prairie as Hawk, Cock, Belly, Lover" in *Black and Secret Man*, with which it invites comparison) in conditional tense: if only, if: a dozen times "if," "If forgiveness were as simple as language" (pp. 33–34). And most vulnerably, most simply:

> I despair of reason, knowledge, my lectures,
> remember only Ann turning away at Udaipur,
> the boat from the palace creating distances.
> We are in a strange land. We are drifting apart.
> India is between us. Across the lake, its sunken
> woman, lie continents:
> > war torture poison
> > an apparatus of romance
> > to keep us apart.
>
> (p. 30)

Many of the poems are nakedly political, perhaps under the influence of Rick Salutin and Martin Kinch, who both appear in the Banff journals. Formally they draw little attention to themselves and they move away from obvious literary qualities. They — I am specially thinking of "Beware the Sick Lion" (p. 23) — are prepared to seek transparency and to insist on the signified. That is part of their aesthetic, but it is part of an ethic as well. Mandel wants their words to speak as simply and to refer as directly as possible. The object is to not lose focus on what must be revealed. And so he minimizes metaphor and rhyme and stylized rhythms. By implication the power and authenticity of his testimony would be endangered if he were to thicken the text reflexively. If he were using the old rhetoric, he would risk obscene evasion, by prettifying horrors in elegant lines. Some pieces, such as "On the Murder of Salvador Allende" (pp. 19–21), fall somewhere between discursive and lyrical phrasing, and evidently draw on the examples of Lorca and Neruda.

Some of the best poems once again fall into a style of self-mockery at which Mandel is so adept and which is so common in Canadian poetry. "Going to Pieces" (pp. 35–36) and "Poem Like a Stone, Like a General" (p. 45) triumph in outrageous invention. Some — "The Geek" (p. 40) — speak gruesomely of sexual transgression and deflected pain; some, such as the superb "In My 57th Year" (p. 51), of regret and longing. Others pay tribute to the courageous and far-seeing. All, I think, locate human evil, whether in domestic politics or public politics, in patriarchy. "*Godfather's Painting*: David Thauberger," which identifies that order deep in our psyches,

ELI MANDEL

even, so help me, in the name of the town (Holdfast) where Thauberger lives, chillingly concludes:

> We stand over the land, fathers,
> and over our homes and over each other.
> We have terrible forces inside us: we can paint them,
> green, acrylic, glitter: the form never lies.
> The truth is in the long dead winters where we live.
>
> (p. 28)

The grammatical ambiguity of "fathers" — is it in apposition: *we*
fathers? or is it in address: you to whom we speak, *you* fathers? —
ensnares Mandel in the circle of patriarchy. The last line, where the
poem goes elegantly formal, eminently conspicuous in iambics —
what could be more final or more certain than that? The monsters
of politics are vicious in their misogyny (at one point Mandel
compares himself to Lear revolted with his daughters' multiple
infidelities) and in their capacity to kill and possess. "Aguirre: The
Wrath of God" (p. 22) shockingly reveals the mad slaughter such
hatred of women (and men) engenders. In "Portrait of Ann," which
echoes the "Aguirre" poem, Mandel writes:

> Her story belongs elsewhere
>   not in this poem
> her ivory face tells of.
> This story is of Incas
>   of men harsher than torture.
> They eat fruit, flesh, fowl
> as though it were female flesh.

The language is fairly literal throughout the poem, but it ends on a
telling lyrical note which serves both to esteem the beloved and to
emphasize how the savagery extends itself into abuses of nature:

> She is stern, royal, alone
> now a tall bird in rain forests
> above enormous trees
> past remote peaks
>
> (p. 47)

Yet the disquiet remains. In the "Thauberger" poem, stricken with
a sense he is bound in a murderous world, Mandel in anguish writes

of his own murders, big and small, of

> how we know how to kill one another,
> metaphors of murder, these are played out night
> upon night and I watch them and watch the painting,
> no longer knowing whether I should write poetry,
> especially poems about land, about Estevan,
> or about why I came back to Regina, Saskatchewan,
> this cold winter of 1979
>
> (p. 27)

But he does, and he writes:

> Not self. Not *setting* in the simple-minded sense of place. But
> *lines* between, among, beginnings, endings. Lines to. Something
> Sagan once said, about the anatomy of the brain being the mind,
> remains with me. As if one's neurology determined the actual
> existence of the world (or the identity of knowledge and
> essence): you are that you know. *It* is what you know . . . not
> experience but lines. (p. 117)

And so he writes on, writing himself, writing himself back. In crisis,
not knowing what comes next. Into existence.

SELECTED BIBLIOGRAPHY

Primary Sources

Mandel, Eli, Gael Turnbull, and Phyllis Webb. *Trio*. Toronto: Contact, 1954.

Mandel, Eli. "Toward a Theory of Cultural Revolution: The Criticism of Northrop Frye." *Canadian Literature*, No. 1 (Summer 1959), pp. 58–67.

————. *Fuseli Poems*. Toronto: Contact, 1960.

————. "Giants, Beasts, and Men in Recent Canadian Poetry." *Queen's Quarterly*, 67 (1960), 285–93.

————. Rev. of *Winter Sun*, by Margaret Avison. *Queen's Quarterly*, 67 (Winter 1960–61), 704–05.

————, and Jean-Guy Pilon, eds. *Poetry 62*. Toronto: Ryerson, 1961.

————. "Lapwing You Are. Lapwing He — A Note on Icarus in Myth and Poetry." *Alphabet*, No. 4 (June 1962), pp. 59–62.

————. Rev. of *Creative Writing in Canada* (rev. ed.), by Desmond Pacey. *The Fiddlehead*, No. 53 (Summer 1962), pp. 61–64.

————. *Black and Secret Man*. Toronto: Ryerson, 1964.

————. "A Lack of Ghosts: Canadian Poets and Poetry." *Humanities Association Bulletin*, 16, No. 1 (Spring 1965), 59–67.

————. *Criticism: The Silent-Speaking Words*. Toronto: CBC Publications, 1966.

————. *An Idiot Joy*. Edmonton: Hurtig, 1967.

————. *Irving Layton*. Canadian Writers and Their Works. Toronto: Forum House, 1969.

————. "Poet of the Obvious." Rev. of *Figures in a Landscape*, by David Helwig. *Canadian Literature*, No. 39 (Winter 1969), pp. 87–88.

————, ed. *Five Modern Canadian Poets*. Toronto: Holt, Rinehart and Winston, 1970.

————. "Toward a Criticism." *The Canadian Forum*, April–May 1970, pp. 50–51.

————. "Modern Canadian Poetry." *Twentieth Century Literature*, 16 (July 1970), 175–83.

————, ed. *Contexts of Canadian Criticism*. Chicago: Univ. of Chicago Press, 1971.

———, and Desmond Maxwell, eds. *English Poems of the Twentieth Century.*
Toronto: Macmillan, 1971.

———. Rev. of *Creation,* by Robert Kroetsch. *University of Toronto Quarterly,* 40 (Summer 1971), 316–18.

———, ed. *Eight More Canadian Poets.* Toronto: Holt, Rinehart and Winston,
1972.

———, ed. *Poets of Contemporary Canada 1960–1970.* New Canadian
Library Original, No. 07. Toronto: McClelland and Stewart, 1972.

———, and Irving Layton. "Nietzche and Poetry: A Discussion." *The Malahat
Review,* No. 24 (Oct. 1972), pp. 23–29

———. *Crusoe: Poems Selected and New.* Toronto: House of Anansi, 1973.

———. "Romance and Realism in Western Canadian Fiction." In *Prairie
Perspectives 2.* Ed. Anthony W. Rasporich and Henry C. Klassen. Toronto:
Holt, Rinehart and Winston, 1973, pp. 197–211.

———. *Stony Plain.* Erin, Ont.: Porcépic, 1973.

———, and Rudy Wiebe. "Where the Voice Comes From." *Quill & Quire,*
Dec. 1974, pp. 4, 20.

———. Foreword. In *The Unwavering Eye: Selected Poems 1969–1975.* By
Irving Layton. Toronto: McClelland and Stewart, 1975, pp. x–xi.

———. "Ecological Heroes and Visionary Politics: Contemporary Primitivism
in Canadian Writing." *Rune,* No. 2 (Spring 1975), pp. 55–67.

———. *Another Time.* Three Solitudes: Contemporary Literary Criticism in
Canada, Vol. 3. Erin, Ont.: Porcépic, 1977.

———. Introduction. *The Poems of Irving Layton.* Ed. Eli Mandel. New
Canadian Library Original, No. 012. Toronto: McClelland and Stewart,
1977, pp. 4–8.

———. *Out of Place.* Erin, Ont.: Porcépic, 1977.

———. "Atwood Gothic." *The Malahat Review,* No. 41 (Jan. 1977),
pp. 165–74.

———. "Writing West: On the Road to Wood Mountain." *The Canadian
Forum,* June–July 1977, pp. 25–29.

———. "The Politics of Art." *The Canadian Forum,* Sept. 1977, pp. 28–29.

———. "The Ethnic Voice in Canadian Writing." In *Figures in a Ground:
Canadian Essays on Modern Literature Collected in Honor of Sheila Watson.*
Ed. Diane Bessai and David Jackel. Saskatoon: Western Producer Prairie
Books, 1978, pp. 264–77.

———. "How Poems Happen." *Transitions III: Poetry. A Source Book of
Canadian Literature.* Vancouver: CommCept, 1978, p. 261.

———. "'Life Sentence': Contemporary Canadian Criticism." *Laurentian
University Review,* 10, No. 2 (Feb. 1978), 7–19.

——. "The Inward, Northward Journey of Lawren Harris." *artscanada*, 35, No. 3 (Oct.–Nov. 1978), 17–24.

——. "Leonard Cohen's Brilliant Con Game." *Saturday Night*, Nov. 1978, pp. 51–53.

——. "The Border League: American 'West' and Canadian 'Region.' " In *Crossing Frontiers: Papers in American and Canadian Western Literature.* Ed. Dick Harrison. Edmonton: Univ. of Alberta Press, 1979, pp. 105–21.

——. "Masks of Criticism: A.J.M. Smith as Anthologist." *Canadian Poetry*, No. 4 (Spring–Summer 1979), pp. 17–28.

——. "Library Checks Out Poet." *Quill & Quire*, June 1979, p. 12.

——. "A Comprehensible World: The Work of Cicansky, Thauberger, Yuristy and Fafard." *artscanada*, 36, No. 3 (Oct.–Nov. 1979), 15–19.

——. *Dreaming Backwards: The Selected Poetry of Eli Mandel, 1954–1981.* Don Mills, Ont.: General, 1981.

——. *Life Sentence, Poems and Journals: 1976–1980.* Victoria, B.C.: Porcépic, 1981.

——. "Strange Loops: Northrop Frye and Cultural Freudianism." *Canadian Journal of Political and Social Theory*, 5, No. 3 (Fall 1981), 33–43.

——. "The Language of Literature: Fantasy and History." In *The Commonwealth in Canada, Proceedings of the Second Triennial Conference of caclals, Part Two, University of Winnipeg October 1–4, 1981.* Ed. Uma Parameswaran. Winnipeg: Canadian Association for Commonwealth Literature and Language Studies, [1982], pp. 13–21.

——. "The Regional Novel: Borderline Art." In *Taking Stock: The Calgary Conference on the Canadian Novel.* Ed. Charles R. Steele. Downsview, Ont.: ECW, 1982.

——. "Atwood's Poetic Politics." In *Margaret Atwood: Language, Text, System.* Ed. Sherrill E. Grace and Lorraine Weir. Vancouver: Univ. of British Columbia Press, 1983, pp. 53–66.

——. "Auschwitz: Poetry of Alienation." *Canadian Literature*, No. 100 (Spring 1984), pp. 213–18.

——. "The Post Structural Scene in Contemporary Canadian Poetry: A Note." *Poetry Canada Review*, 5, No. 4 (Summer 1984), 10–11.

——. "The Death of the Long Poem." *Open Letter* [Long-Liners Conference Issue], 6th ser., Nos. 2–3 (Summer–Fall 1985), pp. 11–23.

——. *The Family Romance.* Winnipeg: Turnstone, 1986.

——, and David Taras, eds. *A Passion for Identity: Introduction to Canadian Studies.* Toronto: Methuen, 1987.

Secondary Sources

Andre, Michael. Rev. of *Crusoe* and *Poets of Contemporary Canada 1960–1970*, ed. Eli Mandel. *Queen's Quarterly*, 80 (Winter 1973), 658–60.

Arnason, David, Dennis Cooley, and Robert Enright. "Interview with Eli Mandel, March 16/78." *Essays on Canadian Writing*, Nos. 18–19 (Summer–Fall, 1980), pp. 70–89.

Atwood, Margaret. *Survival: A Thematic Guide to Canadian Literature.* Toronto: House of Anansi, 1972, pp. 118–19, 132.

———. "Four Poets from Canada: Jones, Jonas, Mandel, and Purdy." In her *Second Words: Selected Critical Prose.* Toronto: House of Anansi, 1982, pp. 55–62; pp. 58–60 deal with Mandel.

Barbour, Douglas. Rev. of *Black and Secret Man. Quarry*, 15, No. 4 (Aug. 1966), 46–47.

———. Rev. of *An Idiot Joy. The Canadian Forum*, Aug. 1968, pp. 119–20.

———. "Mandel's Selves." Rev. of *Dreaming Backwards* and *Life Sentence. Canadian Literature*, No. 95 (Winter 1982), pp. 125–28.

Barthes, Roland. *The Grain of the Voice: Interviews 1962–1980.* Trans. Linda Coverdale. New York: Hill & Wang, 1985.

———. *The Responsibility of Forms: Critical Essays on Music, Art, and Representation.* Trans. Richard Howard. New York: Hill & Wang, 1985.

Bates, Ronald. Rev. of *Black and Secret Man. The Canadian Forum*, Feb. 1966, pp. 259–60.

Beattie, Munro. "Poetry 1950–1960." In *Literary History of Canada: Canadian Literature in English*, 2nd ed. Gen. ed. Carl F. Klinck. Toronto: Univ. of Toronto Press, 1976. II, 305–06.

Bemrose, John. "Poetry." Includes a review of *Dreaming Backwards. The Globe and Mail*, 26 Sept. 1981, Sec. Entertainment, p. 17.

Bennett, Donna. "A Formal Madness." Rev. of *Stony Plain* and *Crusoe. The Lakehead University Review*, 7, No. 1 (Summer 1974), 119–23.

———, and Russell Brown. "Eli Mandel." In *An Anthology of Canadian Literature in English.* Ed. Donna Bennett and Russell Brown. Toronto: Oxford Univ. Press, 1983. II, 115–16.

Bessai, Diane. "Interior Travel." Rev. of *Out of Place. The Canadian Forum*, March 1978, p. 33.

Bishop, A.G. "*Crusoe: Poems Selected and New.*" *Quill & Quire*, May 1973, p. 27.

Bouraoui, H.A. "Eli Mandel: *Another Time.*" *Waves*, 6, No. 2 (Winter 1978), 76–78.

Bowering, George. "Eli and Irving." Rev. of *An Idiot Joy* and *The Shattered*

Plinths. Canadian Literature, No. 39 (Winter 1969), pp. 74–76.

Burrs, Mick. "Celebrating Eli." *Poetry Canada Review*, 6, No. 4 (Summer 1985), 21.

Cameron, A. Barry. Rev. of *Crusoe: Poems Selected and New* and *Stony Plain*. *The Canadian Forum*, Nov.–Dec. 1973, pp. 34–35.

Cogswell, Fred. Rev. of *Poetry 62. The Fiddlehead*, No. 52 (Spring 1962), pp. 62–64.

——. Rev. of *Black and Secret Man. The Canadian Author and Bookman*, 40, No. 3 (Spring 1965), 14–15.

Colombo, John Robert. "Mandel, Eli (as Wolf)." In *Contemporary Poets*. Ed. James Vinson and D.L. Kirkpatrick. 4th ed. New York: St. Martin's, 1985, pp. 535–36.

Cook, Gregory M. Rev. of *An Idiot Joy* et al. *Dalhousie Review*, 49 (Spring 1969), 147.

Cooley, Dennis. "Double or Nothing: Eli Mandel's Out of Place and Another Time." *Essays on/Canadian Writing*, No. 10 (Spring 1978), pp. 73–81.

——. Personal Interview with Eli Mandel. 14 March 1982.

Corsillo, Maria Donata. "Eli Mandel Reflects Imperialist Culture." *Alive*, 4, No. 30 (n.d.), 17–19.

Davey, Frank. "Mandel, Eli." In *Supplement to the Oxford Companion to Canadian History and Literature*. Ed. William Toye. Toronto: Oxford Univ. Press, 1973, pp. 227–28.

——. *From There to Here: A Guide to English-Canadian Literature Since 1960*. Erin, Ont.: Porcépic, 1974, pp. 189–93.

——. "Mandel, Eli." In *The Oxford Companion to Canadian Literature*. Ed. William Toye. Toronto: Oxford Univ. Press, 1983, 503–04.

Dudek, Louis. "Two Canadian Poets: Ralph Gustafson and Eli Mandel." *Culture*, 22 (June 1961), 145–51.

——. Rev. of *Fuseli Poems. Canadian Literature*, No. 7 (Winter 1961), pp. 76–78.

Fee, Margery. "An Interview with Eli Mandel," *Essays on Canadian Writing*, No. 1 (Winter 1974), pp. 2–13.

Fetherling, Doug. "A Poet for All Traditions." Rev. of *Crusoe: Poems Selected and New* and *Stony Plain. Saturday Night*, July 1973, p. 40.

Greenstein, Michael. "Canadian Poetry after Auschwitz." *Canadian Poetry*, No. 20 (Spring–Summer 1987), pp. 1–16.

Frye, Northrop. "Letters in Canada: Poetry. 1954." Rev. of *Trio. University of Toronto Quarterly*, 24 (April 1955), 254–55.

——. *The Bush Garden: Essays on the Canadian Imagination*. Toronto: House of Anansi, 1972, pp. 42 ff., 124, 177, 189–93.

Geddes, Gary. "Lyrical Half-Mad Visions of a Bruised Eye." Rev. of *Stony Plain. The Globe and Mail,* 5 May 1973, p. 37.

Gibson, Kenneth. Rev. of *An Idiot Joy* and other books of poetry. *Quarry,* 18, No. 4 (Summer 1969), 54–56.

Hornyansky, Michael. "Letters in Canada: Poetry. 1973." *University of Toronto Quarterly,* 43 (Summer 1974), 356–57.

Hošek, Chaviva. "Poetry in English 1950 to 1982: 2." In *The Oxford Companion to Canadian Literature.* Ed. William Toye. Toronto: Oxford Univ. Press, 1983, 663.

"An Interview with Eli Mandel." *NeWest Review,* 3, No. 9 (May 1978), 3, 10.

Jaynes, Julian. *The Origin of Consciousness in the Breakdown of the Bicameral Mind.* Toronto: Univ. of Toronto Press, 1976.

Jones, B.W. Rev. of *Black and Secret Man. Queen's Quarterly,* 72 (Winter 1965–66), 696.

Kamboureli, Smaro. "Locality as Writing: A Preface to the 'Preface' of *Out of Place." Open Letter* [Long-Liners Conference Issue], 6th ser., Nos. 2–3 (Summer–Fall 1985), pp. 267–77.

Keith, W.J. "Turning New Leaves (2)." *The Canadian Forum,* May 1961, pp. 44–45.

Kertzer, Jon. "Responsible Dreams." Rev. of *Dreaming Backwards. The Canadian Forum,* Dec.–Jan. 1981–82, p. 41.

Kroetsch, Robert. "For Play and Entrance: The Contemporary Canadian Long Poem." *Dandelion,* 8, No. 1 (1981), 72–77.

——— . Preface. *Dreaming Backwards: The Selected Poetry of Eli Mandel.* By Eli Mandel. Don Mills, Ont.: General, 1981, pp. 9–12.

Lecker, Robert. Rev. of *Out of Place. The Fiddlehead,* No. 117 (Spring 1978), pp. 120–22.

Levenson, Christopher. "Magpies and Nightingales." Rev. of *Crusoe: Poems New and Selected* and *Stony Plain. Canadian Literature,* No. 62 (Autumn 1974), pp. 91–93.

Lewis, Kevin. Rev. of *Dreaming Backwards. Quill & Quire,* Jan. 1982, p. 37.

Lowey, Mark. " 'The best book is coming.' " *Calgary Herald,* 25 Nov. 1984, p. B3.

Lund, K.A. Rev. of *An Idiot Joy. The Canadian Author and Bookman,* 43, No. 2 (Winter 1967), 21.

MacCallum, Hugh. "Letters in Canada: Poetry. 1967." Rev. of *An Idiot Joy. University of Toronto Quarterly,* 37 (July 1968), 359–82, 363–64.

McCarthy, Brian. "Poetry Chronicle." Rev. of *Black and Secret Man. The Tamarack Review,* No. 36 (Summer 1965), pp. 73–74.

McMaster, R.D. "The Unexplained Interior: A Study of E.W. Mandel's Fuseli

Poems." *Dalhousie Review*, 40 (Fall 1960), 392–96.

Mandel, Ann. *Measures: Robert Creeley's Poetry*. Beaver Kosmos Folios, No. 6. Toronto: Coach House, 1974.

Meyer, Bruce, and Brian O'Riordan. "Eli Mandel: Double Vision." Interview. In *In Their Words: Interviews with Fourteen Canadian Writers*. Toronto: House of Anansi, 1984, pp. 106–23.

Miki, Roy. "Talking West: An Interview with Eli Mandel." *Line*, No. 1 (Spring 1983), pp. 26–44.

Munton, Ann. "Eli Mandel." *The New Canadian Anthology: Poetry and Short Fiction in English*. Ed. Robert Lecker and Jack David. Scarborough, Ont.: Nelson, 1988, pp. 147–48.

New, W.H. "This Year Country." Editorial. *Canadian Literature*, No. 77 (Summer 1978), pp. 2–3.

Nowlan, Alden. Rev. of *Fuseli Poems*. *The Fiddlehead*, No. 53 (Summer 1962), pp. 59–60.

Ower, John. "Black and Secret Poet: Notes on Eli Mandel." *Canadian Literature*, No. 42 (Autumn 1969), pp. 14–25.

Pacey, Desmond. *Creative Writing in Canada: A Short History of English-Canadian Literature*. Rev. ed. Toronto: McGraw-Hill Ryerson, 1961, pp. 241–42.

———. "Turning New Leaves." Rev. of *Poetry 62*. *The Canadian Forum*, April 1962, pp. 17–19.

———. Rev. of *Black and Secret Man* and other books of poetry. *The Fiddlehead*, No. 64 (Spring 1965), pp. 71–75.

———. "Some Modern Poets." Rev. of *An Idiot Joy*. *Wascana Review*, 3, No. 1 (1968), 90–94.

Plantos, Ted. "Mandel's Past, Colombo's Candy, Purdy's Earth." *Books in Canada*, 7, No. 2 (Feb. 1978), 16–17.

Reaney, James. Rev. of *Fuseli Poems*. *Queen's Quarterly*, 67 (Winter 1960–61), 703–04.

Rev. of *Trio*. *The Canadian Forum*, Feb. 1955, pp. 257–59.

Rev. of *Fuseli Poems*. *Alphabet*, No. 3 (Dec. 1961), pp. 39–42.

Scobie, Stephen. "If the Old Magic about Words Worked." Rev. of *Dreaming Backwards*. *Island*, Nos. 13–14 (1983–84), pp. 144–47.

Sherman, Kenneth. "Naming or Locating?" Rev. of *Out of Place*. *Waves*, 6, No. 2 (Winter 1978), 79–81.

Simms, Norman. Rev. of *An Idiot Joy*. *The Far Point*, 2 (Spring–Summer 1969), 63–68.

Smith, A.J.M. Rev. of *Poetry 62*. *Queen's Quarterly*, 69 (Autumn 1962), 461–62.

Sonthoff, H.W. "Darkness and Experience." Rev. of *Black and Secret Man*. *Canadian Literature*, No. 24 (Spring 1965), pp. 66–68.

Sorestad, Glen. "A Tribute to Eli Mandel: Estevan Homecoming, April 19/85." Unpublished.

Staines, David. "Eli Mandel's Investigations." Rev. of *Another Time*. *Book Forum. Canada Emergent: Literature Art*, 4, No. 1 (1978), 139–43. A special issue edited by James Carley.

Stevens, Peter. "Poet as Critic as Prairie Poet." *Essays on Canadian Writing*, Nos. 18–19 (Summer–Fall 1980), pp. 54 69.

Suknaski, Andrew. "borges and i; mandel and me." *Brick*, No. 9 (Spring 1980), pp. 16–24.

———. "out of *nārāyan* to *bifrost/the word* arresting entropy." *Brick*, No. 14 (Winter 1982), pp. 50–55.

Taylor, Michael. Rev. of *An Idiot Joy. The Fiddlehead*, No. 75 (Spring 1968), pp. 72–73.

"The Valentine Journals: A Talk with Eli Mandel." *Rampike*, 4, Nos. 2–3 (n.d.), 10–11.

Vernon, Lorraine. "An Exact Madness." Rev. of *Crusoe. Books in Canada*, 2, No. 3 (July–Sept. 1973), 45, 47.

Waddington, Miriam. "Five without a Common Song." Rev. of *An Idiot Joy. The Globe and Mail Magazine*, 13 Jan. 1968, p. 13.

Whiteman, Bruce. "Some Books of Canadian Poetry in 1981." Rev. of *Life Sentence. Journal of Canadian Studies*, 17, No. 2 (Summer 1982), 152.

Wilson, Milton. "Literature in English: Poetry." In *Canadian Annual Review for 1960*. Ed. John T. Say. Toronto: Univ. of Toronto Press, 1961, pp. 316–17.

———. "Letters in Canada: Poetry. 1960." Rev. of *Fuseli Poems. University of Toronto Quarterly*, 30 (July 1961), 383–87.

———. Rev. of *Poetry 62. University of Toronto Quarterly*, 31 (July 1962), 450–52.

———. "Letters in Canada: Poetry. 1964." Rev. of *Fuseli* and *Black and Secret Man. University of Toronto Quarterly*, 34 (July 1965), 354–55.

John Newlove
and His Works

John Newlove (1938–   )

DOUGLAS BARBOUR

Biography

JOHN NEWLOVE was born to Thomas Harold and Mary Constant Newlove on 13 June 1938 in Regina, Saskatchewan. His father was a lawyer, his mother a teacher. Since the family moved quite often, Newlove lived in many districts of Saskatchewan during his child-hood, and, although not simply a poet of landscape, he has made the Prairies he knew as a young boy an icon of imaginative possi-bilities in his work. At one point, his mother taught school in the Doukhobor community of Veregin, the focus of many of his poems of childhood experience.

He went to primary and secondary school in Kamsack, Saskatch-ewan, near the Manitoba border. After one year of university, he worked as a high-school English teacher in Birtle, Manitoba, during 1957–58, as a Saskatchewan government public assistance social worker during 1958–59, and as a radio copywriter, music and news announcer, and news editor for CFSL in Weyburn, CJME in Regina, and CKSW in Swift Current during 1959–60.

In 1960, at the age of twenty-two, Newlove left the Prairies for the west coast. Although he often hitchhiked back and forth across the country, British Columbia was his home for the next ten years, except for a period on the opposite coast in Portuguese Cove, Nova Scotia. In Vancouver he befriended a number of artists: Brian Fisher, another *émigré* from Saskatchewan; Robert Reid; Takao Tanabe; and Roy Kiyooka. In the early years, Newlove dedicated himself to learning his craft and spent much of his time in the Vancouver Public Library, reading poetry, but also studying history and mythology, especially the history of the exploration of Canada. Although the *Tish* group of poets was busy at the University of British Columbia, and although he knew most of them and eventually had some poems published in *Tish* in 1963, Newlove was not a member of that group. Nevertheless, his early published poems indicate that he was learning from some of the same masters as they were.

In 1962 Reid and Tanabe privately published Newlove's first collection, *Grave Sirs*, in a limited edition of three hundred copies, of which fewer than half were bound. Only a couple of its poems ever appeared in later Newlove collections, which is perhaps an indication of his own evaluation of this early work. In 1962, as well, Newlove's poems began appearing in various little magazines. In the following years, his poems graced the pages of periodicals in Canada, the United States, and Great Britain. Almost all of them are remarkably good, and carefully crafted. It is obvious that Newlove served most of his apprenticeship in private, not attempting to publish until he was writing poems of high quality. As a result, he has little early published work to be ashamed of.

In a profile in *Books in Canada*, Newlove talks about his first big break:

> It's such an accidental life. I'd been in a few little mags in the early 1960s. What really set me off from small private-press books was that I was doing my laundry in a laundromat on Fourth Avenue in Vancouver when George Bowering walked in to do his laundry and said there's some guy out East named Colombo who's putting together an anthology for Ryerson. Why don't you send him some of your crap?
>
> So I did and he took 10 or 12, and he was then also connected with *Tamarack* so he took six or seven for *Tamarack*. You get into a few good magazines, an anthology or two, one full-size book, and suddenly you're an "arrived" poet.[1]

The anthology was *Poésie/Poetry '64*, and the poems included are still judged by some to be among his finest. Nineteen sixty-four was also the year Newlove was awarded his first Canada Council writing grant, a sign that his work was receiving critical attention.

In 1966, he married Susan Mary Phillips, a graphic artist and professional organizer for the NDP, who had two children, Jeremy Charles and Tamsin Elizabeth, by a previous marriage. As his poetic reputation grew, Newlove came in contact with poets across Canada, including Al Purdy, who had become a McClelland and Stewart poet in 1965. In 1968 McClelland and Stewart published Newlove's sixth collection, *Black Night Window*, and in 1970, *The Cave*. In 1970, as well, Newlove moved to Toronto and joined the publishing firm as a senior editor, continuing in that position until 1974. In 1973, he won the Governor General's Award for poetry for *Lies* (1972). In 1974 he became writer-in-residence at Concordia University in Montreal, a sure sign of his eminence in Canadian literary circles. He followed that appointment with two more residencies, at the University of Western Ontario (1975–76) and at Massey College, University of Toronto (1976–77). In 1977 he was awarded a Senior Arts Grant from the Canada Council, and in the same year, McClelland and Stewart published *The Fat Man: Selected Poems 1962–1972*, a fitting summation of his extraordinary first decade as a published poet.

In 1979 Newlove returned to Saskatchewan to take up the position of writer-in-residence at the Regina Public Library. He remained in Regina, where his wife worked for the NDP, until the summer of 1982, when he moved to Nelson, British Columbia, to take up a teaching position in the writing program at David Thompson University Centre. When the British Columbia government closed the writing program at David Thompson in the early 1980s, Newlove moved to Ottawa, where he works as an editor for the federal government.

During the latter half of the 1970s, Newlove published little in comparison to his prolific first decade. One longer poem, "The Green Plain," appeared in a privately printed volume, *Dreams Surround Us*, which he and John Metcalf produced in 1977. That year he also edited an anthology of verse, *Canadian Poetry: The Modern Era*, for McClelland and Stewart. He has continued to work as a free-lance editor, one of his projects being *The Collected Poems of F.R. Scott* (1981). In 1981 Oolichan Books published *The Green Plain*, and in 1986 ECW PRESS brought out *The Night the Dog Smiled*, his first collection of new poems since *Lies*. Newlove's poetry is the work of a unique and significant voice in Canadian literature.

Tradition and Milieu

If ever there were a vexing problem, it is that of literary influence, and the old concept of "tracing influences" is simply inadequate to the labyrinthean reality of intertextuality, as it is now understood. Which is to say, perhaps, that "influence" is likely to occur in very roundabout ways. Thus, rather than a *line* of influence, we are far more likely to find a *web* of strange connections, via which certain techniques and concepts spread out among a whole group of writers.

In reference to how he learned to write in a contemporary mode, Newlove says, "Basically, I began in ignorance and had to invent it all for myself" (Moritz, p. 11). This remark is a bit ingenuous, although his further comment that he "didn't know at that time that Saskatchewan was not a fit subject for a poem in the common estimation" (Moritz, p. 11) is certainly to the point. Still, he undoubtedly read a lot of modern poetry in the Vancouver Public Library during his early apprentice days, and although Keats's line "Ruth amid the alien corn"[2] impressed him in school, he obviously realized he must try for something equally striking but in a contemporary mode. Newlove has mentioned liking Browning and Tennyson, along with Keats. He also points to Robert Graves and Wallace Stevens, the latter of whose influence various critics have detected in his work. Finally, he says he has read and been influenced by "George Seferis in translation" during the late 1970s and early 1980s and did get a little Bliss Carman, "Archibald Lampman, who's quite good really, and Robert Service, if he really is a Canadian writer," in high school (Bartley, "Interview," p. 137). Newlove's comments are helpful but they do not tell the whole story by any means.

Newlove chose well when he went to Vancouver to apprentice at his chosen craft, for the early 1960s there was a time of great excitement. He was aware of his many talented contemporaries as well as of such older poets as Irving Layton and Al Purdy. He can be located at a nexus of the twentieth-century intertextual web where the modernist poetics of Pound, the T.S. Eliot of *The Waste Land*, and William Carlos Williams, the more traditional lyricism of Wallace Stevens, and the postmodern experiments of the postwar generation of American and Canadian poets met and meshed for a number of young writers in the sixties. In terms of a personal tone, the importance of Williams and, later, Robert Creeley, is clear. Yet the austere perfectionism of poetic syntax in Stevens also attracted the young writer. Moreover, although his philosophical stance is often opposed to Eliot, Newlove obviously loved some of that poet's cadences, for they can be heard behind his own, especially in parts of "The Pride."

What does all this mean? Nothing more than that Newlove was alert to some of the most powerful and stimulating poetic signals "in the air" around him as he began to write. With an exquisite ear for sound and rhythm, he quickly developed his own voice, but, as is the case with all young writers, he took what he needed from wherever he heard it. Purdy's brash and homey garrulousness is picked up in such "letter" poems as "Dear Al" and "Letter Two" because it fits. These poems do not sound like Purdy — Newlove's personality is too strong for that to happen — but they definitely acknowledge his presence as a new master in Canadian poetry.

Newlove very quickly became a master in his own right, influencing younger writers in his turn. Yet, because he belongs to the largest, most powerful poetic generation yet in Canada, he has had few obvious imitators. His achievement, along with those of such fellow luminaries as Robert Kroetsch and Eli Mandel, undoubtedly helped to make possible the explosion of Prairie poetry, yet his classical purity of form has had less effect on the formal qualities of Prairie anecdotal poetry than has Purdy's easy colloquial storytelling style. Nevertheless, Newlove is recognized by many writers as a "source," someone whose command of rhythm and tone taught them much about the formal possibilities of open verse. Certain of his poems — "Ride Off Any Horizon," "The Pride," "Verigin, Moving in Alone," "The Flowers," "The Double-Headed Snake," and "Crazy Riel," to name but a few of the best-known, most anthologized poems — are *loci classici* for the generation of poets who came to prominence in the 1980s. Newlove's technical mastery is one of his greatest gifts, especially to his fellow poets, and it will continue to influence younger writers who care about form.

Critical Overview and Context

Newlove started writing quite late, after leaving high school and going to work. He says he began accidentally:

> I can't remember the real first attempts or anything. One day, in Regina, I remember sitting at my desk, writing what I guess was an imitation of "Thirteen Ways of Looking at a Blackbird." I know I tried a few other things earlier that year, but I can't really remember when or why I started writing them down. (Bartley, "Interview," p. 141)

Nevertheless, he matured into a poet whose work caught the attention of editors and critics more quickly than most. His poems began to appear in periodicals in 1962, and his first two small-press pamphlets were published in 1962 and 1963. When Colombo featured his work in *Poésie/Poetry '64* and *The Tamarack Review*, he was on his way to recognition. Thus the publication of his first book, *Moving in Alone*, in 1965 was met with serious reviews, of which the most important was D.G. Jones's review article in *Quarry*. Jones precisely discriminates the precise discriminations of New-love's poetry and, in so doing, lays the ground for much later criticism. After pointing out that these "personal, autobiographical, confessional" short pieces "are not lyrics" but "are essentially dramatic, querulous, analytical," Jones further remarks on how they "avoid" mythic and literary allusion, "resist" the usual tropes, and, instead, "rely on statement." He sees "an almost puritanical desire to falsify nothing, to discriminate, to be honest with oneself."[3] Quoting some of the major poems in the collection, Jones offers brief insights into them and begins to map the concerns of the whole book. He suggests that when "discrimination fails, and when self-contradiction fails, there is always silence, a kind of dumb pointing," adding that "silence is also significant, allowing the world to make itself heard" (p. 14). Jones then moves beyond a number of later critics to see the positive side of what many infer is an utterly despairing poetic vision: "And here lies the wisdom of these poems: the simple fact of things, that they exist and endure, is beautiful and terrible, and to be embraced in their beauty and terror" (p. 15). Jones does not try to argue that Newlove's visions are not often hellish, but he insists that a trace or two of heaven is usually present as well, if only by negative implication. Where most reviewers recognized the technical quality of Newlove's poems but also found his vision exclusively pessimistic, Jones perceived the great range of his work, something he would argue further in *Butterfly on Rock: A Study of Themes and Images in Canadian Literature* (1970).

Both *Butterfly on Rock* and my 1972 article, "The Search for Roots: A Meditative Sermon of Sorts," discuss Newlove's poem "The Pride" as a paradigmatic work. In his Introduction Jones uses quotations from "The Pride" to buttress his argument that the poetic imagination has finally firmly claimed Canadian space for its people. Similarly, my essay explores the then-recent upsurge of poems about the native and immigrant past, suggesting that poems like "The Pride," "Ride Off Any Horizon," and "Crazy Riel" are exemplary efforts of that poetic, imaginative, claiming.

Of course, Jones does not simply use one of Newlove's poems to support the basic argument of his study of themes in Canadian literature; in his final chapter, "An Ancient Slang or a Modern," he analyzes a number of Newlove's poems, and, as he did in his review of *Moving in Alone*, he makes a number of suggestive comments about Newlove's deceptive "simplicity" of language. He says of "At This Time," that though the scene is not violent, "... it is part of the crude actuality of place, the isolated moment of experience that the speaker refuses to gloss or distort by referring it to some social or moral or metaphysical idea."[4] Though there may be some irony in the tone, the poem basically speaks of immediate experience as it is, refusing "to betray" it "by some imposing comparison." Jones points to the influence of William Carlos Williams' poetic on a number of Canadian poets, and quite rightly argues that the Canadians share "a common conviction" with Williams and others of a real need "to explore and articulate those aspects of their experience that are ignored or denied or simply distorted by the traditional matrix of language." Newlove, then, is one of the poets who is still building on the Imagist program, seeking to "present an image, the thing in itself; [to] use rhythms that correspond to the emotion felt, the rhythms especially of actual speech" (p. 168). Indeed, Jones clearly identifies the importance of *tone of voice* in Newlove's poetry, and he goes on to suggest that Newlove's continual talking is "his way of taking possession of his world in all its immediacy" (p. 169). Later, Jones suggests that Newlove struggles to *recollect* the roots of his existence as vital "despite [his past's] banality, its occasional violence, its incoherence" (p. 172). In the larger context of his study, Jones sees Newlove not as a simple harbinger of despair but as one of the poets who are "concerned with digesting . . . desolation and affirming the world despite it" (p. 176). Jones is one of the few early critics of Newlove's work to argue that his vision, although unsentimental and often desolate, is not one of unmitigated despair.

In 1972 Margaret Atwood wrote "How Do I Get Out of Here: The Poetry of John Newlove" and also included Newlove among the "elect" of Canadian literature in her *Survival: A Thematic Guide to Canadian Literature*. Much of what Atwood has to say about Newlove's poetry is valuable, but it should be noted that, as is the case with many other poet-critics, Atwood's analyses apply to her own work as much as, if not more than, they do to the works of the writers she is ostensibly studying. Thus when, in her essay, she argues that Newlove's poetry is obsessed with corners and that "... for him it's a life-and-death obsession,"[5] we should recognize that she is pointing to a very real aspect of Newlove's poetry but also ignoring other traits that simply do not interest her.

For Atwood, Newlove's corner is "the world he is stuck in" (p. 59), and it is a bleak place, indeed: there nature is ugly and frightening; animals are terrifying or dead; people are equally destructive of one another; death lurks in every encounter, waiting to spring its trap. "What kind of life is possible for the individual — as man, lover, poet — in such a universe?" asks Atwood, and answers, "Not ... a very enjoyable one," in which the typical stances "are revulsion, guilt, fright and paralysis" (p. 61). Success "is a position he must almost by definition — self-definition — reject. He is a loser and his proper study is loss" (p. 63). The Newlove persona, as Atwood sees him, is "a paralytic or a transient" when alone, and "a treacherous friend" or incapacitated lover when with others. He is often wistfully sad about this, and he attempts, against all the odds, which include the ways in which language itself can lie, to at least be honest about it all: "... the concept of truth, the truth, is perhaps the only piece of firm ground he has to build on" (p. 64).

Because Newlove must believe in the possibility of truth, he is all the more distrustful of the language in which lies can be told. This distrust accounts for the bare-bones quality of his poetry, his and its refusal of the usual rhetorical tropes. But, if lies are ever-present, even in poems, why write at all? This nadir of hope is also the point at which a "beginning of the way out" (p. 65) can also be found. Although she has concentrated on what she believes is the majority of Newlove's poems, which are despairing, Atwood indicates that there are a few in which "... the encounter with the outside world through words, the externalization and transcendence of the self, becomes possible" (p. 66). She points to the poems "in which the function of the poet is seen as praise, though it must be a praise based on the truth" (pp. 66–67). Yet although she mentions some of these poems — "The Singing Head," "The Double-Headed Snake," "The Flowers," "For Judith, Now about 10 Years Old" "Samuel Hearne in Wintertime," and "The Fat Man," among others — her much stronger and longer concentration on the poems that reflect the desperation and even despair sounded by her title leaves the impression that Newlove's work is essentially bleak and harsh. By refusing to talk about Newlove's "craftsmanship," she manages to ignore many of the means by which he creates an almost comic energy of performance even in his darker poems. Nevertheless, Atwood's essay remains an important and influential introduction to his work.

Atwood's essay is the *locus classicus* for those who perceive Newlove as a poet of despair, but she is not alone. Many of the reviews of *Black Night Window*, *The Cave*, and *Lies* emphasize the bleakness of his vision, as Purdy's statement that "Newlove is allied to all the verse pessimists who ever lived"[6] demonstrates. One review of *Lies* that digs much deeper into the complexities of that book is Bowering's "Where Does the Truth Lie," which argues that "New-love has . . . removed himself as subject or observer, to give you despair and pity for the world, and he isn't blaming his father. Somebody had to get our poetry over that obstacle, and wouldn't you just know it would be him?"[7] In the Fall 1974 issue of *Open Letter*, Jan Bartley published a long essay, "Something in Which to Believe for Once: The Poetry of John Newlove," which argued, *pace* Atwood and others, that Newlove's poetry is more complex than these critics have allowed, that "the perseverance of Newlove at least equals his pessimism," and that his "work can be read as a mixture of positives and negatives" written by "a vulnerable explorer who is often uncomfortably accurate."[8]

Although she deals with all the major books published before 1974, Bartley concentrates on the two most recent ones, *The Cave* and *Lies*. She begins, however, with readings of some of the historico-geographical poems of *Black Night Window*, especially "The Pride," which she finds ambitious but finally unsuccessful. She notes, however, that "the search motif [in "The Pride"] is strongly established and it is not the role of explorer which changes but rather the nature of his discoveries" (p. 23). Bartley goes on to begin the necessary examination of *how* Newlove articulates the poetic act of exploration; that is, she pays attention to his technique and to his always "finely crafted expression" (p. 24) of mood and states of mind.

Bartley does not ignore the often devastating clarity of Newlove's unblinking vision, as her discussion of *The Cave* shows. Her analysis of "The Engine and the Sea" as repudiation of the stance he attempted in "The Pride" allows for all the despair the later poem contains, but her reading of the rest of the book argues that Newlove's comic sense of timing, his compassion, and his exact, though often non-"poetic" vocabulary work to complicate the tone and outlook of the whole. "Throughout his work there is a larger difference between the terms disappointment and defeat than most critics would acknowledge," she laconically observes, noting as well how often Newlove "sees despair itself as a personal indulgence" (p. 29). The love poems intrigue her in their insistence on facing the culpabilities of self, on not simply blaming the other, and on continuing to seek hope and happiness despite their elusiveness.

In her reading of *Lies*, Bartley suggests that "the challenge but also part of the fun of *Lies* comes from allowing the ambiguities and puns of the poet to work" (p. 38). Few critics have used the word "fun" when describing their experience of reading Newlove's poetry, yet it is, I think, accurate. Even when, as in "Like a River," Newlove savagely exposes modern humanity's aimless spiritual wandering, he performs his craft with such intense delight in that performance that the reader is drawn into a complex response in which his angry sadness at the argument of the poem is juxtaposed to a kind of joy at how Newlove is once again bringing his magic to bear. Bartley is fully aware of the negative aspects of the poems of *Lies*, but, as her reading of the centrally important "Notes from and among the Wars" reveals, she is sensitive to the whole range of Newlove's "fluctuating moods . . . in his constant exploration of society and his relation to the cosmos" (p. 45). "Throughout *Lies*," she points out, "Newlove despairs of language but refuses to abandon it" (p. 46). Moreover, the final poem of the book insists on making "a positive statement": "The title 'That There Is No Relaxation' echoes the sense of perseverance in the line 'A little more and a little more' which is repeated four times. Speaking in rapid terse sentences Newlove reveals his fear of possible defeat but also his determination" to keep exploring, seeking, writing poems (p. 47). Because she has critically registered something of the full complexity of Newlove's poetic, Bartley has written one of the best essays on his work.

In "Newlove: Poet of Appearance," Brian Henderson suggests that, for Newlove, "things or events themselves are only manifestations, mere appearances" as are the words that attempt to represent them. "We live in a world of harsh phenomena. It is, in Kant's terminology, only the neumena which are true. How do we get at them? Newlove's answer: by negatives. We discard what is untrue by a process of elimination, a kind of gnostic path to knowledge."[9] As Henderson sees it, Newlove profoundly distrusts appearances, especially the appearances of art, of poetry itself; yet he also desires perfection. "It is one of the tensions which make his poems work. He must continually temper his Romantic desire for the world to be a place for heroes with irony and the smell of the real appearances of things . . ." (p. 10).

Henderson sees Newlove's appropriation of colloquial language as an important tactic of Romantic temperance. Moreover, "because of his great distrust of language Newlove eschews metaphor. Metaphors are especially lies. A thing is what it is, not some other thing" (p. 11). This is perhaps too categorical; one wants to know what it means when Newlove does allow a simile or a metaphor to surface in certain poems. At any rate, Henderson perceives in Newlove a disappointment in the lies of appearance, but a recognition that the disappointment is also a lie. If Newlove is akin to Stevens in some of his poetic philosophizing, he also appears to accept Williams' famous dictum "No ideas but in things," which leads to "a poetry of tentative acceptance by refusal" (p. 12). And one aspect of refusal is the fragmentation of form, while another is the seeking of structure through "sound association and suggestion." Despite certain "gnostic" perceptions, Newlove joins Stevens in finding reality "the only thing we can know, even if (unlike Stevens) it is not the perfection sought" (p. 13). Therefore, he will, as he says, "swallow it whole and be strong."[10] Again, like Williams, Newlove seeks an "intensely felt language where words occupy right spaces in a 'vulgar' phrasing and rhythm" (p. 14).

After pointing out that "because of its fragmented nature, a Newlove poem is a concentration of attention rather than an artifact; it is a process of adaptation as opposed to a symmetrical product" (p. 14), Henderson begins a series of evaluative commentaries on specific poems. These are interesting, if open to argument. Although his essay is often as fragmentary in construction as the poetry it seeks to discuss, Henderson nevertheless offers challenging arguments concerning Newlove's poetic and intriguing comments on individual poems.

A more deliberately fragmented essay is my "John Newlove: More Than Just Honest Despair; Some Further Approaches," in which I argue, as I will here, that the energy of Newlove's performance positively cancels the often negative "content" of his poems. The essay also offers readings of poems ignored by other critics, such as the clearly comic "letter" poems and the specifically Heraclitean poems which begin with quotations from that philosopher of process.[11] The essay does not seek to deny such earlier critics as Frank Davey (who says in his short essay "John Newlove" that Newlove's work "displays a self-loathing only slightly less strong than his loathing for the human race and its wretched and treacherous planet"[12]) and Atwood, but rather to augment their views with some glimpses of the more positive, even "comic," vision of Newlove's work.

Bowering's essay "The Poetry of John Newlove" in *A Way with Words* is a revised and expanded version of his perceptive review of *Lies*, already mentioned. He, too, sees the black comic aspects of Newlove's poetic, as well as the maturing of Newlove's vision until, in *Lies*, it achieves an impersonal distance which is all the more haunting for its refusal of self-pity and the confessional mode, that is, for its insistence on a large historical perspective rather than a limited, lyric (that is, too subjective) one. In this larger essay, Bowering also argues the value of the earlier realistic poems and offers a (more than usually) sympathetic reading of "The Pride," which he finds is "arguably the most momentous poem written by anyone in [Newlove's] generation"[13] and analogous, in its attempt to deal with our true history, to Williams' *In the American Grain*.

This is also the view of Susan Wood in her "Participation in the Past: John Newlove and 'The Pride,' " in which she argues that this poem "offers a clear account, even in its failures, of [the] quest for a personal, living sense of an identity based on awareness of the past."[14] Wood offers a close reading of the poem from this historical perspective, one which adds greatly to our understanding of the changing viewpoint of the narrative voice and the narrator's increasingly personal encounter with the past he seeks to know. She is moved by the incantatory power of the poem yet cannot "ignore the reality [Newlove] depicts" in other poems, with their "dead Indians, dead settlers' . . . and a present in which the Indians, isolated from the white crowds on the small town's sidewalks, 'play pool: eye on the ball.' "[15] In this, she appears to agree with Newlove, who has written only one "The Pride" but many of the other kind of poem.

Possibly because Newlove did not publish any new books for almost ten years, criticism of his poetry fell off during the 1980s. W.J. Keith, in his *Canadian Literature in English*, suggests that all Newlove's poems "are united . . . by the theme of discovery within history"[16] and adds that in his work, "we can watch items from the Canadian past forming themselves into a coherent tradition" (p. 10).

He suggests that "Newlove's material is so fascinating and so important that it is easy to overlook his considerable technical expertise," adding that "throughout his work, and especially in the historical poems, he shows an extraordinary capacity to produce the memorable and resonant statement" (p. 110).

E.F. Dyck's 1989 article, "Place in the Poetry of John Newlove," brings a rhetorical perspective to the study of Newlove's poetry, arguing "that *place* in prairie poetry (represented by the work of Newlove) is a *topos* of invention of both argument and style (figure)."[17] Invoking the grand traditions and the tools of rhetorical analysis, Dyck applies them to Newlove's oeuvre and to readings of particular poems in order to demonstrate "that Newlove is a prairie poet in a rhetorical sense" (p. 74). His insights are especially helpful in his readings of three major poems. "Ride Off Any Horizon" is analyzed at length in terms of its "employment of the larger trope of irony (including, as it does, a continuing doubleness and duplicity)" (p. 76). Dyck's readings of this poem, "The Double-Headed Snake," and "The Pride" are full of insights and particular discriminations, and they earn the attention of any critical reader of Newlove's poetry. He is especially interesting on the flaws of "The Pride."

Dyck also offers a lengthy and rewarding analysis of *The Green Plain*, Newlove's "master prairie poem" (p. 84). He contrasts it with *The Waste Land*, "whose title it parodies. Whereas Eliot celebrated (in a mournful way) loss, Newlove celebrates (in a mournful way) recovery; where *The Waste Land* marked an apogee of poetic despair, *The Green Plain* marks a perigee of muted hope" (pp. 84–85). Dyck shows how *The Green Plain* "re-interprets much of what has come before, both in Newlove's and others' works" (p. 85), and argues that its conclusion moves beyond modernist despair to resolve itself in the image of a tree in a fruitful plain. The old centre (Yeats) has not held: Newlove's centre is not an attempted recovery (like Eliot's) of the old images now lying about in ruins; Newlove's centre is the imagination (p. 87). Dyck's essay is valuable precisely because it demonstrates how different approaches can add to our understanding of Newlove's poetry.

As this brief overview of the criticism (which ignores, perforce, many intelligent review articles) shows, Newlove's poetry has fascinated and provoked critical engagement from the beginning. The fact of the critical response is one more testimony to the power of the poetry.

Newlove's Works

In 1962 Robert Reid and Takao Tanabe printed three hundred copies of *Grave Sirs* in Vancouver. Only about half of these were bound, and if Newlove's note in my copy, which adjures me "not to mention it," is any sign, he now wishes it were beyond critical recall. In this, Newlove is being a bit unfair to his younger self though living up to his reputation for tough self-criticism. Although the poems of *Grave Sirs* are no match for his later work, they are nothing for a twenty-four-year-old author to be ashamed of. Indeed, they begin to explore themes that will haunt his later work, while their variety signals a writer capable of many poses and voices.

One obvious reason the older Newlove disdains this book is that the poems lack consistency of technique: the young poet is still finding his way in his craft, and some of his derivative experiments do not quite work. These poems also contain more tropes than he would later allow in his work. Yet the first poem, "Already the Lies," which contains a simile of some subtlety — "Already the lies begin to quiver like lizards / in my head,"[18] which suggests that like the changing colours of a chameleon the lies are a form of camouflage — looks forward to *Lies* (1972) in its view of lying as inevitable yet as something to be fought against. This bleak little speech is followed by the lightly comic "Poem for a Friend," which celebrates in somewhat pretentious archaisms the human capacity to enjoy the world as it is. Other poems reveal other themes he will explore in greater depth later. These are obvious practice pieces, and that is, finally, how best to describe the whole small book.

Elephants, Mothers and Others (1963), although still clearly an apprentice effort, offers convincing evidence from a very early stage of his career that Newlove is a poet of many voices, speaking in a wide range of moods — self-pitying, nostalgic, sardonic, celebratory, lustful, sad, happy, bitter, accepting, ecstatic even — and a variety of complex and subtle tones. Naturally, his control of the various possibilities within that range will increase as he matures, but the variety of these poems is itself a sign that the poet is far more complex than many of his critics have allowed.

Newlove calls himself "a comedian" (Moritz, p. 9), and it is a useful categorization, reminding us that if he is often grittily and even savagely realistic about people's lives, he nevertheless writes as a student of the human comedy. Some of his work is not funny at all, some approaches slapstick tragedy, but much of it, even when the vision it articulates is very black, indeed, is full of wit and a comic energy of affirmation that cannot be denied. The poems of *Elephants, Mothers and Others*, even when they are still apprentice pieces, cover a lot of poetic territory, and some of them have warranted reprinting in later collections.

The first one, "The End Justifies the Means," is one such poem, and an early example of how Newlove finds pretexts for poems in earlier, and in this case well-known, statements. In fact, he denies the famous aphorism, and by playing with its terms, shows why:

> The end does not
> justify the means, there is no end.
> The means are not justified or
> unjustified, they exist.[19]

"Means" becomes "meanings," and then "meanness," and these are neither "justified" nor "unjustified," but simply ". . . exist / in you" and finally ". . . go round you, to no end." In its plain speech and its subtle play with syntax and meaning, this poem exemplifies Newlove's maturing poetic.

The second poem, "The Photograph My Mother Keeps," explores a subject Newlove will return to often: his memories of boyhood in Veregin, the whole problem of roots in a specific social place. The paradox he will grapple with again is that "no part of that me remains" except "The photograph my mother keeps / in her mind . . ." (note Newlove's perfect control of the line-break here); yet he is forced to ask — *not* answer — "and what have I got to do with myself / of that time and flat place, / except I am still the same person?" (No. 2). So the pattern of escape/no escape is established here, though it will be explored in greater detail in later poems.

"The Arrival" is a brilliantly controlled example of open verse, as Phyllis Webb's careful reading of its line-breaks shows.[20] It is also a good example of Newlove's open-eyed recognition, if not quite acceptance, of all that surrounds him in the world: the cleansing ocean, "the sun / just setting," *and* ". . . the sea-going garbage / of civilization . . ." which too-fat gulls gorge themselves on. Despite finding himself ". . . noting / as if they were trivia" the birds and garbage, he concludes with pleasure:

and noting the trees whitely flowering,
took off my clothes and calmly bathed.

(No. 3)

Although aware of the signs of civilization's decay, he nevertheless
sings exuberantly of his delight in having arrived where he can bathe
in the midst of beauty. Even though the tone of this poem is not
present in Newlove's other work as often as the more recognized
tone of despair, it is certainly undeniable when articulated as clearly
as it is here. Thus, it is interesting to note that the title of the next
poem, "On Her Long Bed of Night," sets up bleakly romantic
expectations which the poem subverts at every turn. Indeed, this
witty and intelligent series of descriptions slides easily among various
perceptions to argue through them that the colloquial phrase "no
matter" *is* the matter of the poem. Like "The Arrival," this poem
demonstrates Newlove's increasing technical mastery; when at the
end of part 3 the speaker says "nothing urgent here," we believe him
because the rhythm says it too. Although the poem appears to be an
objective description, the final section shows how compassionately
present to the woman the speaker is:

> Not my child
> Nothing of me
> in this fragile blonde girl
>
> I wish it were but it doesn't matter
> it never matters
>   thinking myself
> how lovely & lonely her thin face is
> she on the bed fallen & me in the chair

(No. 4)

Of course, it all matters; otherwise it would not be the matter of the
poem, which is precisely the "thinking myself" into a sense of
communion, community, with this woman, his friend.

As these analyses show, Newlove is already, in his second small
collection, writing subtle poems. Of the rest, some demand attention,
including "My Daddy Drowned" (No. 6), a brilliantly ambiguous
exploration of the potential psychological cruelty involved in the art
of writing in which the tone never allows the speaker off the hook

but grants him an awareness both frightening and almost comic in its refusal to evade truth about the self. "Verigin" (No. 8) is a poem about roots and routes of ancestry, and the duplicity involved because ancestry begins in a double (mother/father) and keeps doubling further, the further back you go. Along with "Verigin III" (No. 14) and its boyhood memories, this poem points towards the next book. "Arrogant, Unkind" is the first of many such poems of self-accusation, yet the speaker's request that his friends "be with [him] a little longer, / though [he] can offer no promise of change" (No. 9) suggests a human desire to overcome alienation no matter what its circumstances.

"Before the Big Bend Highway" (No. 11) and "Not Moving" (No. 12) are poems of the road and the ironies of the travelling life. They are contemporary hobo poems: no longer able to ride the rails, the new traveller hitchhikes and meets a "mad old man" who insists his guest read "Ezekiel to him, Ezekiel / whom he loved, Ezekiel who prophesied, / he said, The End Of The World" (No. 11), or who crouches, "smoking / nervously / at midnight / 100 miles / to go // & cold / & afraid / on the side of the road // the only animal // not moving / at all" (No. 12). This is another theme Newlove will explore in greater detail in *Black Night Window*.

"Funeral," with its rhythmic re-presentation of the voice of "my / mother that is, or / whoever you like . . . ," might be an explanation for these close, tight-lipped, contained poems: "Don't / cry, don't show anything, don't / don't let them see it," she says, and ". . . Don't expose yourself, / don't let them laugh." The poem's power derives from Newlove's ability to catch precisely the tone of these adjurations while allowing other possibilities their place: "(and what my uncle said is / a different matter)" (No. 17). "For My Friends, Obscurely" is a toughly comic statement of purpose, which begins by refusing the literary romanticizing of such poems as Shakespeare's Sonnet 127, in order to attempt something apparently more ordinary:

I will praise my friends,
telling such lies about them
that you will never believe the truth.

Better for you.

                                          (No. 19)

In its concern with lying, and the possible dangers of "truth" (or is it just "fact"?), this short poem sounds a major theme of Newlove's work. "Smelling Your Blood" (No. 21), with its insistence on the many dangers of life and its freewheeling process of association also looks towards later poems on the same subject. Full of unanswered, and perhaps unanswerable, questions, it artfully mimes the ways in which we think about our friends.

"J.S. Bach" is worth noting only because it seems to be something of a sport in Newlove's work. It is easy to see why the poet would admire Bach's kind of perfect music, but he chooses to praise it in a highly romantic, hortative language. The poet asks this "beautiful music" to "halt my nervous stammering" (No. 22) and then concludes with a fine, if somewhat overwrought, epic simile. Against this, the cool humour and sense of process of "White Cat v" (No. 25) is much more what we associate with the Newlove poem. Once again, as in "Funeral," Newlove's line-breaks provide the sensation of the talk he is recording and allow it to open up beyond the ostensible subject, the possibly sick cat. "Elephants" (No. 26) is a joke, no more, but perhaps important because it reminds us that Newlove is capable of one-liners just like everybody else.

If, despite its individually successful poems, *Elephants, Mothers and Others* is still an apprentice effort, *Moving in Alone* (1965) clearly establishes Newlove as one of the most important poets of his generation. Newlove offers a clue about the poems of his major books in the interview with A.F. Moritz, who suggests that Newlove "seems to construct a book in the same way that he constructs an individual poem" (Moritz, p. 11). Newlove's own comments are helpful here: "History in *Moving In Alone* is very local, it comes from a very small area. Toward the end of *Lies*, it deliberately tries to encompass both the world and time" (Moritz, p. 11). Indeed, these deliberately shaped volumes map a shift in focus from personal history (*Moving in Alone*), through Canadian history and North American history (*Black Night Window* and *The Cave*), to world history (*Lies*), and then, perhaps, to a kind of cosmology (*The Night the Dog Smiled*). Within each of these books, there are many other threads — the personal and the philosophical, especially — but the sense of an expanding historical vision is undeniable.

The first few poems of *Moving in Alone* are personal and contemporary — poems of desire and loss — but they are also parts of a mosaic in which the attitudes struck in the present are rooted in the

life of childhood, which is remembered so vividly in the title poem
and others. Still, what first strikes the reader of these poems is their
almost visceral immediacy of voice, how they speak directly to
various audiences, which overlap and always include, at some level,
that reader. They are arguments, exhortations, explanations,
attempts to fill in the gaps. Equally, they are carefully crafted poems,
examples of how rhythm, sound, tone, and invention cohere to form
a shaped articulation of human possibility.

"With Whom Should I Associate," the first poem, is based, Newlove says, on "a quotation by Confucius about desire" (Bartley,
"Interview," p. 146). The speaker says he will associate with "suffering men":

> ... For all men
> who desire, suffer; and my desires
> are too great for me to hold to
> alone. ...
>
> (p. 9)

It seems, in fact, that people suffer *from* desire, which is why the
speaker seeks the company of others — or, more important, their
acknowledgement — for he realizes that "the greater their desires, /
the more they understand of me" (p. 9). Desire is a condition of being
human, and so, in the following gentle poem of outlawry, "Then, If
I Cease Desiring," he celebrates "how young [he] was," and the
"famous moments" of youthful desire. He does not wish to "cease
desiring," but rather to keep moving, not fall into a stasis of living.
The final stanza is quietly affirmative:

> You may allow me moments,
> not monuments, I being
> content. It is little,
> but it is little enough.
>
> (p. 10)[21]

The ambiguity here is instructive: many readers respond to his work
in terms of how "little" is allowed him, but I feel that his placement
of "enough" as the final word in the poem supports his earlier
statement of contentment. At least there are "moments" of contentment to balance all the other moments of "suffering."

One kind of suffering is intimately connected to sexual desire, and the next few poems lyrically explore its variations. Such "blues" songs of the pain of love belong to an ancient and conventional tradition, and it seems natural that a young poet would try his hand at the mode. Here, as elsewhere in his work, Newlove renews tradition through his uncompromisingly austere poetic: the plain idiom, the refusal of conventional tropes, and the mastery of open verse combine to create great emotional intensity. The poems concern loss, how desire is not enough when its objects are the wrong people, at the wrong time, and anyway, as Newlove says in "She Reaches Out," the other is always "someone else" (p. 11) — there is always some degree of alienation, despite all attempts to reach out and break down, or through, the barriers that inevitably separate people.

Newlove's famous mask of self-pity hovers over these poems. The four "songs" in "No Use Saying to Whom" modulate from third to second person, each shift directed by increasing passion. The final couplet, almost repeating the first, focuses the pain: "No use saying to whom these / songs are addressed; you know" (p. 12). Illicit love, a grand theme of lyric poetry from the troubadours to country and western singers, is given a new twist in "Nothing Is to Be Said," where the physical crashes into the poem — "Your tongue thrusts into my mouth / violently and I am lost" — and leads to the persona's recognition that "I am criminality, there is / nothing I dare do." But it is the comedian who provides the antiromantic turn of the final stanza:

> Ah, I can't go home
> and make love to her either,
> pretending it's you.

> (p. 13)

This is definitely not the standard lover's plaint! Yet it realistically makes new a usually ignored aspect of illicit romance. Newlove's speakers find themselves unloved though still loving; they feel sorry for themselves; they are forced to recognize kindness where they thought to see love ("You Can See" [p. 16] and "This Is the Song" [p. 17]); they are stupid and wily and awkward and afraid — both of love and of the lack of love — and they are very human, their speeches striking us as truthful to the possibilities of the moment and the person. There is a charming ingenuousness to the confession of faults in "This Is the Song":

> The foolish playing at love
> that comes upon me when
> someone is kind (or I am
> suckered in again) or just
> any stupid prettiness
> confronts my young lust
> disenables me too, deceiving
> as I use it on myself

(p. 17)

Newlove's control of the line precisely focuses the shifts of feeling: "someone is kind" *or* he is, but then the next line's shockingly comic colloquial self-accusation is balanced by the possibility of justice in "or just" which, until the syntax of the next line makes it an adjective, is a predicate noun in conjunction with "kind." This balancing of syntax and line subverts a simple reading throughout the stanza, creating a duplicity of statement, and therefore of implied motive in the speaker, which fully supports his later claim that he is "wilier than the fox" when describing "the holes in" himself "as if truth were a virtue" (p. 17). And just what are we to make of that denouement? He has "truthfully" displayed his faults; is he virtuous?

These are lyrics — they offer momentary glimpses of emotions in action. A quick study of despair is simply that: the articulation of that moment's feeling, and good or poor insofar as it captures the feeling or not. "Seeing Me Dazed" catches its speaker at a low point and makes us feel his "numb mind" as it "shuffles / through its depression" (p. 22). This phrase is, by the way, a good example of how Newlove does imply metaphor through minimal means: the verb "shuffle" combined with "depression" conjures up a hospital — the numb patient moving slowly through antiseptic corridors — and a breadline — the down-and-outer seeking some small handout — or it simply strikes the reader as a poignantly precise term for the feeling being described.

Love can lead to anger, too, as the savagely witty "Love Letter" demonstrates. This poem is almost totally tone, and the tone is almost wholly a function of the prosody, how the line and stanza breaks play against the syntax to create surprises and angry jokes, of which the most cynical and painful is the final word, which is only there, we realize, because it is the conventional closing of a love letter. Yet the solitary word "love" (p. 24) followed by a period is simultaneously a denial of what it signifies and an affirmation: that is, so much anger must have a source. The poem is comic, but it is an example of the "laughing to keep from crying" school of humour.

"Four Small Scars" is specifically a poem about signs and how they can be so easily misread. Again, Newlove's control of line and syntax creates a profoundly complex statement out of simple language. It is a good example of what contemporary poets mean when they insist that a poem means exactly what it says. Although the poem reads almost like a syllogism, the logic it upholds is the logic of emotion, where the insistence that some mistakenly call one thing by another's name slides into an admission that anger and love, say, cannot always be told apart; indeed, they often join: one scar

> is token of my imprecision,
> of my own carving, my anger and my love.

(p. 25)

And that "imprecision," placed as it is for greatest emphasis, becomes the human factor that makes differentiation so difficult.

Phyllis Webb quotes Robert Duncan on the "candor" of the short line,[22] a candour which can be felt in Newlove's "You Know":

> You know I can't talk
> When all that goes on.
>
> Would you have me lie
> to please you?
>
> I cannot lie. I would
> to please you.

(p. 27)

Addressed to a personal "you," this also addresses the poet's readers. Apparently lacking any context, the poem actually has many. The "all that goes on" partly refers to the previous poems of love, lust, and loss, but it also points to the world of normal affairs in which each reader lives. And although the lover/poet would like to lie "to please you," he "cannot." This is the bedrock of Newlove's poetic. Nevertheless, as many of his poems will demonstrate, he does not lack imagination, nor the ability to perceive a situation pitilessly and compassionately, in recognition of its human truths.

Webb adds that the short line can also signal "terror,"[23] and this is certainly true of the outrageous comedy of terror and errors that is "The First Time." Again the syntax and prosody push the poem through its human manipulations to its final moment of fear and refusal, a refusal manifested here, as in other poems, other situations, by the speaker's thinking himself away from the moment and its implications:

> Oh, she said, oh that was
> good, was it good for you?
> And oh I said yes, trying to think
> of anything else at all.

(p. 28)

"Lynn Valley: Depression" is a kind of first take on many of the poems in the later *Black Night Window*, including the title poem, but where they eschew all but the perceivable facts, this poem is garrulous and personal, a kind of runaway monologue filled with "the creature noise."[24] The poem is a horribly funny example of "a literary creation of myself" (p. 32) as a *voice* whose mesmerizing power has nothing to do with whether or not ". . . you think / I mean something (no / the fact is that I am more enamoured / of the act of writing than of the act of meaning // (or being))" (p. 31), but is dependent upon shifts of tone to compel our attention, such shifts within and between poems as the rest of the book displays. "For Judith, Now about 10 Years Old," is a deservedly famous example of Newlove's capacity for candour and compassion. The short lines here mime the hesitancy of the act of remembering with such specificity the awful facts of "the scalding water" and "the smell of it, // the smell you had" (pp. 34–35). Yet the poem's refusal to elaborate on the facts is precisely what signals its empathy with its subject. "Eight Dollars Will Do It" (p. 38), a short narrative about economic necessity, also refuses to elaborate upon the specifics of an event. But here the final line opens up possibilities the rest of the poem avoided, as it had to. On the facing page, "Stay in This Room"

303

looks at poetry-making as a kind of vampirism and recalls "My Daddy Drowned" (in *Elephants, Mothers and Others*). The poem seems to be addressed to both a muse figure and the audience, yet, unlike a normal love poem, it speaks in desperate need and makes extreme demands. Indeed, the tone throughout is one of insistent demand: "stay in this poem, stay with me!" (p. 39).

Full of tension and barely suppressed fear and rage, "The Flower" stands with Newlove's finest work. A story of pain, told *in* pain, it provides a perfect example of how Newlove works with perspective in his narratives of character: the poem begins with controlled description from a distance and then moves into a kind of involvement that implicates both poet and reader. The first stanza is suspenseful because suspended; we do not know why the speaker attends to the rain, the buzzing clock, nor why, in stanza 2, he describes a fertility frightening in its intensity. Something is going to happen, but what? Stanza 3 further defines a setting and its alienated observer, increasing the tension with its subtle hint that we might share with the speaker the nature of interlopers but refusing to say why. Why is the world, the sudden contingent violence of the fourth stanza which creates a new victim so quickly, ". . . wrecking his face, his head, / poor hit hurt head" (p. 41)? The alliteration and repetition suggest the psychological ramifications of an accident, which the next stanza clarifies, showing us how the accident changed its victim and drove him to deny any further possibility of change. Here the line-breaks, especially in the final two lines, and the rhythms provide the tone of paranoia, while the simile of the victim's eyes "like some secret / coupled badge" with its implied reference to the "cops" of stanza 3, provides an image of that paranoia. The poem then regains some narrative distance to speak of operations and hospitalization but suddenly returns to the earlier images of rain and flowers growing so profusely they terrify. The victim's hallucinations transform the flowers into diseases and weapons in an act beyond metaphor and therefore insane, but at this point the poet has pulled us in so far that these transformations are ours as well. Thus, though the poem appears to pull back to the outside world in the final stanza, it is a world infiltrated by the paranoia of the poem's subject: the speaker's reference to "My flowery clock" (p. 42) reveals how fully he has been drawn in to the victim's vision. But we have been implicated too, insofar as we have been moved to accept the poem's vision of the cops as dangerous, the flowers as irrepressible, the whole scene as frighteningly out of control. Although the poem's rhythms and images are violent, there is an undercurrent of compassion: it is an elegy for the brother to whom it is dedicated, a man lost though not yet dead. The anger rises above the fear to declare a kind of love for all such victims, and we share it because we have been assimilated into the poem's point of view.

"The Singing Head" (pp. 47–48), a fantasia on a prairie Orpheus — which, with its precise rhymes and rhythms, insists on praising life as it happens under whatever circumstances — introduces a series of poems on travelling across Canada's landscape. What Newlove means by "praise" is variously modified in these poems, but the intent is there, if only, it seems, by the pressure of its absence. Indeed, "East from the Mountains" begins with a song, albeit a ". . . single, faltering, tenuous line of melody / displayed by a thin man's lungs / unsurely, halting in the winter air . . ." (p. 50). It asks, how can one sing to and of the prairie: is there anything to say, really? But the poem's negatives connect positively to assert that huge space's hold on the mind and its inhabitants' living voice of being there, however "tired and halting" their song (p. 51). "Rogers Pass" (p. 52) transcends simple imagism through the analytical, sardonic commentary of the I (eye). "In the Forest" uses double-spacing to slow the poem down, creating a mood of holding back fear by willing thought against it. But thought betrays by thinking us into the surround, ". . . the animals / that may sulk there" (where "sulk" focuses the speaker's fears as "stalk," the expected term, does not), and creating a tension in which neither going nor staying is possible. The tension explodes in the "unthinking" convulsion of "run, run, run" in the final line (p. 54). "The Well-Travelled Roadway" and "By the Church Wall" give us other views of the remembering "I," who saw so much but also had personal problems that prevented him from truly belonging to the moments he records. In "The Well-Travelled Roadway" (p. 55) the mood is sadly nostalgic because "I" cannot *name* the dead animal, having problems enough with his own name. In "By the Church Wall," the "I" speaks his alienation and its roots in "the boy's terrible wish to be good and / not to be alone, not to be alone, / to be loved, and to love" (p. 56), yet his analytical language acknowledges that such self-argument is all he has, or is: ". . . formulating / one more ruinous way to safety" (p. 57). This is not as despairing as it seems: the present participle and "one more" both suggest this activity continues, is an act of living. And the placement of the too sardonic "Where Are You" (p. 58) immediately following further undercuts the self-pity, with a hearty laugh. Travel is, in fact, a way of life, and, like "The Singing Head," Newlove can praise the land, the life, he travels through. Two very different forms of praise are "A Letter to Larry Sealey, 1962," in which he finishes a trip ". . . scribbling on paper towels, / afraid of the ostentation; broke, tired, happy" (p. 62), and "Good Company, Fine Houses," where the Beat poet of the previous poem scorns the bourgeoisie, no longer in comic terms but rather as a seeker who has encountered immanent god-power in the mountains and recognized its terrifying strength while *you* "in your consequential houses" (p. 63) are safely kept from such knowledge.

"I Talk to You" may be about the act of poetry. Like the later "Crazy Riel" (in *Black Night Window*), it proceeds by punning wordshifts to a recognition that such questing talk full of "peculiarities and particularities" (p. 71) is all there is. "Resources, Certain Earths," the first of Newlove's large poems on the Canadian past, is a poem of articulate, argumentative recognition of such "peculiarities and particularities" as they touch the poet's sensibilities and lead to the gnomic assertion that to "swallow [the past] whole" is to "be strong and complete and be saved" (p. 74). The poem states this, but does not perhaps fully convince us that it has enacted it; later poems will more fully engage the materials touched upon here. "Verigin, Moving in Alone" (pp. 82–83), is the final poem and a kind of summing up of the poetic and perceptual discoveries of the other poems in the book. The single long sentence of stanzas 3 to 7 enacts the accumulation of fragments in the memory as they are focused by one particular desire. Then the next sentence of the final four stanzas moves through fear to love to loss, especially loss now of the remembered then. Though specific, the images and names focus emotional shifts in the act of remembering: this is primarily a poem of subtly delineated moods, and a fitting conclusion to Newlove's first major collection.

If *Moving in Alone* signals Newlove's new mastery of craft, *Black Night Window* (1968) represents a consolidation and an extension of that craft. In *Black Night Window*, Newlove brings his technical control to bear on an ever-widening range of material.

Brian Henderson argues that "*Black Night Window* is an ectype of Newlove's pattern" in individual poems: "Beginning in terror and through willed adaptation we end in acceptance" (p. 16). Whether or not we agree that this is the pattern of all Newlove's poems, we can see how the movement of the book towards its finale in "The Pride" is a movement from personal and historical alienation to an attempt at integration. The poems of *Black Night Window* are among Newlove's best-known and most analyzed works, which is why I am going to pass over most of them, in order to discuss some of the later, less well known ones. Nevertheless, they demonstrate Newlove's growing range of material and formal exploration.

The title poem, for example, is both a superb example of the Imagist poetic and a step beyond it. Based on the first stanza of "Lynn Valley: Depression" (*Moving in Alone*, p. 30), the new poem shifts *from* idea *to* thing, yet it actually moves to a large philosophical analogy. Or it does not. Its duplicity lies in its controlled tone: although "dead twig" is accurate and the phrases "the moon dead, / the wind dying" are true to experience and how we speak of it, Newlove's placement of them emphasizes all the connotations of death as a concept. The final three prepositional phrases simultaneously insist upon and resist any wider meaning:

> in the trees,
> in this valley
> in this recession
>
> (p. 11)

That imagination can make us feel that appearances are real is the burden of "Yellow Bear," and the implications of that may explain why Newlove is so chary of metaphor and simile. Beginning with a denial of Eliot's "Little Gidding, v," Newlove insists that it is not the memory now ("the end") that counts, it is the action then ("the start"): "no image but the tree running, / suddenly before my sight // becoming a bear." The imagination is a powerful transformative process and frighteningly transcends the safe comparison of the simile:

> it was my imagination
> began it, thinking, That is like
>
> a bear waiting at the top
> and watching it become the animal.
>
> (p. 13)

If this is indeed the power of poetic metaphor, the poem implies, then one should be wary in using it. And Newlove's poems show just how wary he is.

"Crazy Riel" (pp. 18–19), which I have analyzed at length elsewhere,[25] is the first poem in the book to deal with Canadian history, yet it does so in an utterly subjective manner, its narrative movement dependent not on the historical story but on the linguistic association in the poet's writing mind. The much longer "Ride Off Any Horizon" is similarly structured by the exploratory process of its composition, a process its repeated refrain insists upon: "Ride off any horizon / and let the measure fall / where it may" (p. 34). The "measure" this poem attempts is large, covering both space and time. The refrain is exactly repeated at the beginning of the first five sections, all of which explore aspects of prairie life and death. Only in the sixth and final section does Newlove alter the lines, to carry us to another place that might be measured differently yet is equally human and inhuman, equally a space to be filled, with words and with people desiring words and people. The narrative voice continually adjusts its distance from what it speaks of, these modulations of focus allowing a wide range in tone from nostalgia to sardonic irony. The poem shifts back and forth between personal memory and "vision and history" (p. 34), but the voice is sometimes more involved with the vision than with the memory.

The first three sections deal mainly with the prairie as the settlers knew it. Sections 4 and 5 contrive to shift focus through the satiric comedy of present-day small-town rituals —

> the boys and girls
> are practising against
>
> each other, the men
> talk and eye the girls —
>
> the women talk and
> eye each other, the indians
> play pool: eye on the ball.

(p. 36)

— to a sudden shocking expansive illumination of the violence of white settlement:

Ride off any horizon
and let the measure fall
where it may —

and damn the troops, the horsemen
are wheeling in the sunshine,
the cree, practising

for their deaths: mr poundmaker,
gentle sweet mr bigbear,
it is not unfortunately

quite enough to be innocent,
it is not enough merely
not to offend —

at times to be born
is enough, to be
in the way is too much —

some colonel otter, some
major-general middleton will
get you, you —

indian. It is no good to say,
I would rather die
at once than be in that place —

though you love that land more,
you will go where they take you.

(pp. 36–37)

Carefully playing syntax across his line and stanza breaks, Newlove
seeks to speak from within the historic scene only to recognize his
distance from it and from the "people I will never understand. /
Admire them though I may" ("Crazy Riel," p. 18). The tension here
emerges from the contradiction that he does not wish to, and yet
must, articulate: between the destructive acts of his people then and
his desire now to become "their people [i.e., Indian], come / back to
life" ("The Pride," p. 111). "The Pride," as many critics have argued,
is seductive in its delineation of this desire, but it also tries so hard
that its very positiveness creates a paradoxical sense of failure. In
"Ride Off Any Horizon" the image of assertive pride is quickly

undercut by the officious language of British law, which is immediately rendered empty by the shift to the slang of the conquering army (someone "will / get you, you — // indian"). The language of heroic ideals resurfaces only to be drowned in the coldly pragmatic expression of white power. Newlove achieves great pathos simply through juxtaposing these various kinds of discourse, which contain in their expression all the implications of the relative power of their origins.

Only after this scene of primal historical loss does Newlove turn to the spiritual emptiness of the contemporary cityscape. Suddenly, the rest of the poem becomes a demonstration of fullness: in "vision and history" the vast spaces of the prairie are packed with material for the imagination and the spirit, material which "the concrete horizon" of the city, "stopping vision visibly" (p. 37), prevents us from seeing. The final section of the poem delineates the real loss, which is the loss of the past. The paradoxical affirmation of the poem is its insistence that to know one's past, including all its absences, is to make it present and a presence in one's life. Such knowledge is "the measure" the poem articulates.

Many of the shorter poems are part of what Newlove will call "A Long Continual Argument with Myself" (in *Lies*). Ranging across self-pity, anger, guilt, sardonic good humour, sly wit, and, always, unblinking clarity of insight, they engage us through their direct speech and subtle nuances of tone. "Brass Box. Spring. Time.," for example, is a kind of list, very much a poet's list, each thing named and distinct, as the periods in the title signal. Yet the desperately comic accumulation its one long sentence articulates falls apart in the final couplet following the repeated conjunction conjoining nothing: "I have a brass box for cigarettes, / when I have cigarettes" (p. 46). Though the poem is about loss, the tone is significantly that of the stand-up comedian, as is that of the next poem, "Just About Forty Degrees Off Course," which examines in detail a "comparison to stuff yourself with" (p. 47), only to dismiss the validity of such a simile with a coarse phrase: the poet will hold to plain speech.

"What Do You Want, What Do You Want?" blandly articulates the ultimate macho fantasy and subverts the whole stance by arguing it through to its logical, self-defeating conclusion, shorn of supporting "romantic" rhetoric: "I want a lover / who suffers indignities" (p. 48). "Book II:65" (pp. 54–55) is a different kind of argument, moving from Herodotus to Canada with witty double entendres on politics and sex only to suddenly shift tone to personal reminiscence, and an insistence that the signs of memory (here the coat he and a lover made love in) contain memory. The end of the poem maintains the light tone of the beginning, but, no longer mocking, it gently accepts change.

"The Old Man" is interesting in its presentation of a different kind of memory. Like certain contemporary fictions, notably those of Margaret Laurence and Alice Munro, it represents a double narrator: the older person remembering and telling the behaviour of the younger self. As a poem, it refuses the expansiveness of narration, giving instead two complimentary images: the first three stanzas describe the situation with his father under attack "in the sawdust yard," but does not tell us what happens; the final stanza confesses the speaker's love, not at the action itself so much, but at "hearing him tell / how he made them run!" (p. 57). The poet, here, is honouring the power of the word. "Kamsack" is another poem of personal memories, which moves through its three parts from easy candour through recognition of alienation by language from his Doukhobor peers to ambiguous enjoyment of self-pity at being unloved combined with perception as to why self-love cannot be matched by another's love, except perhaps that of a dumb animal — "that red dog, damn fool / running and barking / away toward the town" (p. 61).

Newlove can be strongly satiric when he wants to be, as "Canada" (p. 74) and "Like a Canadian" demonstrate. The latter is an intriguingly subversive antitext to "The Pride," as it asks, "What does a person want / out of life: images?" and then goes on to attack many of the things Newlove himself has written so movingly about. The poet says he feels "like a Canadian // only when kissing someone else's bum. / It's a hard life . . . // . . . Tough. / But not as tough as living with the Crees" (p. 75). This cryptically sardonic conclusion separates the poet from the heroic figures of the past much as "Samuel Hearne in Wintertime" (pp. 84–85) does, but its jokey tone implies greater resistance to "the romantic stories" of the past ("The Pride," p. 111). This is another, psychological example of "The Double-Headed Snake" (pp. 42–43), where the cynicism and the romanticism do not so much cancel each other out as coexist in uneasy balance, a tension the poet will never be able to break. It is important to recognize that the many contradictory stands the various poems take are simply one mind's re-presentation of the all-too-human capacity to enter every mood available to us, and, in a poet's case, to articulate each one.

Even in *The Cave* (1970), a book many critics feel is narrower in focus than *Black Night Window*, there is a wide range of mood and tone. Although many readers feel the bleak vision of *The Cave*'s opening poem, "The Engine and the Sea,"[26] dominates the book, this is not the case. Rather, to reverse Wittgenstein's famous phrase, the case is the world,[27] in all its ramifications. Although many of the poems continue to articulate subjective moments in the lives of their speakers, two significant shifts occur in others: towards greater historical objectivity, a presentation of the actions of others in time and space, and towards the shared psychological landscapes of dream where anything can happen. (Both these tendencies will increase in *Lies*.) One significant feature of *The Cave* is its many short, though not obviously lyrical, poems. "The Fat Man" (pp. 78–84) is the only poem longer than two pages; most fit easily onto one page.

"The Engine and the Sea" is a bleak poem, offering, not a contrast between the natural life of the ocean and the mechanical life of the city, but a deadly parallel of predatory desire in a mechanically determined universe. Humans and animals alike are trapped by repetitions of "History, history!" and thus the final sentence ambiguously refers to them both: "Under the closed lids their eyes flick back and forth as they try to follow the frightening shapes of their desires" (p. 10). But even here, Newlove implies the need to wake up from the nightmare that is history,[28] and to open one's eyes and see clearly, as his poems insistently do. The further implication is that those who are awake need not necessarily lead mechanical lives but can choose how to live. Of course, as many of these poems demonstrate, what we might choose to do is remember, and that is "a foolish act" ("The Double-Headed Snake," in *Black Night Window*, p. 42), especially when what we remember is loss. Still, it is what many of these poems do: hold onto moments of loss and paradoxically to what has (thus not) been lost.

"These Are Yours" is such a poem. Its ten fragments map how loss remains in terse speech addressed to the lover now gone. It begins in anger, which understated humour tries to control, but the images about the speaker fall to nothing, which the three short lines of part 4, each separated by a line space, carefully mime: "Haven't got / much left / now" (p. 12). The next fragment calls attention to the failure of language: words are only "Shiny remnants / of our future dreams . . ." (p. 12), yet the poet must continue to use words, to speak of what occurred, of how he feels, of how he projects his feeling onto the whole countryside, of what remains, and finally, like one of Samuel Beckett's protagonists, of how he cannot go on and will go on: "My time is past; / but still I must continue" (p. 13) — talking about it, anyway.

The next few poems continue to talk about "it," that is, about various aspects of love lost and found, and though some are sad and resentful, some are happy and grateful, like "Warm Wind." In this poem, contentment in walking with one's lover is enough even to withstand the speculative vision of Armageddon:

> What if the world does end,
> and we are only stained shadows
> the sidewalk photographed? Today
>
> I hold you and have a happiness
> that makes me human once again.
>
> (p. 15)

Indeed, as the final line of the middle stanza implies, the speaker would be happy enough if the end came now, for that atomic photograph would capture them as they are "today" — together.

"You Told Me" is a complex series of repetitions that accumulate contradictions, not clarifications. More important than the truth is the fact that "you told me the truth"; just as the "nothing" that "happened" is clearly something meaningful. "I cannot seduce you" because "you" are honest even as "You lie / in your bed, my bed. . . ." Both "you" and the speaker ask "What do you want?" but this is no longer the blandly comic query of the poem of that title (in *Black Night Window*). No, what a lover wants, this poem implies, is for the beloved to change as he wishes, but what "you / have taught me" is to learn to "be myself again" *because* "Nothing / can stop you from being what you are" (p. 16). If there is some frustration felt at this discovery, nevertheless the poem expresses its complications and a kind of exhilaration in working them out.

That exhilaration can be felt in the other poems here, poems so plain in their speech it seems silly to offer interpretations of them: they mean what they say. The problem is to suggest how they make such plain meaning luminous and resonant, how they renew ordinary language by using it precisely and concisely and with a musician's ear for nuance. At the end of "One Day," for example, after moving from perceiving to thinking to writing and remembering, the speaker pulls back and actually offers a simile to his lover (who in this context, as Roland Barthes would tell us, can be lover, text, and reader, at least)[29]:

> I try to write.
> The Gulf Stream touches
> England as
> you touch me.

(p. 25)

Apparently simple, this is complex in its implications. Does the Gulf Stream *touch* England or only move around it? Either way, it is close and it warms England, just as "you" do for "me." But there is also a temporal statement: "you touch me" now, and at the same time the Gulf Stream touches England. Finally, the stanza insists that only because "I try to write" do "I" fall into such comparisons. Which is not to deny the gentle love it invokes, but is to qualify both why it happens and just how useful it is.

Newlove has said, "Desire is what I write about, mostly" ("Interview," p. 146). This is true of the love poems as well as of the visionary poems of history and memory, where the writer desires to say what he sees so clearly. "A Young Man" juxtaposes both kinds as it circles about desire, its failures and successes. In part 1, "you tell too much," but who is you: the writer's self or the others he turns into his art? "I have / been told" is equally ambiguous: have "I" been told by you, or am "I" being told in the poem, a possible reference to the inescapable autobiographical element in any fiction? Both "I" and "you" could be aspects of the poet, who is still young, still living in desire, the "dream / of the perfect moment occurring" (p. 27). Part 2 suggests how closely poems and dreams are allied: "I have had so many lines; in dreams / I have fixed up so many mistakes. . . ." These mistakes are his, and they possibly caused him to lose a lover; but the dream/poem, in fixing them, has ". . . made it / so she turned . . ." and came to him as he desired, asking "why [he] had waited so long, loosening." But the next stanza confuses the issue: is it he or she who is "unable to sleep," and is it in his dream or in their affair that she asks him "so many times . . . / . . . Why did you wait?" He cannot answer the question except by referring to a vision of death, which claims us all. This vision, which holds him still, waiting, is of the perfect (that is, finished, static) moment of his burial. Given the vision, the poem now cryptically claims us all:

The places of *our* decisions
will be found
in pure places, the perfect moments
endured, exalted the ordinances!

(p. 27; emphasis added)

Are these places the moments — infinitely extended, and therefore "perfect" — of vision, like that of the previous stanza? At any rate they are sacramental moments (one meaning of "ordinance" is sacrament); they are to be endured, and they are not his alone but ours. Part 3 speaks for us, then, not just him. It begins by dismissing part 2: if it is "A Memory / or dream only" and if "the past does not exist," then there is no truth to it. But truth is precisely what the poet desires, because it is the "scaled gauge" by which we "judge." What, however, do we judge? The poet says truth "is enough," but the poem can only assert this if we accept part 2, with its shift from sexual life to universal death, as the evidence that truth is both relative and the measure of our actions. Thus the poem remains determinedly enigmatic, its contradictions the signs by which it asserts its inclusive humanity; yet the subtle rhythms and syntax create a tone that draws the reader into its mood, accepting its claims even if not wholly comprehending them.

One of the things Newlove's poems argue is the difficulty of really knowing an other. "Doukhobor" movingly asserts the necessary incomprehension which exists between people. Its thirteen couplets are one long questioning of the poet's art: "who will be able to say for you / just what you thought . . ." (p. 34) or felt or perceived? The poem seems to argue no one can "say" for anyone else, yet the similes by which the man's death is asserted and the images by which his memories are imagined contradict each other and call that question into question. The poem's paradoxical stance is that we cannot know an other yet we can imagine ourselves as other, and such imagining is the work of art. It is a strangely compassionate poem, prefiguring in its willingness to attempt to get inside another's mind the larger effort of "The Fat Man" (pp. 78–84).

"The Prairie" comes at the problem from a different perspective, that of one's despair over language as a medium sufficient unto the desire to truly communicate. Using repetition and association as he did in "Crazy Riel," Newlove says "the words do not suffice" and goes on trying to make them do so. The long first sentence, with its angry shifts from "compiles" through various forms of massiveness to piles of words and "of buffalo dung" which mark the passage of men and beasts, leads only to a recognition that all this telling is only "invented remembrance" — a form of fiction. What does the poet, despairing of his words, desire? To be "the other's / twin, impossible thing, twining / both memories, a double meaning," but all he manages is ". . . never / to be at ease, but always migrating" across the prairies, "seeking some almost seen / god or food or earth or word" (p. 35). By building up to "word," this order implies that language *is* our best hope for achieving understanding. Although the poet wanders uneasily, he never gives up his quest for the desired words that will miraculously suffice, and that refusal to quit is the poem's hope.

Newlove confronts death in its multitudinous guises with every-thing from wisecracks to elegies. In *The Cave*, he ranges from the curt, sardonic poems of death at sea, like "Atlantic" (p. 49) and "God Bless You" (p. 52) to visionary sermons like "The Last Event" (pp. 38–39) and "The Dream Man" (p. 43). "The Last Event" maps the evasions by which we connive to allow "the businesses of death and war" (p. 38) to continue, on both the political and domestic fronts. A prose poem, it attacks the flashy false art in which "words impart mastery," for words should make us honest, able to perceive "that last animal event" (p. 39) as it really is. Refusing easy outs, the poem appears harsh, but in the integrity of its vision lies its hope for and affirmation of art.

"The Flower" is a deservedly famous poem, assuming the place of an apologia in Newlove's canon. It insists that the tenseness it displays is the mainspring of true poetry, that understatement and implication are more powerful than hyperbole: "The flower / is not in its colour, / but in the seed" (p. 46). Sometimes the seed is buried deep: the paired poems "Otter's Creek" (p. 54) and "The Words" (p. 55) simultaneously make and unmake aphorisms; they resist interpretation yet compel emotional engagement. They are best described, perhaps, as poems of shamanistic transformation; identi-fying with the animal, the speaker will "be pleased to know nothing"

("Otter's Creek," p. 54), thus achieving a sacred ignorance.

Two poems called "Dream" deal with watery death. Both insist on the potential for life in the middle of death, but the first is human in scope — "thin transparent egg strings / fold in layers on dead eyes" ("Dream ['Green sea water washing over']," p. 56) — while the second moves from a vision of earthly apocalypse to one of galactic indifference — "the red and brown vine-tangled land is empty" but ". . . the great galaxial wheel rolls smoothly in its unhuman / silence that contains all sounds . . ." ("Dream ['The luxurious trembling sea']," p. 62). In these dream poems, and others in *Lies*, Newlove moves away from the commitment to minimalism of "The Flower" to a richer, more colourful and even tropic language. They also tend to invoke the famous figure of the drowned poet in their images of death at sea,[30] yet because they insist they are dreams, the sea in which the poet "dies" or is lost is that ocean of uncontrolled images (of desire?), the unconscious.

The images in "The Fat Man" are anything but uncontrolled, yet the fat man's imagination as imagined in this poem is full of the imagery-escaping-control found in bad dreams. A *tour de force* of sliding point of view, the poem simultaneously maintains a judicious distance from its subject and enters his subjectivity. Avoiding the excesses of both satire and sentimentality, the poem partakes of both, achieving a kind of compassionate comedy of contemporary manners. Part 1 begins with an analytically precise description of the man and his flowers in the rain, establishing the character of the speaker as well as the outward picture of the fat man, then ends by slipping into the fat man's thoughts. In the second part, the point of view slides easily from the fat man to the observant speaker and back again, and sometimes, as in the couplet Newlove says mocks his "own . . . feelings of pessimism and gullibility" ("Interview," p. 145) — "Even the worst of dreams / sometimes fails to come true" (p. 82) — encompasses them both. Part 3 begins with the observer but joins the fat man by line 3 and stays with him in his self-pity into part 4, where he imagines how quickly his memory will fade after his death. Part 5 suddenly brings us back to the observer who, the past tense informs us, is recalling this incident from his memory. To the observer, the fat man "was dead already" yet he also ". . . walked down the tunnelling street, / a tarpaper blob retreating with flowers, home / to sleep and dreams and his apple-pie wife" (p. 84). This contradiction between derogatory dismissal and sentimental cliché is the most problematic aspect of the poem. Both renege on the claims to imaginative comprehension of another which the rest of the poem asserts, creating an ethical and epistemological insecurity, which is chilling in its implications.

"The Cave" is, as Jan Bartley points out, "a difficult poem to understand," with its overlapping philosophical, domestic, and science-fiction imagery. Bartley believes its vision is "finally optimistic" ("Something," p. 37), and I agree, partly because of the way it uses the expansive imagery of science fiction to break out of the darkness of the first cave (which is surely, among other things, Plato's cave) into the larger, more magnificent and open one of the whole universe. Although it begins with death, and includes the entropic claims of ageing, it moves "beyond" those to imagination's resurrection at the end. Its rhythm, repetition, assonance, and consonance beautifully express a love of beauty; the poem is so full of light that its tone argues against the death it casually admits. Hope glimmers in all the light beyond Earth, and perhaps beyond death, too. The final lines sing affirmation of the expanding universe of the living imagination:

> . . . Beyond the planets,
> beyond the dark coffin, beyond the ring of stars,
> your bed is in the shining, tree-lit cave.

(p. 85)

Displaying the usual assortment of lyrics sad and sardonic, satiric and savage, *Lies* (1972) also contains a number of longer works which, unlike the earlier long poems of memory or vision, have some of the qualities of Borgesian fictions: that is, they include the discourse of both fiction and essay in the context of the poem sequence. These pieces, often written in a prose notation, are the ones which led George Bowering to argue that Newlove had shifted beyond confessional poetry, which asks us "to feel bad because the poet's world is so terrible": "Newlove says the *world* is terrible, and just as terrible for everyone else . . . ."[31] This is true, but not wholly true: these poems say sometimes the world is terrible, sometimes the world is lovely, but always the world is *there*, and we live in it and should accept that. One of the lies the book explores and exposes is that we can escape through dreams to other, better worlds. That enigmatic fable "The Pool" deals precisely with this desire. At first, ". . . in his dreams he came once to a clear sunken pool / in the middle of the forest of pines, water / from an older continent . . ."[32]: it is an Atlantean place of still "magic" in which the meditative mode is prime. But within this dream "he lay down to sleep" (p. 18) and dreamed of walking out of the forest to a war-ravaged city — under attack by other humans or possibly aliens (the images have a science-fiction tinge) — and this leads to the short final section:

> He woke up, sweating and cramped,
> and said, I won't wake up,
> and woke up.
>
> (p. 18)

The final return is not to the pool world but to our world, present in the poem only by its absence: it is here, the blank space after the final line, that is everything *not* in the poem and to which the poem's protagonist at last wakes up.

Still, the imagination is granted its place: we sometimes try to *make* the world acceptable by agreeing to share a vision of it. This even works occasionally. Like most of its poems, the book's title is ambiguous in the extreme. "Company," a fictional essay on the need to share lies, is an experiment in depersonalization. Its blandly objective portrait of a hopeless loser paradoxically affirms "its" humanity through denying it. Once again Newlove achieves simultaneous distance from and intimate commentary on "its" feelings, partly by allowing shifts of mood and behaviour from section to section. Sometimes the portrait is utterly despairing: women turn away from it; "company is disgusted by it" (p. 21); it has no friends, really. But then it can exchange tales with others of its kind even if "to remember without lying is difficult" (p. 23) and upsetting; it can still dream of other places, the Pacific islands, say, where no one will know, and therefore avoid, it; "When there are no friends / at least there must be companions occasionally" (p. 24). All of which leads to the hope (and sudden compassion) expressed in part 10:

> Perhaps something will happen.
> Perhaps something good will happen.
>
> Perhaps it will meet someone it knows
> or someone who knows it.

Him.

They would talk together about the past.
They would agree with each other.
They would drink beer and smoke and talk confidently
about women
until closing time.

Then they would part,
not contradicting each other.

(p. 25)

You *are* a person when you are recognized as one by someone you *share* company with, even if it involves not seeing the possibility of lies on either part: this is a human need. "Company" achieves its objective of making a social loser a valid subject of poetic sympathy, but there are some problems: it goes on too long and could dispense with sections 3, 7, 8, and parts of 9.

"Harry, 1967" is a more devastating poem because its concision, speed, and blackly comic slapstick achieve a haunting compassion missing in "Company." "Harry, 1967" is a narrative of taking away: it proceeds by negation, each sentence removing more from poor Harry, except his name, the repetition of which is the central means of establishing him as a character in the poem. The descriptions of him and his one lie, or dream, are also important. Thus he strangely grows as a presence in the poem even as it diminishes him. Newlove's sense of comic timing makes the poem work. Each stanza/paragraph builds to a punchline, usually comically expressed loss, except in the tale of Harry's vision, where the blandly unqualified statements call themselves into question partly by their isolation — the pauses between the stanzas inviting dismissal. The poem marvellously mimes the performance of a stand-up comedian, who always waits for the laugh before proceeding. Nevertheless, the dream Harry is somehow affirmative, even in the silly images of his heroism which at least signal that Harry did have an imagination of sorts once. Without imagination, a person has nothing, and so, even if "it's useless to see things that can never happen" (p. 75), it is humanly necessary. The final line places Harry in a horrifying limbo where nothing is possible. Because of the comic tone of the rest of the poem, the deliberate, careful objectivity of "Harry just can't anymore, that's all" (p. 75) is all the more powerful in its implications.

A different kind of fiction, the black comedy of paradox "Or Alternately" is clearly about its narrator's state of mind, despite the apparent omniscience displayed in most of its twenty sections. In witty prose, it explores the process of paradoxical acceptance and refusal, acquiescence and rebuttal, which is pure day-to-day life. In a way, "Or Alternately" is a somewhat manic annotation to the book's epigraph from *The Commentaries of Pius II*: "Lies and perjury were so familiar to him that he often deceived himself and told the truth when he thought he was lying." Part 1 announces the terms of the game this poem plays; the other nineteen sections offer exasperated commentary on it as it carries one along. The poem begins with an entrance to the playing space, and a statement of the problem:

> He moved into the room, alternately believing in everything
> and in nothing; every philosophy, every theology he could
> find comforted him when he first came to it; later, each
> would seem useless or, worse, ridiculous; he was unable to
> make himself forget.
>
> (p. 63)

Part 3 makes specific reference to the epigraph, applying it to the self-in-transit of the poem:

> The lies accumulated and fed each other;
> it became difficult for him to recall their correct order
> and which ones he had told which groups of people. Some he
> believed himself.
>
> (p. 63)

The result of this is the comedy of the following sections, beginning with the single sentence of part 4 — "He lay in the hospital of philosophy and sulked" (p. 64) — in which that final word perfectly renders the childish, all-too-human emotional state of the character. This "hospital" is life itself, as the rest of the poem makes clear, presenting a sometimes satiric, sometimes cruel, sometimes slapstick comedy of mostly domestic behaviour. The exasperation reaches a climax in parts 11 and 12, where the point of view shifts to the first person as the narrator loses his battle to maintain distance from the problem: he sees the futility of "reading books, making notes, notes, writing words, words — words, for God's sake!" (p. 66). This simply does not seem adequate as a response to impossible choices, yet the poem, by its very existence, implies that perhaps "writing words" is one of the few honest responses available to us. The narrator is not at all sure of this, and asks instead, "Why can't I draw?" (p. 66), as if any other art would do better. The following sections manifest a sense of frustration at being always between choices but unable, finally, to choose. Parts 19 and 20 are one sentence, and they present a final, intolerable paradox:

> One changes oneself —
>
> — but expects all others to remain unchanging and unchanged.
>
> (p. 68)

The ambiguity is nicely held here. Is one simply changing or does one will to change and therefore will others "to remain unchanging," which is of course impossible except perhaps in one's perceptions of them, which then become the worst of lies. The poem refuses to resolve the question, yet its comic tone and clear presentation of the problem are affirmative; this is the human comedy, after all, even if it is sometimes grim.

The two other long poems of *Lies* are not fictions; neither are they comic, even in the black modes of "Company," "Harry, 1967," and "Or Alternately." In different ways, both "Notes from and among the Wars" and "Quotations" are historical meditations on humanity's capacity for internecine destructiveness. As Bartley points out in her particularly fine reading of the poem, "Notes from and among the Wars" is an exploration of "the fallacies and vulner-abilities of either the poet or the human condition. The central theme is the desire to dream versus the impossibility of sustaining dreams or transcending reality by means of dreams" ("Something," p. 44). Although he wishes ". . . to dream / through our centuries of blood" (p. 40) and through all that phrase implies, instead the poet forces himself to see these centuries for what they are and to say what he sees. Yet, despite the many horrors the poem exposes, the prayer of section 14 speaks for us all with a kind of exasperated irony:

> The torture goes on forever as we in perpetual motion
> breed and destroy ourselves for any reason
> even intelligent ones

All of which we have always known
in despair and amusement at ourselves

(p. 45)

The balanced contradiction, "despair and amusement," is paradigmatic of Newlove's stance in so many poems, and it is definitely
a statement of the waking mind. Dreams express desires, but the
desire to escape reality is no longer viable, and perhaps never was.
In the final, ambiguous section, the poet avoids "infinity / with
questions" (p. 48), and the final questions simultaneously acknowledge and refuse the temptation of dreamed escape:

Would you want to fly? knowing
below and as you fly
in the green concealed pit
the hunters with their sighted shotguns lie.

(p. 48)

The rhyme sweetens the verse, but the words "concealed" and
"sighted" suggest the brutal deviousness of the real world and insist
we recognize that deviousness in ourselves.
"Quotations" insists on the same recognition, but it is a much more
experimental poem. As Newlove explains,

... that poem is made out of quotations from about 130 books
welded together. Because I wanted them to come randomly so
that they could have come from any civilization, at any time, in
any part of the world, and see what the result would be. It was
a sort of survey of our history, and it became full of death.
(Moritz, p. 11)

The poem is effective because it unites so many different voices from
all "our centuries of blood," and what they say, contradicting and
supporting one another, is appalling. These fragments, "welded"
together, arbitrarily ignoring syntax and grammatical sense, swell to
a near-cacophonous chorale of cruelty and suffering. Newlove's
method of juxtaposition allows each voice its place, but places them
all so each one reflects on the others, calling both them and itself
into question. If they do not speak lies, at least they clearly demonstrate that no one has *the* truth. Since even the voices of historical

commentary contradict one another, the whole quest for simple answers is also called into question. The quotations tell us, and it is Newlove's "voice" in them all saying this, that there are no simple truths, anywhere. The poem begins and ends with references to dreams (another connection to "Notes from and among the Wars"), which contradict each other. The burden of the first statement is that we live in lies, not in "the world as it is" (which is always our disappointment, as he says in "Remembering Christopher Smart" [*The Cave*, p. 57]):

> We only came to dream.
> It is not true, it is not true —
> that we came to live on the earth.

> (p. 83)

But the final lines of the poem suggest that without dreams life is impossible. Both statements sound like Newlove; by discovering "his" voice in other voices, Newlove once again achieves his stance of balanced contradiction, which is the stance of the human, never able to choose finally, always wishing he could.

Although there is much that is uncompromisingly bleak about *Lies*, it is balanced by the comic tone many of its poems display. Moreover, a few poems present images of felicity and pure affirmation. In "The Hero around Me," the poet thinks "of the hero as man in combat only," and then discovers another possibility:

> The day came, but not as war.
> Fields of grain around me were crystal,
> the sky polished, endless gold and blue,
> and in the still heat a meadowlark
> twisted its sculptured tune around me
> once, quickly, a deft feat of superior magic,
> and all time stopped, world without end,
> and I was as a tree is, loathing no one.

> (p. 11)

Beauty exists, and the poet recognizes it. Recognition of such moments (even if they may not be monuments) is one responsibility of an honest poet, as he implies in "A Long Continual Argument with Myself." "As if," he says, "there were nothing to hope for" —

sounding what many think is the basic Newlove note. But no, he continues, and the vision is of human glory in human love:

> when a stranger woman smiles and kisses you
> at someone else's kitchen door, as if
> that tree of gratitude for humans would not bloom again —
>
> which will:
> silver in the silver sun.

(p. 25)

Finally, the last poem in the book, following hard upon "Quotations," reiterates the *cri de coeur* of "Resources, Certain Earths" to "Let me swallow it whole and be strong" (*Moving in Alone*, p. 74). Hortative and contradictory, "That There Is No Relaxation" keeps returning to its central prayer, "A little more and a little more" (p. 94), as it insists that to be alive is all we can ask for and, truly, what we desire.

This sense of life as valuable is to be found in *The Night the Dog Smiled* (1986),[33] in the almost mystic balancing act of "The Green Plain," and in the darkly glowing affirmations of the poet's art in such poems as "The Weather" and "Shakespeare's Sonnets." Of course, Newlove has not gone beyond his visions of human desperation, nor will he ever do so; other poems in *The Night the Dog Smiled*, like "The Cities We Longed For" and "One Thing," continue his explorations of humanity's talent for corruption.

Nevertheless, "The Green Plain" is significant for the way it allows both the negative and the positive their simultaneous place, and moves through balanced acknowledgement of both to full affirmation of the world and our being in it. Usually Newlove has asserted such balance by including in his books poems of both kinds; here the single poem contains and maintains all the possibilities.

"The Green Plain" was published separately in 1981 and deliberately structured as a book.[34] Although the poem has fewer lines than "Notes from and among the Wars" or "Quotations," say, the 1981 chapbook carefully uses the page as a unit of notation, placing each short section on its own for our greater contemplation. Each fragment demands separate attention, yet the poem is cumulative in effect, weaving the individual parts into a complex vision full of resonant reflections and echoes both within itself and outward to

Newlove's and others' work (in its structure it is similar to Phyllis
Webb's *Naked Poems*: a book of coalescing fragments that echo their
context in the tradition). Like "The Cave," it uses a kind of science-
fiction imagery of interstellar space, as well as hints of vast time, to
achieve a sense of immense distance, while simultaneously using the
first-person plural pronoun to create a strange intimacy with its
material and with the reader. We are implicated in its vision, in all
its awfulness and glory.

The poem confronts the usual human problems of Newlove's
poetry, this time questioning the universe as it expands to contain
our vaulting imaginations and desires. Much of what it says echoes
earlier poems, but the tone is gentler, more compassionately accepting. In the first stanza, the poet says, ". . . We praise constancy as
brave, / but variation's lovelier" (p. 19). Later he asks, "How shall
we save the symmetry of the universe? — / or our own symmetry,
which is the same" (p. 20), but the poem keeps insisting that the
symmetry he speaks of must be discovered in variation. He invokes
the galaxies, the far stars and near forests, looks at spring and the
ancient days of the dinosaurs, and unites all these phenomena in his
quest for significant change. I am reminded once again that one of
his favourite philosophers is Heraclitus, who said, "Everything flows
and nothing abides."[35] This quest leads to paradoxical recognition,
as in

> But confusion. The world
> flows past. It is hard to remember age. Does
> this always world flow? Does it? Please say it does,
> not time.
> > Do not say time flows.
> Say: We do. Say: We live.
>
> > > > > > (p. 22)

This section moves from a tone of querulous uncertainty to a certain
assertion of faith. Through such shifts of tone, the poem continually
surprises us into affirmation with it. And because it never seeks to
hide the terrifying aspects of life in the universe, the poem masters
the terror. "Everything is always here, / and burning" (p. 22) the
poet says (once again acknowledging Heraclitus), but he can accept
that. The final section creates from three separate nouns a sentence
of immense metaphoric power, which celebrates the connections

from universe to world to us. It is one of Newlove's most lovingly beautiful affirmations:

> Stars, rain, forests.
> Stars rain forests.
> Sew up the lives together. There is
> this only world. Thank God: this World
> and its wrapped variations
> spreading around and happy, flowing,
> flowing through the climate of intelligence,
> beautiful confusion looking around,
> seeing the mechanics and the clouds
> and marvelling, O Memory . . .

(p. 23)

Newlove has always read widely, and his epigraphs have always brilliantly illuminated the texts they preface. Here is the epigraph to *The Night the Dog Smiled*:

> Unless I understand the conquests of Alexander as a dying soldier's pain and thirst, unless I grasp the ideas of the Inquisition as the torn body of the heretic, unless I feel that these Sufferings are my own, unless in other words I have charity, my ideas of evil are empty.
>
> Jeffrey Burton Russell, *The Devil: Perceptions of Evil from Antiquity to Primitive Christianity*

How fitting that the first poem, "Driving," should speak of both "I" and "you" and manage to break down the difference between them: precisely an inscription of the charity Russell writes of, and also a sign of how the book as a whole will continually refuse us easy outs or identifications. Indeed, it is the way Newlove handles the concept of "voice" and "speaker" in these poems that reveals the continued expansion of his poetic, *and* its growth in grace and charity.

All of Newlove's collections have been meticulously organized, and *The Night the Dog Smiled* is no exception: the order of these poems leads the reader into and through a human labyrinth of desire, fear, terror sometimes, love too, and even hope. Newlove's grand theme of the (dis)grace of human history (how humankind has always found excuses for its destruction of nature, of knowledge, of other human beings) is still the ground of his poems, but there is a new note of optimism, or at least of the desire to discover reasons to believe, because one cannot, in the final instance, deny the need to love. Thus, "A Crescent" tells us, "despair is not a policy" (p. 12), even if, in "A Room," "There is a silence / . . . of waiting for the end, / of killers waiting for their victims' permissions / before the knives descend" (p. 13).

Indeed, the next poem, "The Permanent Tourist Comes Home," is almost a paradigmatic image of the whole book. Beginning with the observation that "To the oppressed / nothing is left but song," which leads to the adjuration, "okay, okay, obey, / since your only function is to die," the poem next shifts to a statement against speaking only in "moulds." The third section raises a lovely "apparition" of "my small mother" only to deliver her message that "Father's dead" (p. 14). Then "I" wakes up, but then, or now? In the fifth part, the speaker will speak against that death with love, but neither "he" nor we can be sure with what effectiveness. Still, the poem can move forward, to this finale:

> Well, to die in the Spring
> and be buried in the muck
> seems reasonable. Enough
> of this. The mountains are bright tonight
> outside my window, and passing by.
> Awkwardly, I am in love again.
>
> (p. 15)

It may be awkward but it surely helps, and it can happen again and again, to which many of these poems testify. Still, the pressures against love, even against charity, are many, and the poems register them, often with curiously comic effects, as in the paranoid vision of a dentist in "Big Mirror." But the voice of that poem, its clipped mania, marks it as craftily "other" from the poems surrounding it, the carefully self-pitying complaint against aging, "Cold, Heat," and the poetically charged statement of poetics, "Shakespeare's Sonnets."

There is a wide range of other voices, here, however, and together they add up to a refusal to deny pain alongside an expressed desire to find in love a means of transcending it. "Concerning Stars, Flowers, Love, Etc." sardonically defies those who say "make it easier. Tell / me something I already know." Watch Newlove's assured prosody, his ability to make the open line *work*, his control of repetition and sound:

> Make it easier, they say, make it easier. Tell
> me something I already know, about stars or flowers or,
> or happiness. I am happy sometimes, though
> not right now, specially. Things are not going
> too good right now. But you should try
> to cheer people up, they say. There is
> a good side to life, though
> not right now, specially. Though the stars
> continue to shine in some places and the flowers
> continue to bloom in some places
> and people do not starve in some places
> and people are not killed in some places
> and there are no wars in some places
> and there are no slaves in some places
> and in some places people love each other,
> they say. Though I don't know where. They say,
> I don't *want* to be sad. Help me not to know.
>
> (p. 17)

This poem is a profoundly disturbing essay in black humour with a moral bite, which pulls us in much further than the average satiric hook by so intertwining the "I" and the "they" that *we* cannot slough our own responsibilities as speakers to and for what "they say." As "White Philharmonic Novels," a stunning poem in ten parts, will say: "I made these voices. / The arrangement is all" (p. 68). This is true of every poem, and of the book as a whole, as well as of that particular excursion through a chorus of demanding and suffering and desiring humanity.

Still, if the texts insist that we have to know what is wrong, some also express the possibility that we can also discover some things that are right. In "The Green Plain," the desire for a new vision is answered, if only tentatively, within the poem itself. This is surely one of Newlove's most important poems, for it manages to incorporate the kind of arranging of other voices he had already achieved in such poems as "Notes from and among the Wars" and "Quotations," while extending their vision to include that charity Russell insists upon. But "Syllables [*via* Sanskrit]" and "White Philharmonic

Novels" are equal to "The Green Plain," and move to even more complete declarations of love. All three join that small group of major mid-length poems in our literature. They repay many readings not only with increased pleasure but with an ever more profound sense of what it is to be an alive and desiring human being.

Having given us visions of the universe and ordinary humanity, and even some small and gently humorous poems about friends, Newlove turns again, in the book's penultimate piece, to offer us a vision of craft separated from charity and compassion that is chilling in its unsentimental rendering of aesthetic madness. "The Perfect Colours of Flowers" is a prose meditation on "art," which carefully and in the subtlest detail describes the slicing of a baby into thin strips which, when held up to the light and looked through, "distorted and disarranged and enriched everything, like some new paintings I have seen" (p. 70). It is a stunning piece of writing, frightening in the intensity of its precise and unwavering presentation of the amoral artist at his work. It is important that the speaker is not the person who makes the equipment with which he can then slice the baby up; but he is impressed, and so admires the *work* that he never seems to notice the murder it entails. Yet the shifts of the narrative, its twists and asides, all work to complicate what it says, as it draws us into its view of things. This brilliant, savage, and frightening piece of writing achieves a deadly stasis in the perfection of death — for its solipsistic speaker. But it cannot do so for us, and that is why it is not the last word in *The Night the Dog Smiled* nor in Newlove's own writing life.

Newlove continues to write powerfully affirmative statements on his art. In "Shakespeare's Sonnets" he says, "This is a business of trying to make things permanent," and concludes with an argument of profound desire:

All the couples of Shakespeare's sonnets
make sense to me. It was another love
other than the Dark One he reached for.

Us.

(p. 41)

Yet he has not forgotten Heraclitus, nor the flow of this only world, and in "The Weather" he acknowledges flow and change in himself as well. "The Weather" is one of Newlove's finest poems, a confession of past failure, a celebration of the necessary desire to try again to say things right, to reach out and touch that other lover who is the artist's audience. And, significantly, in the plainest language, acknowledging ageing, death, and all the weather of living, it does. As the final poem in *The Night the Dog Smiled*, it puts the case of charity up against the "art" of "The Perfect Colours of Flowers." It is simply a beautiful work embracing chance and change, and it gets us all back into the middle of our own human living:

I'd like to live a slower life.
The weather gets in my words
and I want them dry. Line after line
writes itself on my face, not a grace
of age but wrinkled humour. I laugh
more than I should or more
than anyone should. This is good.

But guess again. Everyone leans, each
on each other. This is a life
without an image. But only
because nothing does much more
than just resemble. Do the shamans
do what they say they do, dancing?
This is epistemology.

This is guesswork, this is love,
this is giving up gorgeousness to please you,
you beautiful dead to be. God bless
the weather and the words. Any words. Any weather.
And where or whom. I'd never taken count before.
I wish I had. And then
I did. And here
the weather wrote again.

NOTES

¹ Quoted in A.F. Moritz, "The Man from Vaudeville, Sask.," *Books in Canada*, Jan. 1978, p. 12. All further references to this work (Moritz) appear in the text.

² See his comments on this in Jan Bartley, "An Interview with John Newlove," *Essays on Canadian Writing*, No. 23 (Spring 1982), p. 137. All further references to this work ("Interview") appear in the text.

³ D.G. Jones, "*Moving in Alone*: A Review Article," *Quarry*, 15, No. 1 (Sept. 1965), 12. All further references to this work appear in the text.

⁴ D.G. Jones, *Butterfly on Rock: A Study of Themes and Images in Canadian Literature* (Toronto: Univ. of Toronto Press, 1970), pp. 167–68. All further references to this work appear in the text.

⁵ Margaret Atwood, "How Do I Get Out of Here: The Poetry of John Newlove," *Open Letter*, Ser. 2, No. 4 (Spring 1973), 59. All further references to this work appear in the text. This essay first appeared, in French, in *Ellipse*, No. 10 (1972), pp. 102–18.

⁶ Al Purdy, Rev. of *Lies*, *Wascana Review*, 8, No. 2 (Fall 1973), 70.

⁷ George Bowering, "Where Does the Truth Lie," rev. of *Lies*, *Open Letter*, Ser. 2, No. 4 (Spring 1973), 74. This review now forms part of "The Poetry of John Newlove," in Bowering's *A Way with Words* (Ottawa: Oberon, 1982), pp. 121–34.

⁸ Jan Bartley, "Something in Which to Believe for Once: The Poetry of John Newlove," *Open Letter*, Ser. 2, No. 9 (Fall 1974), 19. All further references to this work ("Something") appear in the text.

⁹ Brian Henderson, "Newlove: Poet of Appearance," *Essays on Canadian Writing*, No. 2 (Spring 1975), p. 9. All further references to this work appear in the text.

¹⁰ "Resources, Certain Earths," in *Moving in Alone* (Toronto: Contact, 1965), p. 74. All further references to this work appear in the text.

¹¹ The "letter" poems include "Love Letter," "A Letter to Larry Sealey, 1962" (both in *Moving in Alone*), "Dear Al," and "Letter Two" (in *Black Night Window*); the Heraclitean poems are "It Is in Changing," "The Sun" (both in *What They Say*), "War Is Both Father," and "You Cannot Step Twice" (in *Black Night Window*).

¹² Frank Davey, *From There to Here: A Guide to English-Canadian Literature since 1960* (Erin, Ont.: Porcépic, 1974), p. 205.

¹³ Bowering, "The Poetry of John Newlove," p. 126.

¹⁴ Susan Wood, "Participation in the Past: John Newlove and 'The Pride,'" *Essays on Canadian Writing*, No. 20 (Winter 1980–81), p. 231.

¹⁵ Wood, p. 238.

¹⁶ W.J. Keith, *Canadian Literature in English* (New York: Longman, 1985), p. 109. All further references to this work appear in the text.

¹⁷ E.F. Dyck, "Place in the Poetry of John Newlove," *Canadian Literature*, Nos. 122–23 (Autumn–Winter 1989), p. 69. All further references to this work appear in the text.

¹⁸ "Already the Lies," in *Grave Sirs* (Vancouver: Robert Reid and Takao Tanabe, 1962), n. pag.

¹⁹ "The End Justifies the Means," in *Elephants, Mothers and Others* (Vancouver: Periwinkle, 1963), No. 1. All further references to this work appear in the text.

²⁰ See "Talking the Line: Phyllis Webb in Conversation with Douglas Barbour and Steve Scobie," *Writing*, No. 4 (Winter 1981–82), pp. 24–25.

²¹ It is probable that Newlove is alluding to Phyllis Webb's poem "Moments Are Monuments," which appeared in *Even Your Right Eye* (Toronto: McClelland and Stewart, 1956).

²² Phyllis Webb, "On the Line," in *Talking* (Dunvegan, Ont.: Quadrant, 1982), p. 67.

²³ Webb, "On the Line," p. 67.

²⁴ Cf., "Crazy Riel," in *Black Night Window* (Toronto: McClelland and Stewart, 1968), p. 18. All further references to this work appear in the text.

²⁵ Douglas Barbour, "John Newlove: More Than Just Honest Despair; Some Further Approaches," *Essays on Canadian Writing*, Nos. 18–19 (Summer–Fall 1980), pp. 258–61.

²⁶ In *The Cave* (Toronto: McClelland and Stewart, 1970), pp. 9–10. All further references to this work appear in the text.

²⁷ Wittgenstein's famous first proposition is "The world is all that is the case" (Ludwig Wittgenstein, *Tractatus-Logico-Philosphicus*, trans. D.F. Pears and B.F. McGuinness [London: Routledge & Kegan Paul, 1961], p. 7).

²⁸ Cf. Stephen Dedalus' remark, "History . . . is a nightmare from which I am trying to awake" (James Joyce, *Ulysses* [London: The Bodley Head, 1960], p. 42).

²⁹ See Roland Barthes, *The Pleasure of the Text*, trans. Richard Miller (New York: Farrar, Straus and Giroux, 1975), *passim*.

³⁰ Cf. Milton Wilson, "Klein's Drowned Poet: Canadian Variations on an Old Theme," *Canadian Literature*, No. 6 (Autumn 1960), pp. 5–17.

³¹ Bowering, "The Poetry of John Newlove," p. 134.

³² In *Lies* (Toronto: McClelland and Stewart, 1972), p. 17. All further references to this work appear in the text.

³³ This discussion of *The Night the Dog Smiled* is a revised and expanded

version of "Weather Report: 'Stars, rain, forests,' " rev. of *The Night the Dog Smiled, Essays on Canadian Writing*, No. 36 (Spring 1988), pp. 90–94.

34 *The Green Plain* (Lantzville, B.C.: Oolichan, 1981); rpt. in *The Night the Dog Smiled* (Toronto: ECW, 1986), pp. 19–23. All further references to this work appear in the text. In *The Night the Dog Smiled*, "The Green Plain" is compressed into five pages.

35 *Heraclitus*, ed. and trans. Philip Wheelwright (New York: Atheneum, 1964), p. 29. And see my comments on Newlove's Heraclitean poems in "John Newlove," pp. 272–76.

SELECTED BIBLIOGRAPHY

Primary Sources

Newlove, John. *Grave Sirs*. Vancouver: Robert Reid and Takao Tanabe, 1962.
────── . *Elephants, Mothers and Others*. Vancouver: Periwinkle, 1963.
────── . *Moving in Alone*. Toronto: Contact, 1965.
────── . *Notebook Pages*. Toronto: Charles Pachter, 1966.
────── . *What They Say*. Kitchener, Ont.: Weed/flower, 1967.
────── . *Black Night Window*. Toronto: McClelland and Stewart, 1968.
────── . *The Cave*. Toronto: McClelland and Stewart, 1970.
────── . *Lies*. Toronto: McClelland and Stewart, 1972.
────── . *The Fat Man: Selected Poems 1961–1972*. Toronto: McClelland and Stewart, 1976.
────── , and John Metcalf. *Dreams Surround Us*. Delta, Ont.: Bastard, 1977.
────── . *The Green Plain*. Lantzville, B.C.: Oolichan, 1981.
────── . *The Night the Dog Smiled*. Toronto: ECW, 1986.

Secondary Sources

Atwood, Margaret. *Survival: A Thematic Guide to Canadian Literature*. Toronto: House of Anansi, 1972.
────── . "How Do I Get Out of Here: The Poetry of John Newlove." *Open Letter*, Ser. 2, No. 4 (Spring 1973), 59–70.
Barbour, Douglas. "The Search for Roots: A Meditative Sermon of Sorts." *The Literary Half-Yearly*, 13, No. 2 (July 1972), 1–14.
────── . "John Newlove: More Than Just Honest Despair; Some Further Approaches." *Essays on Canadian Writing*, Nos. 18–19 (Summer–Fall 1980), pp. 256–80.
────── . "Weather Report: 'Stars, rain, forests.' " Rev. of *The Night the Dog Smiled*. *Essays on Canadian Writing*, No. 36 (Spring 1988), pp. 90–94.
Barthes, Roland. *The Pleasure of the Text*. Trans. Richard Miller. New York: Farrar, Straus and Giroux, 1975.
Bartley, Jan. "Something in Which to Believe for Once: The Poetry of John

Newlove." *Open Letter*, Ser. 2, No. 9 (Fall 1974), 19–48.

————. "An Interview with John Newlove." *Essays on Canadian Writing*, No. 23 (Spring 1982), pp. 135–56.

Bowering, George. "Where Does the Truth Lie." Rev. of *Lies*. *Open Letter*, Ser. 2, No. 4 (Spring 1973), 71–74.

————. *A Way with Words*. Ottawa: Oberon, 1982.

Davey, Frank. *From There to Here: A Guide to English-Canadian Literature since 1960*. Erin, Ont.: Porcépic, 1974.

Dyck, E.F. "Place in the Poetry of John Newlove." *Canadian Literature*, Nos. 122–23 (Autumn–Winter 1989), pp. 69–91.

Henderson, Brian. "Newlove: Poet of Appearance." *Essays on Canadian Writing*, No. 2 (Spring 1975), pp. 9–27.

Heraclitus. *Heraclitus*. Ed. and trans. Philip Wheelwright. New York: Atheneum, 1964.

Jones, D.G. "*Moving in Alone*: A Review Article." *Quarry*, 15, No. 1 (Sept. 1965), 12–15.

————. *Butterfly on Rock: A Study of Themes and Images in Canadian Literature*. Toronto: Univ. of Toronto Press, 1970.

Joyce, James. *Ulysses*. London: The Bodley Head, 1960.

Keith, W.J. *Canadian Literature in English*. New York: Longman, 1985.

Lecker, Robert, and David O'Rourke. "John Newlove: An Annotated Bibliography." In *The Annotated Bibliography of Canada's Major Authors*. Ed. Robert Lecker and Jack David. Vol. VI. Toronto: ECW, 1985, 67–128.

Moritz, A.F. "The Man from Vaudeville, Sask." *Books in Canada*, Jan. 1978, pp. 9–12.

Purdy, Al. Rev. of *Lies*. *Wascana Review*, 8, No. 2 (Fall 1973), 70–72.

Webb, Phyllis. *Talking*. Dunvegan, Ont.: Quadrant, 1982.

————, Douglas Barbour, and Stephen Scobie. "Talking the Line." *Writing*, No. 4 (Winter 1981–82), pp. 22–25.

Wilson, Milton. "Klein's Drowned Poet: Canadian Variations on an Old Theme." *Canadian Literature*, No. 6 (Autumn 1960), pp. 5–17.

Wittgenstein, Ludwig. *Tractatus-Logico-Philosophicus*. Trans. D.F. Pears and B.F. McGuinness. London: Routledge and Kegan Paul, 1961.

Wood, Susan. "Participation in the Past: John Newlove and 'The Pride.'" *Essays on Canadian Writing*, No. 20 (Winter 1980–81), pp. 230–40.

*Joe Rosenblatt
and His Works*

Joe Rosenblatt (1933–   )

ED JEWINSKI

Biography

JOE ROSENBLATT was born on 26 December 1933 in the Kensington Market district of Toronto.[1] He attended Lansdowne Public School and, afterwards, Central Technical High School. Dissatisfied with the routine and monotonous discipline, he dropped out of grade ten. During the years that followed, Rosenblatt restlessly moved from job to job: initially he became a plumber's assistant, then a busboy, then a labourer in a battery factory, then a rubber worker, then a sheet-metal worker. He even went back to school in search of a suitable trade, attending the Provincial Institute of Trades (now George Brown College) to become a welder-fitter. Not content with this training, he joined the Canadian Pacific Railway (CPR) as a freight handler and held this job for seven years.

During his years as a freight handler, Rosenblatt turned to writing poetry. His initial efforts dealt either with nature, far removed from his work for the CPR, or with social injustice, of which he had seen and experienced a great deal while shifting from menial job to menial job. These dual concerns are striking in Rosenblatt's first chapbook of poems, *Voyage of the Mood* (1963). Since his interests at the time leaned towards socialism and political change, Rosenblatt attended socialist meetings. It was at one of these gatherings that he first met the poet Milton Acorn. Acorn read Rosenblatt's early efforts at verse and offered strong encouragement and support. He also showed the young poet's work to others, thereby actively introducing Rosenblatt to Canadian poetry and poets. Al Purdy, a friend of Acorn's, also recognized Rosenblatt's talent and sponsored him for a short-term Canada Council grant in 1963.

From this time on, Rosenblatt was determined to make his living as a writer. He quit his job as a freight handler and left for Vancouver, a city which would, he felt, be conducive to his writing. In fact, many of the poems in *The LSD Leacock* (1966) and *Winter of the Luna*

Moth (1968) were inspired by his people-watching in Stanley Park. Since his initial move to Vancouver, Rosenblatt has lived either in Toronto (from 1968 to 1980) or in British Columbia. He now resides in Qualicum Beach, Vancouver Island, with his wife, Faye, and son, Eliot.

During the ten years following the initial Canada Council grant, Rosenblatt published six new books of poetry — *Bumblebee Dithy-ramb* (1972), *Blind Photographer* (1972), *Dream Craters* (1974), *Virgins and Vampires* (1975), *Loosely Tied Hands: An Experiment in Punk* (1978), and *The Sleeping Lady* (1979) — as well as the selected *Top Soil* (1976). This output is staggering, especially when one considers that, during the same period, he also began to take himself seriously as a visual artist. His drawings illustrate most of his own books, including a story for children (*Tommy Fry and the Ant Colony* [1979]), and his artwork has been collected in three separate publications: *Greenbaum* (1970), *Dr. Anaconda's Solar Fun Club* (1978), and *Drawings by Joe Rosenblatt* (1979). The first two of these collections are books unaccompanied by text. The third is a series of loose prints held together in a green leather folder tied with a ribbon. Many of the india-ink drawings of these collections are of interest because they offer a visual account of Rosenblatt's animal and insect world.

After moving to Vancouver Island in August of 1980, Rosenblatt continued to draw, but he increasingly turned back to writing, publishing *Brides of the Stream* (1983), *Escape from the Glue Factory: A Memoir of a Paranormal Toronto Childhood in the Late Forties* (1985), and *The Kissing Goldfish of Siam* (1989). Unlike his earlier works, these new books show Rosenblatt as gradually moving from predominantly free verse forms to narrative and prose poems. *Poetry Hotel: Selected Poems 1963–1985*, dedicated to Barry Callaghan and published in 1985, is largely a republishing of earlier material, but one that illustrates well the difference between the poetic experiments Rosenblatt explored during his years in Toronto and those he turned to once he took up residence in Qualicum Beach. *Poetry Hotel* begins with the free verse of "Top Soil" and ends with "Life Notes," a section which — in prose — explores Rosenblatt's approach to autobiographical writing.

Since a poet can rarely make his living exclusively from his writing, Rosenblatt took up the teaching of creative writing. He has taught this subject at Three Schools of Art in Toronto, at summer writers' workshops in Toronto and Collingwood, Ontario, and as writer-in-residence at the University of Western Ontario (1979–80), the University of Victoria (1980–81), and the Saskatoon public library (1984–85). He was the senior editor of *Jewish Dialog* from 1972 to 1983 and poetry editor for *The Malahat Review* from 1982 to 1983.

The work of Joe Rosenblatt has not gone unnoticed. He has been included in over fifteen anthologies and featured on several radio and television programs. He has twice been the recipient of Canada Council senior arts awards. More importantly, two of his books have achieved special recognition: *Winter of the Luna Moth* was nominated for the Governor General's Award, and *Top Soil* won that award in 1976. Finally, Rosenblatt's work has also gained recognition outside Canada. An Italian translation of a selected edition of Rosenblatt's prose and poetry is being prepared by Alfredo Rizzardi of the University of Bologna in Italy.

Tradition and Milieu

T.S. Eliot, who greatly influenced Rosenblatt's early career, once said: "It is part of the business of the critic to preserve tradition — where a good tradition exists."² Eliot could have added that, when a critic is tracing any tradition as it affects any individual poet, part of the business of the critic is to determine what the particular poet considers a tradition worth preserving. Rosenblatt, in this respect, finds himself at odds with the most immediate tradition — the contemporary writing of his own country. In 1978 he wrote that

> my poems are not in any shape or form that would be approved of by the mainstream of poets currently writing in this country. Clearly, for them, socioeconomic matters such as reform and Canadian nationalism (or Canadian Nationalism and Narcissism) are the most important subjects. Those kinds of things, however, don't even interest me. More elemental aspects of man are my concern and my personal, even "eccentric," poetic method is used to reveal them to the full. I do not wish merely to enhance the seeming social reality of our world, the social world that might be corrected by a law or two, or a new economic policy. No, I want to show the full force of *reality* and its inherent cannibalistic nature.³

The repudiation of the sociopolitical element of Canadian literature (the one he had initially embraced at the time of meeting Milton Acorn), and of the forms which approve or uphold it, is, in fact, partly a rhetorical overstatement allowable to any poet attempting to justify his ways. The need to repudiate, however, is clear, and the stance Rosenblatt takes explains his desire for a radically different set of poetics. To be true to his view of the world, Rosenblatt feels he

> must distort, twist, the mundane real to its essential *reality*, through craft and art, humour and fantasy, honesty and intensity. Merely describing man is not enough. The poet must expose this creature from his alligator shoes to the electric rose reflecting in his eye. In short, distortion is the essential process of my muse; without it, poetry is but simple photography.[4]

If Rosenblatt feels separated from the present mainstream of Canadian writing, it is because he finds the poetic methods of his contemporaries inadequate for the task of revealing the truth about humanity. Humour and fantasy, in particular, seem to be lacking in the contemporary repertoire of poetic skills. The early E.J. Pratt of "The Great Feud: A Dream of a Pleiocene Armageddon" or *The Witches' Brew*, in effect, represents a better guide for an understanding of Rosenblatt's conception of poetry than the work of any presently living writer.[5] Admittedly, Rosenblatt's animals, reptiles, and insects are not part of the heroic tradition, as Pratt's are, but the fundamentally amoral, cannibalistic nature of the creature-world links the writers. Moreover, the mixture of scientific jargon and poetic diction that characterizes both these authors' works reflects the similarity of their traditions.

To claim that Rosenblatt is indebted to Pratt's work would be unjustified, for the similarities of subject matter and diction connect them only loosely. Rosenblatt has made no conscious effort to model himself on Pratt. The question of tracing a tradition, in such an instance, indicates that the very pursuit of a relationship between one writer and another assumes a poet's commitment to a particular writer or movement. In this respect, Rosenblatt's work yields to no easy analysis. It has been pointed out that Rosenblatt felt dissatisfaction with formal education and training, and a conscious habit of searching for connections, influences, and models was never instilled in him. Rosenblatt's habits of mind as a poet are based on his wide, thorough, and sympathetic reading of writers he finds moving and inspiring. His poetic sight tends to be focused on the discovery of specific lines, rhythms, and isolated poems that he can use for his own purposes, a habit he seems to have acquired from Eliot's method in *The Waste Land*.[6]

Rosenblatt is not among the self-conscious poets who are interested in general and philosophical concepts of tradition and milieu. One must look elsewhere to attain a sense of his link with both the past and the present. In particular one should examine the individual poems that have inspired Rosenblatt, for in his mind the universal quality of a work transcends all loyalties to either an author's self-acknowledged concerns as a writer or an author's commitment to writing in a certain fashion or manner. For an understanding of the influence on Rosenblatt's writing, one should always stress the individual poem in isolation. Poems such as Archibald Lampman's "The Frogs" and "At the Long Sault: May 1660," Pratt's "The Prize Cat" and "The Shark," Milton Acorn's "The Natural History of Elephants," Earle Birney's "The Bear on the Delhi Road," and Irving Layton's "The Bull Calf" are guides to the traditions that influence his work.[7]

If such a hypothesis about Rosenblatt's admiration of individual poems is right, then it is no wonder that his poetry is packed with allusions and echoes to such poems as Blake's "The Tyger," Emily Dickinson's "A Narrow Fellow in the Grass," Ted Hughes's "Crow," and D.H. Lawrence's "Snake." In other words, the tradition of animal poems and fables, far more often than not, identifies the place of Rosenblatt's poetry. The ability to criticize society, behaviour, values, and attitudes has traditionally been made by adding human characteristics to the nonhuman creatures of the world, and Rosenblatt feels most comfortable in this line of writing. One could even go as far as summing up his poetic output as a modern bestiary, as Eli Mandel has.[8] Bestiaries allow for an imaginative integration of realism, fantasy, allegory, and symbolism; the expansiveness inherent in such writing strongly appeals to Rosenblatt's temper.

Such an explanation of Rosenblatt's preference for animal poems, however, does not account for the eccentricities of his poetic method. In Canadian literature, certainly, he has forerunners who offer him direction and guidance. Earle Birney, bill bissett, and bpNichol come immediately to mind. The experimental poems, particularly those of *Winter of the Luna Moth* and *Bumblebee Dithyramb*, strongly reflect the influence of these Canadian poets. Birney may have struck the profoundest chord in Rosenblatt; indeed, *Winter of the Luna Moth* is dedicated to him. When Rosenblatt experiments with alliteration, internal rhyme, and the sonnet form later in his career, in *Dream Craters* and *The Sleeping Lady* especially, he seems to have been powerfully influenced by Birney's effort to take experimentation beyond mere sound and concrete poetry. Rosenblatt has repeatedly stressed the need for rhythm and sonority in poetry, and both the sound poem and the concrete poem have limitations. Since Rosenblatt favours metaphors and similes, in fact delights in expanding them, it is not surprising that he finds the direction of Birney's work in harmony with his own purpose.

Such an outline of Rosenblatt's adherence to the Canadian tradition of the animal poem and to the far-ranging experiments of Birney should not be taken as a circumscription of the poet's range. Rather, Rosenblatt should be viewed as the unmitigated eclectic who is absorbed by his own vision, his own cosmos of personified creatures. Furthermore, his perception of this inner imaginative world seems so inevitably rooted in wit, extravagance, and hyperbole that he is best perceived as a contemporary metaphysical poet reminiscent of the tradition most commonly associated with John Donne.[9]

Critical Overview and Context

The history of criticism dealing with Rosenblatt's poetry is short. With the exception of Frank Davey's two-page overview of the poet's early work in *From There to Here: A Guide to English-Canadian Literature since 1960*, no extended analytic studies exist. Discussion of Rosenblatt's poetry is confined to the review, a form of literary assessment that cannot allow for expansive treatment of a topic. Yet, a consideration of the reviews of Rosenblatt's writing indicates that the central characteristics, tendencies, and qualities of the poet's achievement have been traced, if not delineated. In fact, once the reviews are carefully categorized, the central issues become self-evident. Rosenblatt has found admirers and detractors in relation to five central topics: his imaginative world, his diction, his syntax, his forms, and, finally, his poetic voice.

On the whole, both late and early readers of Rosenblatt's poetry and prose have, at best, mixed emotions. The poet's energetic and novel cosmos, wherein everything is personified, intrigues them, but Rosenblatt's ornate baroque diction and imagery seem, at times, strained or forced. Rosenblatt's most characteristic feature, however, is this preference for odd and striking combinations of the human and the animal: a fruit bat is described as a "municipal bird with varicose veins," and a bee is characterized as a creature with "gland trouble." No matter how critical reviewers may be, Rosenblatt has not altered or tamed his imagery and diction. In *The Kissing Goldfish of Siam* (1989), for example, he describes frogs as "bacchanalian pond humpers," and a trout in *Brides of the Stream* (1983) is a "spoiled dapple bourgeois."

All those who comment on Rosenblatt's poetry have remarked on the quality of his diction and imagery, and their hesitations often lead them to question the poet's unity of design. Victor Coleman, for example, reviewing *Voyage of the Mood* (1963), divides the poems into "social protest" poems and poems that "deal with, somewhat, universal topics."[10] Yet the two categories, though valid, need not be indicative of a lack of focus. Peter Stevens, reviewing Rosenblatt's second collection, *The LSD Leacock* (1966), points out that the two classifications are really united. His commentary is worth citing, for later reviewers only add to his perceptive assessment: "Joe Rosenblatt has been referred to as a proletarian poet and thus one would think he would be resolutely factual, yet he makes a mythically autonomous world of his own, firmly rooted in our consumer society — images of preying and devouring recur. . . ."[11] Eli Mandel later contributes his view that Rosenblatt's peculiarly human chaos of creatures is best seen in the tradition of "medieval writers of the bestiaries, [wherein the poet] seeks in the creatures of the earth not only an image of man but the mystery of creation."[12] Fred Cogswell notes that Rosenblatt's bestiary allows for a vision that reinforces "the one-ness of all life, however ugly or beautiful."[13] Moreover, as Cogswell stresses, the striking and forceful quality of Rosenblatt's work resides in the very conjunction of the human and elemental world, for the transfer of "human values and attributes" to the animal kingdom "provides him with a fresh vocabulary and an original set of images."[14] Later reviewers echo, in a variety of ways, these very comments, and not until 1975 is a new sense of the importance of Rosenblatt's method suggested. F.W. Watt recognizes that the mixture is more than ingenious or refreshing: "Rosenblatt makes us feel what it's like to stand where we really are, semiconscious, in the turgid, murky centre of history, a unique mixture of animal, vegetable and spiritual, living on the mysterious earth which is itself 'a space animal / munching on life.' "¹⁵ In Rosenblatt's imaginative world, as Marya Fiamengo summarizes it, "life emerges as a kaleidoscopic vision of joy and suffering."¹⁶

Where the imaginative world of Rosenblatt's poetry unites the critical responses, the language the poet uses sharply divides them. Most bluntly put, readers either accuse Rosenblatt of being insensitive to language or praise him for taking risks which, while they often fail, also sometimes succeed in attaining new effects. The early reviewers, such as Coleman, Stevens, and Mandel, notice the infelicities of wording; the later reviewers, particularly those dealing with *The Sleeping Lady* (1979), dwell upon the complexity of the diction. David MacFarlane is the most direct about the difficulty: for him, Rosenblatt has a "penchant for seemingly intentional obscurity."¹⁷

The matter of syntax, the next issue of debate in Rosenblatt criticism, is equally divisive. Choosing the right word and putting it in the right place interrelate, and the reviews point out that Rosenblatt's syntax has increasingly shifted towards the wrenched sentence. Early reviewers such as Stevens remark upon the occasional poem which seems unclear because of the poet's word order,¹⁸ and later critics underscore the effusion of awkward lines and stanzas that seem to overwhelm the more recent books. Since metaphors and similes, two of Rosenblatt's favoured devices, must be developed in a linear fashion, the abnormal syntax has divided critical evaluation. Douglas Barbour, in a review of *Dream Craters*, asserts that Rosenblatt's violence to normal word order is a positive feature: Rosenblatt "has discovered an exhilarating and personal syntax."¹⁹ Yet Len Gasparini is exasperated by the habit, charging that Rosenblatt's writing in *Virgins and Vampires* is drenched with "mixed metaphors, and inverted logic."²⁰ Whether early or late assessments are considered, response is certainly mixed on the issues of both diction and syntax.

Rosenblatt's use of form has created equal difficulties. In the early books, short lyrics usually caught the reader's eye. Then, it was the experimental poems that seized the attention, and they have continued to do so. To skim Rosenblatt's poetry, particularly in *Top Soil* (which is really a collection of most of the poems in the first four books), is to skim "practically every kind of 'poetry' going,"²¹ as Barbour puts it. More importantly, Barbour adds, almost every poem fits into the category of "border-blur,"[22] for lyricism and surrealism are almost always intertwined in Rosenblatt's work. Such a mélange has led reviewers to question the success of these mixed and often undefinable forms. Three stances have been taken by the reviewers: one group considers the poems generally flat, dull, and uninspiring; the second group perceives them as interesting, but puzzling; the third finds them exhilarating.[23] There is no doubt that all the readers recognize the validity of the experiments, but there is also no doubt that they are mystified about the direction and purpose of the mixed forms.[24]

Rosenblatt's need to experiment with form leads to the last and central issue of critical debate: his poetic voice. In the earliest reviews, it is considered unique, but later it is called repetitious, monotonous, unexciting. While Rosenblatt seems to be playing a musical instrument with a single string when it comes to imaginative vision, he plays an innumerable series of instruments when it comes to form. Nearly all the reviewers grant Mandel's point that Rosenblatt creates a "bestiary," and they might even concur with Fiamengo in calling him the "Aesop of Canada,"[25] yet many would hesitate to assert that the multiplicity of forms, languages, and modes allows for such a convenient labelling. As Jamie Hamilton voices the concern, after discussing the extreme variety in Rosenblatt's published works, ". . . the variety is two-faced; at times the collection [*Top Soil*] leaves a reader wondering where the man is most at home."[26]

Davey agrees that the problem of voice is the central issue. He grants Rosenblatt the vitality of vision and he finds the use of diction and awkward syntax wholly compatible with that vision, but he considers the poet's unceasing shift from form to form a weakness. To Davey, it indicates an inability on Rosenblatt's part to find a true voice.[27] It is this issue which will receive attention in the discussion to follow, for Rosenblatt does have a true voice, one which becomes clearly identifiable only when the interrelationship of diction, syntax, imagery, and form is assessed.

Rosenblatt's Works

In spite of Rosenblatt's continued and, at times, seemingly oppressive focus upon the minutiae of insects, atoms, reptiles, and animals, in book after book the poet demonstrates an astonishing willingness and ability to change, alter, and transform his writing. The continual metamorphosis of his style and form, in particular, suggests that, for him, no style or form is necessarily or inherently better than another. Yet, despite these variations, his oeuvre is unified, and each book embodies the struggle to convey a central theme: people must shed the ego bound in flesh and take on the cosmos as the outermost skin. To break us of the habit of conceiving of ourselves as an "I" distinct from the world, Rosenblatt creates an elaborate metaphysical swamp opera of human as toad, human as snake, human as butterfly, human as cosmic egg. To compile a list of the variations that Rosenblatt imagines would be a pointless venture; a reader simply needs to recognize that Rosenblatt's bestiary is an effort to explode the comforting, self-pleasing images that limit our self-understanding.

In chronicling the variations of self, the critical scrutiny of language and form plays a central role in Rosenblatt's poetry. The language of the sciences — especially anthropology, biology, physics, and psychology — has, whether we realize it or not, radically altered the self-conceptions available to us. Nevertheless, as the poet knows all too well, society continues to talk about itself and human experience in glib, deceitful, and vapid terms which ignore, or at best overlook, the very implications of the terminology created to accommodate the new views of world and of humanity. Rosenblatt's poetic achievement is to make readers aware of their tendency to use language habitually and mechanically, articulating our understanding *of* ourselves *to* ourselves without thinking carefully or consistently. At times, Rosenblatt will draw on the vocabulary of evolution to point out that if we really *mean* what we say — that we are descended from apes, for example — then we, in part, are apes still. Through the habit of distancing ourselves from evolution through language, we rationalize, disguise, and hide our kinship with the apes by assuming that the ability to verbalize about evolution implies freedom from evolution. However, as the poet declares in the early "Jealousy," "There is an orangutan inside of me,"[28] and no amount of shaving, nor any method of explaining primitive emotions, can make our incomprehensible animal nature disappear. The task is to accommodate, not to reject or ignore, our link with the animal world when attempting to attain self-understanding. To assert that we are part of an evolutionary line, and then to assume that we are somehow improved, enlightened, or advanced because of that evolutionary line, that we are somehow liberated from the natural and untameable forces of nature which form us, is a line of thought that haunts Rosenblatt. If we are part of the cosmic evolutionary force, we can but see ourselves as the most complex animal of all and, therefore, potentially as primitive, inconsistent, and inexplicably motivated as only the "supreme" creature of an evolutionary process could be.

By superimposing one kind of language upon another, or, at other times, by juxtaposing one form of language with another, Rosenblatt is able to demonstrate that our view of ourselves must change if the new ways we have found to explain our world are to have any significance. What some perceive in both the poet's early and late work as patternless language games, mixed metaphors, jumbled diction, and gratuitous surrealistic effects are, rather, an integral part of this poet's serious attack on language to challenge basic assumptions, concepts, and modes of thought in contemporary society. For Rosenblatt, any permanence in language predetermines a permanence in viewing the world; therefore, he continually explores new languages and forms of articulating his vision to avoid stasis, uniformity, and paralysis. The cosmos is dynamic, and the poet, to expand upon the possibilities of allowing us to see ourselves as a part of that dynamic world, must continually reform his own modes of poetry. It is this need, even compelling urge, to modify, alter, and transform language — particularly the traditional language of poetry — which will be analysed in this section.

The immediate surface of Rosenblatt's poetry is often one of wit, contrivance, and distortion (Davey, p. 240). More importantly, his bizarre and disconcerting effects are generated through startling, on occasion seemingly eccentric, uses of diction, image, line, rhythm, syntax, and poetic form. Frank Davey, who in 1974 acknowledged Rosenblatt as one of the few successful experimentalists to have emerged during the 1960s, noted Rosenblatt's delight "in outrageous effects — in the juxtaposition of the sublime and the frivolous, the sacred and the obscene, sophisticated surrealism and the blatancies of pure sound" (Davey, p. 240). Yet, Rosenblatt's strikingly individualistic method of distorting the familiar — his particular method of *ostranenie* (defamiliarization)[29] — should not be viewed as resulting merely from a delight in language play. The experimental poet is often the poet who, consciously or unconsciously, recognizes the danger of a culture yielding to the power of poetry to affect the reader without comprehending its particular effect at any specific moment. The poet's rebellion through experimentation must be seen as an effort to retain poetry's power to make a culture recognize the effects of language. The experimentalist fails to grant the "givens" of the way that a society would like to view itself and deliberately changes the norms of form, rhythm, diction, and poetic structure, so that society will be shocked into reexamining the force of language (and its effect upon understanding) with new objectivity.[30]

In the earliest published poetry, Rosenblatt prefers short, controlled lyrics wherein he can create new self-perceptions through explorations of metaphor and simile. This aspect of his writing becomes increasingly important in the later work, and one might even characterize Rosenblatt as a maker of metaphors. In the early poems, however, Rosenblatt contents himself with implied metaphors and abrupt, surprising similes. People are sensualists who rely strongly on their sense of touch, and in the poem "Love," touch is a Koala bear:

A wee Koala bear
climbs soft branches
of your fingers,
rubs his worldly nose
into the palm's eucalyptus.
Like a wild wallaby,
a loose-skinned tangerine,
the heart leaps out.[31]

Rosenblatt reminds us that every moment of touch is an encounter with a living thing; it is only a matter of reseeing the vitality of our ability to touch and, therefore, feel (in both senses of the word). The title, a single abstract word, forces the reader to actively complete the metaphor: love is a Koala bear; love is touch and feeling; love is the sensual hand's delight in a tangerine. One might even press further here, questioning the extent and range of the metaphors and similes: is a person a Koala bear, or only like one? In the later poetry, the suggestion of links between humans and creatures will become a common characteristic.

The short lyric imposes limitations, however, and in his second book, *The LSD Leacock* (1966), Rosenblatt begins to experiment with other forms. The book attacks our overreliance on abstractions and concepts to order our world into neat, comprehensible categories. To explode our belief in reason, technology, and social order

— the apparently inevitable extensions of our effort to control the world with "ideas" — the poet turns to "automatic writing," attempting to break past or through the need to order experience logically and coherently. In "The World Egg," one in a series of poems dealing with eggs, Rosenblatt creates a stream-of-consciousness prose-poem whose ideas and images are linked by random association.[32] The poet contemplates a particular object and, by allowing himself free rein of thought and feeling, is able to explore the full range of implication suggested by the object. The extended reverie, or meditation, allows the poet to riddle our self-definition as an "I" observer who exists independently of the objects around us. Hyperbole, exaggeration, is the central poetic device of the poem; the common egg of the kitchen table is the object examined:

This egg is supreme
this egg is the invention . . .
the stuff of mental science;
this egg is real
this egg is ahead of Soviet science & U.S. agronomy
& science fiction;
this egg is the link in the space age & market research
&. laughing gas
this egg will take a jet 10 years
to cross its dome perimeter.

(p. 16)

The egg is an egg, but it is also the world, the universe, and the cosmos. Initially, then, the seemingly wild hyperbole shows the simple white egg as "supreme"; yet as the poem continues, the implications of the term "supreme" are traced in detail so that the seeming exaggeration is actually acceptable, if not tame. This technique is often used by Rosenblatt: a poem begins with an overstatement which, by the end of the poem, seems to be transformed into an understatement. Once the reader accepts the interplay of association, once the reader participates in the interlocking of macrocosm and microcosm, the egg becomes the cosmic egg, and our thought is, thereby, liberated from a single view of the single thing: the boundaries of perceiver and perceived have collapsed; we are always both inside and outside the egg.

The dislocation of normal ways of seeing in the egg poems functions to heighten the social criticism. On the one hand, we perceive ourselves as creatures of faith and belief, and in "The Easter Egg I Got for Passover" (p. 19), Rosenblatt teases us into examining our complacency in matters of faith. On the other hand, since we also perceive ourselves as creatures of the material world, the poet, in a poem such as "Egg Sonata" (pp. 22–24), can ridicule our penchant for reducing the cosmic egg to a mere object of trade and commerce. By placing various views of the egg in adjacent poems, Rosenblatt explores the various associations attached to the egg (the cosmos).

Outrageous distortion, in particular, is used in these poems. "The Easter Egg I Got for Passover," to illustrate the point, depicts Christ in appropriately anachronistic terms. The Son of God is described as a "haggard" hippy, who resembles "some of those characters I've seen around the Village, walking the espresso mile" (p. 19). The ascent of Christ is visualized as a climb up a variant of Jacob's ladder to enter the sky-egg from which the ladder descends. The pain and agony of the suffering which the incident suggests, presumably the traditional agony of Christ, is partially cured by two angels "who act as his bufferin" as they assist Him up the ladder (p. 19). The spiritual pain, reduced to a physical headache cured by Bufferin, shocks the reader into reconsidering issues of faith and agony. Materialists, however, receive equal treatment in "Egg Sonata." Once again, the egg is shown as a source of pain, but now the egg is a "sphere of melancholia" because the Canadian egg market has collapsed. Eggs are "pimped away on the market / for practically nothing . . . / soon the eggs will roll out of gum machines" (p. 24).

Our spiritual and material selves are ridiculed as the poet draws on words and images in our everyday world and indiscriminately applies them to issues that "should" be discussed in other terms. The point is that we have developed languages (jargons) that neatly separate issue from issue, idea from idea. The process of categorizing in language, however, indicates how we, at the same time, are fragmenting and compartmentalizing our experience, forgetting again that at all times we are, despite ourselves, both inside and outside the egg.

Rosenblatt, particularly in his early work, often seems an optimistic anarchist who delights in mocking our desire to order our world. For him, the cycles of nature and the actions of animals and insects reveal the true, free, uninhibited, amoral world in which we participate. His writing, therefore, is often marked with unbounded enthusiasm and delight over the unapologetic life-forces which transcend, even defy, our moral and self-conscious order. The method of free association in the egg poems, and their apparent lack of order and form, allow the poet to create a hypnotic effect that captivates the reader and draws him or her into a mood of celebration:

> To an ounce and a half of energy strutting around in the palm of
> my hand
> I say: congratulations . . . , you've made it;
> don't blame you for being mad at me,
> digging your beak into my finger,
> don't blame you for looking up at me with defiance
> like I was responsible for you being in the egg in the first place;
> congratulations! you've made it . . . .
> ("Egg Sonata," p. 22)

The poem sweeps on in its celebration of the defiant energy that bursts from the egg. The repetition of key phrases functions, in part, to create the mesmerizing effect of the poem. Yet, the device has a more serious purpose. The repetition reinforces the speaker's enthusiasm by suggesting an uncontrolled, spontaneous response to life, a response which, because of technique, seems a convincing demonstration of thought that has broken through or past logic, order, and abstraction, without yielding either coherence or comprehensibility. As a result, we can feel unified with the life-force:

> O birdie! congratulations, a thousand times congratulations,
> congratulations! congratulations! congratulations!

> Yes! every morning at breakfast I get kind of religious

> > how fortunate I am
> > breaking the egg
> > from the outside
> > instead
> > of inside
> > > out.
> > > ("Egg Sonata," p. 22)

The sprawling, seemingly uncontrolled repetition of "congratulations," in conjunction with the excessive use of exclamations, suggests that identification is complete and unqualified. The appropriateness of the language is underscored in the use of the periphrasis, the roundabout way of naming the experience: it is "kind of religious." To use the proper word here, to be outright and direct, would be a violation of the very effort to reproduce in poetry an incident where feeling comes first, and the right word, later. For, as the irony of the poem's line reinforces, we are like the chick, although we must break *into* the egg rather than out of it.

In another poem from the same volume, Rosenblatt attempts to shatter the illusion of the ego by identifying wholly with the varieties of butterflies he knows, listing the names as if the words, in themselves, were magical and holy:

> I get high on butterflies;
> their very names:
> > Tiger swallow tail
> > Zebra
> > Pygmy blue
> > Arctic skipper
> > Spring azure
> > Common wood nymph.
> > > ("I Get High on Butterflies," p. 25)

All sense of ego, of "I" as observer, is transcended here as the identity of the speaker merges with the names. The self, or what remains of it, is capable only of listing the things upon which it gets its high. The process of conscious self-evaluation is abandoned as the mind feels lighter, freer, or, as the slang meaning of the word implies, as the mind feels almost drugged by proper nouns, by names. The drug-induced state allows the ego to merge with its world, abandoning all desire for separation between object and viewer.

The ridiculing of the ego, in fact, is often a concern of Rosenblatt's, and his way of attacking the ego is through the use of fantasy, illusion, vision, and humour. In "Waiter! . . . There's an Alligator in My Coffee" (pp. 6–7), the poet captures the heart of the popular jokes about flies in soup or coffee. The implication of the jokes is that creatures — be they insects or alligators — do not belong in our neat, orderly world. Somehow, the products of a capitalistic, materialistic society should be pure, sound, and approved by quality control. Creatures doing backstrokes or swan dives into a cup of coffee point out the discrepancy between unasserted assumptions and reality. In this poem, the poet transforms the familiar fly in the soup into an alligator in the coffee to emphasize our fear of the insect or reptile worlds. The poem moves quickly past the level of allusion. The speaker complains about the alligator, and the waiter is allowed the witty reply: "what do you want for a dime . . . ? / . . . a circus?" (p. 6).

At this point, the joke develops into a poem. The waiter suggests sugar to drown the intruder, but the alligator surfaces to swallow it. The word "circus," initially only the waiter's witticism, now takes on a literal meaning as the poem itself becomes a circus, disordered and chaotic. Simultaneously, the waiter, not the reptile, takes on brutal and frightening characteristics: "Kill him! Kill him! / he said: / BASH HIS BRAINS OUT / WITH YOUR SPOON . . . !" (p. 6). The scene culminates with the entry of the restaurant owner, acting as the *deus ex machina*. Disturbed by the disruption of normal routine, he lifts the coffee and inspects it. Warned that he might lose his nose, he mutters "How absurd" and swallows the "profit motive" to restore order (p. 7).[33] The harsh, realistic term in such a fanciful poem completes the inversion of expectations upon which the poem rests: the everyday world seems more unreal than the most extravagant parody of human behaviour can suggest.

Through wit, conceit, fantasy   in effect by blurring the distinc tion between joke and poem — Rosenblatt achieves in verse what Kafka and Borges achieve in prose: an absurd vision of the world, a vision that measures the seemingly ordinary with distortion, a vision that refracts the norms of human behaviour just forcefully enough to make the reader question human nature and the permanence of our sense of the real. Each figure in the poem has his own motive; the normal situation of a coffee break becomes suspect.

The exploration of joke as poetic form is only one direction in Rosenblatt's effort to find new patterns for poetry. In a totally opposite direction, one which often runs parallel with the experiments in form, is Rosenblatt's determination to break with traditionally accepted poetic diction. Often he will mix words which, ordinarily, apply either to the human world or to the insect world, thereby describing the intersection of human and creaturelike behaviour. A short poem entitled "The Delicatessen" illustrates the point:

355

Beneath the skull cap of the sun
reclines the greatest gastronomer,
the sphinx of death, the hunting wasp
sunning her backside against the system.
With sword extending from her belly
she's the truest gladiator, and a surgeon
and mortician, working through the ganglion
till green Pegasus falls like Morpheus,
a dreamer on a dream estate
and the huntress drags the hopper
to a horse necropolis
which is a catacomb and delicatessen.

(p. 11)

The mixture of images and words, from Jewish skull caps to Roman gladiators to modern surgeons to Greek mythology, suggests a hybrid of allusions. Yet, the mélange forcefully describes the action of a hunting wasp slaying a grasshopper. The devouring of one insect by another in the cosmic delicatessen needs no explanation. Humans recoil instinctively when their own refined form of carnivorousness is pointed out. A word like "surgeon," however, makes the comparison even more unpalatable. Rosenblatt has an eye for minutiae, and his vision has been transformed into word: the insect has a precision and knowledge about anatomy; it pierces the grasshopper with the seeming intelligence of a human and the consummate skill of an expert. Here the exactness of the wording — wording which may initially seem inept — shocks the reader into recognition and reluctant acceptance.

Throughout *The LSD Leacock*, the ingenious verbal humour achieves a complex emotional response. In Rosenblatt's next book, *Winter of the Luna Moth* (1968), the verbal play is often less sophisticated. The words are reduced rather than enhanced by juxtaposition. Rosenblatt cannot seem to resist crude puns, and the depiction of the human world through the animal world becomes uncontrolled didacticism which reads like a parody of the poet's best work. The short poems, in particular, are unsuccessful for this reason.

In one section, for example, the speculations on why "every cat wants to lay a pious pussy"[34] are crude. The puns on cat and pussy are too easy; the implications about humanity too pat and moralistic.

One grants that humans are quite capable of hypocrisy, deceit, and lust; the moral insistence in poems that read like bad allegory neither convinces nor moves the reader.

Rosenblatt seems too outraged to write more than thinly disguised morality tales that attack the shallow, insignificant, misguided follies of humankind. In a short book entitled *Blind Photographer* (1972), Rosenblatt turns to irony in short sparse lines, almost as if he were trying to cure himself of the habit of didacticism; his experiment in this direction, however, was short-lived.[35] He soon returned to forms explored, but not developed, in *Winter of the Luna Moth*.

The importance of *Winter of the Luna Moth* cannot be underestimated, for in it Rosenblatt experiments with other styles of writing. He begins to concentrate on sound and concrete poetry, which leads logically to his next book, *Bumblebee Dithyramb*; and in a series called "The Uncle Nathan Poems," he expands his efforts with surrealism, a style which becomes increasingly important later in his career.

In *Winter of the Luna Moth*, Rosenblatt makes radical innovations in poetic diction, and in the Uncle Nathan series especially he exceeds all his earlier efforts. The poems deal with religious issues, and the "Sabbatical crazed" Uncle Nathan ("Ichthycide," p. 4) abandons his religious uprightness the moment he reveals hedonism in carving and preparing fish. The quarrel with God, the central issue of the series, is not always clear, in part because the radical choice of language tends to disconcert the reader:

> Earth! Earth! is the bitch still green
> liced with people and Aardvark powers?
> And my shop on Baldwin Street
> does she stand? . . . damp and sacred as the Wailing Wall
> under the caterpillar'd canopy of God;
> or has my pterodactyl neighbour
> mogulled up my carp shrined Enterprise
> wherein I cradled images from Lake Genneserat
> to fish fertiled ladies with halvah tongues
> who shred my serpents into shrimp bread,
> for fish food oscillates an old maid's chromosomes!
> Carp, pickerel, transmogrified,
> such is the incantation of Gefilte Fish,

where swimmers have been tranquillized
stomach's the body's palpitating madrigal.
("Uncle Nathan, Blessed Be His Memory,
Speaketh from Landlocked Green," p. 7)

Initially, the allusions to Eliot's *The Waste Land* are recognizable,
but it is difficult to determine whether the deliberate echoes and the
stylized parallels of Eliot's lines in this rewritten form are parodies or
serious reassertions of our mental and spiritual poverty. For example,
Rosenblatt echoes Eliot's question of whether the "dog" has dug up
the corpse again, but the dog has absurdly become a "pterodactyl
neighbour." Furthermore, such phrasing as "the incantation of
Gefilte Fish" seems to break the thread of discernible meaning — the
necessary thread every reader requires to judge the function, significance, and efficacy of language and nuance. Throughout the series,
the juxtaposition of incompatible words creates contrasts like "gill's
epistle" ("The Itch," p. 12), "Lent's locust," and "Kaddish for
aborted caviar" ("Uncle Nathan, Blessed Be His Memory, Speaketh
from Landlocked Green," pp. 7, 6) which, although striking, tend to
obscure rather than clarify the meaning of the poem.

During this period in his writing, Rosenblatt was also attracted to
the possibilities of sound and concrete poetry. North American
writers were experimenting with a variety of forms, ranging from
pictures of alphabet letters, to visual arrangements of lines, to chants
repeated stanza after stanza, to projective verse. Occasionally, the
forms were combined, almost as if the techniques of Hugo Ball, Ian
Hamilton Finlay, and Charles Olson were strung haphazardly
together in a single volume or a single poem.[36] In *Winter of the Luna
Moth*, Rosenblatt's early experiments seem clumsy and artificial. In
"The Butterfly Bat," for example, the spacing of the lines adds little
to the wording of the poem. If the rules of projective verse are being
followed, the breaths are somehow inadequately captured.[37] Moreover, halfway through the poem, the projective style is abandoned
for a combination of sound poetry moving to the concrete:

BUTTER butter BUTT but er FLY

BUTTERFLY Butter fluttering fluttering flittering flittering flit

flit flit flit flit flit flit flit flit flit flit flit flit FLIT

(p. 25)

This portion of the poem seems mechanical and stilted. The picture is neat, tidy, symmetrical, but hardly moving. It does not shock or soothe the imagination. At best, one can recognize the poet's desire to explore the new languages of visual constructions upon the page. The effort to reproduce the butterfly bat on paper, furthermore, has no seeming connection to the Christ image developed earlier in the poem, and the poet's delight in toying with design has apparently carried him away from his opening image. Admittedly, the very experiments that Rosenblatt attempts are, at least in part, a revolt against the poetry so admired by proponents of the New Criticism: the orderly, the cerebral, the deliberately crafted, the subtly ambiguous. Yet, though the revolt is legitimate, a reader can claim that Rosenblatt's obvious enthusiasm has made him overlook the tradition of accomplished visual poetry, poetry wherein sense and image combine, as in George Herbert's "The Altar" or "Easter Wings."

Although Rosenblatt occasionally fails in his experiments, one cannot deny the vigour of his writing, the product of an unqualified enthusiasm and daring. That Rosenblatt entered the poetic world of a tradition to which he could initially not add anything "new" may seem at first glance both foolish and foolhardy, especially since Canada already boasts such accomplished innovators as bill bissett, bpNichol, and Earle Birney; yet, as Eliot warned, in "a time like ours, . . . we are inclined . . . to exaggerate the importance of the innovators at the expense of the reputation of the developers."[38] When Rosenblatt comes to terms with the combination of projective verse, concrete poetry, and sound poetry in his *Bumblebee Dithyramb*, he must be granted the status of a mature developer who, once again, modifies his language and poetic form. In this work he uses one of his strongest features as a poet: the ability to coin striking images for moving effects. His ability to unify our world and the natural world with memorable metaphor works to his advantage: bees are pilots in "football jersies,"[39] "truck drivers of the sky" ("Mother Nature's Proletarians," p. 50), and "ANIMALS / with helicopter / powers"

("Mother Nature's Helpers," p. 34). The deliberate choice of abandoning closed form, the controlled order with which most readers
feel comfortable, supports the effort to show the bee as a creature
beyond law and order:

they weave in & out of morning glories

　　pause in
　　　　neutral gear —
　　　　meditate
　　　　&
　　　　break into
　　　　a kitchen
　　　　without a
　　　　　　　search warrant.
　　　　　　　　　("Mother Nature's Helpers," p. 34)

The implications of Rosenblatt's meditation upon the bee are much
more significant and far-reaching than seems immediately obvious.
One aspect of the combination of concrete and sound poetry here is
Rosenblatt's challenge to his readers to reexamine the language used
to describe reality itself. Neat, ordered, linear patterns predicate an
ideology.[40] To articulate the world in ordered terms is to assert that
reality can be, possibly must be, tamed or controlled. The outrage
readers often feel when looking at strange patterns, such as the one
presented below, is that such stuff is not poetry:

BUZZZZZZZZZ
BUZZZZZZZZ
BUZZZZZZZ
BUZZZZZZ
BUZZZZZ
BUZZZZ
BUZZZ
BUZZ
BUZ
Zz

　　　　　("Bees Are Flies with Gland Trouble," p. 27)

Imposing a pattern on sound such as "BUZZZZZZ" catches the reader off guard, for the device of onomatopoeia seems to be propelled beyond the limits of traditional poetry. One must eventually concede that children or madmen may suddenly raise their arms, claim to be bees, and buzz around a room, driving everyone to distraction. Just as suddenly may a poet seize his typewriter and tap out BUZZZZZZZZZ. The distinction between the madman and the poet is that the latter is deliberately subverting the implied contract between poet and reader, the invisible contract of decorum in form and language. Yet it is the destruction of easy expectation which is central to the poetic method here, for it is Rosenblatt's intention to catch the reader's eye. The forms may be temporary and imperfect, following neither classical nor modern, nor possibly even determinable, rules, but these poems act as they should: they transform the metaphor of a bee entering without a search warrant into an emotional reality. Neither the world nor the language used to explain it can be contained: the world refuses to abide by unspoken contracts between itself and cultured, dignified civilization. The phobia many feel for bees, particularly indoors, has been made real in a poem.

Once the reader gets over the shock, he or she may explore with the poet the chaos of reality in the very language the writer uses to investigate that reality. The word itself may be viewed as a "thing." The word "bee," for example, is itself an object made up of the letters "e-b-e." When the letters are arranged as "b-e-e," readers immediately think of the little black and yellow producer of honey. When arranged properly, words can act like windows; we tend to see what is "behind" them. In this sense, words seem to be "invisible" or "transparent," for readers forget that the image of the insect is, in part, possible in a poem only because of the word "bee."

Whenever a poet, however, rearranges the order of the letters that form a word, the poet can reverse the process of making language almost "invisible." As soon as the poet writes "winwod," the reader is stymied. What does "winwod" mean? It is not in the dictionary! What is a reader to think when no immediate image comes to mind? Now the word is made "visible" — only the odd arrangement of letters strikes the reader's eye, and no exact object or notion or feeling (except possibly confusion) strikes the reader.

With Rosenblatt, the awkward arrangement of letters reminds readers to consider what letters and words can do to the imagination. "Winwod" (a simple inversion of two letters in "window") illustrates how all words on a page are part of the sensory world of experience. We can "see" with words (that is, read the word "bee" and imagine the insect), or we can see the words themselves (that is, recognize that b-e-e represents a particular combination of letters that makes us "see" a certain thing a certain way). The particular way our language makes us think is Rosenblatt's central concern when he points out that "BEES, ARE" ("Bees Are Flies with Gland Trouble," p. 26).

Bumblebee Dithyramb, therefore, uses both poetry and collage [41] in an effort to transcend conventional order and meaning by integrating, rather than just seeing, the world that humans share with creatures, insects, atoms, and letters. Typography is often broken to make bees part of the meaning, yet, paradoxically, devoid of meaning. The bee of words breaks into fragments, into letters, into syllables, into visual movements on the page, just as the bee may, in reality, be only a sound heard or a dot whizzing by. The function of the letters themselves, then, is to reenact the visible and audible elements of the bee. In the process, passion and celebration are substituted for the language effect. In the end, both the bee and the language are brought back to the reader as *things* in the world:

    BEES DO, GYMN,astics
    BEES DO, GYMN,astics
    BEES DO, GYMN,astics
    BEES DO, GYMN,astics
    BEES DO, GYMN,astics
    BEES DO, DO,DO,DO

                              ("Animal Rhythm," p. 24)

Using upper and lowercase letters emphasizes that both language and bees change, move, shift, do gymnastics. The comma, impertinently placed to interrupt verb and object, reinforces how action and thing are united through predication. By interrupting the normal grammatical pattern, Rosenblatt reminds the reader of the mental process that is normally accomplished unconsciously or habitually, but which *must be done* if the reader is to make words "invisible." By the end of the poem, readers sense that the "meaning" of an experience is reduced or simplified whenever traditionally "correct" grammar, punctuation, and typography are applied. A line like "Bees do gymnastics" fails to emphasize how language itself does

"GYMN, astics" in the reader's mind. Straightforward typography would allow the reader to forget that the words on the page are at work; the emphasized typography, however, draws attention to itself. Now the reader cannot simply respond in an intellectual, abstract, and objective manner. Through "visibly" altering "correct" typography, the poet disrupts the normal conventions of reading. The importance of a line of poetry is not simply what it says, but literally how it says it: with letters, with spacing, with punctuation, with typography. In other words, conventional typography makes us respond to our world in a conventional manner. To disrupt that simplified view of reality, Rosenblatt continually resorts to methods of disturbing a reader's view of how language should express either sorrow or joy. For example, two lines of repeated *v*'s in the middle of "Animal Rhythm" reinforce the "unreadable" yet continuous and uninterrupted outbreak of breath, of life, of élan. The collapse of the word into typography suggests the liquefaction of all reality: everything merges, blends, yields, changes. In the end, the reader of these poems is absorbed into the lawless world of bees, becoming part of the cosmos rather than a consciousness observing objectively. Once Rosenblatt has drawn the reader in, he uses more familiar language to describe the bees and their lawless, immoral riot:

^I love to watch them violate the flowers

("Mother Nature's Helpers," p. 34)

Bumblebee Dithyramb, then, contains Rosenblatt's efforts to break language into sounds and letters. The book is his attempt to make letters liquefy, to flow from clarity to obscurity, from representative picture to patternless design — underscoring the active human imagination which, in effect, imposes order and meaning onto a world that shifts and alters.

Experiments with visual designs are only one aspect of Rosenblatt's poetry. The experiments with diction that he began in *Winter of the Luna Moth* continue in his next book, *Dream Craters* (1974). Where the Uncle Nathan poems may represent an excessive attempt to push language to its limits, the poems of *Dream Craters* are often quite successful. The Uncle Nathan poems compel the reader to pursue a linear reading that is constantly denied; the poems in *Dream Craters* work because they eliminate possible linear readings from the outset. Most of the poems are meditations upon a single creature and its relationship to humankind, and the poems read like attempts to unclot the preposterous interrelationship offered, thereby committing the reader to a sustained effort of untangling the various snarls involved. The spatial metaphor of craters acts as a metaphor for psychic states, and the poems resemble efforts to communicate subliminally, as in a dream itself. Surrealism based on dream associations allows the poet to speak through or with the subconscious. It is not the conscious reflection upon dream, or dream's meaning, which intrigues Rosenblatt, but the active state of dreaming itself; poetic devices are used to create the dream in motion, as the dreamer dreams it. The following short poem illustrates the method:

I'm not in my skin today.
I've slept too long in my daylight crypt
& a grey bird in an axeman's hood
pulled the meat out of Cyclop's [sic] window.

"Don't be scared of the birds," said my corpse,
who found me weeping in the hall closet
where seeing-eye nerves scanned their fibre
like human periscopes above the blood,
& I saw the watery eyes of the bird again.[42]

The opening line suggests a play upon the idiom "I'm not myself," but in the dream logic, the mood shift is made concrete. The action of the poem is clear, but its significance is opaque. Does the grey bird of death eating the Cyclops' eye echo a Jungian archetype? Is the bird supposed to be a monster? Such would appear to be the case, for the speaker is found weeping in the hall closet, where he is told not to be afraid. The poetic method seems designed to disrupt a normal sense of personality and self; the personality, as the poems of *Dream Craters* suggest, is more than a series of controllable and recognizable features. The sense of "I" collapses, "moods" turn into "minnows" ("The Birth of Mood and Moodlets," p. 26), and suspicions turn into "snakes / quavering up the trees" ("History," p. 28). Throughout the volume, in fact, Rosenblatt manipulates either the phrases of Jungian and Freudian psychology or the phrases of everyday language about feelings and emotions to turn them into literal visions and dreams. For example, most people in our society accept that snakes, at least in popular psychology, are phallic symbols. The poet wrenches this popular cliché into a vision. The implications of everyday language are made "objective" as they are extended into words. The nuances are expanded, traced, almost as if the poet were exploring the denotations and connotations of words and phrases ordinarily used to describe psychological states. If such a hypothesis is valid, then a poem like "The Birth of Mood and Moodlets" may be seen as a comic extension of the notion that we are "moody" beings composed

> of illegitimate moods, subtle whirlpools,
> tones of progeny atoms adhering to a mood society,
> female mood, male mood, tall mood & short mood.
>
> (p. 26)

Rosenblatt seems determined to explore language and images to make vivid the mental perceptions implied in colloquial idioms and expressions. The language world, therefore, becomes the "real" world in the poet's "craters" — that is, in the pockets of language, the pockets of self-expression and self-understanding.

In *Dream Craters*, the surface metamorphoses of language repeatedly parallel the changes and nuances of human behaviour. In these poems, furthermore, human nature encounters itself in the animal nature implied in everyday idioms and beastly days are transformed from bad weather to beasts' howls and growls in the night of the dream. The poems repeatedly suggest that animals compose society's language because society evolved from the animal world. Through the inversion of references to animals in commonplace metaphors, Rosenblatt revitalizes the reality of humankind's tenuous place in the cosmos of creatures: "we chirp / we laugh / we disappear into the air" ("Suicide Notes," p. 21).

The experimentation with language changes noticeably in *Virgins and Vampires* (1975). Many of the methods and techniques outlined so far still apply, but now Rosenblatt explores them in a new way. Most importantly, he turns to a retelling of popular stories, tracing the implications of folktales and legends wherein humans are either part animal or, at the least, linked to some animal. The most common element of Rosenblatt's retellings may be described as a deliberate aim for *banalization*.[43] Rosenblatt, bent on subverting the language, carefully recrafts an old tale or a modern movie to reveal its banal core. Language perpetuates particular ideologies and social values, and often these ideologies and values are not publicly acknowledged. The "once upon a time" introduction of a fairy story, for example, may act as a buffer, a linguistic device to prevent conscious identification with the characters in the story, inviting instead an inner, private, subconscious identification that need not be examined or admitted. Rosenblatt subverts that pattern. In a poem based on "Jack and the Beanstalk," for example, he eliminates the distancing device, strips away the deliberately archaic language, and retells the tale with contemporary sociological terminology:

> The mentally motherless giant
> has large eyes only for his hen
>
> whose golden eggs have lustre
> for a slum child, a class-conscious manipulator
>
> with a bag of magical beans
>
> always the poor want to move away
> from the neighbourhood
>
> the infectious dreamy ghetto
> where hallucinating juveniles
> dream about fleecing ethno-giants.[44]

The core of the fairy tale has been made banal: the story has always been one of "social improvement." The traditional story, despite its fairy-tale conventions, implicitly defends — even idolizes — materialism. Jack's poverty, it seems, is only dependent upon his lack of material wealth (i.e., gold). If Jack had that gold, he could fulfil his ambitions as a "class-conscious manipulator" who wants "to move away / from the neighbourhood." Rosenblatt, therefore, inverts the conventions of the story. The giant has been maligned. The giant has eyes "only for his hen"; it is the confused "hallucinating juveniles" who are blinded by the "lustre" of the golden eggs. To demean the giant for simply having the hen in the traditional tale is as false today as it was when the story belonged purely to oral tradition. To fault the giant merely for being the giant is as much a mistake as faulting the "ethno-giant" in Rosenblatt's remodelling of the old story. Unjustifiable in any case are dreams of "fleecing" (that is, stealing from) either giants or "ethno-giants" simply because they are different. As contemporary sociologists would have it, they belong to a "visible minority." To make the point, Rosenblatt links the notion of "giantness" to the idea of racial prejudice ("ethno") to illustrate that prejudice underlies much of Jack's thinking. The hallucinatory quality of the traditional language, then, is Rosenblatt's real subject, for the traditional tale never casts into doubt the notion that "wealth" is merely a matter of money, of gold. Human value and "wealth," such as sympathy for fellow creatures — be they human or giant — is totally skimmed over. Furthermore, a language that allows people to fault "giants" of any kind is, if unexamined, dangerous to all. Whether we like it or not, our folk stories often project values that we normally do not share. Language itself can be an "infectious dreamy ghetto" if we allow it to lull us into uncritical habits and patterns of thought.

The popular tale of the vampire is another subject which Rosenblatt banalizes. He delights in making "morals" explicit, direct, and humiliatingly open, thereby revealing their essential triteness. The popularity of the story derives from the presupposition that killers may be antisocial, but that at least they are consistent. There are comprehensible rules for a vampire's behaviour: "Transylvania was free of social warts // he was fair about death / ladled it in wood to mistress, priest, & peasant." Furthermore, the servants of the monster could feel safe and secure, for "he never impaled a blackbird" ("Poem for King Dracula," p. 41). In a society that is uncertain about itself, uncertain whether the monster of modern mass society is aiding or destroying its members, the human-animal vampire shows a consistency in brutality. Rosenblatt reveals, however, that although the modern mind may yearn for comprehensibility and consistency, even in brutality, no such consolation is available:

the brain is dying
in a germless soil, it wants flashes of intense heat
not the pablum of regurgitated theology
but a new violent myth, fresher baby dragons,
bubbling rose trees, butterflies that sting —

our giants are stuffed with chemicals
for before & after television commercials
giant suds, giant life insurance policies
to cover the whole family

we dream about giant sex
& giant shabby skies pregnant with snowflakes
                    ("The Giant as Outlaw," p. 48)

We have been reduced to a vegetable state, existing only on the
"pablum of regurgitated theology," and lacking profound emotions.
Life has been reduced, reduced utterly. In a poem called "Domestic
Scene," the magnificent cat, which Pratt used in *The Witches' Brew*
to represent amoral energy and exuberance, is now reduced to a
kitten:

the television has a degenerate disease
it cries
you have bad breath

you turn the sexual organs
to strange channels

you have bad breath

lights go out in the room
a blue movie

the brain-lobe quakes

you're half alive

kittens move in your guts.
                                        (p. 61)

The validity of the experiment here, even with Rosenblatt's own
imagery, is debatable. Rosenblatt seems to have elected to explore
allegory. He now makes his animal world comparable to the human
world on a one-to-one level: a cat equals amoral energy; kittens equal
the weak remnants of sexual energy aroused only by a blue movie.

Simplistic, yes, but the use of simplified allegory seems appropriate in a book that repeatedly relies on devices of banalization. Everyman is domesticated, and his reduced energy equals that of Everykitten. What Rosenblatt loses in terms of nuance and subtlety he gains in bluntness and directness. If it fails in the details, the book succeeds in its larger efforts — the defence of giants, ogres, and vampires that do not exist. By taking them as more real than they are, the mock seriousness of defending the rights of such mythic beasts can function as a criticism of modern movies and commercials that simply uphold predictable middle-class values and assumptions. Moreover, the puritanical ethos asserted by the middle class Rosenblatt ridicules can be attacked with a simple inversion. The monster of lust and the monster of innocence can be equally ridiculed: the vampire eats TV dinners and the virgin has claws. By banalizing the natural system of implied referentiality — the humdrum and vapid values of the popular myths — Rosenblatt attacks the closure, continuity, and utility of self-contained myths that evade reflection of our true nature.

The poem most important to an understanding of Rosenblatt's poetry, "Somewhere in Argentina," reveals the implications of his choice of popular tales. Here he draws on the post-World War II stories of German war criminals hiding out in South America:

There are those whose brains are pregnant with murder
whose thoughts are cadaverous with blood green
& their sexual glee is a gust of distortion flowing over
the brim with lethal gas & fires of their private
                                        crematoriums
                        somewhere in Argentina

Who the hell won the war?
who cares, history is a blind whore whose bra is lined
                        with fur

It's cold outside the messianic complex
the nose of neurosis runneth over

The public has no memory
a hundred years from every blood bath
the natural public lap their beer like dirty dogs

There are fat people & thin people
murderers are nice guys
they pay their taxes, attend to religion

Morality pulls the switch
millions of corpses salute their super Father
it's a love story in the loser's line of evolution

The fat liberals invented equality
after they were fatter than a slug on a rotten tomato

Pornography stimulates
intellect kills.

(p. 58)

This poem draws together many of Rosenblatt's favourite devices, in particular his preference for definition through metaphor. As is often the case, the metaphor is one that links animal and human behaviour to underline the brutality that is inevitable in human life. Parody, too, plays a strong part in the brilliant substitution of "the nose of neurosis" for the cup of the twenty-third Psalm.

In *Virgins and Vampires*, the irreducible energies of humankind are both attacked and celebrated. Rosenblatt's devices shock and disconcert the reader who catches the continual play upon clichés and trite phrases in poems populated by creatures both real and mythical. The effect is to underscore how little we have progressed. The history of humankind seems "a love story in the loser's line of evolution"; morality and general liberal attitudes are hypocrisy and self-deception in a world which always postulates that "somewhere" in Argentina — never here, never in us, never in ourselves — is the animal nature of humankind revealed. A tone of despair runs through these poems, for Rosenblatt reacts strongly to the persistent abstractions of "public" belief, feeling, and attitude. To force a confrontation with, or reexamination of, the individual self, Rosenblatt disintegrates language. He makes it banal, trite, unthinking, thereby restoring it to us with the reminder of its power to delude, to distort, to evade. Language, here, becomes just as much of a thing as it was in *Bumblebee Dithyramb* — a set of letters to which we tie ideas — but a thing which must constantly be viewed as a transformer capable of clarifying or obscuring human experience.

The achievements, as well as the failings, of *Dream Craters* and *Virgins and Vampires* are largely echoed in Rosenblatt's next book, *Loosely Tied Hands* (1978). Here, for the first and only time, Rosenblatt does not develop or expand experiments with language in any extended or sustained fashion. Only a handful of poems, in fact, meet the promise of the book's intriguing subtitle, "an experiment in punk."

Two of the "punk" poems are worth serious attention, mostly because they indicate Rosenblatt's short-lived desire to flatten language by stripping it of nuance and overtone. In "punk snake poem (for several eunuch voices)," based on the methods and devices of punk rock, the poet attempts to remove depth and resonance from the word:

o yeah yeah yeah yeah yeah yeah yeah yeah yeah
yeah yeah yeah yeah yeah yeah yeah yeah yeah
sheeeeeees pure skin yeah yeah yeah yeah yeah yeah
she turns & twists like a liquorice stick yeah yeah yeah
pure honey skin sweeter than wet wet sin turning round round[45]

Clichés about honey-skinned women blend with abstract images of "wet sin." The trite image and the evocative image sit side by side. That "several eunuch voices" chant these lines is the only hint Rosenblatt offers the reader about his highly critical attitude towards modern rock songs. Rosenblatt packs his poem with absurdities and repetitions, almost as if he were testing the limits of the idiom of the contemporary rock lyric. The inane, tiresome effect suggests a modern consciousness yearning to articulate itself, but incapable of doing so. The repetends are not incremental; they are not expansive. The voice of the modern, the "eunuch," is one of explicit sexual and animal energy without a language to speak, story to tell, or song to sing.

Parody is a second device frequently used in punk rock to ridicule conventions and behaviour. This form of music, it must be remembered, began as a reaction against the popularized, established rock music which had, over the years, become almost conventional. For that reason, the new wave favoured parodies of "establishment" songs. Rosenblatt recognizes this characteristic of punk rock and seizes on it for his own parody of established literature. The central work to receive attention is D.H. Lawrence's "Snake."

Where Lawrence subtly develops the importance of humankind's relationship to ". . . one of the lords / Of life"[46] by stressing the inner moral conflict of the speaker who encounters the snake, Rosenblatt strips the speaker of dignity by removing the capacity for self-reflection. Humans are shown as creatures of habit. The blatantly bald repetition of the urge to destroy suggests the power of even the dullest words to victimize the mind:

> I should beat a snake, with a stick
> I should beat a snake, with a stick
> I should beat a snake, with a stick
> I should beat a snake,,,,,,,,,,,,,,,
> ("philosophical investigations: onto-
> logical argument No. 1," n. pag.)

The repeated commas insist upon the unstated repetition of "with a stick, with a stick, with a stick, with a stick. . . ." This persona's reason has been usurped by mechanical thought, unlike Lawrence's speaker who consciously wrestles with his education. The language Rosenblatt selects lacks dimension or resonance; it is either clichéd or pretentiously sophisticated, but always empty and devoid of connotation, as the title of the poem underscores: "philosophical investigations: ontological argument No. 1."

Rosenblatt, moreover, extends the parody with wit and outrageously ludicrous comedy. In the poem, the snake is sufficiently humanized so that it can talk. The snake asks, "haven't i seen 'u' at the Anaconda Milk Bar?," reminding the speaker of the poem that they live in the same world, even in the same neighbourhood. The inversion is typical of Rosenblatt's humour and irony. In everyday language, people speak metaphorically of their kinship and sympathy with animals, but Rosenblatt, in such cases, makes the metaphor the literal fact, thereby creating seemingly improbable and fanciful unions between human and reptile.

By reducing poetic language until it resembles and parallels the vacuity of contemporary language as reflected in contemporary song, and by parodying traditional poems to attain a similar effect, the poet risks perpetuating the very tediousness of the quality of mind and life he wishes to make fun of. Rosenblatt seems to have acknowledged this danger, for after *Loosely Tied Hands* he abandons the entire experiment.

If Rosenblatt attempts to remove resonance from the language of *Loosely Tied Hands*, he attempts the exact opposite in *The Sleeping Lady* (1979). Never before has Rosenblatt so wholeheartedly committed himself to turgid, opaque, impenetrable diction and contorted, twisted syntax. The following lines best illustrate the point:

Lachrymal eel secretes passionate oil
to liquify mirrors in that mesmerist
— soothes every pore of arboreal fetishist —
& urged into Spin by Love's shivering coil
those aroused ripples desire flesh to despoil,
as eyeball to eyeball in the cool Spiral
low hedonist burns like furious coral
lost in the petals of glorious turmoil.[47]

The primacy of Rosenblatt's experiments is no more forcefully evident than in this untitled poem. Unlike the earlier work, where animals or insects or reptiles are clearly recognizable, now the creatures have plunged into shifting shapes perceivable only in the play of language itself. The "lachrymal eel" is, in fact, the snake, the controlling image of the volume. Its custom of sloughing off its skin and renewing itself is repeatedly stressed in the poems of this book, insisting that the reader too must slough off all traditional expectations about meaning in poetry. The words, if they work at all, work by penetrating subliminally through sonority. Possibly only Swinburne has ever gone as far as Rosenblatt has in trusting to the resonance of words rather than to their clarity or precision.

However, as many reviewers have pointed out, Rosenblatt takes great risks with language, and one can conclude that here, like Swinburne, he has risked too much. The results seem murky and flaccid. But the effects of *The Sleeping Lady* do not arise exclusively from the language in isolation. Rosenblatt, in an effort to give some control to the resonances he aims for, experiments with the sonnet throughout the book. Historically, this poetic form has undergone innumerable alterations since its introduction into English by Thomas Wyatt. Most readers have accustomed themselves to the apparently infinite flexibility of the form, as the acceptance of Gerard Manley Hopkins' and John Berryman's recasting of the sonnet attests. The freedoms Rosenblatt allows himself in manipulating the tradition, however, lead one to doubt his control of fundamentals, particularly since many poems in *The Sleeping Lady* have only a tenuous connection with the sonnet form. The poems that seem to be sonnets following Petrarchan or Shakespearean shape never conform to a predictable set of innovations. For example, poem xx is ordered into one kind of unconventional rhyme scheme (abab cdef gchc ii); in the last six lines of poem xxi, the pattern is unrecognizable (abab cdef egch ij).

The difficulty with the poems, one might argue, lies with a reader's presupposition that Rosenblatt wanted to achieve more than an echo or resemblance of a traditional poetic form. *The Sleeping Lady* deals with Nadine, the poet's dark lady, and the poems centre upon two themes, love and metamorphosis, as the opening lines of poem xxx illustrate: "Break the chrysalis, babe, don't be shy / break through the gauze & viscous webs." Read from beginning to end, the book traces a love affair in which the woman must "break through" the barrier of reluctance — a conventional enough theme. The sonnet-like poems, then, which to most readers will suggest poems of love, help clarify the general direction of the book, although not its specifics. The sleeping lady seems to be the archetypal woman asleep, unaware of the emotions of love.

By linking the sonnet form, admittedly in a loose and tenuous manner, to a book filled with language that intimates yet disguises emotions and passions, the poet gains the advantage of arousing feelings without specifying them. Furthermore, by constantly linking the image of the snake to those various states of consciousness about love, the poet compels the reader to question connections among love, sensuality, and lust. Finally, the transformations of the sonnets, the snake, and the woman of the poems consistently question whether flesh is "but a disguise" (VII) for beings caught in a mystifying, elemental, and primitive world of preconscious and unruly passions. If the aim of the book is to deliberately engage the reader with near forms and near meaning, then the mystification works for those who can read by "feeling" rather than by "knowledge."[48] For those who cannot make this leap to blind feeling, but who can, at least, accept the need for Rosenblatt's risk-taking and experimentation, the poems, in the full oxymoronic sense, are magnificent failures.

Throughout *The Sleeping Lady*, Rosenblatt seems determined to avoid describing any easily recognizable social reality. Instead, by offering uninterrupted, disconcerting, surrealistic effects, he makes every effort to shock. He continually sidesteps ordinary logic and expectation with farfetched similes, metaphors, and oxymora. The metamorphosis of reality, at least in the sense of how rapidly emotions and feelings can and do change — a process similar to the metamorphosis of a larva into an insect — still concerns him most. Yet, despite his every effort to present a vision of "reality" in which things lose their static, well-defined nature, Rosenblatt senses that many of his readers are not carried away in a universal transport that alters the outlines and significance of things. In fact, Rosenblatt comes to accept, as his poems in *Brides of the Stream* (1983) suggest, that his efforts, in this respect, have failed because his readers have misread his poems:

On impulse, they flash upon a painted harlot breathing on it, and then apply the brakes at the last split second. They reject my impressionistic paintings. It seems I've provided the off-spring of an aquatic pervert with some mild entertainment. . . .[49]

Once again Rosenblatt has altered his form. In an interconnected series of prose poems and lyrical verse, he uses a new voice, an "I" speaker who directly discusses his successes and failures. The "voice" may only be a new mask, but for the first time it is a mask that hints at how Rosenblatt's work is increasingly turning to modes of auto-biographical writing, especially in prose-poetry. On one level, for example, the speaker of *Brides of the Stream* is Rosenblatt himself, on his quest to catch the proverbially elusive trout that is supposed to reside in the local stream. The personalized voice is a unifying force in this collection, and *Brides of the Stream* can be seen as a forerunner of two later books: *Escape from the Glue Factory* (1985), which is, as the subtitle promises, "A Memoir of a Paranormal Toronto Childhood in the Late Forties"; and *The Kissing Goldfish of Siam* (1989), an experimental work in the vein of the "educational" novel, beginning in "July 1950 when I was seventeen years old."[50] Leaving behind the puzzling, even opaque, allusions and parallels that link poems in earlier works, Rosenblatt turns to autobiography and chronological order in what seems a determined effort to direct the reader's understanding of Rosenblatt's particular blend of the insect-animal-snake-fish-human.

Poetry Hotel: Selected Poems 1963–1985 (1985) offers the reader a thorough overview of Rosenblatt's continued effort to find a suitable and satisfactory form for his poetic vision. The book, however, is poorly designed and oddly ordered. Rosenblatt's first six books are simply collapsed under the title of "Top Soil 1963–76," his earlier selected poems. No indication of specific dates, titles of books, chronological order, or revisions is offered to the reader in the first ninety-five pages of *Poetry Hotel*. Only the closing "Note on the Text"[51] indicates that the opening section blurs six entire volumes. The next four sections — "Virgins and Vampires," "Loosely Tied Hands: An Experiment in Punk," "The Sleeping Lady," and "Brides of the Stream" — are titled after the original books, which are simply represented in chronological order. The reader misses a rationale or explanation of the selection process for the poems. Why, for example, would three poems selected from *Loosely Tied Hands* (three poems which do not especially reveal Rosenblatt's explorations of the conventions of punk) be granted an independent title and section when *Bumblebee Dithyramb*, a much more powerful work, is left smothered by poems from other collections?

More importantly, the decision to leave the bumblebee poems between pages 44 and 55, while ending the opening section 38 pages later with "Epilogue: A Poetry Manifesto," which celebrates the bee, makes little sense. Had the section been organized to build up to the bee poems, the closing "manifesto" would have seemed stronger and more forceful, especially since it is an outspoken statement of humankind's need to understand what the bee symbolizes:

IF WE COULD LIVE IN THE BODY OF THE BEE BUT FOR A MOMENT
WHILST THE ACT OF LOVE WAS IN ITS STORM WE WOULD KNOW
THE GREAT CLIMAX OF ETERNITY. . . . OUR NERVES WOULD
DANCE. THE BLOOD WOULD FLOW . . . . (pp. 94–95)

If *Poetry Hotel* merits attention, it is for its closing section, entitled "Life Notes." Though less than two pages long, this section (later included in a revised form in *Escape from the Glue Factory*) is the first clear indication of the direction Rosenblatt will follow to explore his own life in prose and poetry, often in a blunt, shocking fashion:

A child starts somewhere on some homicidal bent, and usually substitutes an animal for the person to be murdered. I believe I

started my experiments in murder by dissecting a bullfrog in
class. . . . Was *this* a lesson in biology? ("Experiments," p. 198)

The scientific dismemberment of a frog in biology class, for
Rosenblatt, becomes a typical example of the dangers of a cold,
objective attitude to nature. To merely study the parts, to name them,
then to place "terminal points of the battery to the nerve endings"
(p. 199) while watching the dead creature's legs snap back and forth
creates a false sense of knowledge. Such learning will teach no one,
at least in this poet's view, how and why all beings are part of the
world of living creatures. The quest, for him, is not to dissect (and
thereby to kill while disguising with science our impulses to
"murder"), but to understand nature through sympathetic feeling —
be the emotions ones of sympathy or revulsion, joy or shock,
jubilation or horror. We are neither above nature nor superior to it,
and careful observation of all creatures will tell us more about
ourselves than any biology experiment.

In *Brides of the Stream*, Rosenblatt suggests the need to observe
living nature, not to dissect it. Seeing his darker self, his shadow, fall
on the river filled with life, he realizes his "shadow divides into
minnows" ("The Dark Side," p. 59). Throughout the prose passages
and the short lyrical poems of *Brides of the Stream*, he will follow
these "minnows" (the various moods engendered by the sights in
and along the river) as if they were passing thoughts, associations,
and sudden possible insights into himself and his world.

The first prose passage of the book, "Blind Date," introduces his
theme:

A few miles along the highway from where I live on Vancouver
Island, the Little Qualicum winds under a bridge toward the sea.
I approached the river with some apprehension, my first blind
date. Would she accept elements of my personality, my
"fraudful" flies? (p. 10)

Throughout the sequence, Rosenblatt sees himself as a "Fisher
King," a fisherman who has lost his strength, his vitality, his energy.
The Fisher King, a mythological figure referred to by Eliot in *The
Waste Land* and outlined in James Frazer's *The Golden Bough*,
represents the ruler of a kingdom gone dead. It is the Fisher King's
duty to restore the land, to bring life and vitality back to his

community. Rosenblatt, in *Brides of the Stream*, mythologizes himself into a similar figure, and in his quest to catch the elusive trout of wisdom (presumably a variant of the Holy Grail, which would effectively restore order), he realizes that trout prefer worms to the flies so carefully handcrafted by fishermen:

> I find it incomprehensible that a trout compartmentalizes distinctive images the way an evil file clerk files away a political dossier for some future retribution. How dare they reject my impressionistic paintings for those commonplace hyper-realistic clones! ("Pleased," p. 19)

Rosenblatt, in other words, is beginning to develop a complicated allegory in this passage, one which needs some clarification. The "flies" of the "fisherman" (the poet) in this sequence represent the richly coloured, even gaudy creations (surrealist poems) that are designed to catch the "trout" (the reader). The trout, however, prefers "distinctive images" (realism) and utterly rejects the poet's (fisherman's) designs. In a sense, then, the book is an apology (in the sense of apology understood in Philip Sidney's *A Defence of Poetry* — an "explanation" or "justification") for Rosenblatt's own form of writing. Whether we like it or not, whether it suits our self-image or not, Rosenblatt's "fisherman" insists:

> In the larger sphere we are not far removed from fish. We are corralled, chosen for some upstream demise. A dark minnowy presence swims through every pore. In the Beginning, we gulped down flies. . . . ("Mother," p. 22)

We may have "cast aside a fishly psyche" (p. 22), but we have not necessarily become wiser or kinder. In fact, in our very human impulse even to go fishing, for example, we continue to participate in what the most elusive trout of Rosenblatt's quest (the trout who could explain the link between the lower and the higher animals) calls a "psalm for a cannibal" ("Reflections of Uncle Nathan," p. 36).

The shocking conjunction of the Christian notion of a psalm with the heathen notion of cannibalism is typical of Rosenblatt's determination throughout the book to link seemingly incompatible, even contradictory, notions. In Rosenblatt's poetic world, humankind is the spiritual animal feeding on fellow life, preying as it prays. In earlier works, Rosenblatt largely trusted his readers to make these connections, but in *Brides of the Stream* he goes out of his way to justify why "impressionism" ("Mother," p. 22), rather than realism, will reveal how we can gain a fuller sense of ourselves through murky, heated feelings rather than cool objectivity. As a fisherman, the poet must capture both the elusive trout and the attention of readers, in a sense bringing them together. The task, of course, is difficult — just as it always has been for every fisherman.

The motif of "fishing," of course, is a traditional one, one most familiar to us in the form of Christ as the "fisher" or men. The fisherman, however, has been used by a number of writers since biblical times as a figure symbolic of the need to discover order. Izaak Walton, in *The Compleat Angler*, for example, uses the image to suggest the need to return to nature to discover peace, quiet, solitude. Everyman, like the fisherman, can be restored to himself by turning from the city to the retreats of Nature. Richard Brautigan, in *Trout Fishing in America*, relies on the image to suggest how the "fisherman," in meeting fellow anglers across the country, discovers the variety of attitudes and expectations "typical" of American culture. Brautigan uses the form to comment directly and indirectly on America's strengths and weaknesses as a nation. Rosenblatt alludes to these and other works while also indicating that the image of fishing has been used to illustrate the multiple levels of illusion and deception which surround us all. Where Christ's fishing for men is to save them, to assist them, to help them past nets of illusion and delusion, some writers used the image to show how all fishermen and fish lived in a world of constant deception. Rosenblatt cites from "Claudius Aelianus's *De Natura Animalium*, 2nd Century Flyfishing in Macedonia" to make the point:

> . . . flies apparently seek food above the river, but do not escape the attention of the spotted fishes swimming below. When the fishes observe a fly on the current, they swim stealthily. . . .
>
> But fishermen have planned another snare for these spotted fish, and have deceived them with their craftiness. . . . (*Brides of the Stream*, p. 37)

In Rosenblatt, one level of deception supersedes another; the poet constantly teases, even mocks, those who are either blind or hypocritical about the human mixture of the sacred and the profane. We speak "of holiness, a good atmosphere in the home, how to prepare a carp" ("Poseur," p. 38) without ever realizing that such statements leap from matters of faith to matters of the frying pan. To Rosenblatt, such sudden shifts suggest that we, as humans, are often unaware of our contradictory actions.

To illustrate our vacillating attitudes to life, the different fish presented in the book — from minnow to trout — often function allegorically to represent varying levels of thought about experience. The most important of these thoughts (trouts) is the memory of Uncle Nathan, as Rosenblatt calls the elusive trout at the opening of the sequence in *Brides of the Stream*. (Rosenblatt has referred to Uncle Nathan earlier, in the Uncle Nathan poems, and the figure dominates *Brides of the Stream* and *Escape from the Glue Factory*.) Uncle Nathan is the trout who devours both flies and smaller fish, and then recedes to the deepest pools to evade those out to entrap him. This trout respects the life of the river, the very life that, literally, feeds him.

The Uncle Nathan of Rosenblatt's memory ran a fish shop, where he bred, killed, and prepared fish for his clientele. As a boy, Rosenblatt was, on the one hand, appalled by Nathan's apparent cruelty and insensitivity to fish; on the other, he recognized that people ate these fish with apparent relish (in fact, they would even invent complaints, knowing that Nathan would give an extra fish and so forestall a quarrel). Uncle Nathan was, therefore, a paradox to a young boy: someone with indisputable nobility, yet also someone of unimaginable cruelty (see *Brides of the Stream*, pp. 38–40).

As the young Rosenblatt matures — catches insects, dissects frogs, eats fish, and so on — he realizes that, whether he likes it or not, he forms part of Nathan's world. The degree to which he resembles Uncle Nathan is the key question that echoes through *Brides of the Stream*. Rosenblatt repeatedly wonders, as he wades the river in pursuit of trout, whether he is linked to a family of beings that are cruel and hypocritical or whether that family (both on the personal and the universal level) really cherishes the life that feeds and that has been fed upon. With his sights fixed on the ideals of the Torah, but bound within the constraints of his vision of cannibalism, especially in the prose-poem "And the Lord spoke unto the fish and it vomited out Jonah upon the dry land" (pp. 70–71), Rosenblatt cannot accept that others are simply blind to their vacillating nature — part spiritual, part animal, part insect, part fish. Although at the close of *Brides of the Stream* Rosenblatt's speaker is no closer to catching Uncle Nathan (the trout) than he is at the beginning, he does benefit from the quest and is offered consolation in a vision: "I see Nathan ascend to his Maker // from the lips of that pool" ("Family," p. 88).

Unlike the narrators of his earlier books, Rosenblatt's voice is calmer in *Brides of the Stream*, more steeped in explicit analogy as if to help readers discover why the ordinary language of "realism" is inadequate for the pursuit of the "truths" that lurk in shadows. Rosenblatt's diction, however, is still strained and his imagery oddly comic, as in the final moral of *Brides of the Stream*:

> Carnal toads, forget terrestrial desire and inflamed ambition
> 'else you'll wear his webs with asbestos, in perdition.
> > ("Morpheus," p. 87)

However valid it might be to view humans as toads, to then put these toads in asbestos suits (either in or out of hell) seems to transcend wit. The image is indeed so contrived that Rosenblatt's vision borders on the inane and the didactic, especially since most of the book portrays people as fish rather than toads. In lines that seem neither lyrical nor surrealistic, Rosenblatt is attempting to clarify the values and ideals underlying his methods of depicting humankind's elemental aspects. The diction, however, fails to convince. Regrettably, the theme and the language do not merge smoothly. The surrealistic diction distracts rather than attracts the reader's attention, as in the following passage:

> My brain is vigilant as a Venus's-flytrap and better than a hen leaping for flies. Had the caterpillars matured, they'd have fluttered up to my nocturnal eyes. I engorge on the creatural possibilities of the river. ("Disguises," p. 61)

Had Rosenblatt leaned more towards free-flowing lyrical description — as in the sensual reference to one trout as a "tapered green gowned lady" ("A Tapered Green Gowned Lady," p. 81) — he might have offered a sustained vision of intimate identification with the forces of nature he finds so free, liberating, and attractive. But since he often clutters his prose-poems with awkward phrases like "creatural possibilities" and randomly changes his images from trouts to toads, he adds to the overall inaccessibility of his works and loses, rather than gains, readers.

Escape from the Glue Factory: A Memoir of a Paranormal Toronto Childhood in the Late Forties (1985) echoes many of the themes of *Brides of the Stream*, but now Rosenblatt links them directly to his own boyhood in Toronto. In describing the shock he felt in Nathan's emporium, Rosenblatt writes:

> Nathan seemed inured to the slaughtering of his underwater legions. The question of launching his fish to the stars as an act of immorality never touched his heart and mind. A stronger point would have been: did he ever dine on his own fish? I never got around to asking him a few sensitive questions about the nature of the immutable and the noumenal, let alone fish and whether he felt that they had souls; and did mankind evolve from fish . . . . Nathan, tell me . . . were you clubbing your prehistoric root . . . ?[52]

The need to accept that "fish blood, the ultimate glue" ("The Meditation Tanks," p. 8), links all humankind in the evolution from sea to land was a notion that Rosenblatt, as a boy, sought to escape. Like any child, he wanted to simplify the problem. Yet, where he had hoped to reduce Nathan to an evil figure punished by God, he discovers that the man has been blessed instead: in Nathan's yard grew "the tallest sunflowers in the neighbourhood" ("The Meditation Tanks," p. 15).

What makes Rosenblatt's autobiography so moving is his open and often childlike honesty about his wavering between sentimentality and profound emotion. On the one hand, Rosenblatt realizes "sentimentality had no place in [Nathan's] establishment" ("The Meditation Tanks," p. 8); on the other, the poet realizes that, throughout these memoirs, his "mind roves sluggishly, then slices through birth water, propelled like a channel catfish" ("My Shrine by Numbers," p. 1). The link between grace and damnation seems, for Rosenblatt, to be locked into the secret of the evolutionary process humankind has undergone as if it were an inevitable metamorphosis . . . but to what? Even creativity is implicated, for even creativity is ambiguous:

> Creativity begins in the invention of disguises: a tiny green tree frog like a shift of light on a leaf; a toad reclined against the

trunk of a dead tree, the rough skin blending with the bark, mottled leaves and roots . . . power of instant invisibility. There's nowhere to hide. You stand perfectly still. . . . I've imagined myself as a toad being absorbed by forces in the tree. . . . I feel rootlets running into my arms . . . suddenly so damned radiant . . . . I'm an oily wet creature . . . glue trickles out of my skin . . . a speckled pond fly is stuck on my skin. I feel its pressure . . . trying to free itself . . . it sings a brittle lullaby. . . . ("Dream Frost," p. 104)

The many facets of the predator in animals and humans, whether conscious or not, have constantly disturbed Rosenblatt, and in all of his writings he has brought to his reader's attention the image of elemental creature seeking grace. In *Escape from the Glue Factory*, he constantly blends actual events with memories of films, theological lessons, classroom lessons, and close friendships to illustrate how "bestial" all levels of human experience can be. For example, on the "silver screen" the melodrama dominates, and Eddy — "every celluloid degenerate's name was Eddy" ("Deep Fried Dream," p. 5) — dies "when the rat in Eddy's chest is asleep" ("Deep Fried Dream," p. 7). The confessor makes "small animal noises," and one of the girls in the audience slaps the boyfriend who "drives his tongue with animal joy into her ear" (p. 7). The "lunatic" kid in the school ("every school has its lunatic") belongs in the "bug house" ("Manny," p. 23); the teacher illustrates capitalism with a herd of healthy fat cattle while "the lone Bolshevik cow was the most pathetic of all . . . lonely, thin, emaciated" ("Scott," p. 27); and when the kids in the neighbourhood get into trouble, they have to be "quick on the hoof" ("The Invisible Line," p. 34). Whether original or trite, inventive or clichéd, Rosenblatt's prose illustrates how all levels of life — in the home, the school, the church — are haunted by images of humans as animals. Language is imbued with such links.

The "glue" of the times was a call for blood, for death, be it in the melodramatic movies, where the "bad guy" gets executed ("Deep Fried Dream," p. 7), or in newsreels that recorded the war against the Zionists in Palestine: "The newspapers fed, they gorged on blood and violence. They gave the morning death scores. A bomb went off in a market place, so many Jews had died, columnists glitzed up the grisly details of the dead, the injured and cries for revenge." For "children like me at Lansdowne Public School," the survivors of

Nazi camps "were facing extinction again" — "it sent a murderous chill down our spines" ("Survival," p. 65). Even the children became increasingly brutal, battling among themselves, screaming for revenge, for blood. The anger and the fury became so strong that the Jewish boys of Rosenblatt's community "almost strung up a Jewish lad they mistook as a Brit" ("Survival," p. 67).

At the time, as a boy, Rosenblatt rationalized the act: "Hadn't the Allies fired on their own troops when their logistics got glued up . . . ?" (p. 67). The notion of being "glued up" (mixed up, confused, out of control) haunts the book. The very blood (glue) which seems to link us is also ironically what separates us into beings who can kill and be killed, beings who get classified as Jews, Arabs, Brits. In the closing section of the book, "In His Bandages, the Poet," Rosenblatt explains the impact of the 1936 film "The Invisible Man." The various experiments of the mad scientist to restore himself had failed, as had the young Rosenblatt's experiments of dissecting a frog, as had the Zionist experiments of a new land, as had the experiment of mass education and the belief in church and the unquestioned loyalty to state. The invisible man represents what the late 1940s produced — mad experiments to discover what the world and humankind "really" looked like:

The worm of curiosity got the better of his invisible soul. . .
Panic seized him. He tore at his dressings, pulling them until the tail end of the wrapping was removed. A primal shriek followed. It reverberated throughout the theatre. The experiment to restore his former self had failed. He held up a mirror. . . . Nothing existed from his neck up, not even an eggplant. (p. 111)

Cheap, sentimental, crass, cruel, shallow, melodramatic — the period formed in Rosenblatt the view of humans as well-meaning but essentially naïve creatures as much a part of the environment as any other creatures attempting to survive in an incomprehensible swamp of life.

Unlike *Escape from the Glue Factory*, with its clear effort to be a memoir that clarifies the stultified sensibility of a child constantly haunted by humankind's inconsistently bestial nature, *The Kissing Goldfish of Siam* is an "educational novel" which records the initiation of the protagonist into life, love, and sex. Rosenblatt returns to a much more openly comic-satiric celebration of the amoral energy underlying all life. The protagonist is a self-declared "wimp" ("Hammer," p. 32) who is overwhelmed by his buddy Arnie, a boy who is crude, crass, self-assured, and in the know. They live in "Pontypool" (p. 2), and it is often hard to tell whether they are creatures in a swamp (pool) or humans in a social world that may as well be a swamp of emotions and predators.

The book is a collection of short prose passages, lyrics, and prose-poems about their "swamp" life; at the same time, it makes social comments about popular culture, especially films, newspapers, and newsreels. The variety of popular culture and belief — which is, during the late 1940s, post-war mass hysteria — gives an indication of the boy's sensibility. Overwhelmed by all the things he can neither do nor understand, he gradually recognizes he is a "voyeur" of life ("Angel's Drop," p. 106), an observer who cannot participate. Wavering between prudery and imagined licentiousness, he finally realizes that his "love" for the pond has been "immature."

The girl who teaches him "love" is called July, but she does not initiate the voyeur directly. Instead, she enters the pool and allows the leeches to suck her blood as she has an orgasm. The boy is intimidated by July's uninhibited behaviour, and he retreats from the vision, fearing to be the "humiliated virgin by-stander before angel-lickings, bitings, and her need for a grinding by a pampas bull . . . which I wasn't" ("Angel's Drop," p. 106). At the conclusion of this "initiation novel," the boy, in retrospect, realizes that "the pond, my adolescence" is drying up ("A Dying Lady," p. 108), and that his life has been wasted — the only remaining hope is that one day the dried-out pond will be someone else's "meadowland" ("A Dying Lady," p. 109).

Much of the book, then, centres on the boy's recoiling from a life of animal-like energies, dreaming of easy heroism on the silver screen and finding sexuality in cheap "girlie" magazines, while his "pond" (a confusedly active adolescence) slowly evaporates. It is the portrait of a boy as a frog in a pond, a "voyeur" of nature, who so desperately fears predators and death itself that he is condemned to inertia and loss of energy, life, and vitality. From the moment of the boy's shocked realization that when the goldfish of Siam are kissing, they are actually "fucking" ("Mouth to Mouth Heat," p. 82), he is incapable of acting naturally or spontaneously. The knowledge so horrifies the boy's narrow moral sensibilities (encouraged by cheap books adulating Mike Hammer's "machismo-nourishing pap"

["Hammer," p. 32] and pop movies idolizing "livin' dolls" like Jane Russell ["Livin' Doll," p. 13]) that he cannot survive. The desire for a neat, simplistic, moral world of sharp, clear, indisputable categories utterly cripples him. The message of *The Kissing Goldfish of Siam* is consistent with that of all of Rosenblatt's earlier works: humans must learn to be animals with a spiritual craving, angelic beasts at best, living oxymora who cannot free themselves from the pond.

If there is a difference between *The Kissing Goldfish of Siam* and Rosenblatt's earlier poetry, it is in the harsh, satiric portrayal of the destructively naïve views of the first-person narrator. In the main, however, Rosenblatt's language has not radically changed.

Rosenblatt continues to prefer a baroque style, a style overloaded with metaphors, clichés, jargon, unconventional phrasing, foreign words, and vulgar diction. Even the passages of dialogue in the experimental novel are so marked by these features that Rosenblatt's style is redoubtable, as the following excerpt proves:

> "Too late," Arnie hissed, "even poor bullfrogs in their twilight years have their own evil cumulus. . . ."
>
> "But Arnie," I said, "there's no clouds this evening . . . no candy fluff for that evil bugger to hide in . . . how come this evil cumulus toad?"
>
> "I am not amused by your lack of concern for intelligent life forms in this sea of fecundity."
>
> "So snakes are fucken stupid, huh?"
>
> "Holy Jehoshaphat . . . you are totally unfeeling . . . stone."
>
> "Arnie," I foiled for my ego, "even *schlanges* have to eat . . . and I don't see you crying for all those poor-assed calves that are butchered for your favourite plate, pastrami. . . ."
>
> . . . .
>
> "The *Rana* group," Arnie said, as though he were speaking of a time-honoured corporation, "is inclined to skinny dip like all singularly nocturnal types . . . bats, dizzy stupid moths, and your *monodelphous sirenia*, my favourite aquatic serpent, but alas, their victims . . . even *schlanges*, have to eat." ("The Midnight *Schochet* and the Pond," pp. 99–100)

Such deliberately peculiar, obscure, pompous, and tortuous verbiage characterizes Rosenblatt's dialogues as well as his narrative passages, just as it does in the opening sentence of the chapter called "The Birth of a Voyeur": "On a liquefying chaise lounge, the pond appeared monochromatically smooth, a one-dimensional nude" (p. 86).

The poetry in *The Kissing Goldfish of Siam* echoes the same characteristically odd mixture of words and phrases, as in the poem "Sleep":

> Inside an erebus-cloudy tomb
> shadows repose on vermilion rock.
> Slapping against infinitude
> I am hateful of unborn caviare
> and bibulous virgins.

(p. 51)

Rosenblatt's style consistently resembles a thesaurus of strained similes, illogical metaphors, and jumbled levels of diction. His disruptive diction, therefore, cannot be considered accidental. Whether successful or not — and readers will strongly disagree on this point — Rosenblatt makes no effort to apologize, no effort to write in a clear, controlled "style." Rather, the chaos of words from all levels and fields of language — from science to advertising — reinforces that, for Rosenblatt, human emotion is as mixed, confused, and erratic as the language he chooses to write with. For Rosenblatt, words resemble the eggsperm of frogs, blended with the water, the plants, the dead insects, and the mud stirred up when a predator chases its prey, then left to settle after the pursuit. The jumble of language that Rosenblatt develops, in other words, reenacts the swamp of experience itself, and any effort to "purify" the style would falsify his vision. To smooth the language, to introduce the notion of the "right" word, to level the diction in relation to some idea of "pure" literary style, would only defeat Rosenblatt's purpose — the celebration of the inconsistent, tangled, uncontrollable energy of life and language. For Rosenblatt, language is like adolescent energy — confused, indiscriminate, volatile, explosive. Language, like the inner sexual drive, is amoral, despite our constant effort to control it with glib rules of proper usage. Therefore, by overwhelming the reader with the oddness and eccentricity of all the words available to us, technical and everyday words alike, Rosenblatt crafts an eclectic style that is entirely appropriate to his vision as a writer.

Rosenblatt's work often depends on the violent yoking of opposites. Admittedly, Rosenblatt at times takes too many risks and, as a result, overreaches himself. At the same time, the numerous successes he achieves in reinvigorating not only language but our perception *of* and *through* language justifies his daring. Like Nichol or bissett or Birney, Rosenblatt neither shies away from nor denies a culture's need to confront the varieties and levels of language within that society — be the words colloquial, formal, or technical. Nor, more importantly, does Rosenblatt hesitate to draw upon a vocabulary which is all too easily dismissed as "nonpoetic." For Rosenblatt, the jargon of biology, zoology, physics, and psychology belongs to poetry, whether his contemporaries approve or not. For Rosenblatt, this is the language with which we must articulate and define our world.

Rosenblatt was initially identified as a poet who felt alienated from his contemporaries. Yet, an examination of his poetic methods reveals that the core of his work is closer in spirit to that of his fellow poets than he may recognize. The immediate difference rests in his determination to invert the traditional myth that, when Adam and Eve fell into disgrace, a permanent separation from nature occurred. For Rosenblatt, the old desire for harmony with nature is a false desire; humans and nature have always been inseparable. Human as toad, as snake, as bee, as ape, as human — the evolutionary cycle is made real by the chameleonic voice of this modern Canadian writer. Only by writing in a lawless, even lawbreaking, fashion can Rosenblatt emphasize his vision of an amoral, energetic world. The bestiary he creates, and its cannibalistic nature, is not simply the result of a desire to shock or outrage or even entertain; it is the result of one man's urge to reveal the contradictions, vagaries, inconsistencies, fears, and joys which are inherent in a world full of animal vitality. As far as Rosenblatt is concerned, a law or two, or even a change in government, will not alter or modify the nature of our elemental being. The poet must twist and distort to reveal our fundamental, but inevitable, semiconscious, semi-articulate, and semi-animal state.

NOTES

¹ I wish to express my appreciation to Joe Rosenblatt for providing me with biographical information.

² Introd., *The Sacred Wood: Essays on Poetry and Criticism* (London: Barnes and Noble, 1920), p. xv.

³ Joe Rosenblatt, "The Darkrooms of My Mind," in *Transitions III: Poetry. A Source Book of Canadian Literature* (Vancouver: CommCept, 1978), p. 285.

⁴ Rosenblatt, "The Darkrooms of My Mind," p. 287.

⁵ Pratt always had the desire to "mix phantasy and realism," as he explains in "My First Book," *Canadian Author and Bookman*, 28 (Winter 1952–53), 6.

⁶ The influence of Eliot is noticeable throughout Rosenblatt's work. The Canadian poet is fully aware of his debt to Eliot and, as a tribute to the American-born poet, named his son Eliot.

⁷ In a review of George Bowering's work, Rosenblatt lists some of the poems cited here and explains that he "like[s] to display them as models for [his] creative writing classes" ("No Bowering Toady He," rev. of *The Catch*, by George Bowering, *Books in Canada*, Oct. 1976, p. 29).

⁸ Eli Mandel, "The Poet as Animal — of Sorts," rev. of *Winter of the Luna Moth*, by Joe Rosenblatt, *Wild Grape Wine*, by Al Purdy, *The Animals in That Country*, by Margaret Atwood, and *Black Night Window*, by John Newlove, *The Globe Magazine*, 12 Oct. 1968, p. 17.

⁹ Rosenblatt described his feelings of similarity of mind with the Metaphysical poets to a creative writing class, Wilfrid Laurier University, 8 February 1982.

¹⁰ V.A. Coleman, "The Orangutan Inside Joe," rev. of *Voyage of the Mood*, *The Canadian Forum*, April 1964, p. 22.

¹¹ Peter Stevens, "Facts to be Dealt With," rev. of *The LSD Leacock*, by Joe Rosenblatt, *The Scarred Hull*, by Frank Davey, *Poems for the Miramichi*, by Raymond Fraser, and *Small Change*, by Renald Shoofler, *The Canadian Forum*, Sept. 1967, p. 14.

¹² Mandel, p. 17.

¹³ Fred Cogswell, "One Touch of Nature," rev. of *Winter of the Luna Moth*, *Canadian Literature*, No. 40 (Spring 1969), p. 71.

¹⁴ Cogswell, p. 71.

¹⁵ F.W. Watt, "Why Poetry? Eleven Answers," rev. of *Dream Craters*, by Joe Rosenblatt and ten other books, *The Canadian Forum*, June 1975, p. 41.

¹⁶ Marya Fiamengo, "Canadian Aesop," rev. of *Top Soil*, *The Canadian Forum*, June–July 1977, p. 57.

¹⁷ David MacFarlane, "Inside Jokes, Soporific Vowels," rev. of *The Sleeping Lady*, by Joe Rosenblatt, and *Living on the Ground: Tom Wayman Country*,

by Tom Wayman, *Books in Canada*, Oct. 1980, p. 16.

[18] Stevens, p. 140.

[19] Douglas Barbour, "The Poets and Presses Revisited: Circa 1974," rev. of *Dream Craters*, by Joe Rosenblatt, and twenty-seven other books, *Dalhousie Review*, 55 (Summer 1975), 357.

[20] Leonard Gasparini, "Toading the Line," rev. of *Virgins and Vampires*, *Books in Canada*, Nov. 1975, p. 22.

[21] Douglas Barbour, "Petit Four," rev. of *Bumblebee Dithyramb*, by Joe Rosenblatt, *Angel*, by Eldon Garnet, *The Topolobampo Poems*, by Tim Inkster, and *Tales*, by Gilles Vigneault, *Books in Canada*, Oct. 1972, p. 19. In context, Barbour's comment applies strictly to *Bumblebee Dithyramb*, which is reprinted in *Top Soil*. However, his insight aptly characterizes the whole collection.

[22] Barbour, "Petit Four," p. 19.

[23] Generally speaking, Gasparini voices the most negative view of Rosenblatt's experiments. Someone like Keith Harrison holds a middle stance. Gary Michael Dault is an example of a reviewer with a positive, though not fully enthusiastic, reaction. See the list of secondary sources for complete publication details.

[24] See, for example, Douglas Barbour, rev. of *Winter of the Luna Moth*, by Joe Rosenblatt, and five other books, *Dalhousie Review*, 49 (Summer 1969), 289.

[25] Fiamengo, p. 57.

[26] Jamie Hamilton, rev. of *Top Soil*, *Quill & Quire*, Jan. 1977, p. 32.

[27] Frank Davey, "Joe Rosenblatt," in *From There to Here: A Guide to English-Canadian Literature since 1960* (Erin, Ont.: Porcépic, 1974), p. 241. All further references to this work ("Davey") appear in the text.

[28] "Jealousy," in *Voyage of the Mood* (Don Mills, Ont.: Heinrich Heine, 1963), n. pag.

[29] This term is derived from R.H. Stacy, *Defamiliarization in Language and Literature* (Syracuse: Syracuse Univ. Press, 1977), p. 3.

[30] The theory presented here is based particularly on C.K. Stead, *The New Poetic: Yeats to Eliot* (New York: Harper & Row, 1964), pp. 11–15.

[31] "Love," in *Voyage of the Mood*, n. pag.

[32] Rosenblatt, in the subtitle, identifies only this one poem in the series as "an experiment in automatic writing" ("The World Egg," in *The LSD Leacock* [Toronto: Coach House, 1966], p. 16), but this single comment seems to apply to all the poems in the sequence. All further references to this work appear in the text.

[33] In the revised version reprinted in *Top Soil*, "profit motive" has been changed to "evidence."

[34] "Mystical," in *Winter of the Luna Moth* (Toronto: House of Anansi, 1968), p. 43. All further references to this work appear in the text.

[35] For a further discussion of *Blind Photographer*, see Davey, p. 241.

[36] Walter Sutton discusses the interrelationship of the various styles — including projective verse, Beat poetry, confessional verse, concrete poetry, and others — in *American Free Verse: The Modern Revolution* (New York: New Directions, 1973), pp. 171–211.

[37] My comment is based on Charles Olson's views as expressed in "Projective Verse," *The Poetics of the New American Poetry*, ed. Donald Allen and Warren Tallman (New York: Grove, 1973), pp. 147–58.

[38] T.S. Eliot, "The Music of Poetry," in *On Poetry and Poets* (New York: Farrar, Straus and Cudahy, 1957), pp. 28–29.

[39] Joe Rosenblatt, "Bees Are Flies with Gland Trouble," in *Bumblebee Dithyramb* (Erin, Ont.: Porcépic, 1972), p. 26. All further references to this work appear in the text.

[40] The argument is based upon my understanding of the movement associated with *Tel Quel*, Jacques Derrida, and Roland Barthes as presented by Jonathan Culler in *Structuralist Poetics: Structuralism, Linguistics and the Study of Literature* (London: Routledge and Kegan Paul, 1975). Although Culler is arguing against the poststructuralist movement, he seems to make a more convincing case in favour of it.

[41] *Bumblebee Dithyramb* is illustrated by Rosenblatt, whose interest in line drawings may be seen as one source for his concrete poems.

[42] "The Bird," in *Dream Craters* (Erin, Ont.: Porcépic, 1974), p. 56. All further references to this work appear in the text.

[43] Although the term is occasionally used in Marxist criticism, the meaning here is radically different. Banalization, as I am using it, means to make self-evidently trite through the resources of poetic technique.

[44] "Giants," in *Virgins and Vampires* (Toronto: McClelland and Stewart, 1975), p. 47. All further references to this work appear in the text.

[45] In *Loosely Tied Hands: An Experiment in Punk* (Windsor: Black Moss, 1975), n. pag. All further references to this work appear in the text.

[46] "Snake," in *The Complete Poems of D.H. Lawrence* (New York: Viking, 1964), II, 351.

[47] Poem VIII, in *The Sleeping Lady* (Toronto: Exile, 1979), n. pag. All further references to this work appear in the text.

[48] The emphasis is on the "if," for some of the poems are only loosely connected. In particular, the poem dealing with "John," poem XII, seems to stand apart.

[49] "A Painted Harlot," in *Brides of the Stream* (Lantzville, B.C.: Oolichan,

1983), p. 47. All further references to this work appear in the text.

50 "Birth of a Disorder," in *The Kissing Goldfish of Siam* (Toronto: Exile, 1989), p. 1. All further references to this work appear in the text.

51 In *Poetry Hotel: Selected Poems 1963–1985* (Toronto: McClelland and Stewart, 1985), p. 201. All further references to this work appear in the text.

52 "The Meditation Tanks," in *Escape from the Glue Factory: A Memoir of a Paranormal Toronto Childhood in the Late Forties* (Toronto: Exile, 1985), pp. 9–10. All further references to this work appear in the text.

SELECTED BIBLIOGRAPHY

Primary Sources

Rosenblatt, Joe. *Voyage of the Mood*. Don Mills, Ont.: Heinrich Heine, 1963.
———. *The LSD Leacock*. Toronto: Coach House, 1966.
———. *Winter of the Luna Moth*. Toronto: House of Anansi, 1968.
———. *Blind Photographer*. Erin, Ont.: Porcépic, 1972.
———. *Bumblebee Dithyramb*. Erin, Ont.: Porcépic, 1972.
———. *Dream Craters*. Erin, Ont.: Porcépic, 1974.
———. *Virgins and Vampires*. Toronto: McClelland and Stewart, 1975.
———. "No Bowering Toady He." Rev. of *The Catch*, by George Bowering.
Books in Canada, Oct. 1976, pp. 29–30.
———. *Top Soil*. Erin, Ont.: Porcépic, 1976.
———. "The Darkrooms of My Mind." In *Transitions III: Poetry. A Source
Book of Canadian Literature*. Vancouver: CommCept, 1978, pp. 285–87.
———. *Loosely Tied Hands: An Experiment in Punk*. Windsor, Ont.: Black
Moss, 1978.
———. *The Sleeping Lady*. Toronto: Exile, 1979.
———. *Brides of the Stream*. Lantzville, B.C.: Oolichan, 1983.
———. *Escape from the Glue Factory: A Memoir of a Paranormal Toronto
Childhood in the Late Forties*. Toronto: Exile, 1985.
———. *Poetry Hotel: Selected Poems 1963–1985*. Toronto: McClelland and
Stewart, 1985.
———. *The Kissing Goldfish of Siam*. Toronto: Exile, 1989.

Secondary Sources

Barbour, Douglas. Rev. of *Winter of the Luna Moth*, by Joe Rosenblatt, and
five other books. *Dalhousie Review*, 49 (Summer 1969), 289, 291.
———. "Petit Four." Rev. of *Bumblebee Dithyramb*, by Joe Rosenblatt,
Angel, by Eldon Garnet, *The Topolobampo Poems*, by Tim Inkster, and
Tales, by Gilles Vigneault, *Books in Canada*, Oct. 1972, p. 19.
———. "The Poets and Presses Revisited: Circa 1974." Rev. of *Dream*

Craters, by Joe Rosenblatt, and twenty-seven other books. *Dalhousie Review*, 55 (Summer 1975), 338–60.

Cogswell, Fred. "One Touch of Nature." Rev. of *Winter of the Luna Moth*. *Canadian Literature*, No. 40 (Spring 1969), pp. 71–72.

Coleman, V.A. "The Orangutan Inside Joe." Rev. of *Voyage of the Mood*. *The Canadian Forum*, April 1964, pp. 22–23.

Culler, Jonathan. *Structuralist Poetics: Structuralism, Linguistics and the Study of Literature*. London: Routledge and Kegan Paul, 1975.

Dault, Gary Michael. "Garnet and Other Glows." Rev. of *Dream Craters*, by Joe Rosenblatt, and five other books. *Books in Canada*, Feb. 1975, pp. 24–25.

––––––. Rev. of *Top Soil*. *Books in Canada*, June–July 1977, pp. 16–17.

Davey, Frank. "Joe Rosenblatt." In *From There to Here: A Guide to English-Canadian Literature since 1960*. Erin, Ont.: Porcépic, 1974, pp. 240–42.

Eliot, T.S. *The Sacred Wood: Essays on Poetry and Criticism*. London: Barnes and Noble, 1920.

––––––. *On Poetry and Poets*. New York: Farrar, Straus and Cudahy, 1957.

Fiamengo, Marya. "Canadian Aesop." Rev. of *Top Soil*. *The Canadian Forum*, June–July 1977, p. 57.

Gasparini, Leonard. "Toading the Line." Rev. of *Virgins and Vampires*. *Books in Canada*, Nov. 1975, p. 22.

Hamilton, Jamie. Rev. of *Top Soil*. *Quill & Quire*, Jan. 1977, pp. 31–32.

Harrison, Keith. "Poetry Chronicle." Rev. of *The LSD Leacock*, by Joe Rosenblatt, and four other books. *Tamarack Review*, No. 42 (Winter 1967), 70–77.

Lawrence, D.H. *The Complete Poems of D.H. Lawrence*. 2 vols. New York: Viking, 1964.

MacFarlane, David. "Inside Jokes, Soporific Vowels." Rev. of *The Sleeping Lady*, by Joe Rosenblatt, and *Living on the Ground: Tom Wayman Country*, by Tom Wayman. *Books in Canada*, Oct. 1980, pp. 15–16.

Mandel, Eli. "The Poet as Animal — of Sorts." Rev. of *Winter of the Luna Moth*, by Joe Rosenblatt, *Wild Grape Wine*, by Al Purdy, *The Animals in That Country*, by Margaret Atwood, and *Black Night Window*, by John Newlove. *The Globe Magazine*, 12 Oct. 1968, p. 17.

Olson, Charles. "Projective Verse." In *The Poetics of the New American Poetry*. Ed. Donald Allen and Warren Tallman. New York: Grove, 1973, pp. 147–58.

Pratt, E.J. "My First Book." *Canadian Author and Bookman*, 28 (Winter 1952–53), 5–7.

Stacy, R.H. *Defamiliarization in Language and Literature*. Syracuse: Syracuse Univ. Press, 1977.

Stead, C.K. *The New Poetic: Yeats to Eliot*. New York: Harper & Row, 1964.

Stevens, Peter. "Facts to be Dealt With." Rev. of *The LSD Leacock*, by Joe Rosenblatt, *The Scarred Hull*, by Frank Davey, *Poems for the Mirimichi*, by Raymond Fraser, and *Small Change*, by Renald Shoofler. *The Canadian Forum*, Sept. 1967, pp. 139–40.

Sutton, Walter. *American Free Verse: The Modern Revolution in Poetry.* New York: New Directions, 1973.

Watt, F.W. "Why Poetry? Eleven Answers." Rev. of *Dream Craters*, by Joe Rosenblatt, and ten other books. *The Canadian Forum*, June 1975, pp. 40–41.

INDEX

"Absurd Prayer" 38
Acorn, Milton 8, 339, 342, 343
Adorno, Theodor 245
Advice to My Friends 74, 110,
    130–41, 144, 147–48, 150, 154,
    157, 165, 166, 170
"Advice to My Friends" 130
"Aguirre: The Wrath of God" 268
Alberta 73
"Alexander Trocchi, Public Junkie,
    Priez Pour Nous" 48
Alibi 73, 83
"All men delight in you" 44
"All There Is to Know about Adolf
    Eichmann" 47
Alphabet 202, 203
"Already the Lies" 294
"Altar, The" 359
Altman, Robert 22
"Among These Beings Not This at
    Least" 223
Anatomy of Criticism 200
"Ancient Slang or a Modern, An"
    287
"And Dreamers, Even Then, If
    Dreaming" 128
"Angel's Drop" 385
"Animal Rhythm" 362
Another Time 74, 168, 175, 177,
    190, 193, 194, 199, 206, 250–51,
    254, 264
Arendt, Hannah 33

Arnason, David 196, 200, 202–03,
    217, 220, 246, 261
"Arrival, The" 295, 296
"Arrogant, Unkind" 297
As for Me and My House 6
"As the Mist Leaves No Scar" 57
    n.61
Ashberry, John 217
"At the Long Sault: May 1660" 343
"At This Time" 287
"Atlantic" 316
Atwood, Margaret 13, 24, 181,
    213, 233, 287–89, 292, quoted
    11, 288
Auden, W.H. 118, 191, 208, 213,
    246, 251
"Auschwitz: Poetry of Alienation"
    245

Badlands 73
Bakhtin, Mikhail 79, 83–84
Ball, Hugo 358
"Ballad [My lady was found
    mutilated]" 35, 36
"Banff: The Magic Mountain" 194
Baudelaire, Charles 17, 24
Barbour, Douglas 88, 171, 206,
    286, 291, quoted 11, 33, 86, 203,
    204, 346, 347
Barthes, Roland 79, 83, 259, 314,
    391, quoted 260, 261
Bartley, Jan 284, 285, 299, 314,

317, quoted 289, 290, 291, 318, 322

Bear, The 36

"Bear on the Delhi Road, The" 343

Beardsley, Aubrey 17

Beautiful Losers 16, 17, 21, 24, 25, 28, 29, 30, 34, 38, 45, 47–50

Beckett, Samuel 78, 98, 313

Bedingfield, Dolores 27

"Bees Are Flies with Gland Trouble" 360–61, 362

"Before the Big Bend Highway" 297

Bemrose, John quoted 206

Berryman, John 373

Bessai, Diane 89, 94–95

Best of Leonard Cohen, The 22, 31

"Beware the Sick Lion" 267

"Big Mirror" 328

"Bird, The" 364

"Bird on a Wire" 42

Birney, Earle 28, 343, 344, 359, 388, quoted 171

"Birth of a Disorder" 375

"Birth of a Voyeur, The" 387

"Birth of Mood and Moodlets, The" 364, 365

"birthmark:" 261

bissett, bill 343, 359, 388

Black and Secret Man 192, 198, 202, 203, 205, 223–32

"Black and Secret Man" 224, 266

Black Night Window 282, 289, 297, 298, 303, 306–12, 313

Blake, William 202, 257, 343

"Blind Date" 377

Blind Photographer 340

Blodgett, E.D. 92

Bloom, Harold 79

Book of Mercy 23, 25, 30, 48, 50–51

"Book II: 65" 310

Books in Canada 88, 282

Borges, Jorge Luis 78, 262, 318, 355

Boundary 2: A Journal of Postmodern Literature 73

Bowering, George 9, 132, 148, 164, 167, quoted, 21, 28, 92, 204, 289, 292, 318

"Boy's Beauty, The" 40

"Brass Box. Spring. Time." 310

Brautigan, Richard 379

"Bridegroom Rises to Speak, The" 131

Brides of the Stream 340, 345, 375, 377–81, 382

"Brisbane" 168

Brown, Norman O. 251

Brown, Russell 77, 85, quoted 90, 91, 112–13

Browning, Robert 284

"Bull Calf, The" 343

Bumblebee Dithyramb 340, 343, 357, 359–63, 370, 376

Burning Water 167

Burroughs, William 24

Bush Garden, The 200

But We Are Exiles 72

"Butterfly Bat, The" 358

Butterfly on Rock: A Study of Themes and Images in Canadian Literature 286

"By the Church Wall" 305

"Cabinet Secrets" 254

Cabot, John 134, 180

Cage, John 251

Callaghan, Barry 340

Calvino, Italo 78

Cameron, A. Barry 204, 205

Cameron, Donald 94, quoted 113

"Canada" 311
Canada Gazette 108
Canadian Forum 86, 88
Canadian Literature 88
Canadian Literature in English 292
Canadian Poetry: The Modern Era 283
"Carleton University: January 1961" 228
Carman, Bliss 284
Carpenter, David quoted 86
Carr, Emily 132
"Cassandra" 227
"cause of doubles:, the" 262–63
Cave, The 282, 289, 298, 312–18, 324
"Cave, The" 318, 325
"Celebration" 39
"Ceremony for Rosh Hashonah" 216
Cervantes 80
CIV/n 21
CV/II 88
Champlain, Samuel de 134, 180
"Charles Isaac Mandel" 223, 224, 225
Charles, Ray 49
Chetwynd, Tom 163, 170, quoted 143
Chomsky, Noam 82, 159
Choyce, Lesley quoted 87
Cirlot, J.E. 152, 156, 166, 170, quoted 143
"Cities We Longed For, The" 325
"City Park Merry-Go-Round" 222
"Clean as the Grass" 44
Cogswell, Fred 197, 203, quoted 345
Cohen, Leonard 8, 12, 16–18,

22–65, 192, quoted 25
"Cold, Heat" 328
Coleman, Victor 346, quoted 345
Coleridge, Samuel Taylor 43, 51
Collected Poems of F.R. Scott 283
Collected Works of Billy the Kid, The 24, 224
Collins, Judy 21
Columbus, Christopher 134, 137, 142
"Comedians, The" 230
Commentaries of Pius II, The 321
"Commentary, The" 48
"Company" 319–20, 322
Compleat Angler, The 379
Completed Field Notes: The Long Poems of Robert Kroetsch 74
"Concerning Stars, Flowers, Love, Etc." 328–29
"Congratulations" 34
Conrad, Joseph 71, 78, 142
Contact 24, 191
Cook, Gregory M. 204
Cooley, Dennis 89–90, 94, 189, 190, 191, 192, 195–96, 197, 199, 206, 215, 218, quoted 9, 10, 113, 127, 179 n.49
Cortazar, Julio 78
"Coulee Hill" 72
Crawley, Alan 197
"Crazy Riel" 285, 286, 306, 308, 309
creation 73, 154
Creeley, Robert 198, 232, 260, 284
"Crescent A" 328
Criminal Intensities of Love as Paradise, The 73
"Criminal Intensities of Love as Paradise, The" 96, 111, 126, 128, 129, 130, 134, 135, 150, 173

Criticism: The Silent-Speaking Words 192, 196, 197–98
"crooked gods:, the" 258–60
"Crow" 343
Crow Journals, The 77, 152
Crozier, Lorna 8, 200
Crusoe: Poems Selected and New 193, 199, 200, 204, 205
"Cuckold's Song, The" 44
Culler, Jonathan 391, quoted 177

Dalhousie Review 88
Daniells, Roy 192
"Dark Side, The" 377
Dault, Gary Michael 390
Davey, Frank 148, 195, 344, 347, quoted 9, 11, 17, 55, 181 n.67, 204–05, 292, 349
"David" 223, 225–26
"Day of Atonement: Standing" 225
"Death by Fire" 229
Death of a Ladies' Man (album) 23, 31
Death of a Lady's Man 22, 23, 25, 30, 32, 43, 45, 47, 50–51
"Death of a Poet" 221
"Death of Don Quixote" 243
"Deep Fried Dream" 383
"Defence of Poetry, A" 378
"Dejection: An Ode" 43
"Delicatessen" 355–56
"Delphi: Commentary" 76, 96, 137, 139, 144, 147, 150, 151, 152
Derrida, Jacques 79, 391
"Desert Music" 251
"Desert Words" 251, 254
"Desperate sexual admirals" 49
Devil: Perceptions of Evil from Antiquity to Primitive Christianity, The 327

Dickinson, Emily 343
"Disguises" 48, 381
Djwa, Sandra 24
Dr. Anaconda's Solar Fun Club 340
"Domestic Scene" 368
Don Quixote 80
"Don Quixote Writes to His Priest" 243–44
Donaldson, Allan 26
Donne, John 30, 40–41, 344, quoted 40
"doppelganger:, the" 262
"doppelganger (2):, the" 262
Dostoevsky, Fyodor 16, 190
"Double, The" 262, 263
Double Hook, The 113
"double world:, the" 263
"Double-Headed Snake, The" 285, 288, 293, 311, 312
"Doukhobor" 315
Dowson, Ernest 17
Drawings by Joe Rosenblatt 340
"Dream (Green sea water washing over)" 317
"Dream (The luxurious trembling sea)" 317
Dream Craters 340, 344, 346, 363–65, 371
"Dream Frost" 383
"Dream Man, The" 316
Dreaming Backwards 194, 206, 237–38
Dreams Surround Us 283
"Driving" 327
Dryden, Ken 132
Dudek, Louis 21, 23, 192, quoted 27, 28
Duino Elegies 164
Duncan, Robert 9, 198, 202, 302
Dyck, E.F. quoted 293

"Dying Lady, A" 385
Dylan, Bob 21, 31

Eakins, Rosemary 27
"Earache the Red" 122
"Earthworms Eat Earthworms and Learn" 254
"East of the Mountains" 305
"Easter Egg I Got for Passover, The" 352
"Easter Wings" 359
"Ecological Heroes and Visionary Politics" 194
Edinborough, Arnold 27
"Egg Sonata" 352–54
"Eggplant Poems, The" 104, 144, 147
"Eight Dollars Will Do It" 303
Eight More Canadian Poets 193
"Elegy" 36
"Elegy for Wong Toy" 96, 101
"Elephants" 298
Elephants, Mothers and Others 294, 295–98, 304
Eliot, T.S. 24, 30, 37, 40, 41, 81, 190, 191, 198, 208, 251, 284, 293, 307, 343, 358, 377, 389, quoted 36, 341, 359
Elliot, George P. 72
Elrod, Suzanne 22, 23
"End Justifies the Means, The" 295
Energy of Slaves, The 17, 22, 25, 29, 44, 47, 49, 50
Engel, Howard quoted 86–87
"Engine and the Sea, The" 289, 312
Enright, Robert 89–90, 94, 113, 127, 179 n.49
"Entomology" 219
"Envoi" 244
"Epilogue" 263

"Epilogue: A Poetry Manifesto" 376
"Erie County" 210
"Eros" 150
Escape from the Glue Factory: A Memoir of a Paranormal Toronto Childhood in the Late Forties 340, 375, 376, 380, 382–84
Esquire 22
Essays on Canadian Writing 88, 90, 206, 207
"Estevan, 1934" 10, 254, 255, 256
"estevan, 1934:" 255, 256, 258
"Estevan, Saskatchewan" 191, 211, 214, 255
Estevan the Power Centre 258
Excerpts from the Real World 74, 82, 96, 158, 160, 161, 162–66, 167, 170, 172, 174
"Exodus" 37
"Experiments" 377

"F.P. Grove: The Finding" 96, 101, 102
Faerie Queen 111–12 n.55, 118
"Failure of Secular Life, The" 41
"Fair in Town" 208, 213–14
"Family" 381
Family Romance, The 195, 202
Far Point, The 204
"Fat Man, The" 288, 315, 317
Fat Man: Selected Poems, The 283
Faulkner, William 36, 78
Favourite Game, The 21, 33, 39, 44, 45, 46
"February Thaw" 227
Fee, Margery 191, 193, 194, 195, 197, 200–01, 202, 205
"Fern Hill" 39
Fiamengo, Marya quoted 346, 347
Fiddlehead 88

Fiedler, Leslie 198
Field Notes 1–8: a continuing poem. The Collected Poetry of Robert Kroetsch 13, 74, 75, 87, 88, 92, 96, 97, 105, 107–14, 118, 120–23, 126, 128, 129, 130, 135, 140, 147, 149, 155, 157, 173, 174
15 Canadian Poets 193
"Figuring" 151, 153
"Fiji" 168
Finlay, Ian Hamilton 358
"First Political Speech" 253
First Statement 24
"First Time, The" 303
Fisher, Brian 281
Five Modern Canadian Poets 193
Fleurs du Mal 24, 35
"Flower, The" 304, 316, 317
Flowers for Hitler 17, 21, 24, 27, 28, 34–35, 37, 38, 40, 41, 42, 43, 44, 46, 48
"Flowers that I Left in the Ground, The" 38, 40
"The Fly" 40
"Folk" 42
"For Anne" 45
"For Doug Jones: The Explanation" 134
"For Judith, Now about 10 Years Old" 288, 303
"For My Friends, Obscurely" 297
"For Play and Entrance: The Contemporary Long Poem" 83, 100, 103, 127, 138, 167
Forge 21
"Four Small Scars" 302
"Fragment of Baroque" 37
"Frankfurt *Hauptbahnhof*, The" 96, 130, 137, 147–49, 152, 153, 154, 161, 162

Frazer, James 36, 144, 145, 147, 377
French, William 193
Freud, Sigmund 33
"Frogs, The" 343
"From 'The Pentagon Papers' " 249
From There to Here: A Guide to English-Canadian Literature since 1960 205, 344
Frye, Northrop 13, 14, 26, 197, 198, 200, quoted 8–9, 36, 94
"Funeral" 297, 298
"Fuseli: Girl Combing Her Hair, Watched By a Young Man" 215
Fuseli, Henry 202
Fuseli Poems 192, 203, 214–23, 226, 242

Gasparini, Len 390, quoted 346
Geddes, Gary 192, quoted 11, 12
"Geelong, Victoria" 168
Genet, Jean 24
"Genius, The" 47
"Giant as Outlaw, The" 368
"Giants" 366
Gibran, Kahlil 21
Gibson, Kenneth 204
Gilgamesh 165
Ginsberg, Allen 9, 24
"Girl Toy" 40
"Glass Dog, The" 34
Globe and Mail 193
Go to Sleep World 191
"God Bless You" 316
"*Godfather's Painting*: David Thauberger" 267–69
Godfrey, David 264
"Going to Pieces" 267
"Gold Bug, The" 218
Golden Bough, The 377

Gone Indian 73
"Good Company, Fine Houses" 306
Gotlieb, Phyllis 28
Graham, Ron quoted 30
Grave Sirs 10, 282, 294
Graves, Robert 284
"Great Feud: A Dream of Pleiocene Armageddon, The" 342
Green Plain, The 283, 293
"Green Plain, The" 283, 325, 329, 330
Greenbaum 340
"Groundhogs & Appearances" 15–16
Grove, Frederick Philip 5, 78, 102

"Hallowe'en by St. Mary's Convent" 220
Hamilton, Jamie quoted 347
"Hammer" 385
Hammurabi 165
Hancock, Geoff 70, 71
Harari, Josue quoted 79–80
Hardy, Ann 192
"Harry, 1967" 320, 322
"He was beautiful when he sat alone" 44
"Hebraism" 225
Henderson, Brian 290, quoted 290, 291, 306
Heraclitus 330, quoted 326
Herbert, George 30, 359
"Here was the Harbour, crowded with white ships" 49
"Hero around Me, The" 324
Hiemstra, Mary 6
"History" 364
Hitleriad, The 24
Homer 147
Hopkins, Gerard Manley 191, 373

Hornyansky, Michael 27
"Houdini" 241–43
"How I Joined the Seal Herd" 88, 96, 99, 105, 114, 115–16, 120, 128, 129, 142, 150, 166, 168, 174
Howl 24
Hughes, Ted 343
Huxley, Aldous 257
Huysmans, Georges 17

I Am a Hotel 23
"I am no longer at my best practising" 45
"I am too loud when you are gone" 51
"I dress in black" 45
"I Get High on Butterflies" 354
"I have no talent left" 45
"I Long to Hold Some Lady" 40
"I Met You" 46
"I Talk to You" 306
"I threw open the shutters" 44
"I Wonder How Many People in This City" 46
"I wonder if my brother will ever read this" 49
"I wore a medal of the Virgin" 49
"Ichthycide" 357
Idiot Joy, An 192, 198, 200, 204, 207, 220, 232–43, 250, 251
"If It Were Spring" 57 n.67
I'm Your Man 23, 31, 51
"In His Bandages, the Poet" 384
"In My 57th Year" 267
In the American Grain 292
"In the Caves of My City" 215
"In the Forest" 305
"Independence" 48
"instructions:" 263
"Invisible Line, The" 383

"Ironist" 222
Ishtar 164, 165–66
"Itch, The" 358

"J.S. Bach" 298
"Jack and the Beanstalk" 366
James, Henry 71
Jaynes, Julian 260
"Jealousy" 348
Jewish Dialog 341
Johnson, Lionel 17
Jones, B.W. 203
Jones, D.G. 132, quoted 286, 287
Journals of Susanna Moodie,
 The 24, 181
"Joy of Conquest" 214
Joyce, James 78, 190, 333 n.28
"Just About Forty Degrees Off
 Course" 310

Kafka, Franz 190, 355
Kamboureli, Smaro 73, 83, 124,
 206, 261, quoted 117, 122, 130
"Kamsack" 311
Kant, Immanuel 290
Keats, John 36, 284
Keith, W.J. quoted 292–93
Kerouac, Jack 24
Kerrisdale Elegies 164
Kertes, Joseph quoted 30, 58 n.84
Kertzer, Jon quoted 87–88, 206
Kinch, Martin 267
King, Carlyle 191
Kissing Goldfish of Siam, The 340,
 345, 375, 384–88
"Kite Is a Victim, A" 41
Kiyooka, Roy 132, 133, 281,
 quoted 70
Klein, A.M. 24, 29
Kreisel, Henry 192

Kristeva, Julia 79, 176
Kroetsch, Paul 70
Kroetsch, Robert 8, 13–15, 69–186,
 200, 285, interviewed 70, 71, 73,
 75, 77, 81, 90, 94–95, 96,
 97–98, 116, 117, 136, 154

Labyrinths of Voice: Conversations
 with Robert Kroetsch 70, 75, 76–
 77, 79, 83, 84, 85, 86, 92–94, 96,
 97–98, 100, 124, 125, 155, 174
Lacan, Jacques 162, 181 n.73
Ladies and Gentlemen . . .
 Mr. Leonard Cohen 23
Lampman, Archibald 284, 343
"Lapwing You Are. Lapwing He —
 A Note on Icarus in Myth and
 Poetry" 212
Laurence, Margaret 5, 78, 161, 311
Lawrence, D.H. 343, 371–72
Layton, Irving 24, 27, 28, 29, 192,
 197, 284, 343
"Leaving Greensleeves" 42
Lecker, Robert 85, 94, 100, 110,
 quoted 89, 90, 92, 95, 103, 106,
 114, 116, 126
"Leda and the Swan" 40, 211
Ledger, The 13, 14, 73
"Ledger, The" 80, 96, 104, 106,
 109–10, 112, 113, 148, 150, 157
Lennon, John 31
"Let me swallow it whole and be
 strong" 325
Let Us Compare Mythologies 16,
 21, 24, 26, 27, 35–37, 39, 43
"Letter" 37
"Letter to a Friend's Wife" 73
"Letter to Be Opened Later" 236
"Letter to Larry Sealey, 1962, A"
 306

Letters to Salonika 74
"Letters to Salonika" 137, 138, 140
Levenson, Christopher 205
Levertov, Denise 9
Levi, Primo quoted 46
Levi-Strauss, Claude 175
Lewis, Jane 72
Lies 283, 289, 290, 292, 294, 317, 318–25
Life in the Clearings 181
"Life Notes" 340, 376
Life Sentence 194, 200, 254, 264–69
"Like a Canadian" 311
"Like a River" 290
Line 206
"Lines from My Grandfather's Journal" 38, 46
Lipari, Joseph quoted 87
LiPo 140
"Listen, the sea" 239 40
"Listening to the Radio: For Michael Ondaatje" 132
Literary History of Canada 8, 205–06
"Little Gidding" 307
Live Songs 22, 31, 42
"Long Continual Argument with Myself, A" 310, 324
Loosely Tied Hands: An Experiment in Punk 340, 371–73, 376
Lothian, John 191
"Love" 350
"Love Letter" 301
Lovely Treachery of Words: Essays Selected and New, The 73, 85
Lowey, Mark 190–91
LSD Leacock, The 339, 345, 350–56
"Lynn Valley: Depression" 303, 307

Macbeth 224
McCabe and Mrs. Miller 22, 45
McCarthy, Brian 203, quoted 28
McClung, Nellie 6
McCourt, Edward 191, 257
MacEwen, Gwendolyn 8
MacFarlane, David quoted 346
McKay, Don 92
MacKendrick, Louis 88
MacKinnon, Brian 91, quoted 70, 75, 97, 136
Maclean's 25, 72
MacLennan, Hugh 78, 94
McMaster, R.D. 203
MacNeice, Louis 190
Macpherson, Jay 8
"Madman Smart" 242
"Madness of Our Polity, The" 233
Malahat Review, The 341
Mandel, Ann 85, 193, 260, 261
Mandel, Eli 8, 9–10, 25, 27, 81, 132, 189–277, 343, 346, quoted 74, 84, 96, 168, 175, 177 n.21, 189, 190, 191, 193, 199, 202–03, 212, 250–51, 254, 264, 345
Mann, Thomas 190, 197
"Manner of Suicide" 237
"Manny" 383
"Marina" 236
Marlatt, Daphne 81, 84, 148
Marquez, Gabriel Garcia 78
Martyrology, The 84, 131
Marx, Karl 148, 151
Mary Midnight 202
"Mary Midnight" 226–27, 228
"Mary Midnight's Prologue" 226–27
"Mayor's Papers, The" 230, 231
"Meditation on Tom Thomson" 96, 102

"Meditation Tanks, The" 382
Melody Maker 21
Metamorphoses 80
Metcalf, John 283
Meyer, Bruce 202, 262
"Midnight *Schochet* and the Pond, The" 386
"Migrating Dialogue, A" 41, 47, 48
Miki, Roy 206
"Mile Zero" 76, 83, 113, 134, 154, 155, 157
"Minotaur Poems" 208, 210, 211, 214
Minovitch, Miriam 191
Missing Book of Cucumbers, The 104, 165
Mitchell, Ken 8
Mitchell, W.O. 5, 78
"Modern Canadian Poetry" 194
"Modest Locke" 242
"Montreal 1964" 40
Montrealer 72
Moodie, Susanna 180–81
"Moon in All Her Phases, The" 241
Morenz, Howie 132
Moritz, Albert [A.F.] 284, 294, 298, 323, quoted 87, 298
"Morpheus" 381
"Mother" 378, 379
"Mother Nature's Helpers" 360, 363
"Mother Nature's Proletarians" 359
"Mouth to Mouth Heat" 385
Moving in Alone 286, 287, 298–306, 307, 325
Munro, Alice 311
Munton, Ann 13
"Musee des Beaux Arts" 213
"Music Crept by Us, The" 37
"My Daddy Drowned" 296, 304

"My Life in Art" 43
"My Shrine by Numbers" 382
"Mystical" 356

Nabokov, Vladimir 78
Naked Poems 325
"Narrative Poem" 251, 254
"Natural History of Elephants, The" 343
Neuman, Shirley 74, 85, 86, 92–93, quoted 91, 127, 134, 140, 147, 151, 153
New Skin for the Old Ceremony 22, 31, 42
NeWest Review 88
Newfeld, Frank 26
Newlove, John 7, 8, 10–12, 281–336, quoted 282, 284, 285, 294, 298, 299, 314, 317, 323
Newlove, Mary Constant 281
Newlove, Thomas Harold 281
Nichol, bp 81, 84, 131, 148, 343, 359, 388, quoted 181 n.67
Nietzsche, Friedrich 197, 200–01
Night the Dog Smiled, The 283, 298, 325–31
"No Use Saying to Whom" 300
Northern Review 191
"Not Moving" 297
"Note on the Text" 376
"Notes from and among the Wars" 322, 324, 325, 329
"Notes from the Underground" 215
"Nothing Is to Be Said" 300
Nowlan, Alden 8, quoted 203

"October Light" 99
"Ode on a Grecian Urn" 36
Odyssey, The 80, 138
"Old Man, The" 311

"Old Man Stories" 96, 97
Olson, Charles 9, 82, 198–99, 232, 251, 358
"On Being an Alberta Writer" 172, 174–75
"On Her Long Bed of Night" 296
"On the Murder of Salvador Allende" 267
"On the Renewal of Bombing in VietNam December, 1972" 250
"On the Sickness of My Love" 44
"On the 25th Anniversary of the Liberation of Auschwitz" 245–48, 254
Ondaatje, Michael 24, 27–28, 32, 41, 81, 84, 132, 133, 224, quoted 25, 26, 27, 33, 43
"One Day" 314
"one night I burned the house I loved" 49
"One of the Nights I Didn't Kill Myself" 48
"One Thing" 325
Open Letter 73, 85, 158
"Opium and Hitler" 35
"Or Alternately" 321, 322
"Order" 41, 48
O'Riordan, Brian 202, 262
"Orpheus" 211, 305
"Orpheus and Eurydice" 229
Ostenso, Martha 5
"Ottawa October 70" 244–45
"Otter's Creek" 316, 317
"Our Lady of the Miraculous Tin Ikon" 34
Out of Place 189, 193, 201, 206, 208, 254–64, 265
Ovid 80
Owen, Don 23
Ower, John 205

"Owning Everything" 45, 46
Pacey, Desmond 24, 26, 27, 197, quoted 203
"Pagans" 37
Page, P.K. 8
"Painted Harlot, A" 375
Parasites of Heaven 21, 28–29, 38, 41, 44, 45, 48–49
Paterson 81
Pausanias 104, 144, 145, 147
"Perfect Colours of Flowers, The" 330, 331
"Permanent Tourist Comes Home, The" 328
"petroglyphs at st. victor:" 257, 260
Phillips, Susan Mary 282
"philosophical investigations: ontological argument No. 1" 372
Phoenix, The 21
"Photograph My Mother Keeps, The" 295
"Pictures in an Institution" 234, 236, 263
Pierce, Lorne 197
Playboy 22
"Plaza Mayor" 250
"Pleased" 378
"Poem as Person as Place as Words" 266
"Poem for a Friend" 294
"Poem for King Dracula" 367
"Poem Like a Stone, Like a General" 267
"Poem of Albert Johnson" 96, 101, 102
Poésie/Poetry '64 282, 286
"Poet's Mother, The" 154, 155, 156, 165

"Poetic Process" 222
Poetry Hotel: Selected Poems 1963–1985 340, 375–76
"Pool, The" 318
"Portrait of Ann" 268
"Portrait of the City Hall" 39
"Poseur" 380
"Postcards from China" 96, 137, 141, 150, 151, 159
Pound, Ezra 140, 284
"Prairie" 7
"Prairie as Hawk, Cock, Belly, Lover" 266
Pratt, E.J. 342, 343, 368, quoted 389 n.5
"Prayer for Messiah" 37, 39
"Prayer for Sunset" 37
"preface:" 261, 263
"Pride, The" 12, 284, 285, 286, 289, 292, 293, 309, 311
"Priest Says Goodbye, The" 48
"Priests 1957" 46, 57 n.70
Prism 21
Pristine Forest, A 108
"Prize Cat, The" 343
"Professor as Bridegroom, The" 219
"Projected Visit" 99
Proteus 174
"Psalm 24" 234–35
"Pumpkin: A Love Poem" 100, 102, 129, 173
"punk snake poem (for several eunuch voices)" 371
Purdy, Al 7–8, 282, 284–85, 339, quoted 27, 289

Quarry 204, 286
Queen's Quarterly 21, 88
"Quotations" 322, 323, 325, 329

"Rapunzel" 230
Rasky, Harry 23
"Reading Room: Periodicals" 249
Reaney, James 8, 192, 202, quoted 203
"Reason I Write, The" 45
Recent Songs 23, 31
"Red Wheelbarrow" 16
"Rededication" 36
"Reflections" 194
"Reflections of Uncle Nathan" 378
Reid, Robert 281–82, 294
"Remembering Christopher Smart" 324
"Resources, Certain Earths" 306
"return:, the" 256, 257, 260, 261, 263
Rexroth, Kenneth 9
Ricou, Laurie 132
"Ride Off Any Horizon" 285, 286, 293, 308–09
Riffaterre, Michael 33–34, 41
Rilke, Rainer Maria 164–65
Rizzardi, Alfredo 341
Robert Kroetsch: Essays 71, 72, 76–77, 78, 80, 81–82, 83, 85, 90, 100, 101, 102, 103, 104, 110, 111, 114, 121, 123, 125, 127, 135, 138, 167, 173, 174
Roethke, Theodore 29
"Rogers Pass" 305
"Room, A" 328
Rosenblatt, Joe 8, 15–16, 339–95, quoted 341, 342, 389 n.7
Ross, Malcolm 197, quoted 94
Ross, Sinclair 5, 78
Ross, W.W.E. 11
"Rotorua" 168
Roughing It in the Bush 181
Russell, Jane 386

Russell, Jeffery Burton 329, quoted 327

Sad Phoenician, The 73, 87, 116
"Sad Phoenician, The" 83, 96, 105, 114, 116–18, 120–22, 126, 127, 129, 135, 150–51, 152, 161, 171, 173
Saga of Eric the Red 122
"Sailing to Byzantium" 40
"Saint Catherine Street" 37
Salutin, Rick 267
"Samuel Hearne in Wintertime" 288, 311
Saskatchewan 257
Scobie, Stephen 24, 27, 28, 29, 31, 32, 34, 37, 41, 46, quoted 26, 56 n.54, 57 n.57
"Scott" 383
Scott, Duncan Campbell 11
Scott, F.R. 23, 37, 192
"Sea of Tin Cans, The" 34
"Sea Things" 251
Seed Catalogue 13, 14, 73, 74, 76
"Seed Catalogue" 80, 96, 99, 105, 107, 110–11, 113, 114, 121, 129, 130, 140, 141, 150–51, 162, 166, 167, 168, 173
"Seeing Me Dazed" 301
"Seeing the Bear" 134
Seferis, George 140, 284
Selected Poems 1956–1968 22, 29, 45–46
Semiotics of Poetry 33
"Sentence" 99
Service, Robert 284
Shakespeare, William 37, 39, 113
"Shakespeare's Sonnets" 325, 328, 330
"Shark, The" 343

"She Reaches Out" 300
Shining People of Leonard Cohen, The 22
Shklovsky, Victor 173
"Silences, The" 237–39
"Silent Poet Craves Immortality, The" 120
"Silent Poet Eats His Words, The" 120, 123
"Silent Poet Sees Red, The" 120
"Silent Poet Sequence, The" 105, 116, 120–23, 150
Simms, Norman quoted 204
"Simulation" 249
"Singing Head, The" 288, 305, 306
Sisters of Mercy 22
"Sketches of a Lemon" 125
"Sleep" 387
Sleeping Lady, The 340, 344, 346, 373–75
Smart, Christopher 192, 202, 257
"Smelling Your Blood" 298
Smith, A.J.M. 94
Smith, Patricia Keeney 116, 124
Smith, Rowland quoted 30
"Snake, The" 343, 371, 372
"Snake Charmers" 243
Snow, Michael 244
"So you're the kind of vegetarian" 49
"Something" 322
"Somewhere in Argentina" 369–70
"Somewhere in my trophy room" 49
"Song" (Cohen) 37
"Song"(Mandel) 234
Song of Leonard Cohen, The 23
Songs from a Room 22, 31, 42
Songs of Leonard Cohen 22, 31
Songs of Love and Hate 22, 31

Sonthoff, H.W. 203

Sorestad, Glen 8, 200

"Sounding the Name" 154, 155, 165

Souster, Raymond 191, 228

Spector, Phil 23, 31

"Spending the Morning on the Beach" 76, 111

"Spending the Morning on the Beach — Ten Related Lyrics" 166, 167, 168, 172, 174

Spenser, Edmund 118

Spice-Box of Earth, The 16, 21, 26, 37–42, 44–47

"Spring Harvest" 99

"Spring-time" 36

"stars turn their noble stories, The" 45

"Statue in the House" 233

"Stay in This Room" 303–04

Stead, Robert J.C. 5

Stegner, Wallace 199

Stein, Gertrude 133

Steiner, George 245

Stevens, Peter 346, quoted 206, 345

Stevens, Wallace 284, 291

"Stone Hammer Poem" 14–15, 96, 104, 113, 123, 128, 158

Stone Hammer Poems: 1960–1975, The 13, 73, 99–103, 105–06, 129, 134, 173

Stony Plain 193, 199, 200, 204, 243–54, 255

"Story" 36

"Story of Isaac" 38

"Stragglers, The" 72

"Stranger Song, The" 45

"Streetlights" 236

Studhorse Man, The 72

"Style" 43, 48

"Suicide Notes" 365

"Suite for Ann, A" 263

Suknaski, Andy 8, 194, 199, 206

"Survival" 384

Swados, Harvey 72

Swinburne, Algernon Charles 17, 29, 373

"Syllables [*via* Sanskrit]" 329

Symons, Arthur 17

Tallman, Warren 9

Tamarack Review 21, 286

Tanabe, Takao 281, 282, 294

"Tapered Green Gowned Lady, A" 381

Tempest, The 37

"Terribly awake I wait" 49

"That There Is No Relaxation" 290, 325

"That Yellow Prairie Sky" 72, 73

"Then, If I Cease Desiring" 299

"There Are Some Men" 46

"There Is No One Here Except Us Comedians" 230

"These Are Yours" 312

"These Heroics" 37, 43

"These notebooks, these notebooks" 44

"Thief Hanging in Baptist Halls" 223

"Thirteen Ways of Looking at a Blackbird" 285

"This is the only poem" 44

"This is the poem we have been waiting for" 47

"This Is the Song" 300, 301

Thomas, Dylan 39, 208

Thomas, Peter 85, 88, 100, quoted 89, 111

Thompson, David 257

Thomson, Tom 102–03
"Tidewater Burial" 98
Time 29
Times Literary Supplement 29
Tish 9, 281
"To a Teacher" 38
"To I.P.L." 37
"To My Children" 223, 224–25
"To the Indian Pilgrims" 48
Tommy Fry and the Ant Colony 340
Top Soil 340, 341, 346, 347
"Top Soil" 340
"Toughest Mile, The" 72
"Tower of Song" 51
"Train Wreck" 191, 209
"Travel" 46
Trio 189, 191, 203, 208–14
Trout Fishing in America 379
"True Desire, The" 48
TuFu 140
Turnbull, Gael 191
"Two Dream Songs for John Berryman" 254
"Two Part Exercise on a Single Image" 219
"Tyger, The" 343
Tzu, Lao 133

"Uncle Nathan, Blessed Be His Memory, Speaketh from Landlocked Green" 357–58
"Uncle Nathan Poems, The" 357
University of Toronto Quarterly 88

"Val Marie" 208, 209, 211–12, 214
"various kinds of doubles:, the" 263
Various Positions 23, 31
Venus 165
"Verigin" 297

"Verigin, Moving in Alone" 285, 306
"Verigin III" 297
Virgins and Vampires 340, 346, 365–70, 371
Voyage of the Mood 339, 345

"Wabamun" 252–53
Waddington, Miriam 195
Wah, Fred 9, 81, 132, 148, quoted 84, 173
"Waiter! . . . There's an Alligator in My Coffee" 354
Walton, Izaak 379
"Warm Wind" 313
Waste Land, The 36, 37, 293, 343, 358, 377
Water and Light: Ghazals and Anti Ghazals 131
Watson, Sheila 78, 113
Watt, F.W. quoted 345–46
"Weather, The" 325, 330, 331
Weaver, Robert 27
Webb, Phyllis 131, 191, 192, 295, 302, 325
"Welcome to these lines" 44, 47
"Welcome to you who read me today" 47
"Well-Travelled Roadway, The" 305
Weller, Hilda 70
West, David quoted 87
"What Do You Want, What Do You Want?" 310
"What I'm Doing Here" 46
What the Crow Said 73, 144
"When I Uncovered Your Body" 39
"Where Are You" 306
"White Cat v" 298
"White Philharmonic Novels" 329–30

INDEX

Whiteman, Bruce quoted 87
Whitman, Walt 6, 81
"Why I Happen to Be Free" 57 n.68
Wiebe, Rudy 78, 112, 257
Wilde, Oscar 11, 17
Williams, William Carlos 16, 81,
    109, 232, 251, 287, 291, 292
Wilson, Milton 26, 28, quoted 27,
    203, 205
Wilson, Robert 86, 92–93
"Wind at Djemila, The" 221
"Winnipeg Zoo, The" 105,
    122–26, 129, 131, 161, 169
"Winter Birds" 100
"Winter Lady" 45
Winter of the Luna Moth 340, 341,
    343, 356–59, 363
"Winwod" 361–62
Witches' Brew, The 342, 368
"With Whom Should I Associate"
    299
Wittgenstein, Ludwig 333
Wolf Willow 199
"Woman Being Born, The" 43
Wood, Susan quoted 292
Woodcock, George 32, 197
Woolf, Virginia 78
"Words, The" 316
Words of My Roaring, The 72
Wordsworth, William 80
"World Egg, The" 351
"Writers and Writing" 194
"Writing West" 193
"Writing West: On the Road to
    Wood Mountain" 193
Wyatt, Thomas 373

Yeats, William Butler 24, 190, 198,
    201, 208, 211, 221, 251, 293,
    quoted 40

"Yellow Bear" 307
"Yonge Street Minstrel" 228
"You Are My Country & Western,
    Lullaby" 160
"You Are the Model" 41
"You Can See" 300
"You Know" 302
"You Live Like a God" 46
"You Must Marry the Terror" 150
"You Told Me" 313
"Young Man, A" 314